The Judas Kiss

Justice Denied: The Law versus Donald Marshall, 1986
Unholy Orders: Tragedy at Mount Cashel, 1990
Rare Ambition: The Crosbies of Newfoundland, 1992
The Prodigal Husband: The Tragedy of
Helmuth and Hanna Buxbaum, 1994

MICHAEL HARRIS

The Judas Kiss

M&S

Canadian Cataloguing in Publication Data

Harris, Michael, 1948-
The Judas kiss: the undercover life of Patrick Kelly

ISBN 0-7710-3957-3

1. Kelly, Patrick, 1949-   .   2. Murderers – Ontario – Toronto – Biography.   3. Royal Canadian Mounted Police – Biography.   I. Title.

HV6248.K45H3 1995   364.1'523'092   C95-931767-8

The publishers acknowledge the support of the Canada Council and the Ontario Arts Council for their publishing program.

Typesetting by M&S, Toronto
Printed and bound in Canada on acid-free paper

McClelland & Stewart Inc.
The Canadian Publishers
481 University Avenue
Toronto, Ontario
M5G 2E9

1 2 3 4 5   99 98 97 96 95

For Lynda
Love's morningstar,
my bright and beautiful light.

"Mr. Kelly is either a crafty, cunning, and malevolent psychopath, capable of masterful and adroit manipulation and deception; or he is as he claims, an innocent man wrongly convicted."

— *Myron Schimpf, PhD*
Registered Psychologist

"I have done many things which I am not particularly proud of and these I shall admit and speak of. But I think that the one thing that will become abundantly clear as you progress is that I am not a violent man and I did not commit murder."

— *Patrick Kelly to the author, 1986*

Contents

Layout of Apartment 1705, The Palace Pier

DEATH IN THE AFTERNOON

The lion was going out like a lamb. It was unseasonably warm for March 29: a balmy fifty-four degrees by mid-afternoon. From the Palace Pier, a luxury high-rise on Toronto's Lakeshore Boulevard, you could see six miles across the sunny waters of Lake Ontario. The winter of 1981 had been long and dreary, and residents were airing out their condominiums or enjoying the view from their balconies. Below them, the first strollers of the season ambled along the boardwalk as a southwest wind pushed whitecaps against the breakwater. Amid the pleasant stirrings of spring, no one noticed Death ride in on a sudden gust of wind and coil up on the balcony of apartment 1705.

When Lloyd Eckel saw a dark object hurtle by the window of his apartment, he thought that someone had dropped a bundle of clothing from an upper balcony. Although maintenance man John McGinn knew it was a person, it shot past the apartment where he was working so quickly he wasn't able to tell if it was a man or a woman. It hardly mattered; when the body hit the cement loading dock at the south side of the building facing the lake, it was travelling towards eternity at over sixty-five miles an hour.

Gracie Verge was sewing in her bedroom with her back to the window when she heard a thud so resounding that it rose above the wind keening annoyingly outside the building, a cruciform-shaped tower that seemed to catch and intensify every breeze off the lake. Looking down, she saw a young woman splayed across the loading dock. Answering his wife's horrified shriek, Joe Verge rushed to the window and then headed for the stairs on the dead run.

Philip Adie, who lived directly below the Verges in apartment 404, heard Gracie's scream just after he himself was startled by something that sounded like a sheet of plywood falling on cement. When he saw the motionless form on the loading dock, he called the front desk. The line was busy. Death, it seemed, had sent more than one person scurrying for the telephone.

Concierge Mark Garcia had been fighting to keep his composure ever since Patrick Kelly had screamed into the telephone that his wife had just fallen over the balcony. With trembling fingers, Garcia dialled 911 and asked for an ambulance. At just after 3:45 P.M., it was dispatched to the Palace Pier on a Code 4 alert; the concierge had somehow given the impression to emergency personnel that they had a "jumper" on their hands.

Ellen Bayliss, who was chatting at the front desk when the call came in from Patrick Kelly, was stunned. The Kellys were her next-door neighbours and she immediately called apartment 1704 to break the tragic news to her husband. Don Bayliss listened incredulously. Moments before his wife's call, he had heard a terrific crash from the direction of the Kelly apartment. When Bayliss put down his newspaper and went to investigate, half-expecting to find the cause of the commotion outside his door, the hallway had been as empty as the feeling he now had in the pit of his stomach; over the balcony, from up *here*.

Palace Pier executive Maureen McGuigan had arrived at work that afternoon unnerved by a minor accident she had had on her way into the building. Distracted by a vehicle parked illegally behind the condominium's restaurant, McGuigan had scratched her own car on the entrance ramp to the underground parking garage as she strained to get the offender's licence number.

Fortified by a much-needed cup of coffee, she had just set to work on the pile of paperwork on her desk when Lloyd Eckel called. The frantic tenant told her that there was a body at the loading dock and that she had better "do something about it."

Even though McGuigan had recently been promoted to building manager from her former position as manager of resident relations, tenants continued to come to her with their problems. Just outside her office she ran into Mark Garcia, who was already on his way to see her. He confirmed Eckel's story, adding that he had been personally advised of the accident by the victim's husband.

McGuigan's knees went weak when she heard the name: Patrick Kelly. Just a few days earlier, his wife, Jeannette, had been talking excitedly to McGuigan about her upcoming trip to Italy. She had, in fact, been scheduled to leave that very afternoon. The building manager remembered the conversation clearly because it had been a rare and welcome departure from the usual exchanges with Mrs. Kelly – constant and often picayune complaints about her apartment or the building that McGuigan was obliged to investigate. McGuigan and Garcia hurried through the Palace Pier but they were not the first to arrive at the scene. The loading dock where Jeannette Kelly lay barefoot in the spring sun would soon become the busiest location at the Palace Pier.

Gary Tatti, the son of the building's superintendent, had been relaxing in apartment 101 when he was startled by a loud crash that sounded like a "car accident." Walking outdoors in his blue bathrobe, he found the dead woman's body just outside his parents' apartment. With no one else around, he rushed inside to call for help.

Vitalis Strumila, a nineteen-year-old Palace Pier car jockey who had been sent to investigate the emergency by Mark Garcia, couldn't believe his eyes. He had often parked the Kellys' silver Porsche in the underground garage, and now the woman he had bantered with so many times lay motionless in front of him, the wind ruffling through her long, dark hair. "Mrs. Kelly?" he whispered, inching towards the loading dock. If he offered the familiar greeting in hopes of breaking her awful trance, one close look confirmed there would be no reply: those wide-open, blue eyes were as blank and uncomprehending as the gaping spring sky into which they gazed. It was terrifying to be alone with the newly dead. The teenager was relieved when someone emerged from the tradesman's entrance beside the garage door and ran towards the loading dock.

Patrick Kelly began screaming, then doubled over as if he were going to be sick. Joe Verge arrived at almost the same moment, and the three men stood helplessly beside the lifeless woman. Kelly begged the others to give his wife mouth-to-mouth resuscitation. No one moved. It was obvious to Verge that Jeannette Kelly was beyond human help. Her jeans had split open at the waist, zipper, and crotch from the terrible impact (she had landed squarely on her buttocks), and her twisted neck was clearly broken. As Kelly knelt by his wife and felt for a pulse at her throat, he turned to Verge. "I reached out to grab her and lost her," he gasped, rocking to and fro as he spoke. "Oh my God. Oh my God, Joe."

Suspecting that Kelly was going into shock, Verge tried to pull him away from the body, but he couldn't budge the kneeling man. Patrick Kelly was strong, Verge thought, *very* strong. Kelly then removed his shirt and, bending over Jeannette, spread it over her upturned face.

After surveying the grisly scene, Maureen McGuigan hurried inside to find something to cover the body. She returned with a cloth pad used to protect the elevator walls when people moved in or out of the Palace Pier. With the help of a car jockey, she gingerly lowered it over the corpse, averting her eyes as she performed her last service for Jeannette Kelly. Briefly leaving his wife's side, Kelly walked back to the building and began pounding the wall, cutting his hand on the waffled cement – or so it seemed to Verge. Still overwrought, Kelly returned to the body and clutched the only part of Jeannette he could see – a hand and part of an outstretched arm that protruded from under the elevator pad, as if she were reaching back into the world of the living.

Within two minutes of receiving the emergency call from the Palace Pier, Const. Nelson Andrew of the Metropolitan Toronto Police drove into the service entrance on the southwest side of the condominium. Moments later, he was joined by Const. Theodor Holtzheuser. As they approached the loading dock, both officers heard Kelly cry out, "She's dead, she's dead."

"Do you know this woman?" Constable Andrew asked.

"Yes, it's my wife," Kelly answered, his lips trembling. Though moved by the man's obvious grief, the officer forced himself to ask the standard question: had he and his wife been fighting? Kelly emphatically shook his head.

As Constable Andrew helped Kelly to his feet and escorted him to his cruiser with the help of Maureen McGuigan, Constable Holtzheuser lifted the corner of the elevator pad. The victim was lying on her back with her arms extended above her head in a macabre simulation of the "hands-up" position. The officer felt for a pulse in her right wrist even though it was obvious that the young woman was dead. Where her face wasn't bruised, it was an unearthly, ashen white. Her eyes were open and blood had trickled from her nose and mouth. Holtzheuser noticed that her fingers were tucked inside the sleeves of the blue sweater she was wearing, as if her hands were cold. Through her torn clothes, he could also see that she wasn't wearing any bra or panties.

Leaving the victim guarded by an auxiliary police constable, Holtzheuser called for a sergeant to survey the scene. He then took up a position in the Palace Pier driveway so that he could guide the ambulance to its destination as soon as it arrived.

Huddled in the backseat of Constable Andrew's cruiser, Patrick Kelly was giving the first official explanation of what had happened. Shirtless and shivering, he sobbed out his story to McGuigan in a barely audible whisper. Kelly spoke so softly that McGuigan had to press her ear to his lips to make out his words, which she then relayed to the officer sitting in the front:

Before leaving for the airport, where Jeannette was to catch a flight to Florence, Italy, Kelly whispered, the couple had decided to have a cup of tea. Kelly had been preparing it when his wife walked into the kitchen complaining of a rattle on the balcony. As he busied himself making the tea, she left again with a wooden kitchen stool. Kelly then heard an alarming noise from the direction of the living room. Rushing out of the kitchen, he saw Jeannette toppling backwards over the balcony railing. She had apparently lost her balance and fallen from the stool while trying to fix the rattle she had mentioned seconds before to her distracted husband. He had raced to the balcony and actually reached his wife, but he had not been able to hold on. She had slipped through his hands and plummeted to the cement loading dock 147 feet below.

Suddenly overwhelmed, Kelly complained that he felt sick to his stomach. Constable Andrew let him out of the cruiser to get some air, and the distraught man sat on the curb with his head between his knees, hyperventilating. Afraid that Kelly was going into shock, McGuigan put her arm around his bare shoulders and borrowed a nylon jacket from one of the car jockeys to replace the shirt Kelly had used to cover Jeannette's face.

A few minutes later, McGuigan noticed that Kelly had two small wounds, one on his hand, the other on his face. Glistening brightly, they looked as though they had just stopped bleeding. Could they have been inflicted, she wondered, by the metal zipper of the jacket when he had struggled to pull it on over his head? Her suppositions were cut short by the ostentatious arrival of officialdom in high emergency, that caravan of ambulances, fire trucks, and police cars whose flashing lights and wailing sirens emphasize the gravity of every sudden disaster.

Fifteen minutes after going over the balcony, Jeannette Kelly left the Palace Pier for the last time strapped to a stretcher in the back of an ambulance. She made the trip without her husband. As his passenger had no vital signs and her shattered body felt "like a bag of jelly," driver-attendant Roland Shurian offered no treatment en route to the closest hospital, St. Joseph's Health Centre, less than a five-minute drive away. There, at 4:14 P.M., Dr. Joseph Haninec officially confirmed what everyone at the scene had known for half an hour: Jeannette Kelly was dead.

Just as the first ambulance was pulling away from the Palace Pier on its way to the hospital, a second arrived to transport Patrick Kelly to the same destination. At his request, three Palace Pier residents, Dr. Paul Stewart, Dr. Ernst Lewis, and Gerry Green, accompanied him. While climbing into the ambulance, Lewis (the dentist of two of the country's most famous hockey teams, the Toronto Maple Leafs and Team Canada) accidentally elbowed Kelly in the face. As hard as he'd been struck, Kelly hadn't flinched – a sure sign to Lewis that he was already in shock.

At 4:15 P.M., Maureen McGuigan, Mark Garcia, Const. Charles Perry, and Sgt. Michael Duchak of the Criminal Investigation Branch (CIB) stood in front of the brass doorknocker, double lock, and security peephole of apartment 1705. When they opened the door, they were greeted by the deceased's seventy-five-pound sheepdog, Kelly, who was curious to see which of her owners had returned. McGuigan was afraid of large dogs, so Garcia found Kelly's lead and took her for a walk. Accompanied by McGuigan, the police then conducted a routine search of the premises – a bedroom, two bathrooms, a den, a kitchen, and a combination living room/dining room tastefully decorated with antiques and fine art.

Everything was as Patrick Kelly had described it to the first officers on the scene. Investigators found a CP airline ticket for Jeannette's 6 P.M. flight to Florence, Italy, two white vinyl suitcases in the hall, and $1,900 in cash in an envelope in her purse. A copy of the *Toronto Star* lay on the counter, its headlines given over to the celebrated fight between the Polish government and the world's most famous union, Solidarity: "Let's Talk, Not Fight."

No cups or saucers had been put out, but the kettle that Kelly had plugged in to make tea was still boiling. Beside it, their petals wilting in a plume of steam, was a bouquet of red roses. On the opposite counter, police found several bottles of prescription pills – Librax, Buscopan, and Dalmane – the kind of medication a doctor might prescribe for a sleepless patient with a nervous stomach. The pills belonged to Jeannette.

The radio was playing in the Kellys' bedroom. From atop a bedside bureau, two stuffed rabbits with droopy ears gazed sadly towards the couple's antique sleigh-bed. Its blue comforter was rolled down and the mattress was covered with a fresh white sheet. The dress Jeannette had planned to travel in was neatly laid out on a chair by the bed. Although the room was generally tidy, there were a few signs of the disarray associated with packing: a plastic overnight bag was lying in the middle of the bed, and the victim's underclothing was scattered on the floor of the en suite bathroom. Investigators noted that the towels and bath area were dry. It was the first small puzzle of the afternoon. If Jeannette Kelly had not taken a shower, why would her bra and panties be found on the bathroom floor instead of on her corpse?

The detectives returned to the living room, where the white sheers billowed towards them, pale ghosts rising on the wind off the lake. Sgt. Duchak, who had been briefed on Kelly's account of the fatal accident, including the story of the annoying rattle, noted a humidifier against one wall on the approach to the balcony. It would have been in Kelly's way as he sprinted from the kitchen to the open sliding door, a distance of about twenty-five feet. At that point, he would have needed to make another sharp turn to his right in order to reach his falling wife. The sergeant also noticed that the screen door was off its runners at both the top and bottom.

Stepping over the six-inch baseboard heater that ran awkwardly in front of the balcony door, he found a pair of yellow director's chairs had been set out on the balcony, facing the lake. Dust-covered, it was obvious to Duchak that they had not been recently used. But the object that captured his attention lay a scant inch shy of dead centre on the small balcony – a blond-coloured, wooden, two-rung kitchen stool that was tipped on its side, with its rubber-capped legs at right angles to the railing. When the sergeant tried to upright the stool from which Jeannette Kelly had apparently fallen, its top two legs struck the glass panel beneath the balcony railing. Since the stool could not be set right without its legs hitting the panel, it could not have fallen in that position.

Had Jeannette Kelly really fallen from it, Duchak wondered, or had it been placed there by her husband to support the story he had given to police, a story he hoped would cover up his wife's murder? For a long moment, the sergeant looked out over the lake, listening to the seagulls and the sound of traffic on the Gardiner Expressway as he was buffeted by the March wind; no rattle.

After outlining the stool in chalk, Duchak and two of his fellow investigators set it next to the railing and tipped it over several times, discovering that it always fell approximately fifteen inches from the railing – twice as far as the position in which Duchak had found it. With a puzzled McGuigan watching as the police conducted their experiment, Duchak remembered a troubling detail from earlier in the afternoon.

Before the deceased had been taken to St. Joseph's hospital, Duchak had climbed into the back of the ambulance for a firsthand look. There was an abrasion to the left of Jeannette Kelly's chin that ran along her jaw line, accompanied by a noticeable bruise to the left side of her face. Her fingernails were broken; one on her right hand had been torn from its bed. Could that facial bruise have been caused by a blow, the sergeant wondered? Were the broken and missing fingernails the telltale signs of a life and death struggle between Kelly and his wife, a fight during which the screen door had been knocked off its runners before the victim had been forced onto the balcony and thrown over the edge?

The sergeant was sufficiently troubled to request the assistance of Staff Sgt. Gordon Fenton, a twenty-seven-year veteran of the CIB. When he arrived at the apartment, Fenton spent five minutes on the balcony listening in vain for the rattle. He decided that he didn't like what he saw any more than Duchak had. Nor was he comforted when Duchak told him that Kelly had been suspended from the RCMP while the force investigated allegations that he had burned down his own house to collect the insurance money. His suspicions aroused, Fenton detailed Duchak to St. Joseph's to keep an eye on the widower who just might turn out to be a killer.

At Fenton's request, members of the Identification Branch arrived and began snapping pictures and taking measurements of the balcony to record the scene. Fenton also directed several officers to canvass Palace Pier residents. With luck, someone might have actually witnessed what had happened, or at least heard noises from the Kelly apartment if there had, in fact, been a fight. Just after 7 P.M., Fenton notified Staff Supt. Frank Barbetta that the incident at the Palace Pier was being treated as a murder until further notice.

It was time to call in the men in the death business, detectives from the Metropolitan Toronto Police Homicide Bureau.

Patrick Kelly spent the first hours after his wife's death in an examination room at the emergency ward of St. Joseph's, where he was treated for shock. From the moment he arrived on a stretcher with his arms clasped tightly over his chest, perspiring profusely and crying uncontrollably, nurse Jeanette Lee's principle concern was to calm the patient down. "What am I going to do without her?" he moaned as Lee removed his clothing for the standard medical examination. Through his tears, Kelly recounted the story of how his wife had fallen to her death from a kitchen stool while trying to fix a rattle on the balcony above their own.

Immediately after pronouncing Jeannette Kelly dead, Dr. Joseph Haninec examined her husband. Like Sgt. Duchak, Dr. Haninec had noted a large bruise on the left side of the deceased's face and had been struck by the lack of external bleeding, an obvious anomaly in a death caused by a fall from a great height. His curiosity piqued, he asked Kelly what had happened.

Still crying and hyperventilating, the patient replied that he had seen his wife "falling over the balcony." When Haninec pressed for more details, Kelly became "very uncooperative" and tense, giving only yes or no answers to his queries. The doctor administered five milligrams of Valium intravenously. A few minutes later, Lee gave the patient an intramuscular injection of five more milligrams of Valium to ease his tension. It seemed to work. Less than an hour and a half after his wife's death, Kelly had coffee and a sandwich, an uncommon display of appetite for a shock victim. By 6:45 P.M., his vital signs were normal. When Haninec returned to check the patient, Kelly smiled and said that he felt much better now. It was uncertain who was talking – the patient or the Valium.

Kelly was reclining on a bed talking to fellow Palace Pier resident Dr. Paul Stewart when the chaplain of St. Joseph's arrived. George Couto had already been briefed that a woman had died in a fall and that her husband was in shock. While Couto prayed for Patrick and Jeannette, Kelly's emotions flared again, the mantra of his grief reduced to a single line: "Oh God, she was so beautiful."

Couto inquired if there was anyone he could contact on Kelly's behalf. The soon-to-be ordained chaplain was usually asked to call relatives, so he was mildly surprised when the patient gave him the name of Dennis Morris, a Toronto lawyer. Kelly explained that Morris was not being summoned in his professional capacity, but rather as a friend – someone who could help make funeral arrangements for Jeannette. Morris soon arrived and was overheard by police telling Kelly how much he disliked hospitals. At 7:30 P.M., Kelly was discharged by Dr. Haninec. Following the orders of Sgt. Duchak, constables Andrew and Perry escorted their charge to 21 Division to meet with the homicide detectives who were investigating his wife's death.

Morris, the friend who also happened to be a lawyer, would be present for Kelly's interrogation.

While Patrick Kelly was being attended to at St. Joseph's, Staff Sgt. Ed Hill and Sgt. Ed Stewart of the Homicide Bureau were on their way to the "accident" scene. Both detectives had been off-duty and about to tuck into their Sunday dinners when they were called into the case. As they began their half-hour drive from headquarters to the Palace Pier through the suddenly chill March evening, Hill briefed his partner on the details he had so far been given by officers at the scene. The deceased was Jeannette Kelly, the thirty-three-year-old wife of former RCMP undercover officer Patrick Kelly. In the opinion of the initial wave of investigators, the young woman's death was highly suspicious.

After a brief visit to the loading dock, where the victim's final position had been preserved by a chalk silhouette, Hill and Stewart took the elevator to apartment 1705. The officers there gave them more detailed briefings, and Sgt. Duchak conducted the stool experiment for their benefit. The homicide detectives agreed that Kelly's version of the day's dire events was at the very least questionable, particularly after they failed to detect the slightest evidence of the annoying rattle that Kelly claimed had drawn his wife to the balcony and her untimely death.

By the time detectives Hill and Stewart arrived at 21 Division, Kelly had already been waiting for them for more than an hour. Before interviewing him, they huddled with constables Andrew and Perry, who had been at the scene and then bird-dogged Kelly to St. Joseph's. Perry reported on Kelly's grief-stricken demeanour at the hospital and the nature of his conversation with Dennis Morris – a rambling exchange about real estate, mutual friends, holidays in various parts of the world, some of Kelly's undercover cases as an RCMP officer, and the trip Jeannette was to have taken that day to Italy.

Andrew repeated the account of the afternoon's events that Kelly had given him from the backseat of his cruiser. He also noted that the suspect had two small cuts on his person. Just before the detectives left to question Kelly, Andrew recounted a curious remark that the ex-Mountie had made to him at the hospital. "He said if I didn't like my job or ever became dissatisfied with it, to give him a call, that he would get me something with better money."

The first homicide interview with Kelly lasted only an hour. He told the detectives that he had been with the RCMP for nine and a half years and that he now worked for K&V Enterprises Ltd., an investment company based in Victoria, British Columbia. Jeannette had worked as a reservations agent for CP Air at Pearson airport. She was originally from Glasgow, Scotland, and her father, James Hanlon, still lived there. (The detectives had already found Hanlon's telephone number in an address book at the Kelly apartment.) It was his and Jeannette's first marriage and there were no children. As Kelly talked, Stewart made note of the wounds Andrew had reported to them, a small cut on the knuckle of his left hand and another nick under his left nostril.

"Any marriage problems?" Hill asked.

"We had arguments," Kelly replied. "We had a hassle about nine months ago, but we had no intention of separating. . . . Lately we were getting along pretty well, the odd spiff [*sic*], nothing heavy."

As diplomatically as possible, Hill asked about Jeannette's deadly fall. Kelly again explained that he had been in the kitchen making tea when Jeannette complained that "'the thing on the balcony is still rattling.' She grabbed a stool and went out of the kitchen." A moment later, Kelly heard an alarming noise and rushed to investigate.

"I ran out to the balcony and she was falling backwards. I reached over and tried to grab her," the now sobbing man told them. "Part of her legs. She was gone."

Twenty minutes after the interview began, Hill left to take a telephone call. Investigators at apartment 1705 had just retrieved a potentially important document among papers found in Kelly's dresser – a seventeen-page letter in his handwriting listing the couple's assets and liabilities. Dated August 16, 1980, the letter laid out what appeared to be a separation agreement, complete with financial arrangements for each of the Kellys to rent separate apartments. When Hill returned, he steered the conversation back to the state of the Kellys' relationship in the months leading up to Jeannette's death.

"Were you having any marriage problems?" he again asked.

"Ten months ago she was depressed and was seeing Doctor Allen, but she was happy lately," Kelly answered.

"Have you been having any trouble with your patio door to the balcony?" Hill inquired. The detectives wanted to know why the screen door was off its runners. One possible answer was that Kelly had dislodged the door carrying his wife from the apartment to the balcony before throwing her over the railing.

"The screen door comes off the hinges all the time," Kelly told them. "The doors to the balcony have been open for the last three days. I believe the door was intact."

Hill knew otherwise from his personal observations. So the question stood: how had it come off its runners?

"When you rushed out to the balcony did you hit the screen door?" he persisted.

"I could have, I don't know."

"Did you ever have the screen door repaired?"

"I don't believe so. I believe we complained about the screen door last year," Kelly told him.

Police had already recovered papers from the Kelly apartment that told a different story. Although the Kellys had lodged written complaints about everything from blades of grass coming up through the cement at the condominium's patio restaurant to graffiti on the walls of the loading dock where Jeannette's life had ended, there was no record in the thick file of work orders covering apartment 1705 about trouble with the screen door or, for that matter, a rattle on the balcony.

Their conversation was again interrupted by a telephone call for Hill. Investigators at the apartment had just found the Kellys' insurance policies. As a result of his wife's death, Kelly was about to come into a healthy sum of money. When he was asked about insurance, his answer was matter-of-fact and detailed.

"I met with the insurance man two weeks ago," he told the detectives. "There is $190,000 on both of us. . . . We have wills. She leaves to me, I leave to her."

Hill saved his biggest problem with Kelly's story for last. Why would anyone get up on a kitchen stool to fix a rattle, or anything else, seventeen storeys above a cement loading dock, let alone a person who had to be at the airport in less than an hour to catch an international flight and who had not yet showered and dressed? His scepticism was veiled in a disarmingly simple question.

"Was your wife scared of heights?"

"No, I am," Kelly replied. "She used to paint our house. I used to hold the ladder."

When the interview ended at 10:25 P.M., Kelly had not allayed Hill's suspicions. The detective now knew that Kelly's marriage had been in serious trouble less than a year earlier, that Kelly stood to gain by his wife's death, and that no one other than Kelly had heard the mysterious rattle that Jeannette had allegedly been trying to fix when she fell over the balcony. He informed the ex-Mountie that there would be a post-mortem on his wife's body the following morning and asked where he could be reached if the detectives needed to ask him additional questions. Kelly said that he would be staying at suite 4005 of the Palace Pier with his friend, Dr. Paul Stewart.

Before booking off for the night, the detectives visited the city morgue. The living human being of a few hours before had already taken on the depersonalized identity of the dead: cadaver 100 in locker 52, with a face the colour of chalk and both hands bagged in plastic. As Hill and Stewart knew, understanding who she had been in life would go a long way towards unravelling the riddle of her sudden and suspicious death.

2

THE RESTLESS PRINCESS

Nestled at the end of a cul-de-sac in the fashionable Glasgow suburb of Newton Mearns, Jimmy Hanlon's custom-built house declared to the world that he had arrived. By Scottish standards, the place was an architectural curiosity – a sprawling, American-style bungalow with a double garage in a city of nineteenth-century row housing built on lilliputian lots. It was a long way from The Gorbals, the tough Glasgow tenement district where both Hanlon and his wife had grown up. No one knew that better than the cocky businessman, and he was justifiably proud whenever friends or visitors referred to the Hanlon home as "Jimmy's palace."

The road to Newton Mearns had been decidedly uphill. After a wartime stint in the merchant navy, Hanlon started a taxi business in Glasgow with a single car and himself as driver. Jocular, eccentric, and boundlessly energetic, he was an instant hit with customers. An accomplished raconteur, he ended his stories with a raspy chortle and a conspiratorial wink that made people feel like they had known him all their lives. He was full of friendly advice and wasn't averse to turning off the meter for a quick pint with a thirsty customer. As the business grew, he added five drivers to the payroll and began to make a solid living.

But the former sailor was too ambitious to rest on the oars of a single accomplishment. With one business success behind him, he attempted another – Hanlon Autos, a car dealership in Paisley in the city's west end that catered to the carriage trade. Like the passengers in his original cab, his wealthy customers were charmed by the engaging rogue with the shock of silver hair and a taste for expensive suits. (Hanlon was so obsessed with keeping fresh that he showered and changed his clothes twice a day in the summer.) Combining wheeler-dealer ethics with a swaggering personal style, he soon repeated his earlier success in the taxi business. For the industrious Scot with a drop of pirate blood, the sky seemed to be the limit.

The initial beneficiaries of Hanlon's hard work were the members of his family – his wife, Charlotte, known as "Lottie" to distinguish her from their eldest daughter of the same name, and Jeannette. Like the stylishly elegant Mrs. Hanlon, both girls were always impeccably turned out and had travelled extensively, giving them a cosmopolitan air well beyond their years. They attended the best schools in Glasgow and had private tutors to instruct them in French, Spanish, and German.

Jeannette showed herself to be a gifted linguist. She followed up her private language lessons with a stint at the Sorbonne in Paris and completed her education at a Swiss finishing school in Neuchâtel, which had been recommended to the Hanlons by Jeannette's French tutor, Madame Felks. To her doting father, Jeannette was "twice as sharp" as his more reserved eldest daughter, the avowed favourite of his wife. "Jeannette was so much like me in many ways that Lottie never really loved Jeannette the way she loved Charlotte," Hanlon recalled.

Witty, fun-loving, and something of a daredevil, Jeannette was the queen of Newton Mearn's young smart set, the undisputed leader of the pack. Ensconced behind the wheel of the gleaming sports cars provided by her father (Hanlon saw to it that they were washed every day), she cut a glamorous figure racing from Glasgow to Loch Lomond for an afternoon's water-skiing or a picnic in the country with friends. Although she was just five-foot-three, the girl with the flashing blue eyes and long, dark hair was a superb athlete, who particularly excelled in skiing. Everyone knew that if you wanted to race down the mountain with Jeannette Hanlon, you had better be prepared for the expert hill and the run of your life.

Not satisfied with routinely outperforming her male companions, Jeannette relentlessly egged them on to riskier exploits. If they failed to rise to her challenges or patronized her, they were quickly knocked down by her bowling-ball bluntness; like her father, Jeannette Hanlon didn't mince words. One of her male companions, struck by the way Jeannette had somehow transformed herself into "a man's man," thought that she might have been carrying some psychological baggage on behalf of Jimmy Hanlon: "Quite frankly, I think that Jeannette was trying to fill the boots of the son that never was."

Whatever was behind Jeannette's derring-do, it proved as magnetic to the girls in her orbit as it did to the boys. Abby Latter, who met Jeannette when they were both sixteen, thought her friend was much more exciting than the proper heroines she had been forced to read about at the Warren Academy for girls, the hated boarding school in Sussex, England, that made her feel like she was "back in the time of Dickens." Painfully shy and deathly sensitive about her weight (her brothers did little for her self-esteem with their standard introduction: "This is my sister, Fatso"), Abby was mesmerized by her friend's good looks, easy confidence, and worldly ways.

While everyone else was so drearily predictable, Jeannette was always full of surprises. On a solo vacation to Tunisia when she was eighteen, Jeannette had decided on a whim to stay. She took a job as a travel guide in Sousse, a palm-fringed beach resort a hundred miles outside Tunis, ushering tourists around the catacombs and escorting them on tours of the town's famous "souks," or street markets. When Jeannette's Tunisian exploits were featured in an article in the *Scottish Daily Mail*, complete with a photo of her relaxing on the beach, her sun-starved friends back in Glasgow could only marvel at her adventures. "Last week I went to a Moslem wedding that lasted three days," she told the newspaper. "The following day we got up at dawn to attend a camel market. Honestly, I'll need a holiday when I get home."

Despite the obvious differences between them, and Abby's impression that Jeannette had been spoiled by her father, the two girls became close friends. Abby was captivated by Jeannette's zest for life and wicked sense of humour, and hung on every detail of the stories from her exotic travels. The girls shopped in the chain of exclusive women's clothing stores owned by Abby's father and visited regularly at each other's homes. The Latters, Russian Jews who had emigrated to Scotland in 1900, eagerly embraced their daughter's dazzling friend, encouraging Jeannette to let herself in if no one was home when she called. "Jeannette loved my parents, you know, and my parents treated her like a daughter," Abby remembered.

By the mid–1960s, the Latter home had turned into more of a sanctuary than a social destination for Jeannette after it became increasingly obvious that her parents were headed for the marital rocks. For more than ten years, Jimmy Hanlon had been openly keeping a mistress and cultivating a drinking problem of legendary proportions. To family friends, it appeared that Lottie tolerated the arrangement in order to maintain the comfortable lifestyle that she and her daughters enjoyed. On those inevitable occasions when her husband's infidelities brought Lottie to the boiling point (she was also known "to take a wee dram"), Jimmy insolently told her to get a divorce if she wanted one; he "didn't give a shit."

Their relationship eventually became so strained that Jimmy took to communicating with his wife via messages scrawled on the bathroom mirror. Using the last of his shaving cream, he once wrote a foamy directive that Lottie displayed to some of Jeannette's friends: "Get shaving cream." But their battles weren't always conducted with such creative incivility. "It was really a horrible situation," Abby Latter remembered. "I know that at one stage, her mother was thrown through the plate-glass window of the door by her father."

Caught in the middle of her parents' disintegrating relationship, a lonely place to be now that Charlotte had married and moved to the north of England, Jeannette didn't know whose side to take. She loved her father but knew that he had grievously wronged her mother. Her divided loyalties eventually took their toll, and her relationship with both parents suffered. All moneys were cut off and Jimmy stopped providing his favourite daughter with expensive automobiles. Working now as a communications officer with British Airways at Glasgow airport, she realized that the time had come to leave home. As most of her friends knew, she had high hopes that it wouldn't be long before she exchanged Jimmy Hanlon's gloomy castle for a palace of her own.

Although Jeannette had a host of male companions, she had had only one boyfriend since the age of sixteen. In many ways, Dan Coyle, the eldest teenage son of a prosperous Glasgow family, was an unlikely Prince

Charming. Shy and reserved, Dan had spent his entire life since leaving school working from dawn until dusk in his father's fruit and vegetable business, a blinkered vocation that had left him even more socially awkward than he was by nature. With his future as eventual owner of D. C. Coyle assured, his family had long since decided that higher education or leisure pursuits were unnecessary diversions for their hardworking son.

Lacking schooling and experience, Dan was a poor fit in Jeannette's local "jet set." He didn't join in the boisterous repartee, had no travel stories to swap, and couldn't do a lot of the things that the others did with such effortless grace. But it was his very status as a diamond in the rough that seemed to most attract Jeannette. Even when he sent Jeannette a card that in Abby Latter's opinion was illiterate, the obvious difference in their educational levels was of no importance to her friend. Abby thought she knew why. It was *Pygmalion* in reverse, a desire to improve Dan that was perfectly in keeping with Jeannette's lust to be in control. She would turn the small, insecure son of a prominent merchant into a power in his own right and in the process make herself indispensable and happy.

Dan's fascination for Jeannette was less complicated. He admired her beauty, self-assuredness (he thought that she sometimes carried confidence to the point of cheekiness), and rugged spirit of adventure. Although few people knew it, he had always chafed under the pressure that his parents had put on him to work in the family business. He was especially bitter over the fact that his free-spirited younger brother had lived the life of a wastrel but still enjoyed his father's love and support. Tired of being the dutiful son, he longed to be his own person and envied the way that the carefree Jeannette seemed to do as she pleased. But he had no illusions about his "domineering" girlfriend's long-term plans: "She had given herself to me in a loving fashion and perhaps was hoping that I was content and we might have got married."

It was no secret in Jeannette's circle that she wanted to be Dan Coyle's wife, and it was taken for granted that the couple would eventually tie the knot after the customary game of pursuit and retreat. The prospective match had the blessing of both the Coyles and the Hanlons, who knew and respected one another as working-class families who had pulled themselves up by their own bootstraps and were enjoying the fruits of success. The Coyles were fond of their son's charming girl-friend, and Jimmy Hanlon thought that Dan was "a great guy from a very, very wealthy Glasgow family." There was only one problem; Dan Coyle wasn't ready to take a wife.

"I think she thought the relationship was a lot deeper. I certainly wasn't ready to settle down. There were always these hints of, 'Oh, you know so-and-so has just got engaged and so-and-so has just got engaged.' I still had a lot of things I wanted to do."

The young man's main item of unfinished business was to find out whether there was life beyond the stultifying and unjust world of D. C. Coyle and his ne'er-do-well younger brother. Dan moved to London and took a job in Covent Garden, where his practical experience would be highly prized in one of the world's biggest fruit and vegetable markets. Jeannette was bitterly disappointed with his decision to leave Glasgow and wouldn't accept the fact that their four-year relationship was apparently over, even when Dan failed to send her his new address. She made several trips to London in an effort to rekindle the romance, and on one occasion even tracked Dan down at his undisclosed lodg-ings in Epping Forest thirty miles outside London. Her romantic sleuthing failed to produce the desired result. "It was nice to see her," Coyle recalled, "but I felt I was being hunted."

Jeannette came down to London a final time to have lunch with Dan in a restaurant beside Harrods. They lingered over their favourite wine, talking about old times in Glasgow as the afternoon crowds flowed by. As former lovers often do, she mistook nostalgia for romance and began talking about where they would go that evening. When it became clear from Dan's awkward reaction that they had just had their last date, there was a brief, bitter argument. After doing his best to say a gentlemanly goodbye, Dan got into his car and drove away.

"But there was the usual traffic jam and I hadn't got very far. She just came up and smacked me on the face. It says a lot about her character that when she wanted something, she was going to get it. That's what maybe drove me away from her."

Disappointed in love and unable to live in the war zone of her parents' embattled marriage, Jeannette decided to leave Scotland. She moved to New Zealand and landed a job with QANTAS Airlines working as a ticket agent. But even though they were half a world apart, she continued to carry a torch for Dan Coyle. Over the next two years she sent him cards and letters inviting him to visit. He declined. When she returned to Glasgow in the winter of 1974, she saw Dan a final time. After their meeting, it was obvious to Jeannette that they would never again be anything but friends. "I think she was trying to hang on to me as long as possible before she made a commitment to someone else," Coyle remembered of their last meeting.

But this last farewell didn't leave Jeannette high and dry. On her way back to Scotland, she had taken a vacation in Acapulco, where she had had a brief fling with a Mountie from British Columbia. Now that she knew she would never be Mrs. Jeannette Coyle, she was free to test her intuition that the handsome stranger might become the new man in her life.

His name was Patrick Kelly.

3

THE SECOND SON

Crouched at the top of the stairs, Patrick Kelly was transfixed by the conversation that rose in whispers from the kitchen below. At first he thought that his mother and father must be sharing a private joke. But when he held his breath to listen more intently, the twelve-year-old realized it was not laughter that filled the lengthy intervals between their hushed words, but sobbing. Hugging his knees, he was rocked by that special anxiety children feel when they hear their parents crying. Tough, practical Winnifred Kelly was no more given to tears than her husband, "Big John" Kelly, a roistering police officer with a generous heart and garrulous streak as broad as his working-class back. What, the boy wondered, could be so wrong?

The cause of their sorrow was the Kellys' youngest child, Timmy. Ever since Patrick had gazed through the nursery window at the new addition to the family, there had been disquieting hints that this child was different from him and his fourteen-year-old brother John, Jr., and two-year-old sister Candice. The doctor's prognosis, delivered with the gravity of a death sentence, had mystified and frightened him: *mentally retarded*. Hoping for the best, Winnifred and John had taken their son home anyway, but as predicted, the severely handicapped infant didn't respond to his mother's nurturing. Adding to everyone's misery, Timmy developed epilepsy and soon began experiencing fits of terrifying intensity.

Winnifred did her best to look after him, instructing her sons how to prevent their baby brother from swallowing his tongue during his "spells." But even with the strongest medication, the infant's condition deteriorated to the point where he needed constant attention. Since a single day of private care would cost more than the Kellys made in a week, there was only one solution – make Timmy a legal ward of the state and have him institutionalized at Glendale Lodge.

The mystery of his parents' tears was solved. For Patrick, it was like the day he had brought home a frozen cat and asked his mother to "fix it." To the growing list of things that adults couldn't control he now added another: Timmy had to go to a home because his parents couldn't afford to keep him.

Hardship was nothing new to John and Winnifred. They had met and married in Toronto shortly after John was discharged from the navy, and life had been a struggle ever since. The boys had come along soon after John parlayed his electrician's papers into a job with Ontario Hydro. Always restless, John pulled up stakes and moved to British Columbia just before his second son's sixth birthday. In October 1955, they arrived in Campbell River where John went to work for B.C. Hydro. But the hard-living electrician with the short fuse didn't like the job and moved to Victoria, where he took up a position with B.C. Telephone. As it often would, his temper got the better of him. "I got into an argument with my foreman in front of the police station, so I quit and walked into the station and put an application in and ended up with the Victoria Police," he recalled.

The fact that his father was a police officer was at best a mixed blessing. Patrick revelled in the reflected glory whenever Constable Kelly arrived home for lunch on his gleaming Harley-Davidson, a spectacle that always attracted an admiring crowd of neighbourhood children. But Big John drilled it into his sons that they carried a special responsibility because of his new line of work. "I think my kids had a strike against them, like a minister's son," he said. "'I'm a policeman, don't you ever do anything wrong. I've got to answer for it if you get in trouble.' This was how they were raised."

For the most part, Patrick took his father's words to heart. But they didn't stop him from skipping school, disappearing into forbidden parts of the forest, or pelting passing cars with rocks from a railroad crossing in the company of other young desperadoes. Although their father was the one who laid down the law, it was their mother who enforced it, paddling the children with her leather moccasin when they broke the more serious household rules. But Big John was ready to wade in if matters called for a heavier hand. "I asked Patrick to put the garbage out one time and he got cheeky with me and I ended up cuffing him. So he took Judo up and went into martial arts, and I've never been able to lay a hand on him since."

To supplement his modest salary, John repaired radios and televisions on the side. He installed makeshift workshops in their succession of rental houses (the family moved five times in its first year in British Columbia), and young Patrick was impressed with how his father tackled any job whether or not he initially knew how to do it. If you couldn't manage something yourself, the trick was to find the right teacher. "My father used to say, 'Don't reinvent the wheel, somebody's already done it for you. Find out what works and go do it,'" Kelly said.

Even with John's part-time job, money was still in short supply, and Winnifred took a clerking job at Woodward's to help make ends meet. Despite her outside responsibilities, she kept her house spic and span and managed the Kelly finances like a true child of the Depression. There were many more meals of fried bologna than of steak, and it was always a special event when Big John returned from a hunting expedition with plastic bags of freshly butchered venison that Patrick helped his mother lay up in the freezer.

At Christmas, Winnifred brought home the broken cookies and candies that the store could not offer for sale, and she always had a jar of money that appeared from its hiding spot in time to deal with minor emergencies. "My mother held the house together," Patrick remembered. "During some of the crises that came when I was a kid, it was usually Mom that was able to dig a little deeper and make the good out of a bad thing."

Despite the constant economic struggle, family life was pleasant enough for the Kelly children. The boys shared a bedroom in their various houses, and Patrick enjoyed being included in the activities of the older brother he idolized. When he wasn't with John, Jr., Patrick played with Dinty, the Kellys' beloved boxer dog. Dinty would trot along beside the boy's bicycle as he rode past the glowing arbutus trees and mountain vistas that made Victoria a child's paradise. One of Patrick's favourite pastimes was archery. After hours of solitary practice in the forest near his home, he became a dead shot with his bow and arrow, exhibiting the same steady hand that would later make him an expert marksman with pistols and shotguns.

Both sets of grandparents lived nearby, and the Kellys paid regular weekend visits. Patrick enjoyed playing soccer with Grandpa Kelly in the backyard while waiting for his grandmother to call them in for the buttertarts and cupcakes she always baked for her grandchildren. Grandpa Kelly worked as a hospital cleaner and taught Patrick that all work had dignity and "it didn't matter what you did as long as you did it right." Grandpa Locke, a mechanic who owned and operated two small boarding houses, brought Patrick along when he made repairs to his properties. When the work was done, he would sometimes take his "little handyman" fishing. Patrick caught his first salmon, a five-pound beauty, on one of their expeditions, though it was his grandfather who actually landed the fish.

Beyond the family, life was not nearly as congenial for Patrick. Because of their frequent moves during his early years, Patrick had always been the new boy in school, an uncomfortable outsider circling the periphery of long-standing playground clans and alliances. There were so many schools – Glanford, Margaret Jenkins, Richmond, and MacKenzie Avenue – that their names were a blur. Even Patrick's teachers didn't seem to really know their young pupil. "Pat has been in this school for such a short time that it is impossible to write out a report for him," his Grade 2 teacher observed.

It was good to have John, Jr., around to look out for him, but not even his brother's fists could silence the teasing Patrick took over his obesity. When their unhappy son became a "complete butterball," his parents finally sought medical help. The family doctor put Patrick on a strict diet and monitored his progress. By insisting that Patrick report to his office every day to be weighed, a bicycle ride of several miles, Dr. Donald Horton ensured that the patient's new eating regime was supplemented by regular exercise. A year later, Patrick was "one fit kid" who no longer had to worry about taunts from his peers. He enjoyed his transformation so much that he developed an inflexible habit of working out that gave him the body of a finely tuned welterweight, a physique he has maintained ever since.

Patrick's difficulties with his schoolwork were much harder to overcome. From the earliest grades, he was a poor reader who had trouble spelling and pronouncing certain words. Placed in remedial reading classes and speech therapy in elementary school, he still had difficulty "keeping up to the grade three level." Frustrated by his slow development, his teachers wondered if he was making the extra effort he would need to be promoted to the higher grades. "I am disappointed in Pat's lack of progress," his Grade 5 teacher commented. "Is Pat reading an *easy* library book each night for 10 minutes? Does he study his timetable cards?"

Despite his poor performance in language studies and mathematics, and the fact that he "hated school with a passion," Patrick was promoted from the primary division to Colquitz Junior High School. Many years later Patrick discovered that he was dyslexic.

Although it didn't sit well with him that he had to meet a higher standard of behaviour than his peers because of his father's line of work, it was a sad day for Patrick when Big John announced to the family that he was quitting the police force. The job had lasted seven years, and it had been a period of relative stability for the family. But everyone was proud of Big John when they found out why he had turned in his badge. At a retirement party for Victoria's chief-of-detectives, the deputy chief had insulted him, telling Kelly that if it wasn't for his retarded son, he wouldn't have a job. The man never saw the punch that laid him out.

"I lashed out," John, Sr., later explained. "I was going to kill him. I was mad. I walked into his office two days later and threw him my badge. 'I quit,' I told him. He said, 'If I was ten years younger . . .' And I said, 'Don't open your mouth, cause if you do I'm going to shut it.'"

Big John had no trouble resuming his career as an electrician in B.C.'s booming construction industry, though he often had to travel to distant job sites. With his father away and his mother occupied with two small children, Patrick began to expand his horizons beyond the home. He went to work after school at the bowling alley in the Strathcona Hotel, where he was paid five cents a game as a pin-boy. Later, he worked part time at the Crystal Springs Beverage Company as a shipper's helper and the Carey Road Home Service Station pumping gas. By the time he left Colquitz Junior High, where he continued his unremarkable academic performance, Patrick had saved almost enough money to buy the car he would soon be driving – a green Pontiac Parisienne.

Through his four years in Junior Forest Rangers and regular work-outs at Victoria's YMCA, Patrick made a number of friends, but none as long-lasting as Victor Simpson. Although he first met Victor at Colquitz Junior High, he and the "roly-poly little kid" who shared his interest in cars and girls didn't become close until they reached Mount View High. Victor's parents, Bert and Pat, "took a shine" to Patrick and treated him like the second son they never had. Patrick and Victor played pool in the basement, watched television, and tinkered endlessly with their cars in the Simpson garage. As an only child, Victor had the run of the house, a luxury Patrick appreciated. At his house, the daily routine was orga-nized around the needs of the younger children. With his father so often travelling and brother John married and living up the coast, the mundane responsibilities of the Kelly household now rested uncomfort-ably on Patrick's shoulders. Victor's house became a sanctuary, and Patrick went there every day for lunch and virtually lived with the Simpsons during summer vacations.

Even though he was a year and a half younger than Victor, Patrick was an impressive companion. Years of judo instruction and intense physical workouts had turned him from a playground target into a for-midable opponent. When he and another student got into an argument in the music room, Patrick broke his antagonist's nose. But his physical prowess was not the only thing worthy of his friend's admiration. Patrick had a way with the opposite sex, once amazing Victor and his girlfriend by arranging three dates in a single day with different girls. "It was inter-esting because we doubled with him on all three occasions. He arranged a date for the morning, a date for the afternoon, and a date for the evening."

Patrick was generally popular in high school, but some of his peers were turned off by his tall tales, a habit they put down to his constant desire to be the centre of attention. If there was a car accident, Patrick had witnessed it, a fire, he had somehow been on the scene before the authorities. Unlike his friend's detractors, Victor was close enough to Patrick to know that his improbable stories were often an accurate portrayal of events.

"Action followed him around. It was not something that he caused, it was something he was just involved in. So, he could tell very lurid stories about things," said Victor. "Maybe it was the way that he told the stories, maybe it was the fact that he was always involved in something that was a little more exciting than someone else's life that made people think he was making it up. But from the perspective that I had, I could see that a lot of the things that he was saying were true."

If anyone was entitled to the opinion that Patrick was a lightning rod for trouble, it was Victor. One afternoon the boys were cruising in Victor's car when they were broadsided by a mechanic test-driving a hot rod. Their car was ripped in half on impact and the boys had to be cut out of the wreckage. Miraculously, Victor was unhurt, but Patrick's neck and back were injured and his doctor told him not to participate in heavy physical activities. The one thing that made school enjoyable, sports, had been snatched away in a heartbeat on a lazy Saturday afternoon.

Patrick's academic record at Mount View was even worse than his performance in the lower grades. Out of nine subjects on his Grade 10 report card, he scored four Ds and an E, prompting his teacher to sum up his situation in a glum, three-word sentence: "A poor start." Bored, and still struggling with his learning disability, Patrick began to think of Mount View as a torment that would never end. He fell behind in his assignments and started skipping school as often as he could. But thanks to a painful infection that laid him up for several months later that year, there was no need for excuses.

"I remember the doctor talking about this being analogous almost to gangrene, and it started eating away at the meat at the bottom of my feet," he recalled.

His teachers promoted him to the eleventh grade, but it was an act of compassion rather than impartial judgement. Lacking a solid grounding in French and English, he failed the following year.

It was during his second stab at Grade 11 that Winnifred Kelly's tenacity began showing up in her son. With the end to his school years in sight, Patrick buckled down and pulled his marks up to a satisfactory level. Kenneth Galbraith, who taught English, law, and music at Mount View, supplied some of the inspiration. He introduced Patrick to the pleasures of music and whetted his appetite for travel with films about life in other countries. Patrick admired his worldly air and the easy rapport he established with even the most uninterested student. There was one other thing that Patrick liked about him; Mount View's renaissance man drove a Jaguar XKE. Whenever Patrick saw the powerful sports car pulling out of the school parking lot, he imagined what the world would look like from behind its wheel.

The final year at Mount View was a time for seniors to begin making serious plans for the future. Although it now looked like Patrick would be graduating from high school, he knew that his marks weren't good enough to get him into university. Patrick was undecided about what to do next. Unlike Victor, who wanted to be a dentist, he had no particular ambition. After graduating with a 60 per cent average, he began talking to a weightlifter at the YMCA about becoming a Mountie. As the local staff recruitment officer for the RCMP, Sgt. J. B. Tufford was well qualified to offer advice. Tufford told Patrick that the force could offer a young man an exciting career that would take him across the country and, if he had the talent, around the world. The prospect appealed to Patrick, and he found himself warming to the idea of following in his father's footsteps – albeit with important differences. He would drive a sleek sports car, not a Dodge sedan like Big John, and he wouldn't have a houseful of kids to support.

Even at his high-school prom in 1968, where the class song was "To Dream the Impossible Dream," Patrick was thinking about becoming a Mountie. His date that night was Heather Mackay, whose father was the RCMP's assistant commissioner for British Columbia. Patrick had dated Heather fairly steadily during the last year of high school, and her father was always encouraging him to apply to the force – even after Heather wrecked Patrick's car during an illegal driving lesson.

Victor was mildly surprised when Patrick began talking about becoming a Mountie. (Before deciding to go to university, Victor himself had applied to the force but failed to pass the physical; he was a quarter of an inch too short.) He thought that his maverick friend would never be comfortable in a paramilitary organization like the RCMP with its extensive protocols and iron discipline. "He seemed to be an individualist, a loner, one that would want to do his own thing."

Patrick's misgivings were more practical. He was worried that his old injuries might make it impossible for him to complete the rigorous physical training that RCMP recruits undergo. Although he had continued light workouts as part of his rehabilitation, he decided for the time being to take his doctor's advice and look for less strenuous work. A few weeks after graduation, he landed a job with the Bank of Montreal as a management trainee that paid $3,875 a year. If he passed the course, he would end up as an accountant, an odd occupation for a student who had struggled with mathematics since his earliest school-days.

Patrick Kelly's career in banking lasted just over a year. After nine months in Port Alberni on Vancouver Island, he was transferred to the bank's Dawson Creek branch. At times he found the work fascinating, but as Victor had predicted, he was not made for the mind-numbing protocols of routine business. It irritated Kelly that his questions about procedures were met with glassy-eyed indifference. He soon realized that his superiors were less interested in why things were done the way they were than in following the rules for every procedure as laid out in the bank's handbook.

During his posting to Dawson Creek, part of Kelly's job was to calculate interest on mortgages up for renewal. It was a tedious and time-consuming task, exactly the sort of assignment that he abhorred. After three days of coming in early and working until midnight, he had still not completed his calculations. When one of the supervising accountants grumbled about how slowly the work was progressing, Patrick demonstrated that Big John Kelly wasn't the only family member who didn't like being hassled. "I said, 'Excuse me, that's it. Goodbye, I'm out of here.'"

After a brief stint as a millworker with Sooke Forest Products, Kelly finally applied to the RCMP. The heavy work in the logging industry proved to him that his injuries from the car accident were sufficiently healed to handle any physical training the force would require. He also had the strong feeling that being a police officer would supply the excitement that had been missing in the bank. "I believe that a career in the Force would be interesting, challenging, and most rewarding," he wrote.

With those words on his application, Kelly entered the selective and highly competitive process of joining Canada's national police force. He scored 64 per cent on the initial test, which covered his basic knowledge of mathematics, geography, science, social studies, and English. Despite his misgivings, the twenty-year-old was judged to be physically sound at a preliminary medical at Victoria Veterans' Hospital. With these hurdles out of the way, it was time for an intensive interview with a staff selection officer who would make the first in a series of subjective assessments of Kelly's fitness for the RCMP. The recruitment officer who conducted the interview was none other than his old friend from the weight room of the Victoria YMCA, Sgt. J. B. Tufford.

Kelly came off as sociable, athletic, and fairly well educated, though Tufford noted he was "not well-informed on current affairs." The applicant's stated hobbies were as wholesome as they were incompatible: judo and ballroom dancing (Kelly had recently enrolled in a three-month dance course that offered lessons twice a week). His childhood had been "happy and normal" and he enjoyed a good relationship with his parents. Like them, he was an Anglican, but he no longer attended church. Although he had no savings, his indebtedness totalled only $700 – $600 to a finance company for a car loan and $100 to the Hudson's Bay Company for clothes that he was paying off at the rate of $7 a month. His only other expense was room and board, $65 a month. Kelly, who appeared unremarkable to his interviewer, passed the first official sniff.

"This applicant is small [5'9", 150 pounds], somewhat soft-looking with short neck, round, broad face, clear complexion and a full head of dark brown hair combed to the right side. With training he would no doubt present an average picture in uniform. . . . While there is nothing outstanding about him, he has the potential to make normal progress in the Force."

The next stage of scrutiny was a detailed background check, a crucial part of the winnowing-out process designed to save the force from recruiting public-relations disasters. RCMP investigators checked whether the applicant had a criminal record, and delved into his family and work history, personal finances, education, and character before deciding if he was worthy of wearing the red serge.

Investigators learned that Kelly's only brush with the law had been for making an illegal right-hand turn in December 1969. There was no sign of political subversion in his family, his credit rating was good, and teachers at Mount View High attested to his stated educational accomplishments. Neighbours and several of Kelly's former employers gave enthusiastic character references, telling police that he was "a good all-around youth . . . a very stable and thoughtful person."

His landlady in Port Alberni told investigators that Kelly was an ideal boarder "who stayed in quite a bit and who neither drank nor smoked." Although he had only been with Sooke Forest Industries for four months, his boss reported that Kelly had an "excellent working relationship with management" and was currently being considered for a more responsible position at the mill. Nevertheless, when local RCMP authorities submitted their findings to recruiting headquarters in Ottawa, their report cast a shadow over the would-be Mountie. "The only detrimental information which has come to light is the applicant's HONESTY."

The compromising assessment was based on the shadowy findings of the two RCMP officers who were assigned to investigate Kelly's employment with the Bank of Montreal. When Const. E. R. Roe interviewed personnel from the Port Alberni branch where Kelly had worked from July 1968 to April 1969, he was told that Kelly had been one of ten employees at the bank when there had been several mysterious cash shortages. Four or five times the bank had been short as much as $200, and it had never been determined how the money was taken or by whom. In reporting this information, Constable Roe was careful to point out that Kelly was not being accused of the thefts by his former employer, who considered him to be trustworthy. "The source does not suspect Kelly but mentioned the occurrence as a matter of fact."

The picture that emerged from Kelly's four months at the bank's Dawson Creek branch was also unsettling. Although bank personnel again said that they believed Kelly to be honest, they told Corp. R. L. Belter about an episode that raised doubts about his character. After resigning from the management trainee program with the explanation that "the bank wasn't for him," Kelly had shown up three months later at a branch in Victoria with six or seven "unprotectographed," or blank, personal money orders that he wanted to turn in. He explained that he must have inadvertently packed the money orders in his private papers when he left Dawson Creek. When pressed by bank officials about exactly how the financial instruments had come into his possession, the young man declared that he really didn't know.

J. L. Cotter, the officer in charge of recruitment at RCMP headquarters in Ottawa, was troubled. He made his feelings clear in a confidential memo to the commanding officer of the Victoria detachment: "It is difficult to understand how personal money orders from the bank could possibly make their way into Kelly's luggage by mistake. It would appear that there is some question here as to Kelly's honesty and further enquiries should be made with the banks involved to ascertain if there is any possible way an employee could take personal money orders home by mistake and the exact circumstances concerned in the ultimate return of the money orders at Victoria. Kindly have the necessary enquiries conducted and report accordingly."

His instructions were carried out, but the report simply confirmed that there was "no way that the money orders in question should have left the bank." At this point, the Criminal Investigation Branch (CIB) became involved in Kelly's screening process. Insp. G. L. Dalton wrote a confidential letter to the commissioner of the RCMP in Ottawa that made clear where he stood in the matter: "In view of the information obtained during the investigation of the applicant's honesty, I would suggest that there is sufficient doubt to render him unacceptable as a member of the force."

Curiously, Dalton's letter remained in Victoria with the notation "not forwarded" handwritten across the bottom. A week later another CIB investigator was dispatched to the bank's executive offices in Vancouver for a more precise assessment of its former employee. Once again, the bank's response was damaging but not damning.

Inspector Dalton was unsatisfied with what he saw as the bank's coyness. He wanted to know if bank officials suspected that Kelly was a thief. On June 23, 1970, RCMP investigators returned to the bank a final time to ask Kelly's former employer if they would rehire him. If they were hoping for a definitive answer to help them in their screening process, they were to be disappointed: "They would not go so far as to say that they suspected Kelly of any dishonesty," Corp. G. S. McDonald reported, "but did say subject had reapplied for employment with the Bank and that they did not rehire him."

In his final letter to the commissioner of the RCMP, Inspector Dalton resolved the doubts about Kelly's honesty in the applicant's favour – a turn-around from his earlier assessment based on the same evidence. After noting that Kelly should not have had the blank money orders in his possession, and that the Bank of Montreal would not rehire him, he pointed out that bank officials still insisted that they did not suspect him of dishonesty. (In fact, one bank official in Port Alberni told an RCMP investigator that he did suspect Kelly of stealing money from the bank but didn't want to make a formal accusation without definitive proof.) "This concludes enquiries in this regard and it would appear the applicant is suitable material for consideration."

On Tuesday, November 3, 1970, the RCMP finally gave the green light to the applicant who had caused it so much trouble over the previous several months. At 6:30 P.M., the recruit boarded a train in Vancouver bound for six months' training at RCMP boot camp in Regina.

Patrick Kelly was going to be a Mountie after all.

4

THE NATURAL

$\mathbf{A}$s he drove west from Toronto along the Queen Elizabeth Highway towards a rendezvous with the target, an attractive blonde with heroin for sale, Patrick Kelly glanced at his image in the rearview mirror and permitted himself a tight smile. He had always known it would come to this: alone, without a badge, gun, or body-pack, and about to enter the deadly world of heroin trafficking as an undercover agent of the RCMP.

In the left breast pocket of his sports jacket, he could feel the bulge of the envelope containing the $5,000 "flash money" he would use to facilitate the deal. It wasn't as reassuring as a gun (by choice he never carried one), but it was all he had to get him through the assignment. He hoped it would be enough. His senses honed to a razor's edge by a mixture of fear and exhilaration, he rolled down the window and took a deep breath of cool spring air.

As a member of the Toronto drug squad, he had made dozens of arrests and often assisted other agents in covert assignments, but this was the first time he himself had worked as an operator with a full cover team. Although he lacked formal training for his new role, there was no shortage of backup to help him make a successful début. The new Monte Carlo he was driving had phony plates, and Kelly's false driver's licence matched the bogus registration that had been prepared for him back at the Jarvis Street headquarters just in case the drug dealers, as they often did, ran a check on his car.

Manoeuvring through the evening traffic, Kelly occasionally spotted the ghost cars that carried the ten or so other RCMP officers taking part in the operation. Their presence wasn't as reassuring as it should have been. Even with "the cavalry" close by, Kelly knew that he would soon be disappearing into an apartment building far from the friendly eyes, ears, and guns of his colleagues. It was, he thought, a little like disarming a bomb; you could take every precaution in the book, but there was no guarantee that it wouldn't blow up in your face.

Every undercover operation had its share of imponderables, but this one was unusually ticklish. Kelly had been introduced to the target by Réjean Chenard, a French-speaking informant who had approached police with details about a heroin trafficking operation involving a young woman named Jackie Beth Whilan and her addict-boyfriend. Deeply involved in the drug trade himself, Chenard was looking for both money and "consideration" from the RCMP in return for his information. Since Kelly was the only member on the drug squad who spoke French, he had drawn the undercover assignment.

At an initial meeting at a shopping plaza in Mississauga, where Kelly was introduced as Chenard's relative, Whilan agreed to meet with him at her apartment. There, she promised, he would be able to buy heroin. Kelly made it clear that he was not a user but a connection, someone trying to establish a line of supply for others – the handiest way of avoiding the unwanted invitation to sample the drugs he was after. Wary about providing him with her precise address, Whilan instead gave Kelly directions to a Mississauga apartment complex, a pair of high-rise buildings that faced each other across a circular driveway. The building with the blonde waiting in the lobby would be the right one.

It was an arrangement designed to put a police officer in touch with his sweat glands. Kelly didn't know the identity of Whilan's boyfriend or who he would be "scoring" from, so it was impossible to prepare properly for the meeting. He couldn't even be sure that the people he was about to do business with didn't already know him from his work as a street-level drug investigator. Worst of all, he couldn't give his cover team the number of the apartment where the deal was to go down. Once inside, whether he got out again was entirely up to him.

As promised, Whilan met Kelly in the lobby. After making sure that he hadn't been followed, she guided the undercover agent into the elevator and pressed the button for the fifth floor. As they surged upwards, Kelly was sure that his cover team would now be inside the lobby, watching the indicator to see the floor where the deal would take place. Soon, he thought, his colleagues would have every exit covered in case things went wrong.

Once Kelly and Whilan were inside the apartment, Whilan's boyfriend expertly frisked the new customer, confirming for Kelly one of his cardinal rules as an undercover agent: never wear a wire when making a buy. Satisfied that the stranger was clean, Whilan's boyfriend asked to see Kelly's money. After producing his flash roll, Kelly ordered two "bundles" of heroin for $700. (A bundle is twenty-five capsules of the drug wrapped in a condom.) Whilan made a phone call and casually announced that "Sammy and Johnny" would be over in a few minutes.

Kelly shivered. Salvatore "Sammy" Gallo and Johnny Woods were well-known hoods with loose connections to the mob. Woods had gained gruesome notoriety in the police community a few years before when the gun he was carrying in his waistband accidentally discharged and blew off part of his penis. But Kelly had more to think about than Johnny Woods' unfortunate aim; just a year earlier, he had personally arrested the two men who were now on their way over to sell him heroin.

Kelly considered pulling the plug on the buy but decided instead to play it out. For one thing, a lot of time had passed since his encounter with Gallo and Woods, and sporting a new hairstyle, he looked quite different than he had when he'd busted them. A second factor was the strange phenomenon he had often witnessed since joining the drug squad: at the time of arrest and interrogation, a subject was usually under such intense stress that he tended to see the badge but not the police officer behind it. If the subject was also under the influence of drugs, as Gallo and Woods had been, it was Kelly's experience that "they couldn't recognize you if they tripped over you the next day." It was a risky call, but better than aborting his first undercover mission.

To a man who was happiest living on the edge, it seemed like an acceptable enough throw of the dice until Theresa and John Gunning, without buzzing up from the lobby or bothering to knock, walked through the door of Whilan's apartment. The Gunnings were heroin addicts anxious to score from Gallo and Woods. Theresa, who had been arrested by Kelly just weeks earlier, took one look at the well-dressed man sitting on the couch and turned in horror to Whilan.

"He's a fucking cop," she shrieked.

It was every undercover agent's nightmare. Without a word, Kelly leaped over the coffee table and "really drifted" his accuser in the face, knocking her over the chesterfield. Then Kelly grabbed John and shoved him up against the wall, pressing his knee against the terrified man's groin and hissing at him through clenched teeth.

"Who the fuck is this bitch? I'm not here for this kind of shit."

Already unnerved by Kelly's calculated "animal act," the Gunnings quickly admitted their mistake when Whilan unexpectedly waded in on Kelly's side for reasons of her own. As the person who had invited him to the apartment, it was in her best interests to convince her associates that he wasn't a narcotics agent, particularly with Sammy and Johnny about to arrive with a supply of heroin.

"What the hell do you think you're doin', Theresa?" Whilan said, applying a cold cloth to her friend's swollen face. "I know this guy. We used to live together in Montreal." Kelly could only marvel at her timely lie.

"Yeah, honey," John chimed in. "You must have made a mistake."

"Maybe I did," the injured woman slurred, still dazed from Kelly's punch. "Come on Johnny, let's get out of here."

Five minutes later Gallo and Woods showed up. Luckily for Kelly they were clearly "on the nod" (high on heroin) and their recall wasn't as good as Theresa Gunning's. Two and a half hours after he arrived, Kelly left the apartment with two bundles of heroin, the first physical evidence in an investigation that would go on for months and eventually lead to a successful infiltration of the intensely secretive drug trade of Toronto's Little Italy.

Kelly's RCMP handlers were "real impressed" with his bold handling of the Gunnings and his "ballsy" approach to Gallo and Woods. The point of the evening wasn't lost on anyone. If an unschooled Patrick

Kelly could make a heroin buy that would lead to higher level transactions on his first outing as an undercover agent, what could he do with specialized training?

No one who had helped train the recruit from Victoria would have guessed that he would one day be a star of the drug squad. During the six months that he was at RCMP boot camp in Regina, Kelly's performance had been resoundingly average. His record in academic subjects was satisfactory, his assignments were prompt, neat, and complete, and he asked good questions in class. Although his instructors and fellow recruits occasionally found him "overly talkative," he got along well with everyone in his troop.

Given his personal commitment to fitness and the five years of judo instruction, the results of his physical training were surprising. Merely average in self-defence classes, he was a bona fide slouch on the parade square, where instructors tried their best to drum discipline into recruits from the shoe-leather up. Bored by the incessant marching, Kelly thought that his instructor was a "prick" and remembered foot drill as the "ultimate hell" of basic training. Things were not much better in vehicle training, where his instructor noted that he had several "poor" driving habits to overcome, particularly in a city setting.

The recruit was apparently slow in getting the message. Just a week before he graduated, Kelly was given an official RCMP warning after Regina police caught him speeding, 78 m.p.h. in a 60 m.p.h. zone. Calling his actions "totally unacceptable," his superiors reminded him that he had a special responsibility as a peace officer not only to enforce the law but to set an example for others. It was as if Big John Kelly had just tapped him on the shoulder. Policeman's son or policeman, it seemed he had to meet a higher standard than everyone else.

Kelly graduated from boot camp on May 18, 1971, tying for twenty-first place among the thirty-two new Mounties of Troop 18. In most subjects, Memory and Observation, Public Speaking, Practical Training, Driving, Foot Drill, and Self Defence, he received a C. His best mark, an A, came in Typing; his worst, a D, in Physical Training. Not surprisingly, Kelly was given a less than glowing assessment by his RCMP trainers after six months of intensive training and close scrutiny.

"A square-jawed member of small build and little over minimum height, who presents a good appearance in uniform. A youthful looking and somewhat diffident member who flushed easily and impressed as not being too forceful. Nevertheless, he spoke up readily and expressed himself well. Described by his troop supervisor as a quiet, independent member, a bit of a loner and one who tended to do things his own way. Kelly appeared to have enjoyed training, feeling that he had learned a lot, and particularly, to curb his temper. Motivation for the future appears to be satisfactory, with fair to average potential indicated."

Patrick Kelly may not have set the world on fire in the eyes of his instructors, but that didn't matter to the friends and family members who gathered for his graduation. For two days, the RCMP put on quite a show for its guests. There were guided tours of the famous training facility, whose red brick dormitories and leafy grounds were reminiscent of a university campus, and the recruits gave lively demonstrations of their new skills that were carefully designed to showcase each man at his best.

John and Winnifred Kelly squeezed each other's hand when Patrick finally marched into the drill square in his red tunic and tan Stetson for the passing out parade. Bert and Pat Simpson, who hadn't thought twice before agreeing to attend Patrick's big day, were almost as proud of him as his own parents. Victor, who attended Patrick's graduation with his new bride, Kay, was particularly impressed with his boyhood friend's success: "It was something to be proud of. There was a lot of people that attempted to do that and didn't make it. I had just come out of law school and was nice and plump, and there he was, looking great in his red serge, climbing ropes and doing all this fabulous stuff."

A week after he graduated, Const. Patrick Kelly was assigned to "O" Division in Toronto and posted to the City Court Section where he prepared and served summonses. He performed his duties punctually and required a minimum of supervision, but his immediate superiors saw no more in him than a "very adequate policeman."

Although the work was routine, Kelly made the most of his first posting. Since it was his job to help select the court dates for RCMP agents set to testify, he became familiar with their files and got to know the members of the drug squad on a first-name basis. They began inviting the personable young Mountie to the dinner parties they threw at restaurants like Old Angelo's when they cracked a big case. Kelly was fascinated by their stories about the drug world with its big money, fast living, and heart-stopping danger. As their often complex cases, featuring everyone from the sorriest junkie to the most organized drug lord, worked their way through the system, Kelly paid close attention to the way the best agents handled themselves on the stand. With luck, he thought, some day it would be him taking the oath before testifying on behalf of the Crown.

Shortly after he was sent to the RCMP Detachment at Pearson airport for more general policing experience, Kelly formally applied for a transfer to the Drug Section. It was not just that he found routine police duties boring, he was also discovering that he didn't like working in uniform, preferring the individuality and anonymity of civilian clothes. But his casual and cocky demeanour during the interview about his requested transfer convinced Staff Sgt. C. R. Hine that Kelly wasn't ready for specialized police training just yet: "I was left with the feeling that this man is still a little immature. He is a very friendly and talkative person with an abundance of confidence . . . I believe if he were to be selected for the Drug Section at this time, that it would increase his ego and possibly not permit the development . . . into a reliable member. . . . that he has the potential for."

Kelly's request was turned down. Instead, he was posted to the Owen Sound Detachment on February 20, 1972, for a further six months of general duties. Although it was not the transfer he had wanted, he performed his mundane tasks promptly and efficiently, and his superiors noted that he was always willing to put in extra duty without complaint.

But as Victor Simpson had once remarked, no matter where Kelly went, drama was just a step behind. That July, Kelly and a fellow constable rescued two men whose boat had overturned three miles outside Owen Sound harbour in the rough waters of Georgian Bay. The incident earned Kelly his first commendation from his commanding officer. Kelly and his partner, wrote Insp. L. C. Winters, "no doubt saved the lives of these two boaters."

When it came time for a transfer, Kelly's internal personnel assessment expressed only one reservation about the young member. His fellow officers in Owen Sound noticed that Kelly frequently "over-exaggerated" in an attempt to impress them with his personal exploits. A senior officer discussed the criticism with Kelly, who flatly denied telling tall tales. Others had simply "misconstrued" his stories because of the vivid way in which he had related them, he said.

After he was transferred back to "O" Division and the City Court Section, Kelly completed his Recruit Field Training Program with a three-hour written test. If, as his superiors feared, he was given to stretching the truth, this time there would be no need for exaggeration. On a test in which the previous six trainees had averaged 81 per cent, Kelly scored 90 per cent. A few months later, on June 4, 1973, he was rewarded with a transfer to the Toronto Drug Section.

Kelly was assigned to the heroin squad as a street investigator and sometimes cover man for the secret operations of other agents. It was fascinating duty, and it didn't take long for the rookie to figure out that this particular branch of law enforcement operated by its own rules. Before leaving RCMP headquarters to conduct one of his first searches, Kelly was asked by a senior officer if he had his "drop." When it became clear that he had no idea what the man was talking about, the officer opened his desk drawer and tossed Kelly two bundles of heroin. If things went wrong during the search and someone was shot, an investigator had to be ready to explain why he was there in the first place. In this business, the officer said with a wink, a person could never have enough insurance.

Within a few months, Kelly became a specialist in one of the most difficult drug transactions of them all: the "cold" buy of opportunity. Unlike a covered operation, where the agent would be introduced to the target by a paid informant and supported by a team of investigators, Kelly went in "cold" to buy drugs after identifying dealers through his own street investigation. It was a dicey job, since it frequently triggered the dealer's primary tool of survival – a well-developed sense of paranoia. Since the dealer didn't know Kelly, and no one that he *did* know had introduced him, how did Kelly know that he sold drugs? It was up to the RCMP investigator to invent a plausible story to allay the dealer's fears and make the buy. Kelly's lines were obviously convincing. During his first year on the drug squad, he made more than forty buys of opportunity that led to dozens of arrests.

Kelly worked hard at his new job, logging up to sixty hours a week. Making heroin and cocaine purchases by night and investigating and testifying in drug cases by day, he began to attract attention from other areas of the force, which led to even more work. Because of his martial arts skills, Kelly was occasionally seconded for "internal ring" security that the RCMP routinely provided for VIPs. The members of the ring were chosen in part because they were good with their hands. Their task was to deal with "close-quarters" threats – people who managed to penetrate the external ring provided by the Security Service.

Kelly demonstrated how proficient he could be during a general security assignment for Prime Minister Pierre Elliott Trudeau when he made a public visit to a Mississauga shopping plaza. As he hung back on the periphery of the media entourage flowing along with the prime minister, Kelly received instructions to "take out" a placard-waving demonstrator that the SS had determined might be a threat. Kelly approached the target and knocked him out with a karate blow "across the throat." He then threw the man over his shoulder and deposited him in a nearby shoe store, explaining to flustered clerks that he had "passed out" in all the excitement.

Suddenly, the unremarkable recruit from Regina was looking like a winner. In addition to his excellent street record, he had become an expert in lock-picking and electronics and had successfully completed French-language courses at the Ontario Institute for Studies in Education. His service with the City Court Section had acquainted him with how drug prosecutions were conducted and the most effective way of giving evidence. Most of all, Kelly had ably demonstrated that he could handle himself in a physical confrontation, a valuable attribute for the undercover work that so attracted him. The icing on the cake had been Kelly's admirable performance in his first undercover operation, where he had made the buy from Sammy Gallo and Johnny Woods that paved the way for further heroin purchases closer to the source of the drug in Little Italy.

His superiors on the heroin squad were pleased when their "energetic worker" took their advice and formally applied for the RCMP's Undercover Training Course on April 16, 1974. On his application, Kelly listed his favourite sports as karate, judo, scuba-diving, and skiing. In his sedentary leisure time, he wrote, he liked to read books about cars and browse through *Playboy*, *Penthouse*, and *Reader's Digest*. Given six categories in which to compare himself to the average citizen, he listed his agility, endurance, and energy as superior, and his speed, physical strength, and courage as average. Although the officer who interviewed Kelly acknowledged the applicant's obvious credentials for the course, he sounded a cautious note: "Domineering personality. Maybe too good with B.S."

This reservation was put aside when Const. Patrick Kelly became one of sixteen participants chosen from a nationwide field of applicants for Operational Undercover Training – Drugs, Course #4 that took place in Montreal from April 24 to May 15, 1974.

Facing the eight members of the opposing team in an empty Montreal warehouse, Patrick Kelly – whose official identity once he began the RCMP's top-secret undercover training was HQ 208 – understood exactly what was expected of him. He and his teammates were to score on their rivals' untended goal as often as they could during the next thirty minutes and remain on their feet until the game was over. There were no rules, just the single objective of scoring at any cost, a fitting metaphor for the dark business many of them would soon be facing in the real world of the drug trade.

With a shrill blast from the supervisor's whistle, the mayhem began. Players on both sides punched and kicked one another in scrums, gang-tackling the ball carrier or running him into the brick wall if they couldn't drag him down. While Kelly was struggling with an opponent trying to score on his goal, one of his teammates "threw the man into a choke" and kept him there until he passed out in a heap on the ware-house floor. Scooping up the ball and warding off a few defenders along the way, Kelly sprinted down the floor and scored. The supervisors watched silently from the sidelines, recording the performance of each player on clipboards. A second whistle signalled the end of the game, and the trainees were sent back to their hotels to lick their wounds and rest, with orders to return in an hour and a half for further "instruction."

A senior member of the RCMP's Ottawa Drug Section had opened the course with a "pep talk." He told them that the specialized work they were being trained for was dangerous, unorthodox, and controversial. They would be away from family and friends for extended periods, criticized in court for their methods, and targeted for reprisals by the drug dealers they took down. They might also become objects of jealousy within the force because of their unconventional and ostensibly glamorous work, which involved international trips and expense-account living. Other than the challenge and excitement of the job, there wasn't much to balance that dismal prospect, certainly not the dollar-a-day danger pay they would be entitled to as undercover agents. Before finishing his speech, the officer made a final point that he urged his handpicked audience to take to heart. Despite the fact that they were being asked to assume the role, methods, and psyche of criminals, they must *never* forget that they were still law enforcement officers.

To bring home just whose side they were really on, the RCMP brought in a drug prosecutor and a judge to lecture trainees on the courtroom aspects of their work. The Crown attorney explained how he would assist them in court by carefully leading them through their testimony. He told them how he wanted their notes organized and stressed that it was important to attend pretrial meetings to discuss how to camouflage or totally avoid weaknesses in the case before proceedings actually began. If the agent had a particularly damning piece of information, they should work out a way of "sliding it in" where it would have the most damaging effect on the accused. If at any time during cross-examination by the defence they got into difficulty with the prearranged testimony, they should pause, clear their throat, or in some other way signal the prosecutor that it was a good time to object, interrupt, or ask for a recess. Under no circumstances were they to volunteer information beyond the scope of the precise questions they would be asked. The key was to keep to the game plan regardless of what the other side did.

When the Crown attorney was finished, the judge underscored the need for professional police witnesses and the Crown to get their act together before the first witness took the stand. After lecturing the trainees on what he expected from them when they testified in his court, he recommended that they jointly review all police and Crown briefs to resolve "innocent inconsistencies" that might be seized upon by the defence if they were brought out in open court. He also noted that grooming often had an impact on juries: a presentable witness was more apt to be believed than an ill-kempt one. It was a tip that Kelly never forgot: image was an important element of credibility.

The classroom component of the course was offered by experienced officers like Ben Soave, famous in RCMP circles for his illustrious career in the drug squad, including the successful infiltration of the Toronto Mafia while working undercover. The trainees were taught how to work with informants, how to simulate the effects of drugs like cocaine during a buy, and how to carry out the all-important search for incriminating intelligence. They were reminded that the security operations of banks and telephone companies were usually run by ex-police officers who would often make information available to the RCMP on an informal basis. For those more difficult situations where it was undesirable to go through official channels, the trainees were taught how to pick locks and make surreptitious entry into a suspect's home or business – a practice with which Kelly was already familiar.

"Warrants were never used for these information searches," he remembered. "You B&E the place, get your info, and get out. Often we would cover the searches by having someone in the area who had a 'writ of assistance.' If you got caught in the act of checking a place, you would simply grab the intruder and call in the guy with the writ and *voilà*, instant legal search! The other alternative was to whack him on the head and run like hell."

An operative from the U.S. Drug Enforcement Agency lectured the group on some of the international aspects of the drug trade, including how the Colombian cartels laundered their huge profits by investing in dummy companies in North America or by using couriers to transport cash out of the country to the safety of foreign banks. The world's leading crime groups, including the Mafia and the Oriental Triads, were discussed in detail, from their organization to some of their bloodthirsty deeds. As course instructors constantly tried to remind their students, they would be dealing on a day-to-day basis with people for whom life meant nothing and murder was a normal means of conducting business.

Every aspect of undercover work was dealt with in detail: working with informants, surveillance and counter-surveillance, safe houses from which agents were based during an operation, negotiating techniques, and survival methods. Since a key skill of the future agents would be their ability to deceive a target, they were lectured about the fine points of a good cover story. Experienced operators like Soave suggested that trainees adopt "covers" that closely resembled true facts, inventing only those few elements that were necessary to hoodwink the target. A cover that became too elaborate was a cover that was easily blown. Whatever persona they chose to adopt, the RCMP could provide them with false identification, from driver's licences and credit cards to official passports. But the trainees were cautioned against over-using fabricated documentation. The force would not be able to protect an agent if he ended up in custody with phony but untraceable documents that the RCMP had illegally produced. In such circumstances, it was tacitly understood, the agent was on his own.

Since the RCMP didn't want its people using public money to buy bogus product, the trainees were given chemical kits supplied by Health and Welfare Canada to test the nature and purity of the drugs they bought. (Long before he attended the course, Kelly carried a small ampoule in which he ran his own tests on the heroin and cocaine he purchased on the streets of Toronto. The bulkier Health and Welfare kits were almost exclusively for the use of cover men.) By watching how certain drugs dissipated in water, or by heating them in a piece of tinfoil and noting the colour of the smoke and the residue, Kelly could ascertain purity levels and the cutting agent used.

When it came to those sensitive areas where drug enforcement agents are left straddling the line between legal and illegal acts, the trainees got official RCMP policy by day and another story by night. Although the force made it clear that it never sanctioned the sampling of drugs by its agents in the course of their undercover work, Kelly was told by experienced agents that there were going to be times when he would have to "use a little something" in order to maintain his cover. He was also told that whatever a Crown prosecutor may say about the need for full disclosure by the police, the only sacred partnership was between an undercover agent and his cover man. Given the nature of their work, they would sometimes have to rewrite, reshape, and mould notes, hide things from the Crown, and even lie on the stand. After all, "the Crown was a nice guy, but he wasn't an undercover cop." The basic rules of engagement came down to a single imperative: doing "whatever had to be done to survive" regardless of how your superiors wanted you to play.

"These conversations were off the record and usually held while socializing in bars or taverns in Montreal. . . . It was this extra instruction that many felt was the most beneficial because it was the real stuff of the real situation. . . . It was a brainwashing game and one that was played by two sets of rules – the official ones in the classrooms and the unofficial ones which were taught after hours," Kelly recalled.

The most important element of the course was the extensive role-playing that trainees were put through by operators, cover men, and acting coaches. Here a trainee's mastery of street jargon, cover story, and the all-important element of personal poise could be put to the test in a practical situation. The "drug plays" in which the trainees took the parts of traffickers, users, and connections were then critiqued by experienced agents and informants. (It wasn't always acting. A particularly dramatic part of the training took place when a heroin addict who was also an RCMP informant shot up in front of the trainees so that they could see firsthand the effect of the drug in order to be able to recognize it in the field.)

With their classroom work completed, the trainees were sent out to make real buys from known traffickers in the Montreal area. They were instructed to make their purchases and then return to a safe house where they would hand over their drugs to instructors, write up their notes, and relate their experiences to the group. It came as an unwelcome surprise to some of the students when the "traffickers" they had scored from turned out to be RCMP drug personnel who showed up at the safe house with tape recordings of the various transactions. Instructors then played back the buy as it had actually happened and noted any discrepancies with the trainee operator's notes and verbal report. Those who had embellished or in any way misreported their dealings were humiliated in front of the group. Keenly aware of the potential for abuse in the field of undercover operations, the force was anxious to remind the trainees that a dishonest undercover agent could never be sure who he was buying from or when he himself might be under surveillance.

After having their mock purchase critiqued, the group was sent out a second time to make a "cold buy" in Montreal's bar district. Kelly, who had impressed his instructors to this point with his savvy and adept role-playing, returned with heroin he claimed to have purchased from a black drug dealer he met in a bar on Crescent Street. The instructors were immediately suspicious. The heroin he brought in was in capsule form, typical of how the drug was sold in Toronto; in Montreal, it almost always came wrapped in tinfoil. Since the instructors knew that Kelly had already made dozens of heroin purchases in Toronto, they accused him of "setting up his own buy" with drugs he had brought to the course. Kelly denied the allegation, and since he had not made the purchase from an RCMP officer posing as a dealer, there was no alternative but to take his word.

Near the end of the course, the RCMP sprung yet another surprise on the trainees. When they showed up at the safe house they had been using as a base for their practice drug purchases, they were told that they would be spending the next twenty-four hours on the street, after being stripped of all money, jewellery, and identification. Officially, this was an exercise in urban survival, a dry run in living like their targets that might well save their lives in future operations; unofficially, it was a game to see which trainee came back with the most money and drugs.

Short of resorting to physical violence, there were no restrictions on how that might be done. Each trainee was to avoid the police and return to the safe house at a predetermined time. If they were arrested, they were not to talk about the course or the fact that they were members of the RCMP. Instead, each of them was given the telephone number of a lone Montreal police officer who knew about their presence in the city and would arrange their bail. No one had to be told that if they had to use the telephone number, their future did not lie in undercover work.

In his first hour on the street, Kelly approached a girl and asked for money. Dressed in blue jeans and a T-shirt, he explained that he'd just gotten out of hospital after a car accident the day before. To make matters worse, he had lost his wallet somewhere along the way and was now quite hungry. Instead of giving him the price of a meal, the attractive French Canadian girl invited him to lunch. They talked amiably for over an hour and before his benefactor went back to work, she had given Kelly the key to her apartment and invited him to spend the night.

"She gave me twenty bucks and I bought some stuff, shaving stuff and some shampoo and stuff, went to her place and got all cleaned up and she came back and we made whoopee and wound up going to a party that night."

The party provided even better opportunities to advance his private agenda. While some of his less imaginative course mates were sipping coffee at the Salvation Army, Kelly was inveigling a drug dealer he met at the party into fronting him a pound of hashish. He then sold a portion of the hash at a Montreal bar and used part of the proceeds to buy a new set of clothes the next day. When his taxi pulled up in front of the safe house the following afternoon, Kelly had $1,200, a quantity of hashish, and the name of the dealer who had fronted it to him. As the member with the most money, drugs, and usable intelligence, Kelly was the hands-down winner of the exercise.

"Some guys came back with a little bit of weed, a little, you know, a gram of hash. I guess my attitude at that point was to do what I did best."

His RCMP trainers agreed. The officer-in-charge of training and development, Supt. R. G. Moffatt, called Kelly "a natural" for covert operations and recommended him for undercover drug work: "Cst. Kelly is very well motivated and enthusiastic regarding this field of investigation. He was rated as one of the top candidates on the course. He blends well into the target surroundings with his bearing, appearance, and speech. He proved capable of sizing up new situations with exceptional speed and adjusting to meet requirements. He appeared very persistent in any task undertaken and was able to take necessary and appropriate action on his own. Cst. Kelly's . . . natural ability for undercover work should make him an excellent operator. He is considered capable of a long term operation in any area of drug enforcement at any level. He has the potential to work up to the higher levels of a trafficking organization and should be used in that capacity. Recommended for a metropolitan area."

Besides his obvious affinity for the work, there was another thing that made Kelly an appealing choice for undercover work – he was single. "While Kelly enjoys the companionship of a number of young ladies," one of his superiors wrote in a 1974 assessment, "he has no marriage plans."

The RCMP's newest undercover agent may not have been thinking about a trip to the altar, but it was a different story for the determined young woman who was by then living with him. After a long distance telephone romance, Jeannette Hanlon had crossed the Atlantic and a personal Rubicon to live with the Mountie she had so briefly met in Mexico. With her parents' marriage in ruins and the failed relationship with Dan Coyle still a bitter memory, she had no intention of returning to Scotland as a single woman.

5

THE PURSUIT OF HAPPINESS

The sight of his bride climbing the steps of St. Catherine of Sienna Church took Patrick Kelly's breath away. Her long, white veil fluttered behind her and her shoulder-length brown hair shone in the autumn sun. From the moment he first saw her, he had been attracted by Jeannette's regal bearing, and today she swept into the suburban Mississauga church like a princess entering a medieval cathedral. A small woman, Jeannette Hanlon could still fill up a room with her larger-than-life presence.

At the church, Kelly was so taken with his bride that he almost missed it when Jeannette's maid of honour, seven months pregnant with twins, swooned just before the ceremony began. At the last moment, Kelly recovered and caught Joanne MacLean, steadying her until the fainting spell passed. Standing in front of the altar, which was bedecked for the occasion with yellow and white chrysanthemums, he barely heard Father Joseph Pranzo intone the words that made him and Jeannette husband and wife.

It hardly seemed possible to Kelly that a year and a half had passed since their brief affair in Acapulco. When he and Jeannette had met in a queue in front of Carlo's and Charlie's, one of the resort town's most popular restaurants, matrimony had been the last thing on Kelly's mind. He enjoyed his work on the heroin squad and the carefree bachelor's life that came with it, racing around Toronto in his Mini-Cooper with a variety of pretty girls when he wasn't laying traps for drug dealers. Vacationing with his roommate and fellow Mountie, Wayne Humby, the twenty-three-year-old police officer had simply been looking for a little fun, just as he had when he and Victor Simpson doubledated as teenagers back in Victoria. "Patrick was never very close to girls," Simpson recalled. "He took a lot of girls out and enjoyed their company, but he didn't want long, lasting relationships with them."

From the very beginning, Jeannette was an exception to Kelly's rule. He found himself deeply attracted to the pretty, well-dressed, and obviously cosmopolitan young woman whose dark hair was streaked with premature strands of silver. He teased her about her accent and the duck emblazoned on her expensive sweater; she was charmed by his playful attentions and boyish good looks. They arranged to meet later for dinner and were entranced by each other. They made love that first night under the famous wooden cross overlooking Acapulco's harbour and spent the rest of their holiday as if it were a honeymoon, sharing candlelit dinners and midnight trysts on the beach.

The young Mountie quickly realized that Jeannette was a woman with a lot to offer beyond the bedroom. Fluent in several languages, she showed off her Spanish in a haggling session in a local market, helping Kelly buy an onyx chess set for half the asking price. Jeannette impressed him with her easy grace in every social setting, displaying a degree of "polish" he had never seen in any of his dates back home. Whether in evening dress or a T-shirt and cutoffs, she "moved well" and was in command of herself and the situation, high virtues to a man who had undergone intensive training to be able to do the same things.

Even though he knew nothing about the daredevil of Loch Lomond, he soon found out that his new companion was far from being all elegance and *savoir faire*. Against the advice of the resort, the couple rented a Jeep and drove into the hills around Acapulco, a risky outing given the rampant crime beyond the protective confines of their hotel. Patrick was delighted to find that Jeannette was every bit as confident and adventurous as he was. With her languages, social gifts, and brimming self-confidence, he couldn't help thinking that she had all the essential ingredients of a good undercover agent.

Their time in the sun went by all too quickly. Before Jeannette departed for Scotland, Patrick invited her to visit him sometime in Toronto. She didn't tell him that part of her reason for flying home was to see an old flame in Glasgow. A few weeks later, when it became obvious that Dan Coyle was no longer romantically interested in Jeannette, she shifted her attentions to her Canadian Mountie.

In March 1974, she flew to Toronto on a free pass from Quantas Airlines and stayed with Patrick at the Hurontario Street apartment he shared with Wayne Humby. They doubledated with Humby and his girlfriend, dined out in the city's excellent restaurants, and even attended an RCMP party thrown by one of Kelly's superiors. The four-week visit persuaded Jeannette to move to Canada. Patrick said he would act as her sponsor and, depending on how things turned out, perhaps much more.

Although she never told him, Jeannette was following an agenda of her own. She was twenty-six years old, and as far as she was concerned, ready for marriage. With her dreams of Dan Coyle finally dashed, she was in the market for a replacement, and this charming and confident young man with so many rough edges for her to smooth seemed like the ideal candidate.

After Jeannette returned to Scotland, the couple engaged in a long distance romance by letter and telephone. When his monthly phone bill began to eat into his share of the rent, Kelly had to put their transatlantic love affair on a budget. But the smitten young man had more on his mind than his finances, as the poem he wrote about their fateful meeting in Mexico boldly declared:

Making love beneath the cross that's on the hill . . .
Who put it there and why? . . .
Perhaps for sailors who entered in the harbour . . .
Maybe it has been put there just for us to watch,
And gaze upon as we make love for this first time.
Maybe it's to tell us of a future, of hopes, of unity, of covenant,
Of permanence, of something more than let's play and be gone.
Acapulco, the cross upon the hill . . .
It leads us to the altar . . .
I met Jeannette here.

The plodding pace of Canada's immigration bureaucracy was no match for the lovers' ardour. The impatient couple decided to take a European vacation while Jeannette awaited permission to come to Canada. They stopped first in Glasgow where Kelly did little to endear himself to Jeannette's family and friends. They were distinctly cool to her North American love interest, citing the same trait that had bothered Kelly's colleagues in the Owen Sound Detachment of the RCMP: his overly dramatic accounts of his exploits as a Mountie. Jeannette's father in particular took a dislike to the cocky young man who had won his daughter's heart.

"He kept rambling on about breaking into a guy's house and getting him with drugs . . . and the guy set a dog on him," Jimmy Hanlon recalled. "He told us he shot the dog and after he shot the dog, he told me he put the gun in the guy's mouth. I couldn't take to this young guy at all."

With her parents' marriage in ruins (the Hanlons were now formally separated and on their way to a divorce), Jeannette couldn't have cared less that her father had misgivings about the man she hoped would be her husband. She and Patrick drove south from Scotland through England and then crossed the Channel to the continent. Jeannette revelled in tutoring her street-smart but otherwise unsophisticated charge. As for Patrick, travelling with Jeannette was like the university education he had never had. She talked knowledgeably about the famous places they passed through, switching from English to perfect French when they docked in France and began the beautiful drive south. Jeannette captivated Patrick with her tales of the marvels of Nice, Monte Carlo, and the Riviera. They were lessons he never forgot. "That's where I became very fond of the south of France," he later recalled.

Jeannette's immigration papers came through in the late summer of 1974, and she arrived in Toronto in early September. After a brief stay at Patrick's Hurontario Street apartment, the couple found their own place at 1055 Bloor Street East in Mississauga, a "much nicer" address in Jeannette's opinion. Hanlon was furious when he learned about his daughter's decision to move in with Kelly and abruptly stopped making his weekly Sunday phone calls.

Undeterred by her father's bitter displeasure, which with all the confidence of a favourite child she rightly suspected would pass, Jeannette went about the business of settling into her new home. She used her fluent Spanish to land a job in downtown Toronto as a reservations agent with Avianca Airlines, the national carrier of Colombia. The second income would help them to have the kind of life she had known in Newton Mearns; Kelly's meagre salary of $21,000 a year clearly would not be enough.

During their leisure time, the couple kept to themselves, shunning for the most part the RCMP functions that other members and their wives found so important. Jeannette made it clear after the first RCMP party she attended that she didn't particularly enjoy the macho and often uncouth antics of Patrick's colleagues. As for Patrick, he was just as happy to boycott these social events because he was always afraid that a fellow officer would let slip to Jeannette how dangerous his job really was. Whatever her friends and relatives may have thought about him, Kelly's "tall" stories about his life as a drug agent were much closer to fact than fiction than any of them could imagine.

On February 7, 1975, the *Globe and Mail* carried a story about a series of predawn police raids around Toronto that smashed a major heroin and cocaine ring. The RCMP arrested twenty-one people, issued warrants for thirteen others, and closed down an illegal "speed" lab that had been operating out of a legitimate Weston, Ontario, business office. Among those arrested were Salvatore Gallo and Theresa Gunning.

The *Globe* reported that the arrests were the result of an eight-month investigation by an unusually resourceful RCMP undercover operator who had posed as an out-of-town drug distributor. The investigation had originally been aimed at heroin traffickers, but the agent had managed to work his way into an international cocaine syndicate as well. Over the course of the lengthy operation, he had purchased 558 caps of heroin and 11 ounces of cocaine with an estimated street value of $100,000. Although Kelly's name did not appear in the story, his superiors clipped the article to his RCMP service record.

Unaware of the details of his work and preferring it that way, Jeannette saw herself and Patrick as a cut above his RCMP associates and enlisted his help in keeping their social distance from them. By nature a loner, Patrick didn't need much persuading. "They [the RCMP] liked to sit around and drink beer and watch football games," he said, "and that was very boring to both Jeannette and I."

Instead, they preferred to dine out at least twice a week in fashionable bistros like La Petite Place on Eglinton Avenue and go for long walks around Grenadier Pond in High Park. Jeannette was an avid movie and television buff and would often sit in front of their TV set knitting while Patrick lifted weights in their spare room. One of their favourite pastimes was dancing, which they pursued with the same discretion that directed their approach to the social aspects of RCMP life: "We would pick and choose the places very carefully, and if we went dancing, it would not be at the discos but in the finer hotels," Patrick recalled.

Jeannette was as particular about her friends as she was about her dance clubs. Normally disdainful of anyone associated with the RCMP, she made an exception in the case of Joanne MacLean, the wife of sometimes RCMP informant Ian MacLean. Patrick and Ian were already friends and Jeannette struck up an independent relationship with the shy young nurse who initially found her totally intimidating. "My first impression of Jeannette was of somebody much older than myself and in fact older than she herself was. She was very sophisticated."

But when Jeannette Hanlon liked someone, she quickly dropped her aristocratic airs and turned on the charm. Like so many others who had experienced her winsome side, Joanne was soon won over, and the two women began spending a lot of time together. Always happiest when she was directing the affairs of others, Jeannette helped the MacLeans pick out their first house and took the lead hand in decorating it.

Far from being offended, Joanne appreciated the tasteful interventions of her cultured friend. Nor did she mind when Jeannette borrowed her silver, china, and placemats for dinner parties with the terse explanation that for now, at least, she and Patrick couldn't afford such things. From the way her friend said it, Joanne had the feeling that it wouldn't be that way for long if Jeannette Hanlon had anything to do about it.

The other couple that made it into Patrick and Jeannette's restricted circle of friends was John Pinkerton Hastey and his American fiancée, Dawn Taber. A fellow member of the drug squad, "Pinkie," as he was known on the force, often worked as part of Patrick's cover team. The burly police officer had met Dawn, a native of Calais, Maine, in his hometown of St. Stephen, New Brunswick, when they were both teenagers. After John was transferred to the Drug Section, he invited Dawn to live with him in Toronto while they planned their wedding.

A sweet-natured "country girl" with auburn hair to her waist and soulful grey-blue eyes, Dawn had briefly been a member of the police force in Calais, where she spent a short time on the street as an under-cover drug agent. Unlike Dawn's future husband, the happy and guile-less young woman was an immediate hit with Jeannette. Again, Jeannette adopted the comfortable role of self-appointed tutor, advising Dawn on everything from how to dress to matters of personal grooming. The two couples went out together, and John and Dawn were frequently treated to the *cordon bleu* cooking that Jeannette had learned at Neuchâtel. Although Dawn had not been to finishing school, she made an impor-tant contribution to these gourmet feasts whenever Patrick and Jeannette went shopping at the Dominion Store where she worked part-time as a check-out girl. "I'd shove through these big roasts and legs of lamb and steaks and ring up the potatoes," she recalled.

Shortly after John and Dawn's wedding that summer, Patrick notified the officer-in-charge of the Toronto Drug Section that he planned to marry Miss Jeannette Hanlon on September 20, 1975. A week later, the RCMP approved his request to take a four-week Spanish course in Bogota, Colombia, commencing August 1. His holiday in France had left Patrick interested in international police work, and he hoped the Spanish immersion course would be the first step towards earning a transfer to Europe as a drug liaison officer. In addition to the language skills that the RCMP hoped its "mature and dedicated young member" would acquire, it also wanted him to establish contacts in Colombia since much of the cocaine sold in Toronto originated in that country. If he could accomplish his dual mission, the $744 fee for the course would be taxpayers' money well spent.

Although her own employer, Avianca Airlines (along with Javeriana University and the Colombian government), sponsored the course, Jeannette had misgivings about Patrick's South American trip and shared them with Joanne MacLean. It was bad enough to be left alone for so long, but she also feared that she might be in personal danger given the nature of Patrick's work. Although he never consciously showed any signs of the pressure of his underworld role-playing, Patrick had begun to grind his teeth so severely at night that the RCMP had provided him with a custom-made mouth guard to wear in his sleep. The force concluded that his bruxism was directly related to job stress. With Patrick away, Jeannette was terrified that the demons that pursued him in his restless dreams might come after her in the real world.

Joanne MacLean tried to calm her friend's nerves by focusing her energies on her upcoming wedding. The two friends planned the reception back at the apartment and the wedding feast to follow at the Old Mill restaurant. Joanne even arranged for a top Yorkville fashion designer to make Jeannette's wedding dress. When Patrick returned from Colombia, his wedding was still a few weeks away but everything was in place.

The guest list was an embarrassing and intractable problem. Apart from the MacLeans, the Hasteys, and Wayne Humby, most of the bride and groom's friends lived in distant countries or provinces, leaving only the RCMP members who made Jeannette so uncomfortable to fill a few rows of the church. His opinion of Patrick unchanged, Jeannette's father flatly refused to attend the wedding. Since Patrick had asked his parents not to fly in from Victoria because of the cost, the only immediate family member in the wedding party was the bride's mother. But Lottie Hanlon's presence turned out to be more of a burden than a blessing. The night before the wedding, she took her daughter aside and pleaded with her to reconsider her decision.

"Jeannette, I really don't think he's your match. I just don't like him. There's something about this chap I just don't like."

"I know what I *want*," the young woman frostily replied. On the day of the wedding, the bride and her mother were on such bad terms that they stopped speaking halfway through the festivities. Jeannette fumed to Joanne MacLean that her elegantly dressed mother was "trying to steal the show" on *her* big day.

Conspicuous by his absence was Victor Simpson. The best friend who had once travelled from Victoria to Regina for Patrick's RCMP graduation was not only not invited, he wasn't even told about the wedding until several months later. Simpson later attributed Patrick's strange omission to his new role with the RCMP. "Things started to change after he got into the drug squad. That's when he became very tight-mouthed with everything that he did."

Six months after their wedding, the Kellys bought their first house, a gingerbread-style, red-brick Victorian surrounded by mature elms in the small community of Cookstown. John and Dawn Hastey helped them move in. Jeannette gave up her job at Avianca Airlines and went to work for a travel agency in nearby Barrie. Since they couldn't afford city prices, it had seemed like a godsend when Patrick's second cousin, John McKay, offered them his Cookstown property for only $68,500. When the MacLeans drove up from Mississauga to see it for the first time, Joanne was astonished and impressed. "It was a big, big house for two people," she remembered.

It was also an ideal place to start a family. Although she had been indifferent to the idea of having children when she married Patrick, Jeannette began to reconsider her views during Joanne MacLean's pregnancy. When Joanne went into hospital, Jeannette doted on her "like the mother of the mother." After the twin girls were born, she bought them sleepers and stuffed animals and decided that she wanted children of her own after all.

For several years, Jeannette had been using injections of DepoProvera as a means of birth control. Now her gynaecologist told her that the effects of the powerful drug could take up to a year to work their way out of her system. Further complicating her maternal aspirations was the considerable scar tissue resulting from previous abdominal surgery – an appendectomy and the removal of ovarian cysts. Getting pregnant would not be easy.

Reluctant to believe that she alone was the cause of the problem, Jeannette wanted a full fertility workup done on herself and Patrick. He refused. After five months of unsuccessfully trying to get pregnant, Jeannette abruptly gave up and announced that she was going to have her tubes tied instead. She didn't appreciate it when other RCMP wives expressed their disapproval of so dramatic a procedure for such a young woman. The finality of her decision hinted at the vengefulness that lay behind it.

"This followed about three weeks of hostility towards Pat where she'd throw a remark at him that it was probably his fault, at which point he'd get quite angry and she'd back off again," Joanne MacLean recalled.

With time heavy on her hands, Jeannette threw herself into renovating the Cookstown house from top to bottom, even adding a new room. Unhappy with the furniture that had come with the property, she began collecting early Canadiana antiques, which Patrick taught himself to restore. After only a few months of concentrated effort, the couple had transformed the rundown house into a local showpiece. But Patrick's frequent absences on assignment meant his unhappy wife was more often than not alone in the big, empty house. The Kellys had no friends in the neighbourhood and Jeannette lavished her attentions on their sheepdog, Kelly, doting on her like the frustrated mother she was – or so it seemed to her friends.

"The dog seemed a sort of surrogate child for them," Ian MacLean said. "If you invited them over for dinner, it was understood that the dog was coming too. They hand-fed the animal from the table, and whenever they went grocery shopping, they bought the dog its own peanut butter. Jeannette told us how she would dress the dog up in nightgowns, which we thought was bizarre, to say the least."

Beset with strange medical problems that left her feeling totally enervated, Jeannette left the Barrie travel agency shortly after the move to Cookstown and went on unemployment insurance for most of 1976. Suffering from inexplicable nausea, headaches, dizziness, lower abdominal pain, and loss of appetite, she badgered the doctors at Women's College Hospital in Toronto to find out what was wrong with her. After an internal examination, X-rays, and an exhaustive battery of tests that stretched over many months, they finally concluded that her problem was a spastic colon brought on by stress.

The news came as no surprise to Patrick. Even though he made it a point not to discuss the details of his work at home, he knew that Jeannette constantly worried about his safety. Sometimes the realities of his job struck home with a vengeance. Shortly after a colleague told Jeannette that Patrick had had "a close call" on a case he had just cracked, another agent the couple knew was nearly murdered. Paul Nadeau, who had been on the undercover course with Patrick in Montreal, and who had frequently dropped into the Kellys' apartment when they lived in Mississauga, was lured into a target's car and savagely beaten with the butt of a shotgun. Unconscious and bleeding profusely, he had been dumped in a ditch and left for dead by his assailant. It was the last straw for Jeannette. She hadn't come to North America to have a police officer show up at her door with the news that she was a widow. Reminding Patrick of their plans to live well and travel, she pressed him to apply for less dangerous work closer to home.

Concerned about Jeannette's health, Patrick suggested to his superiors that he be transferred out of the Drug Section to a detachment in the vicinity of Cookstown. The report generated by his request showed that the RCMP was sympathetic to his predicament but reluctant to lose one of its top undercover agents. Kelly had excelled as an operator, as a cover man, and as a courtroom witness during his three years on the drug squad. In fact, he was so highly thought of by his superiors that he was recommended for corporal even though he hadn't served long enough to qualify for the promotion. But in the end, the force agreed that a change would be beneficial for his "excellent development potential" and his marriage. A handwritten addendum to the report recommending that he be posted to Barrie, Ontario, effective August 3, 1976, drew the administrative lesson from the Kellys' unhappiness: "We should monitor the family situations of all drug undercover operators to ensure we are not destroying the health of the next of kin or marriage relationships."

Things did not improve much for Jeannette after Patrick's transfer. Kelly was expected to finish his ongoing cases in London, Newmarket, and Toronto before taking up his general detachment duties in Barrie. But even after he had completed these jobs, his file showed that he found little "relief from the rigours of extensive undercover activities." He was simply so good at what he did that the Barrie Detachment began using him to make buys of opportunity for its own drug investigations. This happened so frequently that Supt. D. H. Heaton, the officer-in-charge of drug enforcement, stepped in with a blunt directive: Kelly was not to be assigned to further drug investigations since this was defeating the purpose of his transfer.

Since Patrick's ostensible change of duties wasn't giving the Kellys more time together, Jeannette turned her energies in a new direction. In the spring of 1977, she took out a small bank loan and opened a craft store in Cookstown called The Quilt Shoppe. Just as she was getting the business going, her life took an unexpected turn for the better when the MacLeans reappeared in her orbit. Joanne MacLean wanted to stay home with the twins, but while the family lived close to Toronto, they needed her income as a nurse to make ends meet. By moving north, they hoped to cut their living expenses to the point where Joanne could give up her job. Patrick helped by finding Ian a job with the Bradford Paper Group in the advertising department, which supplemented the money MacLean was getting from the RCMP's Security Service as a freelance undercover operator who infiltrated subversive groups. Jeannette was delighted when the MacLeans moved to the small town of Gilford, just a few miles east of Cookstown.

At first, the two couples picked up their friendship where it had left off nearly a year before, going out once or twice a week for dinner or a movie and visiting in each other's houses. It seemed to Ian that the Kellys were "less content" than before, and he sensed that Patrick was bored with his posting in Barrie where he was "less of a celebrity" than he had been in Toronto. As for Jeannette, he got the impression that she was fed up with life in the country, Patrick's job, and his waning physical interest in her. "Jeannette would oftentimes jocularly, but at times with an element of truth or fact in it, complain that she was not getting enough sexual marital relations with Pat. He was either always tired or he was out of town or he was disinterested."

Jeannette called Joanne every morning and the women frequently travelled to Toronto to buy stock for the shop. Recalling the couple that couldn't even afford their own dinner plates, Joanne wondered where they were getting the money for the tasteful renovations to their house and their increasingly lavish lifestyle. Patrick's explanation that he had a polar bear rug business on the side didn't strike Joanne as a plausible explanation. "She would spend a great deal more money than I would on her groceries, and I used to envy her all her gourmet food that she used to buy at that time."

Within a few months, strains began to appear in the friendship between the two couples. Patrick and Jeannette began regularly dropping in on the MacLeans around dinnertime, expecting to be "fed and entertained." Ian thought the Kellys were "taking advantage" of them. Nor did he appreciate Patrick's habit of stopping in for tea with Joanne in the middle of the afternoon.

Though she still had deep feelings for Jeannette, Joanne, too, had her misgivings. Generous at first in occasionally giving Joanne small items from the shop, Jeannette had suddenly begun pressing her to buy expensive items whenever she came by, leaving the impression that things were not going well with the business. Then came the night when Patrick put on an unwelcome demonstration of his physical prowess in the MacLeans' backyard after a barbecue.

"I don't think he meant to knock Ian out, but by doing one manoeuvre he basically knocked him out for a few seconds and flipped him," Joanne recalled. "Telling me that he could pick me up with a finger, he lifted me with one finger under my forearm which I hardly even kept rigid. He lifted me right off the ground like that, seemingly without any effort at all."

After less than a year, to Patrick and Jeannette's dismay, the MacLeans decided that country life wasn't for them and moved back to Mississauga. Although it wasn't the main factor behind their decision to move, putting some distance between themselves and the Kellys was among their reasons. Ian got another advertising job with the *Mississauga Times* to supplement his RCMP pay, but it didn't last long. A few months after he started work, the paper received an anonymous telephone tip that Ian was in fact an RCMP informant using his position at the *Times* as a front. MacLean was fired after an uncomfortable confrontation on his doorstep with one of the paper's senior managers. Although he never found out who had blown his cover, both he and Joanne had their suspicions: "We didn't believe it could be either Pat or Jeannette, but then not too many other people knew."

Increasingly unhappy in Cookstown, Jeannette decided that she, too, wanted to move back to Toronto. They put their house up for sale. The idea of country living had proven more attractive than the reality, and she missed the excitement of the city and the friends she had made there. But more important than any other consideration, she and Patrick had fallen in love with a luxury condominium they had seen at the Palace Pier on Lake Ontario. Situated on nine acres of landscaped lakefront gardens in Etobicoke, just west of the city of Toronto, the apartment tower had everything that any status-conscious couple could ask for — a six-hundred-foot pier with day moorings for sailboats, an elegant ballroom, a glass-enclosed gourmet restaurant, a heated, indoor swimming pool, bellhops, a concierge, a fully equipped health club with three squash courts, and even a sophisticated security system.

As a first step towards realizing their dream of moving into the Palace Pier, Kelly sent a memo to the officer in charge of RCMP staffing and requested a transfer back to the Toronto Drug Section. Questioned about his wife's medical condition, he said that Jeannette was much better since her operation (she was sterilized in December 1976) and because he was making a practice of being more open with her about the general nature of his police work. Referring to Kelly "as being particularly adept at undercover work," the RCMP granted his request, and he was transferred back to Toronto on October 24, 1977.

Jeannette sold The Quilt Shoppe, and the Kellys appeared to be headed for the Palace Pier. There was only one problem; nearly a year after the Cookstown house was put up for sale, there hadn't been a single nibble.

6

SHADOWS BY FIRE

When the first volunteer fire fighters arrived at just after 2 A.M. on August 19, 1978, the flames were shooting out of 16 George Street, Cookstown, like a blowtorch. A gold Plymouth was parked in the driveway beside the old brick house, and the volunteers' immediate concern was that someone might still be asleep inside. One of the fire fighters pounded on the door at the north entrance, while another cupped his hands and shouted until he was hoarse; no one appeared in the second-storey windows.

Volunteer Fire Chief Raymond Taggart, Sr., ordered two of the volunteers to don their Scott Air Paks and see if they could make it up the staircase just inside the front door. Seconds later, they stumbled backwards into the night, choking from the smoke that mushroomed from the open door so furiously it looked as though it were chasing them. The fire was spreading very quickly. By the time the pumper truck arrived, flames were breaking through the roof at the south end of the new addition.

Neighbours who had seen the fire through the trees gathered on the street, some offering help, others watching in stunned silence. A boy wearing only his pyjama bottoms ran round and round the burning house, transfixed by the throbbing red glow inside. Two more fire fighters tried to get through the front door, knocking down the Lambert Real Estate sign on the lawn with the hose they were dragging. Six feet inside the door, they were driven back by an impenetrable wall of smoke and blistering heat. At the back of the house, the fire fighters scrambled up a ladder, chopped a hole through the roof, and tried to put out the fire in the eaves. When it became obvious that the pumper alone couldn't cope with the flames, Taggart called in the water truck. Before the night was out, it would make five frantic trips back to the fire hall to be refilled.

After a few hours of training their hoses through broken windows, Taggart and his crew were finally able to enter the house and make their way to the second storey, where they tried to douse the flames from the top of the east stairwell. As the fire fighters edged more deeply into the structure, the ceilings suddenly caved in, forcing them to retreat down the stairs. Shifting their efforts to the west side of the residence, they climbed a ladder and turned their hoses on the attic. Just before dawn, their faces red and raw after four hours of battling the fire, the men finally got the blaze under control.

With steam rising from the smouldering ruins and the air heavy with the smell of smoke and charred timbers, the early-morning sun revealed the extent of the damage: 85 per cent of the house had been destroyed. Standing around the scorched foundation of a burned-out house always gave him a strangely empty feeling, but Taggart knew that he and his crew had done all that they could. Now it was a job for the Fire Marshall's Office and the police, since this was as clear a case of arson as he'd ever seen.

Earlier that morning, Taggart had gone inside the house to search for occupants. Pushing open the door to the new addition, he had crouched low and shone his flashlight at floor level, its beam penetrating the darkness just beneath the smoke. A few feet away, he spotted a red container that looked like a gasoline can.

When the fire finally subsided, Taggart and one of his volunteers toured the gutted premises. The chief retrieved the open gas can he had previously seen, concluding that the arsonist had probably panicked and left it behind after the flames spread more quickly than he'd expected. He also recovered a 38.-calibre pistol bearing the stamp of the RCMP, surmising that it was probably the service revolver of the young Mountie who lived here. It was a good thing that the Kellys hadn't been at home in their beds last night, Taggart thought.

At 6:15 A.M., Cookstown's volunteer fire chief handed the .38 and the blackened five-gallon gas can to an OPP officer and headed home to get ready for work. His suspicions about the cause of the fire were quickly confirmed. Forensic tests established beyond a doubt that gasoline was present at the origin of the blaze in the family room, as well as on the floor of the entrance to the adjoining hallway. There was no doubt that somebody had deliberately set fire to 16 George Street; the only question was who.

That summer, the Kellys had been spending as much time as they could at Edwards Kingscote Lake Lodge in Algonquin Park, ninety-five miles northeast of Cookstown. The lodge was owned by Scotty and Joan Calder, who also ran an antique business in Flesherton, Ontario. The Kellys had purchased several small items at the Calders' shop, and the couples had become casual friends, getting together two or three times a year when they were in each other's neighbourhoods.

In the spring of 1978, the Calders told the Kellys about the lodge they had purchased in Algonquin Park not far from Bancroft. The posh resort consisted of a main house, a bunkhouse, and several cabins built beside a lake. The new owners were hoping to attract an international clientele to their unspoiled wilderness retreat and had high hopes of making a success of their latest business venture. They gave the Kellys a brochure showing Kingscote's facilities and prices and invited them to stay for a weekend as their guests.

Patrick and Jeannette fell in love with the place. Rather than paying for future visits, they struck a deal to help out around Kingscote in exchange for free room and board. Since Scotty planned to continue the antique business, it was a mutually beneficial arrangement. Jeannette helped Joan in the kitchen and Patrick assisted the Calders' young handyman, Bobby, with the outside chores. Patrick and Jeannette slept in the main house, where the Calders lived when they were at the lodge, or in one of the outlying cabins with their sheepdog, Kelly, curled up at the foot of their bed.

After the work was done, the Kellys were free to do as they pleased. Jeannette enjoyed hiking the nature trails with her own and the Calders' two dogs, while her husband swam or canoed in the lake. The more strenuous the activity, the better Patrick liked it. To the athletic Mountie for whom workouts had become a personal ritual, there was no substitute for physical exertion to work off the stress of his increasingly dangerous life in the RCMP.

By the summer of 1978, Kelly was under more pressure than he had ever experienced during his five years undercover. His bruxism had become so bad that he had broken his protective mouth guard and had to have a new one made. If anyone had a reason to grind his teeth, it was the man who made a living out of taking criminals into his confidence and then betraying them in the name of the law.

For the past fourteen months, Kelly had been at the centre of two large-scale drug investigations. One of them was a Joint Forces Operation (JFO) with the Metropolitan Toronto Police aimed at an international heroin and cocaine ring based in Ontario. Even though he preferred to work alone, Kelly had been paired up with Toronto police officer Allison Buchanan. The arrangement was based on the fact that the Metro police had the informant on the case, as well as the intelligence on the principle targets, a pair of former Israeli commandos suspected of smuggling large quantities of drugs into Canada from the Middle East.

The RCMP provided the drug money for the covert action and Kelly's undercover expertise. Buchanan, who assumed the role of Kelly's wife for the operation, was a relative newcomer to the world of undercover police work. She had drawn an excellent teacher. To the delight of both police forces, Kelly infiltrated the group and bought heroin and cocaine directly from both Michael Mizrahi and Moshe Savion in the Markham gas station they used as a cover for their trafficking. The pair was arrested after they agreed to sell Kelly two kilograms of cocaine for $64,000.

The RCMP was impressed with its crack undercover operator, as the officer-in-charge of drug enforcement, Supt. D. H. Heaton, made clear in a memo to the officer-in-command of the Toronto Drug Section: "I realize it was a difficult assignment and Cst. Kelly handled it in a most commendable manner. I was particularly pleased to hear that Cst. Kelly not only succeeded in developing the case but was able to take the initiative and direct the purchase in such a manner as to implicate not only Savion but Mizrahi. In order to develop this case Cst. Kelly has spent some six months in periodic contact with the targets and there is no doubt that this tenacity coupled with his expertise led to the matter being brought to a successful conclusion. I would ask that Cst. Kelly is made aware of my appreciation for a difficult job particularly well done."

The rave reviews for Kelly continued to come in after Mizrahi and Savion were convicted, including glowing praise from the federal lawyers who attributed their successful prosecution to the poise and daring of their star witness: "Specifically, we would like to highly commend Cst. Patrick Kelly, the undercover officer in the case, both for the role he played in the investigation and for the manner in which he conducted himself at trial. Cst. Kelly displayed singular skill as an undercover officer and, more importantly from a prosecutor's point of view, an ability to give evidence at trial in the manner that all professional police officers might hope to emulate. Cst. Kelly seems to succeed in doing a difficult and dangerous job well, while conducting himself with a degree of professionalism which is a credit to your force."

Kelly and Buchanan continued their covert assignment after Mizrahi and Savion were convicted, accounting for several more arrests and successful prosecutions before the JFO was terminated on August 10, 1978. In the end, Kelly's cover had been blown, and before getting down to the demanding task of preparing for his upcoming court cases, he decided to get out of the city and drive up to Kingscote for a few days of restorative solitude.

Patrick and the family dog made the trip alone. On the spur of the moment, Jeannette had decided to visit her father in Scotland and flew from Toronto to Glasgow on August 14. As Kelly would later explain, his wife's parents were going through their final divorce agony and Jeannette wanted to lend her moral support to her father during the bitterly contested property settlement. But when Jimmy Hanlon got his daughter's phone call from the airport asking to be picked up, he was dumbfounded.

"I'm in Glasgow," Jeannette announced.

"What do you mean you're in Glasgow?" the astonished man replied.

"I'm here," she replied.

All the way to the airport, Hanlon couldn't shake the feeling that something was wrong. Jeannette always called to let him know her travel plans when she came home, if only to make sure he wasn't off in Kenya where he regularly vacationed and did business. He also knew that she was no longer travelling on airline passes and that this unexpected trip would be expensive for the Kellys, who had only recently returned to Canada after a five-week holiday in Europe. The more Jeannette insisted that everything was fine, the more convinced Hanlon became that it wasn't. His daughter's "very unsettled" behaviour during the first few days of her visit did nothing to persuade him otherwise.

Leaving his RCMP ghost car parked in the driveway beside his house, Patrick slid into his new Volvo stationwagon at 7:30 A.M. and headed north. After a stop in Orillia to tidy up some police business, he arrived at Kingscote just before noon on Friday, August 18. While Kelly frolicked with the Calders' dogs, Patrick told Joan Calder about Jeannette's sudden trip to Scotland and crowed a little about his new car. He and Bobby then chopped some wood for the lodge and spent the rest of the afternoon carting boulders to an area of the property the Calders wanted filled in. After tucking into one of Joan's delicious dinners, improved by a day's work in Kingscote's cool, pine-scented air, Patrick retired to his room at the rear of the main lodge at around 9:30 P.M. It was the last the Calders saw of him until the following morning.

Just before 7 P.M. on Saturday, August 19, Ian MacLean got his second mild surprise from Patrick Kelly in a matter of days. After six weeks without hearing from his friend and mentor, MacLean had received a phone call from Kelly on August 17. He told MacLean that he might be able to get him a job with the Calders stripping antique furniture. Although he found Kelly's offer "a little bizarre," since it would mean a brutal commute from Mississauga to Flesherton, MacLean didn't want to appear unappreciative and said he was interested. The truth was, he still hadn't found work since he was fired from his newspaper job in Mississauga. With the twins to support, he and Joanne couldn't afford to be choosy about employment matters, particularly since Ian's only other source of income was the $1,500 in cash he got each month as a paid informant.

Kelly said he would find out more about the position when he saw the Calders that weekend and call MacLean back on either Sunday or Monday when he returned from Algonquin Park. So when MacLean's phone rang Saturday evening, he was surprised to find that it was Kelly calling a day early to say that the furniture stripping job was his if he wanted it. In the circumstances, MacLean thought, acting as a one-man employment bureau should have been the last thing on Kelly's mind.

MacLean had mistakenly assumed that Kelly knew about the fire and was just being his usual cool and collected self. He and Joanne had found out about the calamity that morning from a mutual friend, Jimmy Culbert. After Culbert's call, MacLean had immediately contacted the Mississauga RCMP to track Kelly down. Although Kelly had explicitly indicated on RCMP location sheets that he would be spending the weekend at Kingscote Lodge in Algonquin Park, it became apparent to MacLean from his friend's casual conversation that he still didn't know what had happened in Cookstown.

"I'm afraid I have some bad news for you, Patrick," MacLean said.

"Is it my mother?" Kelly asked, his voice suddenly tense.

"Your house was destroyed by fire last night."

Kelly momentarily lost his composure, then thanked MacLean and abruptly hung up. Joan Calder, who had accompanied Kelly to Pine Grove Point to use the pay phone in front of the general store (the lodge had no telephone), knew from her friend's face that something terrible had happened. Kelly immediately called Cookstown's fire chief, then the Bradford Detachment of the OPP to get more information. Const. David Kyte read the details of what had happened from an occurrence sheet made out the morning after the fire, noting that "Kelly seemed very upset, sounded like he was almost in tears, and was swearing a lot and really not believing it." Kelly then told the constable that his life had recently been threatened and asked him what he should do. Before hanging up, Kelly apologized to Kyte for his momentary loss of composure.

"I never had my house burn down before," he explained. "I feel as if someone just kicked me in the balls."

After spending the night at Kingscote, Kelly set out at 6:15 A.M. for Cookstown. Not knowing where he was going to sleep that night, he left the dog with the Calders. Eager to help out their distraught friend, the couple lent Kelly some money for immediate expenses. After making a brief stop at what used to be 16 George Street, where he talked to a neighbour about the fire, Kelly drove to the Bradford Detachment to claim some personal belongings, including his service revolver, that the OPP had recovered from his house. Before Kelly left, the duty corporal asked him if he owned a red gasoline can.

"Yes, I do," Kelly replied. "It should be in the shed."

"A can was found *inside* the house," Corporal Feir told him.

"I would never leave a can there."

Feir escorted Kelly to the evidence vault and showed him the gas can found at the scene.

"Is this your gas can?"

Kelly hesitated before answering.

"I don't know. I will have to check the shed and see if my can is still there."

"You don't know if this is your gas can or not?" Corporal Feir repeated.

"I can't be sure, but I don't think so. I will have to check."

The next day at noon Kelly called the OPP to report that his gas can was still in the shed where he'd left it the last time he cut the grass. Since he had only the one can, the container they had shown him in the police vault must have belonged to the arsonist.

After borrowing some clothes and making arrangements to stay with a friend in Alliston, Patrick called Scotland to break the news to Jeannette. She was playing tennis with the widowed mother of her old friend, Abby Latter, but hurried back to her father's flat to return Patrick's call. As soon as she heard that the house had been burned to the ground by persons unknown, Jeannette made travel arrangements to return to Canada. The next morning before leaving, she called Abby Latter to tell her what had happened. "She seemed very frightened. She had always been scared that something like this would happen because so many people had threatened Patrick," Latter recalled.

Jimmy Hanlon held a different opinion of his daughter's reaction, a view more in keeping with the uneasy feeling that there had been more to Jeannette's sudden and unannounced appearance in Glasgow than a spontaneous visit. "You know, she got the call and she said, 'Oh, well, that's Patrick on the phone, I'll have to go.' She said, 'The house has burned down.' But like I had the impression that she knew what was going on. I must be honest . . . I think she knew what was going on . . . The visit was just too quick."

On his way to Flesherton to see Scotty Calder about the job Kelly had lined up for him, Ian MacLean arrived at a crossroads that presented him with the first decision of the grey Monday morning: to the left lay an unwanted career in furniture stripping; to the right, the ruins of his friends' house. Curiosity won out over commerce, and he turned right.

When he first laid eyes on the devastation, MacLean almost wished he had continued on to Flesherton. It was painful to see a house where you had once socialized with friends reduced to a pile of rubble on an empty lot. By coincidence, Kelly was at the site, sifting through the debris for anything that was salvageable. As the two friends talked, MacLean had the "niggling suspicion" that Kelly's loss wasn't as great as he let on. After all, the Kellys had been trying to sell the house without success and already had an option on an apartment at the Palace Pier; an option, if MacLean remembered correctly, that was fast coming up for renewal.

The two friends chatted as Kelly absentmindedly poked through the ashes with the toe of his running shoe. Jeannette was due to arrive from Scotland that evening, and he asked MacLean to meet her at the airport and take her back to his townhouse. He explained that the RCMP had assigned a security team to the Kellys to protect them from further attacks by the people responsible for the fire. He would come by for Jeannette as soon as his bodyguards authorized it. Anxious to help, MacLean agreed to go to the airport on Kelly's behalf.

For someone who had just lost everything, Jeannette seemed remarkably composed to the MacLeans, although they didn't have much time to make their assessment. Half an hour after they got back from Pearson airport, Kelly stuck his head through the door of the MacLeans' townhouse and told Jeannette "it was time to go." Without coming in, he explained to his friends that he and Jeannette were going into seclusion and that for an indefinite period no one would be allowed to see them.

The MacLeans watched as the Kellys were led away by two RCMP cor-porals, Al Assance and Mike Atkinson, for the drive back to their tem-porary quarters in Toronto, the Holiday Inn at Yorkdale Plaza. Befitting the realities of Kelly's undercover life, they were registered under false names.

From the very beginning of the police investigation, the one person for whom the fiery events of August 19 held no mystery was Patrick Kelly. The people responsible for torching his house were drug dealers that he had put out of business at some point in his undercover career, and their purpose in setting the fire had not been arson but murder. He didn't need to remind the OPP that drug traffickers lived in a payback world where life meant nothing and the only good undercover policeman was a dead one.

With more than four hundred drug buys to his credit, and fifty trips to the witness box in courts across the country, there was no shortage of felons who might want Kelly dead. Back in 1975, Roman Perdes, a drug enforcer Kelly described to police as "a real arm and leg man," had allegedly put out a contract on the Mountie's life. After Stewart Lunn went down for seven years as a result of Kelly's work, informants told the RCMP that certain members of Lunn's family were plotting revenge on the "Mountie rat" who had turned in their relative.

More recently, Kelly had given testimony at the trial of Gordon Frith, a Toronto private investigator he had linked to cocaine trafficking and enforcing. Frith's co-accused in the case had appeared at 225 Jarvis Street claiming that her lawyer had told her that "a Mountie could be removed" as a consequence of their arrests. The next day an anonymous letter addressed to Kelly arrived through the mail. Its spare message seemed to back up the woman's story: "You hurt me emotionally and financially. Now it's my turn." The letter was followed by a series of threatening phone calls that were traced to Frith's enraged father. The man said he would blow Kelly's head off if four charges against his son weren't dropped.

After speaking with RCMP Staff Sgt. Chuck Martyn, who confirmed the many death threats against Kelly, Det. Insp. Fern Savage of the OPP checked out some of the more likely suspects, quickly ruling out the possibility that any of them could have been involved in the arson. But the OPP did discover that around 11:30 P.M. on the night of the fire, a man delivering a bulldozer to the house next door to 16 George Street had seen a van parked behind Kelly's police car. Some of Kelly's neighbours also told police that, on the night before the fire, they had noticed a pair of cars slowly circling the block before driving off. As tantalizing as these reports were, they led police down a cold and ultimately empty trail.

There was, as everyone knew, another possibility: that Kelly had burned down his own house and then used his work on the drug squad to cast suspicion on others. Regardless of how uncomfortable Detective Inspector Savage felt about delving into the affairs of a fellow officer, it was the duty of the experienced investigator and his colleagues to explore all avenues that might lead them to the perpetrator.

The OPP established that the Kellys had been trying to sell their Cookstown home for nine months. During that time, the couple had gone through three real estate companies and dropped the asking price from $99,000 to $82,500. There had been no offers. Since the Kellys had bought the property from Patrick's second cousin two years earlier, the insurance on 16 George Street had risen from $40,000 to $110,000, with another $55,000 on the contents. Although that seemed like a big jump in such a short time, the Kellys' insurance agent told police that the amount was in line with replacement costs for the renovated house.

Then there was the matter of the luxury condominium in Toronto. Kelly told Savage that he and Jeannette had made a conditional offer to purchase one of the units at the Palace Pier subject to the sale of their Cookstown property. The Kellys had agreed to pay $15,000 down, and the management company that ran the development would take back a $72,000 mortgage based on the couple's stated assets. That would leave the Kellys with a monthly payment of $786.54, which included maintenance costs.

But when OPP investigators talked to the Palace Pier's director of marketing, they got a different story. Anna Marie Read told police that in April 1978 the Kellys had signed an *unconditional* offer to purchase an apartment at the Palace Pier for $87,000. Under the terms of the sale, the Kellys had written a cheque for $3,000 and had to pay the remaining $12,000 of their downpayment when the deal closed on October 16, 1978. Although the closing date could be extended if the Kellys paid

$1,000 each month they went beyond the original date, they would lose their deposit if they didn't follow through on the purchase after ninety days. By failing to close, they would also be laying themselves open to a lawsuit, although company executives also told the OPP that Kelly would still be eligible to apply for a lease-back arrangement if for some reason he couldn't come up with the rest of the downpayment.

The information provided police with the haziest outline of a possible motive for the arson, but they were a long way from being able to seriously suggest that Kelly had burned down a house he couldn't sell in Cookstown to pay for a luxury apartment he wanted in Toronto – particularly when they found out from Patrick's real estate agent that he had never been pressured to bring the couple an offer. At this point, only one thing seemed clear. Both the OPP and the Fire Marshall's Office were in for lengthy investigations before the mystery of 16 George Street could be solved, assuming it ever would be.

After a week of wandering the halls of Yorkdale Plaza under RCMP guard, Patrick Kelly returned to active police duty. His superiors deemed it too dangerous to send him back into undercover work, so he was assigned to a surveillance team on a drug stakeout. For security reasons, he was also provided with a full-time partner. Kelly and his wife were still living at the Holiday Inn until the time came to move to the Palace Pier, although Jeannette spent two weeks in hospital after undergoing tailbone surgery to ease the pain from an old auto accident. But as the weeks slipped by, it became obvious that the Kellys would have to pay the final $12,000 of the downpayment on apartment 1705 from the substantial overdraft that their bank had extended to them and not from insurance money.

More than six weeks after the fire, neither Waterloo Mutual nor Wawanesa Mutual had honoured the Kellys' claim. Although there was some disagreement over the schedule of loss that Patrick had filed, the main reason for the delay was the ongoing arson investigation. Both insurance companies insisted that they wouldn't settle with the Kellys until the Fire Marshall's Office had completed its investigation.

By October 3, 1978, Kelly was so frustrated with the bureaucratic delay that he instructed his lawyer, Dennis Morris, to call the Fire Marshall's Office and find out when the seemingly endless forensic tests would be completed. Morris talked to Walter Halliday, an inspector with thirty years' experience as an arson investigator, who had some interesting information to pass on. The two gasoline cans found at 16 George Street were being re-examined with a new laser technology capable of picking up fingerprints that couldn't be detected using the traditional dusting procedure. He promised to let Morris know the results of the examination as soon as they were ready. Morris couldn't reach Kelly that afternoon, but telephoned him the following day to pass on what Halliday had told him.

The same day that Kelly found out about the fire marshall's plans to re-examine the gas cans with a laser scanner, the OPP was busily pursuing its end of the investigation through more conventional means: pounding the pavement in Canadian Tire stores in the vicinity of Cookstown to see if anyone remembered selling a red five-gallon gas container to someone in the last week. Police knew that the one found in the house had been purchased at the chain store because the scorched can still bore the company's distinctive sticker. OPP Const. D. G. Woolway was in the middle of conducting interviews with store personnel when he got a message to call Patrick Kelly collect at RCMP headquarters at 225 Jarvis Street.

The constable was in for a surprise. Kelly told Woolway that he had been driving past a Canadian Tire store when he suddenly remembered that he had, in fact, purchased the five-gallon gas can that was found in his house, the same can he had denied was his when Corporal Feir showed it to him the day after the fire. Sounding appropriately sheepish, Kelly explained that he had bought the can from a Canadian Tire store on Highway 27 near Woodbine Racetrack after borrowing a friend's lawnmower to cut the grass.

The second can had been necessary because Jimmy Culbert's lawnmower was gas-powered, while Kelly's ran on a mixture of oil and gas. Since his old gas can was filled with the oil and gas mixture, he needed the new one for the straight gas needed to run Culbert's mower. When he finished the lawn that day, Kelly had refilled the new gas can and stored it in the shed, planning to give it to Culbert in return for the use of his mower. In the stressful aftermath of losing his house, he had simply forgotten the entire episode.

It was a disturbing revelation. Was it plausible that he could totally forget about buying the second can for more than a month? And was it just a coincidence that Kelly's belated recollection came on the same day that he found out about the laser re-examination of the gas cans by the Fire Marshall's Office? Or was he trying to advance a non-incriminating explanation of the facts in case the new technology turned up his fingerprints? And if Kelly was telling the truth, what did the new information say about the unknown perpetrator? Had the arsonist really begun his work that night with a scavenger hunt of the victim's premises in hopes of finding a topped-up can of gasoline with which to start the fire? If so, it was a very casual approach to the premeditated murder Kelly believed was the real motive behind the burning of his house. Most disturbing of all were the forensic tests that would soon cast a cloud of suspicion over Kelly's explanation for buying the second gas can. When analysed by the Fire Marshall's Office, both the can taken from Kelly's shed and the one from inside the house were found to contain straight gasoline. So if Kelly hadn't needed the second can for the straight gas mixture burned by Jimmy Culbert's lawnmower, why had he needed it?

The OPP's ongoing investigation was edging closer to the theory that Patrick Kelly may have been involved in the burning of his house. There were other mysteries to unravel in addition to the gas can controversy. Why had the Kellys left their sheepdog's pedigree papers with the Calders just before the fire, as Const. John Taylor learned when he visited Kingscote? And was it true, as reported by an OPP sergeant to Constable Woolway, that some of the items from the Kellys' house that had been included in their schedule of loss had in fact been sold at a local auction?

As a suspect, Kelly had both the motive and the opportunity. It was at least arguable that he needed the insurance money to close the deal on the Palace Pier luxury apartment, and it was possible that Kelly had driven from Kingscote to Cookstown on the evening of August 18 and back again before breakfast the next morning, since he had gone to bed early on the night of the fire. Unsatisfied with the Mountie's explanation about the second gas can he now remembered buying, Constable Woolway applied for a search warrant to delve into Kelly's bank records.

Suspicious of what he found, Woolway paid an official visit to RCMP headquarters to find out more about the numerous international trips Kelly had apparently taken.

Meanwhile, the notion that Kelly had burned down his own house was already being openly considered over the back fences of Cookstown. Joanne MacLean was so upset after hearing from a girlfriend that there was a feeling in town that Kelly was responsible for the fire that she called Jeannette and told her what was being said. Joanne had expected her friend to be angry, but she was totally unprepared for the call she received from Patrick a few hours later.

"He didn't raise his voice, he more or less hissed at me through the phone. Who the hell was I to phone her and say something like that? I had no right to tell Jeannette anything like that. If I heard things like that, I should come and tell him. And who's the bitch anyway? And he wants to call her and what's her name and he's going to get to her."

It was the first time that she had ever seen Kelly lose control, and Joanne was frightened. In her opinion, Kelly had hugely overreacted to what she had told Jeannette, unless there was more to it than idle gossip. Joanne began to wonder.

Whatever the wagging tongues of Cookstown or their colleagues in the OPP may have thought, the RCMP continued to stand solidly behind Kelly. In the fall of 1978, Insp. H. A. Palmer placed a memo in Kelly's personnel file making note of the arson investigation into the burning of his house. Palmer observed that Kelly had "successfully investigated some major criminals in the drug trade" and that "it is quite likely that the fire could be revenge motivated." Still, Palmer was cautious. "I am also advised from the OPP investigation, Cst. Kelly's financial status may be in question. I recommend that this aspect be followed up by his Line Officer in the interests of the Force and particularly when considering Cst. Kelly's future role as an undercover operator. I would stress that such personal enquiry of Cst. Kelly *not be* conducted until the OPP investigation is completed. Any query on our part at this time could easily be misinterpreted by outside investigators as interference."

The mere fact that one of their premier undercover agents was the subject of an arson investigation was both embarrassing and inconvenient for the RCMP. Not only had Kelly covered the force in glory on a number of occasions, he had also provided the key pieces of evidence in dozens of trials where his word had been relied on to secure convictions. Reflecting his outstanding police work, Kelly's performance assessment profile for 1978 contained the recommendation that he be promoted to corporal. But his superiors agreed that, as long as he remained under investigation, he could no longer function in his former capacity, depriving the Toronto Drug Section of one of its best assets. And if he were ever connected to the Cookstown fire, dozens of convictions where his word had been the deciding factor in establishing the accused's guilt would be called into question.

Two senior RCMP officers thought they saw a way out of the dilemma without interfering in the investigation by the OPP. In a fall meeting with Kelly, Supt. D. H. Heaton and Insp. Will Stefureak recommended that he take a polygraph examination to help establish his innocence. Although neither officer suggested that he be tested by an RCMP or OPP polygraph operator, Kelly got the distinct impression that was exactly what they wanted him to agree to. Angry at being treated like a suspect, Kelly refused, citing his "total distrust" for both police forces who were not, in his opinion, giving him "a fair shake."

Instead, Kelly conferred with his lawyer, Dennis Morris. Morris's opinion was that Kelly should take a lie detector test to establish his total innocence, but with a private polygraph operator who had no knowledge of the case. Kelly agreed, and Morris hired John Jurens, an investigator who had testified as an expert witness, lectured at various law schools, and worked with several police forces over his twenty-five-year career. Jurens impressed Morris with his remarkable claim that in more than fifteen thousand lie detector tests he had administered, he had never once been proven wrong in his opinion. That, Morris thought, ought to be good enough for the RCMP and the OPP, and might even carry weight with his client's still tightfisted insurance companies.

A week after his client submitted to the polygraph test, and the same day the Kellys moved in to the Palace Pier, Jurens reported that in his opinion Patrick was being truthful when he denied burning down his own house or being in collusion with the people who had done it. The results were immediately sent to the RCMP, the OPP, and both insurance companies. The RCMP was delighted with the results, and Waterloo Mutual was sufficiently impressed to release an interim cheque of $10,000 against the full amount. Gil Coates of Waterloo Mutual revealed that his company now wanted to settle quickly, but the second company, Wawanesa, was still holding out for more information from investigators.

More good news for the embattled Mountie was on the way. The Metropolitan Toronto Police informed the RCMP that it had seized three notebooks from the homes of suspected drug dealers at the end of the joint forces operation in which Kelly and Buchanan had been involved. Const. Bill Henderson, the Metro officer who had the notebooks, advised Kelly that one of the suspects in the case, Paul Donnelly, a known hashish and cocaine importer, was facing pending arson charges. Kelly reported the news to his supervisor, Staff Sgt. Chuck Martyn, who directed him to borrow the relevant notebooks from the Metro police, copy them, and then study their contents to see if they shed any light on the fire at 16 George Street.

Kelly couldn't contain his excitement after reading two of the notebooks belonging to Donnelly. In them were the words "Yel. Volvo Wa.," Kelly's licence plate number, "NLX 873," and what looked like rough directions to his house, "Hwy. 27&89."

It was the kind of smoking gun the RCMP had been hoping for to clear its man. As soon as he received the notebooks from Kelly, Staff Sergeant Martyn informed OPP investigators of the new information and provided them with a copy of the threatening letter Kelly had recently received at 225 Jarvis Street. He then investigated the information gathered by the Metro police, which looked even more promising as a means of establishing Kelly's innocence.

The RCMP learned that Donnelly had been picked up on a Metro wiretap on September 14, 1978, in which he admitted to setting a barn fire in 1977 and a warehouse blaze in Toronto in August 1978. The first attempt on the warehouse had failed, but Donnelly completed the job on August 19, 1978, between 2:15 and 3:30 A.M. The *modus operandi* had been very similar to the George Street fire set earlier that same night. The arsonist had forced open a door, poured gasoline on newspapers, and then set the building ablaze. A red gas container had even been recovered from the warehouse.

The RCMP also checked a scribbled out phone number found in Donnelly's notebook and discovered that it belonged to Peter Straw, a suspected cocaine trafficker who owned a black Ford Econoline van, which fit the description of the vehicle in Kelly's driveway seen by a witness on the night of the fire. Best of all, Donnelly had spent the weekend of August 18 to 20 at a farm near Tottenham, just a fifteen-minute drive from Cookstown. Donnelly could have easily set the fire at 16 George Street and still had time to drive to Toronto to burn down the warehouse.

As far as Staff Sergeant Martyn was concerned, the evidence clearly supported the theory that vengeful drug dealers and not Patrick Kelly had torched 16 George Street. In his report on the arson investigation, Martyn noted that he was unaware of any evidence pointing to Kelly as the guilty party, referring to him as an "excellent" officer. If there was a prime suspect in the case, it was Donnelly, since he had the motive, was an admitted arsonist, had the opportunity, and associated with the "right" people.

Kelly didn't waste any time taking the new information to his insurance companies, notifying them that the RCMP now knew the identity of the arsonist and would soon be taking him into custody. Faced with the Mountie's performance on the lie detector test and testimonials of good character from the RCMP, Waterloo Mutual and Wawanesa Mutual agreed to settle the Kellys' claim of $123,430, a course they felt obliged to follow lacking any "concrete" evidence from the OPP or the Ontario Fire Marshall's Office implicating Kelly. When the Mountie and his lawyer appeared on December 18, 1978, to pick up the cheque, Kelly told representatives of the companies that the arsonist had, in fact, been arrested by the RCMP but for the time being it was not being made public. After receiving the money, Kelly lost his temper. He berated the insurance executives over how he had been treated during the four long months it had taken to settle the claim, an understandable reaction from a frustrated man who had effectively been asked to prove his innocence without ever being charged with a crime. When he submitted his bill for the arson case to Kelly, lawyer Dennis Morris sent an accompanying letter in which he made note of the "terrible emotional turmoil" the Kellys had endured during the settlement of the claim:

"Mrs. Kelly especially in my observation has suffered a terrible emotional strain as a result of the accusatory atmosphere which prevailed throughout the case. . . . It is my understanding that the arsonist is now in custody and hopefully will not be let loose in our society for many years to come. It is reassuring to realise that the RCMP has stood behind you throughout this ordeal and now that this matter is concluded I can only hope that you are the one who is able to forget this awful nightmare experience."

The Kellys made a good start at putting the past behind them when they hosted a New Year's Eve get-together for a few close friends at the Palace Pier. Everyone was impressed with the opulence of apartment 1705, Dawn Hastey all the more so since it had somehow been acquired on the same salary as her RCMP husband John was making: $21,000 a year.

Whatever the Kellys and Dennis Morris believed, in fact, the investigation into the burning of 16 George Street was far from concluded. While it was true that Paul Donnelly was in custody at the time Kelly collected the insurance money from his house, it was for various drug offences and the blaze at the Toronto warehouse; he was not, and never would be, charged with setting the Cookstown fire. And while the RCMP was satisfied that its man was now exonerated, OPP investigators became even more suspicious of Kelly when their investigation into the so-called notebook evidence took a surprising turn.

After being apprised of Donnelly's notebooks by Staff Sgt. Chuck Martyn, OPP investigators had taken copies of the documents back to the Metro police for verification. Bill Henderson, the Metro constable who had seized the notebooks from Donnelly's apartment, and who had them in his possession until he turned them over to the RCMP, couldn't believe his eyes as he leafed through the material. He told Constable Woolway that he was "positive" that the references to Kelly now in the notebooks hadn't been there before. It became clear to Woolway that the Metro police believed Kelly had forged the references to himself in an attempt to fabricate evidence against Donnelly, a man the Mountie knew was already under suspicion for another arson. "Thinks the whole thing stinks," Woolway wrote in his notebook. "Advised Kelly had the notebook before they photocopied it . . . would be a good idea if I sent it to the centre for handwriting checks to compare suspect."

On January 5, 1979, Woolway obtained control samples of Donnelly's and Kelly's handwriting and forwarded them to the Centre of Forensic

Sciences along with the notebooks in question. Even though expert examination of the notebooks failed to reveal significant similarities between the allegedly "added" notes and Kelly's handwriting, neither did it definitively say that the writing belonged to Donnelly. A little over a week later, Superintendent Heaton wrote a memo to the Toronto Drug Section, asking if the OPP had eliminated Kelly as a suspect in its arson investigation. It had not.

Angry at being treated like a criminal, and feeling emotionally raw over his four-month ordeal with the insurance companies, Kelly decided that he shouldn't have to bear the financial penalty of having had to defend himself from the shadowy but persistent suspicion that he had burned down his own house. On January 26, 1979, he asked the RCMP to pay Dennis Morris's legal fees of $7,446.38. Sympathetic to the plight of this justifiably disgruntled member, who had been taken off undercover work and restricted to routine investigations since the fire, Superintendent Heaton supported Kelly's request, noting in a February 2, 1979, memo that "in the absence of any additional information, it would appear that Cst. Kelly may well be the victim of his rather successful undercover operations."

In order to get authorization from headquarters to pay members' legal bills, the RCMP conduct a standard investigation into their finances. When they looked into Kelly's accounts, the investigators were shocked: between mid-1976 and 1978, on his credit cards alone, Kelly had spent $42,000 above and beyond his salary. Where had all that money come from?

7

MOONLIGHTING

When Patrick Kelly pulled the fully silenced, small-calibre machine gun out of his bag and handed it to one of the two men who had been waiting for him in the hotel room in Houston, Texas, he mistakenly assumed that his assignment was over. One man removed the Houston Telephone Book and Yellow Pages from a drawer, placing them upright and back-to-back against the pillows on the bed, while the other slipped a clip into the machine gun known as the "Buzzsaw." He then picked up the phone and ordered two steaks from the hotel kitchen. Twenty minutes later, there was a knock at the door.

"Who is it?" the man holding the machine gun asked.

"Room service."

Snapping the silencer into place with a single twist of his hand, he pointed the muzzle towards the bed and pulled the trigger. As the nine-millimetre slugs thudded into the telephone books, the machine gun itself made a sound like a very quiet sewing-machine stitching its way through a piece of cloth. Thanks to the weapon's unique filtration system, there was barely a trace of cordite in the room. The shooter stowed the machine gun under the bed and nodded to his partner, who answered the door.

"Gee, I thought you'd never get here," he said. "We're *starving*."

Taking charge of the food gurney, he paid the bill in cash and peeled off a healthy tip for the bellboy.

"Oh, by the way, did you hear anything strange?" he asked, furrowing his brow.

"No, sir," the bellboy replied.

"Okay, thanks again."

The man smiled at Kelly and backed away from the open door. *Now* the assignment was over.

On his way to the airport, the undercover Mountie couldn't help thinking how smoothly things had gone during his ten-day "mission." Travelling under a passport obtained with false documents originally issued to him by the RCMP for his drug work, he had flown to Italy with the milling plans for the silenced machine gun. There, he turned them over to another contact who took them to the famed Berretta gunsmiths in Milan. Three or four days later, the prototype that Kelly had agreed to smuggle back to the United States was delivered to his hotel room.

Kelly packed the weapon and drove over the Italian border into France, crossed to England, and flew from London to Montreal, where he rented a car and drove south. When he reached U.S. customs, he flashed his RCMP identification and "waltzed right across the border" with the Buzzsaw in his briefcase. He then flew from New York City to Texas, where he turned the weapon over to the men he had arranged to meet in a downtown Houston hotel. With his task behind him, he looked forward to getting back to Toronto for his reward: a cash payment of $30,000 U.S. from the intimidating man who had hired him.

Kelly always felt an undercurrent of anxiety whenever he met the Fat Man. It was like the feeling he used to get as a boy when he swam too far out in the creek and the water turned black and bottomless beneath him. Even though Kelly had learned not to ask questions of the person who had provided him with such a lucrative sideline, it was obvious to him that Edgar X (a pseudonym) was powerful and well-connected. He had found out just how well-connected during their first private meeting at Edgar X's apartment, which he immediately noted was fitted out with a closed circuit television camera trained on the elevators. His 350-pound host had greeted Kelly with an engaging

Southern drawl and a glass of wine from behind a stack of very interesting documents.

"He produced my files, my red files. The red files are the original files," Kelly later explained. "He had 'em all. I mean my undercover file, HQ 208. I don't know who this guy is but he's sitting in an apartment in Mississauga with my undercover file. Got my attention right away."

Thinking that Edgar X was a heavyweight from the upper echelons of the force, Kelly asked if he was SS, the initials for the Security Service of the RCMP, the forerunner of Canada's civilian spy agency, CSIS. Kelly had occasionally worked for SS, the National Crime Intelligence Unit, (NCIU), and the U.S. Drug Enforcement Agency (DEA), and their approaches to him had sometimes been unorthodox. Speaking in the riddles he used whenever he talked about himself, Edgar X laughed off Kelly's question: "You wanna know who I am? I'm a member of Catholics In Action," he joked.

To Kelly it was a novel yet noncommittal way of saying the CIA. Edgar X talked generally about the U.S. government and its occasional need for people with Kelly's background and training. Towards the end of their session, he told Kelly that he was very impressed with his record as an undercover drug operator and asked him to consider doing some work for Catholics In Action.

When Kelly informally asked his contacts at SS and the NCIU to find out more about his would-be patron, he had the feeling he had touched a nerve. People seemed to know who Edgar X was, but nobody wanted to talk about him. Even Howard Saginur, the Toronto lawyer who had introduced Edgar X to Kelly as a "businessman" at their first meeting, didn't seem to know much about him. A few weeks after their private meeting, the Fat Man had offered Kelly his first "assignment" – delivering the milling plans for the Buzzsaw to Milan and smuggling a prototype back to Texas. Pleased with the Mountie's performance, Edgar X paid him in cash in the back of a chauffeur-driven limousine behind the U.S. embassy on University Avenue in Toronto.

When Edgar X called on him again several months later, he found the young Mountie eager to do business. Although the Fat Man wondered if Kelly could carry out this particular mission without arousing the suspicions of his superiors, Kelly knew that his unique style of undercover work, in which he often acted as operator, investigator, and intelligence gatherer, was tailor-made to cover periodic absences from the RCMP.

"It wasn't unusual for me to go to a guy like Nev' Gillespie or Chuck Martyn, my other boss, and simply say, 'Uh, listen, I'm doing an investigation, I'm gonna be gone for three or four weeks, I'll check in periodically. Reports weren't an issue because you'd say you'd been doing surveillance. And then, you know, you just say, 'Nothing happened.'"

This time out Edgar X had something more ambitious in mind. He wanted Kelly to devise a means of transporting an unspecified cargo to Nicosia, Cyprus, and then to oversee its delivery. The cargo was in the form of two four-foot-square pallets loaded with eighteen-inch-square plastic packages. Although he never asked what the packages contained, Kelly had his suspicions: "Best guess? Dope."

After studying the problem for a few weeks, he met again with Edgar X and two associates who looked like "ex-military types" in the boardroom of a lawyer's office in Mississauga. No lawyers were present. When Kelly arrived, the boardroom table was covered with photographs and maps that the Fat Man gathered up and put into his briefcase before the meeting began. As Edgar X and his men sipped coffee, Kelly presented his idea: that the cargo be repackaged as blood products in a refrigerated unit packed with legitimate medical supplies and delivered to Cyprus in a vessel disguised as a Red Cross ship. Edgar X seemed delighted with the idea and promised to be in touch.

Three weeks later, they met again. This time Edgar X produced a picture of an old PT boat he said could be fitted with oversized fuel tanks for a transatlantic voyage and disguised along the lines Kelly had suggested. The vessel was currently available at a military auction in the United States. Edgar X would supply the registration for the vessel and false identification for Kelly and his five-man crew, including passports, major credit cards, international drivers licences, and inoculation certificates.

At the end of the meeting, Edgar X gave Kelly a brown envelope and told him he would call when the vessel was ready. Back in his car, Kelly opened the envelope and thumbed through the $20,000 U.S. inside. Like the rest of the proceeds from his highly specialized sideline, it would be hidden in a safety deposit box, never to appear on his income tax return. Even though he knew that he was breaking the law, Kelly thought of his freelance activities as enterprise rather than crime.

"I saw the economic opportunity. I was fairly skilled in a particular area and somebody wanted to buy my services. It was moonlighting."

Despite the RCMP's stern prohibition against its members making any form of outside income, the force had long since lost its moral authority to control or pass judgement on anyone's activities, or at least it had as far as Patrick Kelly was concerned. From his very first raid, when he was told to carry drugs into the target's residence, Kelly had suspected that the world of narcotics enforcement was not what it appeared to be. After a few years on the Drug Section, he had concluded that it was "rotten to the core," a shadowy underworld of deception, manipulation, and betrayal that took place against a backdrop of big money, fudged statistics, and sudden death.

Kelly's disenchantment deepened with each new unsavoury practice he witnessed. But instead of spawning a reforming zeal in the young Mountie, it triggered a towering sense of personal licence. There were the cases where the RCMP orchestrated arrests by providing drugs to its own criminal informants who then used them in "setup" buys. The drugs would come from legitimate seizures but would be diluted by police and selectively dispensed to informant-addicts or dealers who would in turn sell them to carefully chosen targets.

"There was a constant traffic between Toronto and Montreal. Seizures would be made in Montreal and pieces of the seizure would be buffed up in the vault in Montreal and brought to Toronto for dispersion. Toronto informants were sent to Montreal to do the exact same trip, back and forth. It comes down to a numbers racket and you have to justify why you're here. It's very much like an *agent provocateur* situation. I mean they're real sales and they *are* hypes and drug dealers, but what I'm saying is it's an obvious form of entrapment."

It was a system that sometimes had Kafkaesque consequences for the informant. Allan Kirzner was an addict recruited by the RCMP's Montreal Drug Section to provide information on drug distribution in Canada. Even after he had attempted a cure for his heroin addiction, Kirzner was actively encouraged by the RCMP to return to his former duties as a junkie-informant. After acceding to their request, Kirzner was working for the Montreal Drug Section when he was arrested by the RCMP in Toronto with a substantial quantity of heroin and a small amount of cocaine, drugs he claimed to have as part of his role as an agent of the police. Despite his defence that, at the time of his arrest in Toronto, he was merely following the instructions of his RCMP handlers to infiltrate the drug market, he was found guilty of possession for the purposes of trafficking and sentenced to three and a half years in prison. When Kirzner took his case to the Ontario Court of Appeal in 1976, the heroin addict learned a painful lesson in the course of having his conviction upheld: in Canada, entrapment by police is not recognized as a defence to a criminal charge.

According to Kelly, the courthouse wasn't the only place where informants were abused. Valerie Thistle, a thirty-year-old heroin addict and hooker, was one of his most reliable contacts. She and her boyfriend, "an old-style rounder and hype," had introduced Kelly to traffickers in Asian brown heroin around Toronto that led to several drug seizures and arrests. The drug cop and the hooker had hit it off from the very beginning.

"I recall the very first time I ever met her. We were walking up the street and she said, 'I have to tell you. You gotta be the best-looking Mountie I ever met in my whole life. I hook on the side, but for you I'd be doin' it for free.'"

It was up to the individual agent to establish the cash award for the informants he was running, and Kelly always treated Thistle generously, sometimes paying her as much as $2,000 for an introduction and always making sure that she got her money on time. For one thing, he believed that she and her boyfriend had potential as informers from deep in the twilight world of Toronto's heroin trade, and for another, he had gotten to know Thistle and sympathized with her plight. The daughter of a well-to-do Toronto family, she had been "thrown in the ditch" by her own parents after getting hooked on heroin. One of Kelly's private pleasures was treating Thistle like a person rather than an investigative tool. Occasionally he took her flowers, and one evening he picked her up on Yonge Street and took her out for a gourmet dinner, something of a change of pace from her life in the rundown Ford Hotel.

"I'd take her to some place really nice, like really, *really* posh," Kelly said, adding that the bill for his chivalry went on his RCMP expense account. "I'd order a steak and lobster and wine. It was really a nice relationship."

Because of the way he treated her, Kelly wasn't surprised when he got a call from the Etobicoke General Hospital one day saying that a woman named Valerie Thistle had overdosed on heroin and was asking to see him. He showed up in Valerie's hospital room with a bouquet of flowers and sat by her bed holding her hand while she talked. She explained that a member of the drug squad had given her heroin instead of money to set up an introduction to a dealer she and her boyfriend were then using.

"And I said, 'Valerie, how much stuff did he give you? She said three bundles. That's a lot of stuff. You're talking seventy-five caps. It's total Christmas for a junkie. And she said, 'Well I guess the stuff was hotter than he knew and I knew and here I am.'"

Despite his sense that informants were often abused, Kelly had witnessed firsthand how effective they could be against dealers who were cunning enough to foil the RCMP's more conventional investigative methods. In early 1973, he had been a member of a surveillance team assigned to a raid in London, Ontario. The target was a trafficker who had managed to elude local authorities, even though it was common knowledge that he was selling heroin. En route to the raid, Kelly's superior told him to pull over so he could talk to a man who had apparently been waiting for them at the side of the highway in his own car.

Kelly recognized the man as Tony Mellilo, a Toronto heroin dealer he had often had under surveillance at a Harbord Street pool hall where Mellilo carried on his trafficking with the full knowledge and co-operation of the police. The trade-off was that Mellilo had to supply the names of his customers to the RCMP. In addition to keeping the profits from his drug sales, he was also paid hefty informant fees by his Drug Section handler.

"Every time that Mellilo would sell, certain people we would take down, certain people we wouldn't, and it was strictly setups. He had a complete licence to sell out of his pool hall, out of his home. In the London thing, Tony Mellilo was met by my superior in my sight."

When Kelly's superior returned to the cruiser after the meeting, he ordered the formal surveillance to begin, and Kelly followed Mellilo to the target's place of business, a pizza shop on the outskirts of London.

After Mellilo sold twelve bundles of heroin to the target, the surveillance team "kicked down the walls" and made their arrest. "Mellilo had his money and was written up as an informant, and I know that more funds were designated. This was a straight setup job," Kelly said.

Occasionally, Kelly had taken a more active, if allegedly unwitting, role in setting up a target with RCMP drugs. Approached by a colleague on the Drug Section to make a buy from a Toronto businessman named Freddy Kubesch, Kelly agreed to an introduction to the target through a high-level informant known as "French Paul." In the end, French Paul, a heroin user and trafficker from Montreal, did not come through with the introduction, and Kelly attempted a "cold" buy from the target. He met Kubesch in a Yonge Street drugstore, a well-known haunt of pushers and users. Armed with the names of some of Kubesch's associates gleaned from RCMP files, Kelly instilled enough confidence with his cover story to set up a buy. Kubesch said that he personally didn't have anything at the moment but that he could score from another source. That source turned out to be French Paul, who sold Kubesch heroin he had been given by the RCMP. Kelly in turn bought it back from Kubesch, and the Mounties got their arrest.

"I believe I bought a couple of times off of Kubesch and he went down for three or four years," says Kelly. "By the time the information got to me that we had sold him our own dope, Mr. Kubesch was well into doing his time, bloody near ready for parole. I took no action."

Stage-managing offences and arrests using criminal informants wasn't the only way the RCMP dealt with difficult targets, according to Kelly. Early in his undercover career, Kelly was introduced to a contact in postal intelligence who he claimed frequently gave the RCMP access to the mail of suspected drug dealers without proper authority. In one of Kelly's cases, which involved a large marijuana importation ring operating on Canada's West Coast, suspicion had come to rest on a particular Toronto lawyer. Kelly commented to the postal intelligence liaison officer that although the lawyer's correspondence with one particular client might be useful to his investigation, it was clearly privileged and couldn't be intercepted.

"Our contact at postal intelligence said 'no problem' and invited me back to his office," claimed Kelly. "He explained that they had their own printers, so they could take an envelope, match the paper, and simply duplicate it. In another section of the office they had a complete collection of postal stamps and cancellation stamps. So if you were mailing something from Bogota, he would simply take down the equivalent Colombian stamp, prepare a cancellation stamp, redo the envelope, seal it, and out it would go after it had been photocopied. I actually saw a set of the old and the new side by side and I couldn't tell the difference. He handed me a photocopy of the actual letter, made it and supplied it to me, and then shredded the original envelope."

Occasionally the rules were bent in the other direction when unexpected quarry showed up in the snares of the RCMP's undercover operations. During a one-man operation in southeastern Ontario connected to the notorious Peter Lord case, Kelly followed a trafficker named Patrick Rousseau to a motel just outside Kingston. After checking in carrying a briefcase, Rousseau left to make a phone call. Kelly broke into the premises and found a large quantity of cocaine in the briefcase.

Returning to his surveillance position, he watched as first Rousseau and then a second man, whom Kelly thought he recognized, arrived and entered the motel room. A few minutes later, the second man came out with the briefcase Kelly had already searched, carrying it to his car in the lot of a nearby motel. While he jotted down the licence plate number, it dawned on Kelly why the man had seemed so familiar: he looked just like a judge from Magistrate's Court in Toronto.

When he got back to the motel, the first man's car was still in the parking lot. Kelly kicked out one of the tail-lights and then called Kingston police to "roust" Patrick Rousseau. Using the broken tail-light as an excuse, the police pulled Rousseau over and searched his car. They found $17,000 in the trunk but no drugs. When the Kingston police turned this intelligence over to Kelly, it seemed pretty clear what had happened; since Rousseau had the money and the other man had left with the briefcase, a deal had just gone down. Ordering a motor vehicle check on the second man's car, Kelly discovered that it was registered to the judge he had indeed recognized leaving Rousseau's motel room.

The next day Kelly handed in a report of the motel room meeting to his superiors and was told that others would "take care of this." In itself, that wasn't unusual, since there was an entire branch of the RCMP in

Ottawa that dealt with sensitive matters. The normal procedure was to forward Ottawa a photocopy of the intelligence in question, while retaining the original on file at Jarvis Street. But according to Kelly, the officer-in-charge requested Kelly's notebook in which he had made a two- or three-page entry about the judge. After ripping out the pages dealing with that part of the surveillance, he handed Kelly the remaining notes and then reached into his drawer to get something.

"He handed me another notebook and he said, 'Well, you got a court case coming up pretty soon, haven't you? I'd advise you to start writing.' And that was it. He kept the pages and handed me the notes and told me to rewrite them."

The lesson was clear to Kelly. If the RCMP could use its power to bend or break the rules when it suited its needs, using and discarding people at will, what was so wrong with an undercover agent doing the same thing in the furtherance of purely personal goals? After all, it was the RCMP that had taught Kelly that when breaking the law, there was really only one rule: anything goes, just as long as you don't get caught.

A month after he received the $20,000 U.S. for his smuggling plan, Kelly got word that everything was in place for the voyage to Cyprus. A few days later he flew to Fort Lauderdale, Florida, where he was met by a crew member who took him to an out-of-the-way yacht basin near Fort Myers. The falsely registered PT boat had been converted to Kelly's specifications, and he personally directed the loading of the cargo into custom-made containers.

"I ordered the boxes to be made," he later said. "They were made of a material very similar to the stuff used in Airstream trailers, a silvery metal. The boxes were of the kind used for transporting plasma."

To avoid creating undue attention during a refuelling stop in Morocco, Kelly selected a port that had a lot of paramilitary traffic as well as a Red Cross station. From Morocco, they steamed to Gibraltar and then to Nicosia, known in intelligence circles as "Microwave Alley" because of its international reputation as a listening post on the Middle East for the world's intelligence community. The delivery of the contraband cargo went off without a hitch, and Kelly received another $50,000 U.S. for his troubles.

Well satisfied with Kelly's work, Edgar X would later compare him to a U.S. marine who had dreamed as a child of becoming a Mountie: "Patrick was Canada's Ollie North, a can-do sort of guy."

Unknown to his RCMP superiors, Kelly's "moonlighting" had started long before he ever met the Fat Man. In fact, his career as a smuggler had actually begun as a spinoff of his Spanish-language training in Bogota, Colombia, in the summer of 1975, just weeks before he married Jeannette Hanlon.

On the surface, Kelly had accomplished everything that the RCMP had asked of him during his stay in Bogota. He took four hours of grammar instruction every day and studied for another four to keep up with his courses. When his grades came back through the Specialized Training Unit of the Police College, he had scored a respectable 71 per cent in the intermediate level of the course and impressed his teachers with his diligence. He had also held meetings with a man known as "Gonzales," the U.S. Drug Enforcement Agency (DEA) station chief and CIA liaison officer, the Canadian Consulate, and local drug authorities that the RCMP believed would be valuable to the Toronto Drug Section. The force was particularly happy with the cover stories Kelly worked up on the basis of contacts made in Bogota, knowing that they could now be used in Canada by other agents if the need arose.

After a DEA introduction to Carlos Campeau, the head of the Colombian National Narcotics Enforcement agency known as "F2," Kelly was invited to accompany his South American colleagues on a drug raid. The target was a warehouse in Bogota that had been under surveillance for several months. Suspecting that it was a full-fledged "drug factory," authorities expected to seize large quantities of cocaine and the chemicals and equipment that had been used to refine it.

As the forty men of the F2 raiding party left their operational base, an old building off El Centro, the famous roundabout in downtown Bogota, Kelly observed that each agent took two items from the locked cupboards that ran along both sides of the broad hallway they left by: a submachine gun and a kilogram brick of cocaine.

"They simply put it in their flak jackets," Kelly remembered. "The kilos were probably ten inches long, maybe two or three inches wide, wrapped up in cellophane. Because there's forty people on this raid and they got forty kilos of cocaine, no matter how you cut it, there's gonna be a helluva lot of dope found."

Although Kelly suspected that the agents of the F2 carried their own cocaine for the same reason that his colleagues on the Toronto Drug Section did when they went on a raid, there was no need of insurance this night. The Colombian narcotics police and its Canadian guest walked into a drug factory in full swing, arresting sixty people, seizing hundreds of kilograms of cocaine, and three-hundred-pound bales of coca leaves stacked to the rafters of the old warehouse. As the F2 loaded the fifty-gallon drums of ether used in the distillation process onto trucks and took axes to the huge vats where the raw product was filtered during refining, one of the agents turned to Kelly with a smile that was in keeping with the generally festive atmosphere of the raid.

"This isn't a cocaine factory," he said, holding up a stack of U.S. twenty-dollar bills seized by F2. "This is a *money* factory."

From what Kelly already knew about the cocaine trade, it was hard to disagree. At source in Colombia, Ecuador, or Peru, the drug sold for between $4,500 and $6,800 a pound, depending on purity. By the time a pound of 70 per cent pure cocaine made its way to North America or Europe, it would sell for $180,000. The drug would be then be "stepped on" or diluted with dextrose, procaine, or lidocaine, so that the buyer of one pound of 70 per cent pure cocaine would now have two pounds of 35 per cent pure cocaine. These two pounds would then be sold to others who would further cut and dilute it into half-pound lots until it was eventually "ounced or grammed out" for final sale. By the time the cocaine turned up at the parties of Toronto's wealthy recreational users or filled the syringes of the city's hardened addicts, it was usually between 5 and 15 per cent pure. The message for would-be traffickers was as simple as it was seductive: anyone who could get ten pounds of cocaine into North America had just won the lottery.

Although Kelly's official report of his training session contained everything he had learned about the cocaine business, including the police contacts he had made in the various drug enforcement branches in Bogota, there was one side of his trip that he kept to himself. During his language training, Kelly was billeted with a well-to-do Colombian family who moved in Bogota's better social circles and often invited their handsome and athletic young guest to come along. (Even though he was about to be married, Kelly later admitted he "went kind of wild" in Bogota and slept with a few of the women he met at his host's fashionable tennis club.) During a dinner party attended by U.S. embassy personnel and DEA officials, Kelly was approached by an affable Franciscan priest who told him that he had heard good things about him from the nuns who were also taking the Spanish course in preparation for church postings in South America.

After hearing from his friend Gonzales, the head of the DEA, about what Kelly was doing in Bogota, the priest invited him to a weekend retreat at a closed cloister run by the church in a village called Villa d'Eleva, sixty miles southeast of Bogota, saying that the beautiful and tranquil mountain village was the perfect place to lay down the worries of the world and relax. Kelly had already observed that the priest and Gonzales appeared to know each other very well, and was curious enough about what was on the man's mind to accept his invitation.

"It was pretty obvious that the priest was tight with the guy who was in charge of the DEA. They got along very well, and the chap in the DEA apparently had known the priest from earlier dealings, from some work he had done in Texas or New Mexico."

During the long, hot ride by Jeep to Villa d'Eleva, Kelly kept his eyes peeled for any sign of the rebel soldiers then causing government troops and foreign businesses in Colombia a great deal of trouble from their mountain strongholds. His host seemed unconcerned about the dangers everyone back in Bogota had warned Kelly about, smiling and calling out friendly greetings to the villagers they met along the way. Noticing Kelly's skittishness, the priest tried his best to put him at ease. "There is no danger, Patrick," he said. "Here, the only guerrillas are Franciscans!"

That night, as the two men sipped wine and huddled in front of a fire to keep off the cool mountain air, the priest asked Kelly if his trip to Bogota was "a onetime shot" or whether he would be travelling back and forth from North America to Colombia. Kelly said that his work would be bringing him back to Bogota as the need arose, and the priest asked if he would be interested in "assisting the Church" in a special project.

Certain wealthy parishioners who were worried about Colombia's volatile political situation were anxious to transfer their money out of the country to the safety of American banks, he explained. Since the authorities would prevent them from doing that if they used conventional banking procedures, they needed a reliable courier who could be trusted to carry their money to the United States. To such a person, the nervous rich of Colombia would be willing to pay $20,000 U.S. per trip, or so his new friend claimed.

"I recall being a little curious." Kelly said. "I said, 'Surely you people have been doing this for a while, why me?' He was just very blunt and commented that they had had some problems in the past and that they had been looking for someone who could do the job discreetly and who could be trusted. I take it I must have fallen within those categories because the first transfer was made shortly thereafter."

Kelly did not personally handle the money in Bogota, but used "Church connections" to carry it from parishes scattered around the Colombian countryside through Central America to Mexico. He selected the best border points for their crossings, and told the couriers how and when to travel. The smuggled funds were always delivered to a church in Acapulco, where Kelly picked them up for the last leg of the trip into the United States.

It was the riskiest part of the enterprise, but Kelly's RCMP training stood him in good stead. He took the money north from Acapulco by car to a small town called Hermosillo on the Sonora River not far from the Arizona border. Once in Hermosillo, he paid Mexican farmers to hide his suitcases in the back of their vegetable trucks. In the heart of a vegetable growing area, several hundred trucks a day crossed the border from Hermosillo to Nogales, Arizona. Once across the border, he would make his way to a major centre like Phoenix or Tucson and then fly to New York City, wearing either a collar or the dark-brown habit of the Franciscans. There, he would turn the funds over to another priest who would be waiting for him at a church.

"I could quite easily complete an entire trip within three or four days and also fit in my schedule with the RCMP. They would not have even known that I was out of the country. I often used false ID for these trips, and initially I travelled as a Catholic priest. I went by the name of Father Patrick Michaels. All payments to me were made in cash."

Years later, Kelly acknowledged that the money he delivered to the church in New York City may well have belonged to Colombian drug lords trying to launder their illicit profits in the United States. After all, there had to be some explanation for the fact that the large amounts of currency he claimed to be smuggling on behalf of wealthy and nervous Catholic parishioners were always in U.S. dollars.

Wherever the money was coming from, one thing was certain: the subtle and not so subtle improvements that Kelly's moonlighting began to bring to his private life in the mid-1970s weren't being financed by polar bear rugs.

8

THE END OF THE RIDE

When Abby Latter came to Toronto in the spring of 1979 to visit Jeannette Kelly, the events that would lead to the arrest of her friend's husband a year later were nowhere in sight. Not that Abby had been looking for them. The purpose of her two-week vacation was to get away from the cloying world of Glasgow, where her domineering brothers had already mapped out her life, a dutiful combination of working in the family clothing business and caring for their recently widowed mother. Resisting what she saw as an attempt to turn her into an old maid, Abby longed for an opportunity to test her own wings and make a new start; she got it after a chance meeting with a vacationing Jeannette and Patrick Kelly in a Glasgow pub in 1978.

Although Abby had lost track of Jeannette for nearly five years, the old friends picked up where they had left off as teenagers. Jeannette gave Abby a shorthand account of her new life, and Abby in turn confided that she felt smothered by her family obligations in Scotland. Before they parted, Jeannette invited Abby to come to Canada, where she promised her friend that she could get a taste of independence from the secure base of the Kellys' Cookstown home. Jeannette extended the invitation again when she returned to Glasgow in August 1978 on the surprise trip that ended as suddenly as it began with a call from Patrick with news of the fire. After she returned to Toronto and moved into the Palace Pier, Jeannette kept up the phone calls until Abby finally agreed to come to Toronto.

To the starry-eyed visitor from Glasgow, the city by the lake had been everything her friend had said it was and more. Abby was impressed by Massey Hall, the CN Tower, High Park, and, not the least, by the opulent lifestyle of her hosts. Jeannette made a point of including Abby in everything, just as she had in Scotland when others chose to treat her friend like an ugly duckling. Deciding that she needed a man in her life, the Kellys even indulged in a little matchmaking, introducing Abby to Harry Morozowich, an OPP officer and the brother of Patrick's lawyer, Dennis Morris. Abby began dating Harry, and for the first time in her life felt young and free. The only cloud on the horizon was the prospect of returning to Glasgow.

Sensing Abby's dread of going home, Jeannette did everything she could to make the most of the visit, hoping to persuade her friend to emigrate to Canada. One day, they picked up Dawn Hastey from work and the three women went to the Eaton Centre for lunch. Abby liked Dawn, who seemed so young, pretty, and full of life. Even though Dawn was originally from the United States, Abby could tell that the former police officer had fallen in love with Toronto in the same way that she had. She was sorry to hear that Dawn was having such problems in her marriage and couldn't imagine why her RCMP husband preferred to drink and stay out late instead of coming home to such a vivacious and attractive woman.

Abby couldn't help thinking how different things were for Jeannette. Not only was Patrick suave and considerate, he had somehow been able to shower his wife with luxuries that seemed to Abby to be well beyond a police officer's salary. She was dazzled by their apartment at the Palace Pier, the new car, Jeannette's expensive clothes and jewellery, and the trips the Kellys were always taking. The only oddity was the lack of food in their refrigerator, which was explained when Abby realized a few days after her arrival that her hosts preferred dining out in elegant restaurants like Winston's to cooking at home. When Abby finally got up the nerve to ask how they could afford their lavish ways, Jeannette said that Patrick made extra money restoring and selling antique furniture.

The trip to Canada was such a success that Abby applied for landed immigrant status as soon as she got back to Scotland. Jeannette couldn't wait to have her childhood friend in Canada and wrote her soon after her return to see how her emigration plans were going:

"How are things progressing with your papers? If you need any help please call us and don't forget – the very day you send them in, let us know, because Pat has to get in touch with the guy at this end who's going to help you, so please don't forget . . . Harry went off to Puerto Rico for 2 weeks, he's due back this Saturday, so no doubt we'll be seeing him . . . Pat is fine and sends his love. Please write soon with all the news."

That August as Abby boarded the plane for Toronto where she intended to await her final immigration approval, it was as if her life in Europe had come down to a single, withering memory: the biweekly supervised baths at boarding school where Matron kept a sharp eye on the water level to make sure that the girls didn't use more than their allotted two inches. How different things would be for her now, she thought, far from the dour roots of her childhood where she could start her life over in a new and exciting city.

The Kellys were at the airport to give Abby a rousing welcome. Even though she wanted to rent her own apartment, Jeannette wouldn't hear of it, insisting that she stay with them at the Palace Pier. It would give Jeannette a chance to repay the many kindnesses Mrs. Latter had shown her back in Glasgow in the tumultuous days of her parents' disintegrating marriage. Besides, Abby needed to learn more about North American ways before striking out on her own, and who better to teach her than Jeannette?

It had only been five months since her last visit, but Abby was astonished at the change in the atmosphere of apartment 1705. The Kellys told her that criminals had burned down their home in Cookstown, and that even though the insurance companies had settled the claim, the police still suspected that Kelly himself may have been involved in the fire. Patrick said that the apartment was "bugged" and told Abby that if she wanted to talk to him about it, they would have to go outside.

On the third day of her stay, her formerly gracious host presented her with a $270 telephone bill for long distance calls to Scotland. Although Patrick had placed the calls, their purpose he explained, had been to "advise" Abby on immigration matters, making them her responsibility. Not wanting to add to the stresses that were taking such an obvious and terrible toll on her old friend, she paid the bill.

Although she said little in front of Patrick, Jeannette confided to Abby that she had been experiencing strange mood swings and a profound depression that she couldn't seem to shake. Abby wondered if they could be connected to the fact that the Kellys still didn't have any children. Jeannette replied that she had had her tubes tied because there was a "genetic" problem in Patrick's family – an oblique reference to her husband's institutionalized brother, Timmy. When Jeannette had sought professional help for her depression, Dr. Joseph Allen had been unable to find any medical cause, and instead attributed her low spirits to the distressing fact that her husband was being investigated by the police. Jeannette's salt and pepper hair had turned silvery-white almost overnight, and there were regular trips to the hairdresser to have it dyed. The only time she was happy was when the apartment was full of girl-friends like Sheree Brown or Dawn Hastey, frequent visitors who seemed to help Jeannette temporarily forget her troubles.

Their lively visits were in sharp contrast to life with her Mountie husband. From the very first night in the apartment, Abby noticed a subtle tension between Patrick and Jeannette that hadn't been there in her previous visit. Instead of acting like a happily married couple, they seemed more like brother and sister now; still affectionate, but in an oddly formal way. Their bedroom door was always open and during the six weeks of her stay Abby never saw them hug or kiss. Thinking that the couple needed privacy to carry on with their normal sex life, their considerate guest began inventing excuses to come home late. But Jeannette's steely looks made clear that, far from pleasing her, Abby's strategic absences were distinctly unwelcome.

Not knowing why her friend got so upset whenever she strayed from her side, Abby decided that it was just the same old Jeannette she had known in Newton Mearns; the leader of the pack who was never happy unless she was setting the agenda for everyone else. But Abby had not come to Canada to find a new mother, and she began to resent it when Jeannette tried to tell her how to dress, which jobs to apply for, and whom to date. She was completely mystified by her friend's shrewish disapproval when Abby told her that she was considering an invitation from Harry Morozowich to move in with him. After all, it had been the Kellys themselves who had introduced her to the police officer in the first place. If he had been good enough for Abby then, why wasn't he good enough for her now?

Abby raised the matter with Morozowich himself, but wished she hadn't when she heard what he had to say. The OPP officer cautioned her to be careful in her dealings with the Kellys, telling Abby that the ongoing investigation into the Cookstown fire was raising serious questions about Patrick's conduct as a police officer. A number of Patrick's colleagues, including Harry, were now keeping their distance until the investigation was over, and she would be well-advised to do the same.

Still loyal to her friends, Abby told Morozowich that she didn't appreciate his constant jokes about Patrick's credibility, although the truth was, she had her own reasons to doubt her host's claims. Patrick's "guarantee" that Abby would be accepted into Canada fell flat when her initial application was rejected, leading her to suspect that the self-assured Mountie wasn't nearly as powerful or well-connected as he had led her to believe.

As her relationship with the Kellys deteriorated, Abby noticed that she was being replaced in their favour by Sheree Brown, a girl who worked with Jeannette in her new job as a reservations clerk at CP Air. Like Abby, Sheree was on her own in Toronto and didn't know anyone. The Kellys constantly fussed over the young woman, chauffeuring her to and from work, bringing her to the apartment for dinner and socializing, and even setting her up with a twice-divorced resident of the Palace Pier, who, according to Patrick, ran a private investment fund. Sheree idolized the Kellys and listened attentively to Jeannette's motherly advice about the wisdom of marrying a wealthy man, even if, as was the case with the Kellys' male friend, he happened to be twice Sheree's age. According to Jeannette, it was always wiser to put security above matters of the heart.

The more the Kellys coddled Sheree, the more distant and even unfriendly they became with Abby. Jeannette began telling friends that Abby was ungrateful for all that the Kellys had done for her, while Patrick starting making snide personal remarks in her presence. Abby took to going to bed early to avoid unpleasant scenes, and finally told Jeannette that it would be best for all concerned if she moved out. Given how the couple had been treating her, Abby thought that Jeannette would applaud her decision. Instead, she became angry, as she always did whenever the subject of Abby's leaving came up. When Jeannette saw that there was no changing her unhappy friend's mind, she reluctantly helped Abby pack and agreed to act as her guarantor after she found suitable accommodation in a building near High Park. The day Abby moved to an apartment on the seventeenth floor of Glenlake Towers, Jeannette and Sheree arrived for a tour of the premises. During the inspection, Jeannette opened the door to the balcony and gingerly stepped outside. Refusing to look over the edge, she turned to Abby and, in the grave tone of a mother impressing a warning on a child, told her to be "very careful about going out there."

A month after Abby left the Palace Pier, Jeannette showed up at the office of Dr. John Hall, complaining of severe pain in the tailbone he had operated on only the year before. After examining her, Dr. Hall asked his patient how she had reinjured herself. Jeannette told him that she had been kicked by her husband during a quarrel. When Abby later found out about the attack, she thought that she finally understood Jeannette's obsession with having her around. It wasn't that she had wanted to control Abby's life: she just hadn't wanted to be alone with Patrick.

By the summer of 1979, the OPP investigation into the fire at the Kellys' Cookstown home had reached an impasse, as Det. Insp. Fern Savage made clear when he sent his report to the Criminal Investigation Branch: "I strongly suspect that Kelly caused his house to be burned, however, I don't feel at this point in time that there is sufficient evidence to support criminal charges." The OPP left the file open, but its investigation slowed to a crawl.

By contrast, the parallel probe by the RCMP into whether Kelly's undercover work was related to the burning of his home was building momentum through the spring and summer of 1979. By the time Abby Latter came to stay with the Kellys for the second time, Patrick's relief that the OPP appeared to be off the case had been spoiled by persistent rumours that the RCMP was digging even more deeply into his activities than its provincial counterparts and was very unhappy with what it was finding. The rumours were well-founded. By November 1979, Insp. Will Stefureak sent a confidential memo to M. S. Sexsmith, the assistant commissioner, commanding officer, "O" Division, stating that he had serious concerns about Kelly.

When Supt. D. F. Heaton heard this, he was glad that he'd handled Kelly's latest internal performance rating the way he had. On September 19, 1979, Kelly had been given a glowing appraisal by Corp. L. H. Polehoykie, his supervisor for the past six and a half months. Polehoykie reported that Kelly had performed all his job functions with intelligence and vigour and had displayed an unusual amount of leadership and initiative. Kelly had performed so well in both an operational and administrative capacity that he was, in the opinion of Polehoykie, a future candidate for the key role of international liaison officer in the intelligence arm of the Drug Enforcement Branch, as well as being worthy of being promoted to the rank of corporal.

Superintendent Heaton had once been nearly as enthusiastic about Kelly as Polehoykie was, but the rumblings out of the OPP arson investigation had persuaded him to be cautious. On September 27, 1979, Heaton supported a downgrading of Polehoykie's exceptionally high rating of Kelly, though he agreed that Kelly was an "above-average" member. But when he heard the initial results from the RCMP's investigation of Kelly, Heaton wondered if he had been too generous to Kelly. If what his investigators were telling him was true, the force had a rogue cop on its hands.

Stefureak's suspicions rested in part on a careful re-examination of the OPP's investigation of the Cookstown fire, as well as the results of a continuing RCMP audit of Kelly's finances. Like Constable Woolway, Stefureak found Patrick's belated recollection of the second gas can unbelievable; he was equally suspicious of the convenient entries in the Donnelly notebooks that Metro Const. Bill Henderson said hadn't been there when he first seized them. After resubmitting the notebooks for forensic examination, Stefureak concentrated on finding out how Kelly had been able to spend $42,000 above and beyond his RCMP salary between mid-1976 and 1978.

The RCMP's investigations turned up a very disturbing coincidence. Between August 13 and December 14, 1977, Kelly discharged $9,695.14 of personal debts, including $1,580 on his Eaton's card, which he had paid in cash. At the time he settled these accounts, Kelly had been given over $10,000 by the RCMP to buy heroin and cocaine in a JFO with the Metro police, a case Kelly had brought to a successful conclusion with the arrest of the targets.

Several months later, Metro sergeants Don Kidder and Don McAndrews received an official letter of complaint from the now convicted traffickers. Michael Mizrahi and Moshe Savion insisted that Kelly had framed them with his own drugs, an allegation which, if true, would have allowed him to keep the money he had been given by the RCMP to make the deal. Although an RCMP internal investigation had concluded at the time that the accusation against Kelly was groundless, now investigators weren't so sure. The money given to Kelly to buy the drugs and the cash he subsequently used to pay off his Eaton's account had both been in twenty-dollar denominations.

Suspecting that part of Kelly's motive for the arson may have been to defraud his insurance companies on the contents of 16 George Street, RCMP investigators turned their attentions to the schedule of loss he had filed, conducting interviews with everyone who had submitted supporting documentation. Their inquiries led them to Jimmy Culbert, who had written and signed three letters to support various parts of Kelly's overall claim. Under intense questioning, Culbert told the Mounties a very different story than he had given Kelly's insurance companies.

Culbert said that although he had attested to the fact that the total value of antiques lost in the Cookstown fire was $25,000, the true figure was closer to $10,000. He also admitted that $3,550 worth of furniture that he had said he had sold to Kelly, and which subsequently turned up on his schedule of loss, had never in fact been purchased by the Kellys. Finally, he told police that $1,560 worth of antiques he had confirmed was destroyed in the fire had actually been removed from the ruins by him and Kelly, refinished, and sold. One of those items, a walnut gunstock chair, was now in Kelly's possession, even though it appeared on his schedule of loss for insurance purposes at $150.

When he was asked why he had written the letters, Culbert gave the investigators their final surprise of the interview; he hadn't. The letters had been typed up at 225 Jarvis Street by Kelly, who told his friend that the RCMP wanted the matter handled that way. Culbert signed the letters

Kelly had written as a favour, wondering if this was how his friend intended to become a millionaire by the time he was thirty, the goal that Jeannette had once said Patrick had set for himself. The antique dealer assured investigators that he never received any money for his accommodating deceits.

The time had almost come to put the squeeze on Kelly. But before doing that, the RCMP investigators had one more matter to take care of: confronting the only other man besides Kelly they suspected might have set the Cookstown fire.

It may have been St. Patrick's Day, but Ian MacLean knew that the men waiting for him on his doorstep when he came home from work weren't in a festive mood. The two RCMP officers, Will Stefureak and Gerry Milligan, escorted the Security Service informant to 13 Division, where they borrowed one of the interrogation rooms and spent the next two hours of March 17, 1980, grilling MacLean about his relationship with Patrick Kelly. The tenor of their questions made clear that they suspected MacLean of being involved in the Cookstown fire. If it wasn't so serious, MacLean thought, it might even have been comical.

In the fall of 1979, Kelly had begun showing up to take MacLean out for early-morning coffee, explaining that he couldn't talk at the MacLeans' home because it was probably bugged. The subject of their meetings was always the same: the continuing investigation into Kelly by the RCMP and his growing anger at his suspicious and ungrateful colleagues. After all, the insurance companies had settled his claim, the Fire Marshall's Office had closed the case, and the OPP hadn't laid charges after investigating for over a year and a half. So why were his own guys putting his balls in a vice?

After venting his anger, Kelly was usually full of questions. MacLean believed that his friend was pumping him for the gossip going the rounds at 225 Jarvis Street because Kelly was cut off from all official information about the case and desperately wanted to know where he stood with his RCMP superiors. Kelly theorized that some members of the force were out "to fuck" him because of his lone-wolf investigative style and told MacLean that if they were going to charge him with arson, they should just get it over with. He said that he planned to write an exposé about RCMP dirty tricks, a subject much in the news thanks to the current McDonald Commission on RCMP wrongdoing, and asked MacLean if he wanted to collaborate, giving the perspective of the Security Service. MacLean declined, wondering if Kelly's book project was really a subtle threat against the force that he wanted MacLean to report back to the SS in hopes that it might persuade the RCMP to back off from its investigation. As they sipped their coffee and talked, neither Kelly nor MacLean knew that their morning bull sessions were taking place under the watchful eye of an RCMP surveillance team.

Investigators thought they might be on to something when they witnessed MacLean taking money from Kelly during a morning meeting in December 1979. But the two men's actions at subsequent meetings presented a puzzle; if Kelly was paying off MacLean for his part in the Cookstown fire, as police initially theorized, why would MacLean hand money over to Kelly when they met again? The answer was nothing more sinister than Christmas presents. MacLean explained that Kelly had lent him $500 just before Christmas, and he had been repaying him in cash instalments after each payday, accounting for the transactions witnessed by the RCMP.

After checking out MacLean's story, investigators were satisfied that his meetings with Kelly weren't connected to a conspiracy involving the Cookstown fire. The RCMP was finally ready to interview the man who it now believed had set the blaze and disgraced the uniform of one of the world's great police forces.

It was almost a relief for Patrick Kelly when he was finally ordered to present himself at RCMP headquarters on March 19, 1980, for an interview with Stefureak and Milligan. In the month previous to his questioning, he and Jeannette had both been off work on sick leave, suffering from headaches, stomach problems, and insomnia, which doctors attributed to stress caused by the prolonged police investigation into Kelly's activities. Even a post-New Year's trip to Hawaii, where Patrick, Jeannette, and Sheree Brown stayed in a condominium in Molokai that the Kellys had recently bought, had only temporarily buoyed their spirits.

As soon as they returned to Canada, Jeannette's nervous problems flared up again and she began experiencing severe chest pains. Joanne

MacLean recommended a battery of doctors to treat her friend's rapidly multiplying ailments even though she had privately concluded that Jeannette had been turned into a hypochondriac by her husband's continuing problems with the police. The MacLeans now believed that Patrick had burned down his own house, a conviction that deepened for Joanne the day that he stopped by for tea and asked her if she would look after Jeannette because he would soon be leaving the country without her. Certain that Jeannette knew nothing about the arson, Joanne felt deeply sorry for her and worried that her mental anguish might even lead her to commit suicide.

In the middle of their miseries over the arson investigation, fate handed the Kellys a casualty of married life run amok. Dawn Hastey, the wife of Patrick's RCMP colleague, John, turned to her old friends when her shaky marriage finally fell apart. Sensing that the couple would never be able to settle their differences over John's alleged drinking problems, abusiveness, and chronic financial difficulties, the Kellys advised Dawn to end the marriage. Patrick even drew up a list of the couple's assets so that Dawn would have some idea of the property settlement she could expect, telling her that she could stay with them until she got her money and could afford a place of her own. As Sheree Brown had once assumed Abby Latter's place in apartment 1705, Dawn now replaced Sheree as the other woman in the Kellys' lives.

Patrick thought it was natural that Dawn should come to the Kellys in her time of trouble. He had always believed that his relationship with John had been clouded by a certain "animosity" over the Kellys' superior lifestyle, which so clearly impressed Dawn. While John and Dawn struggled to keep up the mortgage payments on a house in an Orangeville subdivision, the Kellys were living in a beautiful period home in Cookstown and, later, a luxury lakeside apartment in Toronto. When the Kellys went on vacation, it was to Europe, Hawaii, or Mexico; a holiday for Dawn meant a trip to New Brunswick to visit John's relatives. "We had to dress and tone ourselves down a bit when we went out with other officers," Kelly remembers, "including Dawn and John."

Apart from a few late-night attempts by John to see his estranged wife, which were headed off by the strategic intervention of the Palace Pier's doorman, Dawn's presence in apartment 1705 made for a pleasant

addition to the Kelly household. Both of her friends were on tranquil-
lizers and Dawn did her best to calm their jangled nerves. She helped
out around the apartment, walked the dog, and most important of all,
provided Jeannette with a sympathetic companion. When Dawn got
home from Citadel Life Insurance, where she had just begun a career as
an agent, Patrick was grateful for her company on the squash courts of
the Palace Pier, where he tried to work off the anxieties of the police
investigation that was threatening his career with the RCMP, and a great
deal more that no one but he knew about.

Convinced that his apartment was still bugged, Patrick talked to
Dawn during long walks together along the waterfront and through
High Park. It felt good to Kelly to be around the young woman who
was up for anything and was always ready to laugh, even in the darkest
moment. Dawn liked and trusted Patrick, and even after he told her
that "he just wanted to run away," using an identity change to start a
new life, it never crossed her mind that he may have been guilty of
arson.

After the first five minutes with Stefureak and Milligan, Kelly realized
that they were as convinced of his guilt as Dawn Taber was of his innocence. Their tone was hard-nosed and accusatory and became even
more aggressive after Kelly refused to give a voluntary statement. Since
the interrogation was part of an official In-Service investigation,
Stefureak ordered him to answer his questions, warning Kelly that if he
didn't, he would be charged under the RCMP Act with failing to obey a
lawful command.

The officers hammered him with questions about the gas cans, the
Donnelly notebooks, and details of his insurance claim, which Kelly
told them had been accurate and truthful. Stefureak and Milligan were
briefly joined by Tom Bell of the Commercial Crime Section, who had
a complete record of Kelly's charge cards that showed the extra $42,000
he had spent over an eighteen-month period. When Bell asked where
all these additional funds had come from, Kelly explained that he
refinished and sold antique furniture on the side – a practice that in
itself was strictly forbidden by RCMP regulations. When pressed for
financial records to back up his claim that he was Cookstown's most

financially successful part-time furniture dealer, Kelly said that they had been destroyed in the fire. Bell knew that it was impossible for Kelly to have generated that much money from antique sales and told him that the funds had to have come from another source.

At 9:20 P.M., after ten and half hours of relentless questioning, Kelly refused to sign the statement recorded by Stefureak and Milligan. The RCMP officers read him his rights and informed him that he may be charged with arson, the fabrication of evidence, defrauding his insurance companies, and disgraceful conduct.

"Do you wish to say anything?" Stefureak asked.

"No, I do not," Kelly replied. Although no one knew it, earlier in the month, he had applied to renew the false passport he had obtained when he first joined the drug squad in the name of Patrick Shannon Ryan. The direction that things appeared to be going, he was glad that he had.

The day after his interview, Kelly was suspended with pay and ordered to turn in his badge and police identification, his two revolvers (a regular issue .38, as well as a .38 Smith & Wesson snub-nose used in undercover work), and a pair of handcuffs. Shortly afterwards, his top secret security clearance was rescinded, and he was given strict instructions not to exercise any authority vested in him as an RCMP officer. When he asked to travel to Hawaii with his wife for a March 22 to April 5 holiday, permission was denied, and he was expressly prohibited from leaving the jurisdiction pending the outcome of the ongoing internal investigation.

Shortly after Kelly's suspension, Assistant Commissioner Sexsmith initiated internal proceedings against the former undercover agent whose case he viewed as extremely serious. All told, the RCMP saw five elements to what was known inside the force as the "Kelly caper": perjury/theft, arson, fraud, the payment for Morris's still unpaid fees, and suspension/discharge.

In addition to its far-reaching legal and bureaucratic implications, the case was also highly embarrassing in the short term. Kelly was currently involved in several court cases in which he was set to testify, including a trial resulting from a cocaine purchase he had made at the Sheraton Hotel in Toronto on February 25, 1978.

Thanks to his tainted credibility, Kelly's past undercover operations were now suspect. Eventually, the Crown decided to stay proceedings in two investigations involving trafficking and conspiracy charges based on Kelly's work, and not to proceed with new trials following two successful appeals of previous convictions, including the high-profile case of Michael Mizrahi and Moshe Savion. As demoralizing as such a course of action was for the RCMP, it was clearly preferable to being hit with huge damage suits as a result of Kelly's possibly corrupt police work.

With these internal matters dealt with, Sexsmith contacted the commissioner of the OPP to inform him that any evidence of criminal activity by Kelly uncovered during the RCMP investigation would be turned over to his investigators for appropriate action. He left no doubt about what he had in mind: "For reasons you well understand, I would appreciate charges being laid as quickly as possible in relation to the insurance fraud and having this matter processed through the Courts as expeditiously as possible."

To facilitate the legal proceedings, Sexsmith directed Stefureak and Milligan to provide OPP Constable Woolway with the evidence they had gathered to show that Kelly was guilty of insurance fraud. At virtually the same time that the two police forces and a Crown attorney were preparing their case against him, Kelly sent a dunning letter to the officer-in-command of the Toronto Drug Section, reminding him that the legal bill he had submitted from Dennis Morris, and which the RCMP had agreed to pay, had still not been settled. If the force did not remit the moneys at once, Kelly wrote, he would take out a personal loan and add any interest charges to the amount the RCMP had already agreed to pay.

In the same letter, Kelly also demanded to know where he stood with his employers. This was necessary, he wrote, "so that I can perhaps begin to once again feel that I am an active Member in this Force with a future in the Force and not something that will be supervised and viewed with caution for the rest of my service."

At 3 P.M. on April 10, 1980, the Kellys returned to their apartment to find the door was unlocked; the special cylinder Patrick had installed for security purposes was malfunctioning. Before going out to pick up his laundry, Kelly called the concierge, who said he would send up a locksmith. When Kelly returned to the apartment an hour and a half later, the locksmith was still examining the front door, and two OPP officers were sitting in his living room with Jeannette. Even though she had just returned from the two-week holiday in Hawaii that Patrick had been unable to share because of travel restrictions imposed by the RCMP, she looked pale and drawn. Not knowing what to do, she had refused to talk to the police when they telephoned just after Patrick had gone out. But she had had no choice but to let them in after they showed up with a search warrant at her front door, escorted by the Palace Pier's apologetic manager of resident relations, Maureen McGuigan.

Kelly suddenly thought he knew what had been wrong with the front-door lock. Other officers must have surreptitiously entered apartment 1705 before constables Woolway and Ryder made their official call to execute the search warrant. That way, if Kelly lied or tried to mislead the investigators in any way, they would be aware of it from a previous intelligence briefing and could conduct their interview accordingly. Kelly had done the same thing himself on a number of investigations and understood the advantage it gave to the OPP officers who now rose and extended their right hands when he walked into his living room.

The officers were clearly hesitant to talk in front of the locksmith, so Kelly showed them into the den and closed the door. Constable Woolway showed Kelly his search warrant and asked him if he had a walnut gunstock chair on the premises that had been claimed on his schedule of loss from the Cookstown fire. (At the same time, other officers were executing a search warrant at the MacLean residence, looking for any articles that had been claimed for insurance purposes. They found nothing.) Kelly acknowledged that he had the chair, which he said had been refurbished by his good friend Jimmy Culbert. Although the chair had been deemed to be unsalvageable after the fire, Culbert had especially restored it because he knew that it had been an anniversary present from Jeannette to Patrick and wanted the couple to have a memento from their former home.

Kelly led the OPP officers to a storage room in the basement of the Palace Pier, which struck the officers as an odd place to keep a piece of furniture with such great sentimental value. Kelly himself carried the chair to the police cruiser and told Woolway and Ryder that it was the only piece of furniture that he had from the fire. If they wanted to check on it, they could contact his lawyer.

After getting a copy of the search warrant and checking the correct spelling of their names, Kelly turned to go when Woolway asked him an unexpected question based on something he had been told earlier in the day by Maureen McGuigan. Was it true that Kelly owned another condominium in the Palace Pier? Kelly looked up abruptly, hesitated for a moment, and then admitted that he did. When Woolway asked him who was renting it, Kelly bristled: "I know my rights and I have to draw the line somewhere. . . . If they are going to push this investigation, then we will settle it in court." In fact, Kelly had already solicited appraisals on both apartments in case events forced him to liquidate his assets in a hurry. The day before, he had put apartment 1907 up for sale.

Back at 225 Jarvis Street, Constable Woolway and Inspector Stefureak prepared the briefs to be used in charging Kelly. After reviewing the briefs, Crown attorney John Murphy requested additional material for the informations to be laid against Kelly and then directed that he be charged with arson and two counts of fraud against the Waterloo Mutual and Wawanesa Mutual insurance companies.

The axe was finally about to fall.

The Kellys and their new boarder, Dawn Taber, were sipping tea in the elegant living room of apartment 1705 when a sudden ringing from the kitchen set butterflies fluttering in everyone's stomach. By April 1980, it had reached the point where no one wanted to answer the telephone. In fact, for the past several months, the Kellys had left it off the hook as much as possible, hoping to keep the forces they felt were closing in on them at bay. After a long moment in which no one made a move to get up, Kelly put down his teacup and walked towards the kitchen, a slim shadow moving through the spring dusk.

It was the call he had been expecting – and Jeannette had been dreading – ever since the RCMP had suspended him from active duty a month before. Austin Cooper, the crack criminal lawyer Kelly had hired to take over from Dennis Morris, broke the news to his client as compassionately as he could. The OPP was formally charging Kelly with fraud and arson in connection with the burning of his house in

Cookstown nearly two years earlier. As bad as the news was, Cooper had managed to negotiate a small concession from the authorities. Kelly would be allowed to turn himself in to the police the next day, April 23, 1980, rather than submit to the usual procedure in such matters: being arrested at his residence in the middle of the night under the curious eyes of his neighbours.

Jeannette was devastated. Crying hysterically, she alternated between berating the police for what they were putting her through and haranguing her husband for not be able to "control" what was happening to them. How could the OPP charge him with arson when there was no evidence? How could the RCMP turn against him after he had risked his life for them so many times as the "fair-haired boy" of the drug squad? After everything they had been through with the insurance companies and the Fire Marshall's Office, now she would have to tell her father that her husband had been arrested. It was so humiliating.

Despite the fact that she had problems of her own, Taber was overcome with pity for her two friends. With the exception of her own mother, there was no one she admired more than Jeannette, particularly after she had invited Taber to move in to the Palace Pier. She felt just as strongly about Patrick, seeing him as a larger-than-life figure and an ideal husband who "walked on water." Eager to return their many kindnesses, Taber resolved to do whatever she could to help the unhappy couple through their ordeal.

The job began early the next day. After a sleepless night, the Kellys, Taber, and the family dog set out on the one-hour drive to the Barrie Detachment of the OPP, where Austin Cooper had arranged for Kelly to surrender to Const. D. G. Woolway. Cooper's associate, James Ramsey, also made the trip to represent their client at his bail hearing. As they drove north past the wet spring fields that flanked Highway 400, the passengers in the Volvo stationwagon talked quietly, even exchanging a few nervous jokes to relieve the tension. Ashen and silent in the front seat beside her dapper husband, Jeannette didn't join in. She saw nothing funny about the fact that her world was falling apart all around her and, worst of all, that everyone would soon know all about it.

After he was arraigned, Kelly drove a few miles south to Bradford, where he dropped Jeannette, Taber, and the dog at Jimmy Culbert's home, asking his friend to look after them while he went to be finger-printed and photographed. As upset as he was to see Kelly and his wife in such misery, the furniture restorer had reasons of his own to feel nervous about their sudden appearance on his doorstep. Wondering if Kelly knew that he had changed his story to the police, Culbert hastily made coffee and offered Jeannette the use of his telephone to call Glasgow. As soon as she heard her father's voice, Jeannette started to wail, and Taber had to take the phone and explain what had happened to a bewildered Jimmy Hanlon.

At the Barrie Detachment of the OPP, Kelly was formally booked and his personal information entered into CPIC, the police intelligence computer used to keep track of felons. Accepting the OPP's contention that the accused might flee to Scotland where his in-laws lived, justice of the peace E. J. Burton ordered Kelly to surrender his passport. Bail was set at $1,000 with the condition that the accused man report to 51 Division of the Metropolitan Toronto Police every Friday until his case came to court.

That night back in Toronto, Jeannette was wretched. When the three-some went up to the Palace Pier's rooftop club for a drink, she sat by herself in an out-of-the-way corner, not wanting to be seen by other residents, while Patrick talked with Dawn at a table in the middle of the crowded lounge. Sipping Courvoisier as he looked out over Lake Ontario, he made her shudder when he delivered his grim bottom line on all that had happened. "He said, 'I can never go to prison. I will commit suicide rather than go to prison,'" she remembers.

The next morning, Kelly was introduced to another reality of life on the wrong side of the badge. In contrast to the days when press reports of his exploits as an undercover agent had been obligingly anonymous, news of his alleged crimes came with stark and numbing attribution: "A Royal Canadian Mounted Police undercover officer was charged today with arson and two counts of fraud following a 19-month investigation by the Ontario Provincial Police," the *Toronto Star* reported. "The charges were laid against 30-year-old Patrick Kelly of the RCMP "O" Division drug squad in Toronto in connection with a fire at his former home."

Like the price of gold and last night's sports scores, the undercover life of Patrick Kelly was suddenly down in black and white for all to see.

Two and a half months after he was charged with fraud and arson by the OPP, Patrick Kelly was summoned to a July 4, 1980, interview with RCMP staff sergeants Norm Harvey-McKean and Wayne Horrocks concerning the disbursement of the force's moneys to informant 0.1255. He again refused to provide a voluntary statement and was ordered by Harvey-McKean, a former supervisor and staunch Kelly supporter, to answer questions regarding the allegation that he had pocketed $3,500 of $4,000 the force had given him to pay one Phillip X (a pseudonym). Based on intelligence partially supplied by the U.S. Drug Enforcement Agency, Kelly had reported that Phillip X not only had information about a major marijuana smuggling ring based in Toronto, but was also privy to a Florida drug operation that exported most of its product to Canada. In return for sharing what he knew with police, the informant wanted to be paid.

The normal procedure in such matters was for the RCMP agent involved to submit an application referred to as a "990" to his supervisor requesting authority to make a cash payment to an informant. The amount of the "award" depended on the quality and importance of the informant's intelligence, which was why a synopsis of what the agent expected to get for taxpayers' money was always included on the application. To protect the agent from allegations of non-payment by the informant, and the public from the theft of its money by the agent, the actual cash transaction was always "covered" by a second RCMP member. After he counted the money and witnessed the payment, this second officer then added his name to the receipt that the informant had already signed. The receipt indicated the precise time, date, place, and amount of the transaction, as well as the name of the RCMP agent who made the payment.

According to the documentation in RCMP files, Kelly appeared to have followed force procedures when he twice paid Phillip X awards of $2,000 for drug information, first on October 27, 1978, and again on December 14. The payments were both made in downtown Toronto restaurants, and the receipts were properly made out and duly co-signed by RCMP Corp. Al Assance of the drug squad. But despite the signed receipts, Harvey-McKean had reason to believe that the documents didn't tell the real story.

"Did you withhold any of the money from these payments for yourself?" Harvey-McKean asked.

"No," Kelly replied.

After eliciting more details about the time and place of the witnessed payments, he asked a question he hoped would take Kelly by surprise.

"Do you believe in the polygraph test?" he asked.

"Yes, to a certain extent," Kelly answered.

"Would you take one in connection with this?"

"No I would not," Kelly replied. He explained that he wouldn't take a polygraph on this or any other matter, since the one he had taken during the arson investigation had obviously been disregarded by the RCMP.

"Is there any reason that you can think of why 'Phillip X' would say he didn't receive the money?" Harvey-McKean continued.

"I can think of a good one," Kelly shot back. "I took the same approach with 'Phillip X' as any other informant – promise them the sky and only give them what they're worth. He wanted more money after he saw the write-up in the newspaper on the SIM project [an undercover drug investigation]. For a long time he kept phoning me from Florida, coming on to me about more money and I would hang up on him."

Looking calmly into Kelly's face, Harvey-McKean dropped his bombshell.

"If I told you he was working in Florida on December 14, 1978, what would you say?" he asked.

"I'd say he wasn't," Kelly replied, fully aware that the receipt Phillip X had signed showed that the December 14 payment had been made in Toronto.

Harvey-McKean showed Patrick two receipts, each bearing the name of the informant and each in the amount of $2,000.

"Do both signatures on the receipts look alike. Do you think they are both his?" Harvey-McKean asked.

"They say 'Phillip X,' so I'd have to say yes," Kelly answered, ignoring the implication that he had forged his own informant's signature on the receipt.

At 7:10 P.M., the lengthy interview was interrupted by Insp. Will

Stefureak, who personally served Kelly with a notice of intent to recommend discharge. If it was a tactic designed to wring a confession from Kelly, it failed. He read the official document impassively, even when he got to the part that made obvious what his superiors believed he had done:

"You were clearly involved in the commission of an offence under an Act of the Parliament of Canada of so serious a nature and in such circumstances as would significantly affect the proper performance of your duties under the RCMP Act, thereby rendering yourself unsuitable to continue service in the Force. . . . You submitted two signed receipts of $2,000 each in support of your claim to have paid the $4,000 to Informant 0.1255. In fact, Informant 0.1255 was paid only $500 more or less in the first instance, and nothing in the second. Your action constitutes theft or fraud of approximately $3,500 against the Government of Canada."

A few days later, Harvey-McKean travelled to the United States, where he and a DEA agent took a formal statement from Phillip X, who said that he had been working in Naples, Florida, on the day that Kelly was supposed to have made the second $2,000 payment at the Kozy Restaurant in Toronto. A check of the records of the Deltona Corporation, the company that employed him, confirmed the informant's story. As for the first alleged payment of $2,000, Phillip X repeated that he had only received $500.

Back in Toronto, Phillip X's story was corroborated in part by Corp. Al Assance, who told internal investigators that on October 27 he had indeed witnessed Kelly pay Informant 0.1255 at the McDonald's Restaurant at Pape and Gerrard in Toronto's east end. But since Kelly had asked him to observe the transaction from a distance of forty feet, allegedly because strangers made his contact nervous, Assance could not swear that $2,000 had actually changed hands. As for the second documented $2,000 payment, Assance admitted that he had not witnessed it at all. Instead, he had signed the receipt after Kelly presented it to him with Phillip X's signature already affixed. Since Assance had previously witnessed a transaction with the same informant for the identical award, and because Kelly had been a trusted and admired member of the drug squad for several years, the corporal had merely done his colleague a favour. Assance acknowledged that what he had done was against RCMP regulations and told investigators that he had warned Kelly at the time never to ask him to bend the rules again.

The RCMP was faced with the choice of whether to pursue Kelly's alleged theft of informant fees criminally or administratively. In a secret memo dated June 30, 1980, the force made it clear it believed that it had "sufficient evidence" to warrant laying criminal charges. But just two days later, there was an official about-face. In a confidential memo, Supt. D. H. Heaton wrote: "While there has obviously been a misappropriation of funds with respect to this informant payment, it would seem doubtful that sufficient evidence will exist to support criminal action. Notwithstanding, a decision must be made on whether to refer the matter to either the Provincial Crown Attorney or the Police Department having jurisdiction to avoid any criticism in the future."

Even though an official in the Attorney General's Office told Supt. R. M. Culligan and Insp. Will Stefureak during a July 4, 1980, meeting that there was sufficient evidence to support a charge against Kelly, the RCMP ultimately opted for an administrative solution to its problem, appointing three senior officers to a Discharge and Demotion Board for the purposes of conducting an In-Service hearing on the matter. Whatever the reasons for the decision, its advantages to the RCMP were obvious. Its policy of chequebook police work, in which the force paid known criminals from public funds in exchange for intelligence on the murky world of drugs, would remain secret, as would the identity of Informant 0.1255, who might otherwise be killed. And by the time Kelly was convicted of arson, assuming, as the RCMP did, that he eventually would be, the embarrassing matter of his employment with the force would no longer be an issue.

On July 23, 1980, Kelly admitted under further questioning in preparation for his official hearing that Corporal Assance had not, in fact, been with him when he paid Informant 0.1255 the second award of $2,000, contrary to what he told Staff Sgt. Norman Harvey-McKean on July 4. He now said that he had arranged for Assance to witness the payment, but when he called him at the Pretzel Bell Tavern with the time and place of the meeting with Phillip X, his fellow officer refused to leave the bar. Kelly claimed that Assance instructed him to proceed with the payment without him and bring the receipt to the tavern, where, according to Kelly, it was ultimately signed.

When he was confronted with company records that Informant 0.1255 had been working for Deltona Corporation in Florida on the day Kelly claimed to have met him in Toronto, the accused officer insisted that he had made the award on the date indicated on the signed receipt, December 14, 1978; Phillip X was simply lying. Even though Kelly had passed a private polygraph test administered by Ben Silverberg, who reported that his subject was telling the truth about the informant payments, the RCMP was unimpressed when Kelly's lawyer gave them the report.

As the date for his demotion and discharge hearing drew near, Kelly exercised an option that had been available to him ever since the force had commenced internal proceedings against him on July 7; he resigned. Assistant Commissioner Sexsmith tried to deduct $3,500 from Kelly's superannuation cheque to recoup the money the RCMP believed he had stolen instead of paying Phillip X, but to no avail. The Attorney General's Office advised the force that the Crown would not likely succeed in an action to recover the informant fees and that the cost of an unsuccessful action would be prohibitive. Heeding its legal advice, the force instead wrote off the money, and on July 28, 1980, Kelly entered civilian life with a full superannuation settlement from his disgruntled employers. By voluntarily leaving the RCMP, Kelly escaped the fate of being drummed out of the force as "unsuitable," the equivalent of a dishonourable discharge; instead, he was given a certificate of service that looked like a university degree, vouching for the 9 years and 268 days he had served as a member of the Royal Canadian Mounted Police.

Kelly's file, HQ 208, was, in the parlance of the force, a closed volume, or so the RCMP thought.

While the events that brought about the end of Patrick Kelly's undercover career in the RCMP were playing out in North America, Jeannette Kelly was doing her best to forget her sorrows on the beaches of Italy and Greece. Believing that her husband's preliminary hearing on the arson and fraud charges would be held in July, she had arranged to take a lengthy European vacation until his legal battles were over, getting a medical leave from her job at CP Air based on her doctor's opinion that she was on the verge of a nervous breakdown.

Joining her on the trip was Dawn Taber, who informed her employers at Citadel Life Insurance that she, too, was under doctor's orders to take a leave of absence to deal with a debilitating case of bad nerves. Because she had no money and her property settlement with John Hastey wouldn't come through until October, Kelly obligingly gave Taber the money for the trip.

From the first glorious days in Ostia on the Tyrrhenian Sea, she was grateful that he had. During their European idyll, Dawn and Jeannette shared secrets and adventures that drew the two women closer than they had ever been before. Jeannette was gaining some comfort in another man's arms and openly saw her Italian lover in Dawn's presence, confiding to her friend that her husband's indifference had finally driven her to adultery. There was even talk of Jeannette moving to Italy where she would become the mistress of the married man she had met at Rome airport during a trip she had taken to Kenya to see her father just after Patrick had been charged.

Happy to be taken into Jeannette's trust, Dawn shared a confidence of her own. Before leaving for Europe, Patrick had taken her to the Eaton Centre, where he had given her $4,000 in cash for the trip. Then came the secret part. According to Dawn, Patrick dictated a letter to her which for the first time made her believe that he had, in fact, burned down his Cookstown home. After Dawn signed her name to the bottom of the last page, Patrick had instructed her to address it to Austin Cooper, the lawyer who was representing him on the arson and fraud charges. Dawn did as she was told and mailed the letter from a post box on Lakeshore Boulevard in front of the Palace Pier just before they picked up Jeannette for the trip to the airport.

But as close as they had become, Dawn didn't tell Jeannette all her secrets. She didn't tell her that she had slept with Patrick shortly after moving in to the Palace Pier, or that on May 22, 1980, she had drawn up a proposal to increase the Kellys' life insurance to $500,000, a fact Patrick wanted her to keep from his wife. But as they walked the moonlit beaches of Mykonos, Dawn did ask her friend a question that had been on her mind ever since Patrick had asked her to run away with him to the south of France.

"Do you think Patrick would ever hurt you?"

Stopping in her tracks, Jeannette looked straight into her friend's eyes.

"That's one thing I don't have to worry about."

Turning away, she swung down the beach at a lazy pace, tossing a pebble into the sea.

9

THE GENTLEMAN
ENTREPRENEUR

Joanne MacLean couldn't believe her eyes. The new Porsche 924 crouched in her driveway looked less like a car than a powerful cat poised to spring. Judging from Jeannette's broad smile as she stepped into the September sun, swinging the driver's door closed with an expensive thud, the Kellys had a new acquisition. Joanne rolled her eyes, then hurried to the front door to greet her friend. It wasn't that the sleek sports car didn't go with the swank apartment at the Palace Pier, the designer clothes, and the exotic trips; what the working mother of two wanted to know was how an ex-police officer without a salary still managed to live like a millionaire.

This visit from Jeannette was quite different from their last contact just two weeks earlier. Joanne would never forget Jeannette's pathetic voice over the telephone on the night of August 16, 1980, after Patrick had smashed her into the refrigerator during a violent quarrel. Injured from the encounter and cowering in her bedroom, Jeannette kept whimpering that she didn't know what to do. Joanne knew that her friend needed help, but didn't want to go over on her own because Patrick was still in the apartment and she distinctly remembered their frightening exchange over the arson. Instead, she called Dr. Joseph Allen and persuaded him to make a house call at the Kelly apartment. After treating Jeannette for an injured leg, Dr. Allen told her to go to the hospital if she didn't feel better by morning. Looking sternly at Kelly, the doctor also advised the couple to seek marriage counselling.

The next day, Jeannette's leg was still swollen below the knee, and she drove herself to the emergency ward of Toronto General Hospital. The injured woman explained that she had fallen at home the day before and heard a crack when she hit the floor. After doctors put her leg in a Jones Splint for what they diagnosed as a sprained knee, Jeannette called Dawn Taber to drive her back to the apartment. When Dawn, who had been staying with friends in Burlington, walked into the hospital lobby and saw Jeannette, she felt a lump in her throat. Slouching in a wheelchair with her leg in a cast, her normally elegant friend looked faintly clownish in the baggy surgeon's pants the hospital had given her. Gone was the tanned and confident travelling companion of their European holiday; in her place was a frightened and forlorn woman who looked suddenly older than her thirty-two years.

Jeannette's girlfriends gradually found out what had happened. After an earlier argument on the night before she was injured, Patrick had drawn up a seventeen-page letter, listing their assets and debts, which he proposed to use as the basis for a separation agreement. Included were the two apartments at the Palace Pier, the condominium in Hawaii, shares in a British Columbia gold mine, restaurant equipment from a previous investment, jewellery, furs, and antiques.

But on paper, at least, the couple's liabilities more than outweighed their assets. There was even a reference in the letter to possible tax problems over Kelly's "undeclared" extra income. According to Kelly's proposal, the separation could either commence immediately or after the disposition of assets, in which case they could continue living together until the disposition, but not as husband and wife.

Even so, he left the door slightly ajar for a possible reconciliation, suggesting that if both parties agreed, they would start seeing a marriage counsellor or a psychiatrist. The proposal's concluding line struck the tone of a displeased executive who had all but decided to terminate a troublesome employee: "I think the above is reasonable, justified, and accurate. Should there be any questions, I am free to discuss it."

Leaving the proposal on the dining-room table, Kelly went out for a game of squash, his favourite form of blowing off pent-up energy in times of high stress. When he returned, Jeannette, who had been stewing for hours, flew into a rage. Red-faced and shrieking, she demanded to know how he could have written such a cold document and then just walked out without discussing it. Working herself into a fury, she slapped his face and then attacked him. "She attempted to grab me by the balls," Patrick recalled, "and I simply took her by the shoulders and twisted her to the ground. She twisted her knee slightly, and that was it."

Less than a week later, at 2:30 A.M., Jeannette was back in the emergency ward of the same hospital, claiming that her seventy-five-pound sheepdog had accidentally struck her in the face during a late-night "grooming session." Remembering the patient from her recent visit, hospital personnel listened silently as she related her improbable explanation. Jeannette was diagnosed as having painful jaw joints and numbness on the right side of her face and referred to her family doctor.

That autumn she was a frequent visitor to her family doctor, Joseph Allen, and the specialist John Hall suffering from a variety of physical and psychological ailments. During a visit to Dr. Hall over recurring problems with her injured knee, the subject of spousal abuse was raised. Not only did Jeannette deny that her husband had injured her knee, she now said that he had not, in fact, kicked her in the tailbone as she had told the surgeon just a year before. Having seen enough battered women to know that denial was one of the saddest parts of the syndrome, Dr. Hall dutifully recorded what she had to say on her medical file, even though he was personally convinced that her new story was no more than a protective or self-deluding lie.

But there was no sign of marital problems on Jeannette's face at the end of August when she breezed into Joanne MacLean's living room bursting with news about the Porsche and what had made it possible: Patrick's new career as executive manager of K&V Enterprises Ltd., a West Coast investment firm owned by a Victoria lawyer. It was the first time since the arson charges that Joanne had seen her friend in good spirits. Obviously Jeannette was delighted that her husband had found new employment less than a month after leaving the force and that they were once again "secure."

After the short visit ended, Joanne watched from the front door as Jeannette got into the Porsche and gingerly backed down the driveway.

She didn't approve of her friend's decision to put up with an abusive husband, but Joanne knew there was nothing that she or anyone else could do about it. During a previous heart-to-heart, in which Jeannette admitted that she was no longer happy with Patrick, she told Joanne that she hadn't invested several years of her life to get what she had just "to leave the marriage and go live in a lousy one-bedroom apartment."

Jeannette Kelly enjoyed the good life as much as she demanded it: the last thing she planned to do was end up like her father, on the wrong side of a ruinous divorce.

By 1974, it would have been tempting to conclude that Victor Simpson, Patrick Kelly's boyhood friend, had become a professional student. After abandoning his early aspirations of being a dentist or a police officer, the soft-spoken young man with the dark, expressive eyes had earned an undergraduate degree from Notre Dame University in Nelson, British Columbia. He and his wife, Kay, had then moved to Ontario, where he got his master's degree in sociology from the University of Waterloo. Back in B.C. after completing his thesis, and still undecided about his future, he dabbled in computer science and sociology courses, while working for B.C.'s law reform commission. The bespectacled scholar toyed with but finally rejected an academic life, taking a position as a probation officer, which he abruptly left after being accepted into law school at the University of British Columbia.

His family and friends smiled knowingly at what they saw as Victor's latest educational enthusiasm, but he proved them wrong. He stayed the course at law school, and after a year of articling was ready to begin practising law in his hometown of Victoria. Bert and Pat Simpson couldn't have been prouder. Their only son had finally put down roots and set his course in life, and the doting parents could now look forward to having Victor and his family close by as they grew older.

Kelly had maintained sporadic contact with Simpson when he and Kay were living in Ontario, spending the occasional Christmas together in the early 1970s, but he became a fixture in their lives when his old friend began practising law. After the Cookstown fire, Kelly started flying to Victoria every two or three months for lengthy talks with his trusted friend, increasing the visits to once a month after he was suspended from the RCMP. Patrick flew out when Victor moved into smart, new offices at 1012 Douglas Street in Victoria, never missing an opportunity to show him how much he admired Simpson for what he had accomplished. The two men became very close again and began talking about potential joint ventures based on Kelly's business activities in Toronto. It was the same Patrick whom Victor loved and remembered from their Victoria days with one major difference: his formerly outgoing and talkative best friend had grown extremely secretive. "If it was business-related, then he would not talk on the telephone, he would not speak in the office. If you had business to conduct, you went on the streets and walked the streets and talked business. He never talked in front of females, be they wives, lovers, secretaries, or office managers," Simpson recalled.

The arson investigation was a frequent topic of conversation. Kelly told Simpson that the police probe had put tremendous strain on his marriage, and even admitted to an affair with a young woman named Dawn Taber. He made clear that he blamed the RCMP for much of his trouble, and accused the force of persecuting him for his unorthodox investigative style, his impressive record, and his knowledge that some of his colleagues were on the take.

Although Kelly denied any role in the fire, which he said had been set by organized crime figures out to kill him for his undercover drug work, their talks strayed into some strange territory. Kelly asked his lawyer friend teasingly hypothetical questions about "how would you, or how could you, form a new person out of documents and paper?" With the preliminary hearing on his arson charge looming, Kelly also asked Simpson to research Canada's Extradition Act to find out the sorts of crimes and the various countries that were covered under the treaty. Just as Kelly had told Dawn Taber and Joanne MacLean that he intended to leave the country, he now raised the subject with Simpson. Simpson didn't know exactly what Kelly meant by "running away," but it was obvious to the lawyer that he was at least contemplating some profound change in his personal life and was actively preparing for it.

In particular, Kelly talked about the possibility of transferring the title of both his Molokai condominium and apartment 1907 at the Palace Pier to K&V Enterprises. The Hawaiian property was, in fact, transferred and Simpson arranged for a nominee to put in an offer on the Toronto property. If the offer was accepted, the joint title of the property would be transferred, and his client would end up as the sole owner. Kelly left little doubt in the young lawyer's mind about his motives for the property manoeuvres: "The concern that Mr. Kelly expressed at that time would be that if she [Jeannette] were to separate, or divorce him, the way that he had set up the finances, or was trying to set up his finances, at the time may have been of benefit [in] a divorce situation."

After he was forced out of the RCMP, Kelly made an unusual proposal to Simpson. He wanted a job with K&V Enterprises, ("K" for Kay and "V" for Victor), the management company that ran Simpson's law practice. His self-appointed task would be to find investments for the company; in return, he would be provided with a car (the Porsche) and a monthly salary of $1,200. When Simpson replied that his firm didn't do that kind of work, Kelly took Victor and Kay for a ride along Beach Drive, where one of the most opulent houses in the wealthy Victoria neighbourhood happened to be for sale.

"We had talked about how much money we could make. I looked at a house that was going for an exorbitant amount of money and we laughed and said, 'Oh, maybe in a couple of years we could afford it.'"

K&V hired Patrick. As odd as it might seem for a lawyer to engage someone who stood charged with fraud and arson to handle financial investments, Simpson was convinced that Kelly would bring business to the firm. "I thought he could sell refrigerators to the Eskimos," he said. There was one other peculiar but attractive feature of the deal. Kelly would pay his own salary and benefits from funds he brought into the company. It was not the lawyer's money he apparently wanted, but a position that would give him another role to play now that he was out of the RCMP. Kelly the undercover agent was about to become Kelly the gentleman entrepreneur, complete with an official title, a professional address, and a business card. In the parlance of his former profession, he had arranged cover for his next operation.

Although Jeannette didn't know it, Kelly had been doing business with K&V for months before he came home with the welcome news about officially going on Simpson's payroll. Just two days after his arrest on the fraud and arson charges, K&V wired Kelly $5,000. The money came in the form of a loan from K&V at 17 per cent interest. Two days after Kelly's resignation from the RCMP, K&V sent him a promissory note in the amount of $8,000. What the paper transaction concealed was that the moneys had been paid into K&V by Kelly from the proceeds of his "moonlighting." Simpson had merely sent him back his own funds. Between March and September 1980, when Jeannette was worried sick about how they were going to pay their bills, Patrick sent $65,000 to the company that now employed him, receiving most of it back in the form of salary and loans. Simpson never asked where his client got the cash, and Kelly never told him.

Money wasn't the only thing the former Mountie brought to K&V. During a meeting in July 1980, Kelly gave Simpson a parcel for safe-keeping, which the lawyer was not to open unless something happened to Kelly. Simpson put the sealed package in K&V's safety deposit box at the Toronto Dominion Bank branch in the Town & Country Shopping Centre in Victoria.

Although Simpson wouldn't know it for eighteen months, the package contained a passport bearing Kelly's photograph but not his name. If the arson case took a turn for the worse, Kelly intended to disappear, leaving his assets and his wife in the hands of Simpson. The only other person who knew the details of the plan was the person he planned to take with him.

Dawn Taber arrived back in Toronto from her European vacation a few days after Jeannette Kelly in the middle of a severe thunderstorm that knocked out the radar and closed Pearson airport. After spending the night in Montreal, she flew to Toronto the next day and called Jeannette from the airport. Jeannette came to pick her up in Dawn's car, which, judging from the odometer, Patrick had obviously been using in her extended absence. Dawn was annoyed. She had expressly asked him not to drive it. She was also angry that he hadn't called her mother as he'd promised to tell her Dawn's whereabouts. This was all the more important because neither Dawn nor John had been able to tell their parents about their marriage breakup. So when Dawn's mother had called John looking for her daughter, she had grown frantic when she hadn't been able to find her.

But these were minor matters compared to something else Patrick had done. Why, she wanted to know, had Patrick left a message at the Hermes Hotel in Athens saying that her mother was dying when that was completely untrue? Jeannette explained that Patrick's preliminary hearing on the arson charge had been fast approaching, and he was afraid that Dawn wouldn't come back from Europe in time to testify about the letter she had written to Austin Cooper about Jimmy Culbert. But now it didn't matter because the preliminary had been postponed again, this time until January 29, 1981.

After smoothing Dawn's feathers over the car and the phony message, Jeannette took her to breakfast and briefed her on what she should tell Patrick about their vacation. Because the two women had separated in Europe and come home on different days, Patrick might well ask what had happened; above all else, Jeannette didn't want her friend mentioning anything about Marcello Rodocanachi.

After leaving Dawn in the Holiday Inn off St. Peter's Square, Jeannette had gone to Ostia, Capri, Florence, and Venice with her Italian lover. Afterwards, she and Dawn had reunited in Ostia at the La Scalletta Hotel and then followed Marcello and his family to Mykonos, where they were holidaying. Marcello and Jeannette used to slip away together, and even though Dawn viewed Marcello as completely unattractive, "an overweight mole with very thick glasses," she could see that her friend was in love. For the first time since she had married Patrick, Jeannette could now imagine starting a new life without him, or so she told her friend.

Although Marcello was her principal worry, Jeannette was also concerned about another encounter she and Dawn had had with a pair of Greeks they'd met in a restaurant, who had invited the women back to their ship. Jurgos, a handsome, rugged man who told the women he was a multimillionaire, took Jeannette to his stateroom, while an exhausted and tipsy Dawn retired to one of the many empty cabins. The other man, Feliciano, "a small, fat, disgusting man with six days' growth," scratched at the door to get in but eventually went away when Dawn ignored him and Jurgos told him to leave her alone.

"Well the next thing I hear is this ungodly scream from Jeannette," remembered Dawn. "And so I open up the door and I ran down through the hallway and I slide open the door into this huge master bedroom and there are Jurgos and Jeannette under the covers and Feliciano is standing on the end of the bed with shot spots all over his bikini underwear. I thought I was going to die. It was so funny. And poor Jeannette says, 'You know, all I could think of was this wicked threesome.'"

The next day when Jurgos drove the women back to their hotel, Jeannette lay on the floor in the backseat, terrified that Marcello might see her with another man. With her head pounding from too much ouzo the night before, she insisted on being let out several blocks from her hotel in front of a Catholic church, where she immediately went to confession. While her friend cleansed her soul inside, Dawn waited on the church steps, considering the state of her own conscience and what, if anything, lay waiting for her back home.

Everything with Patrick had happened so quickly. She could still remember the April morning shortly after moving in to apartment 1705, when she had awakened in the den to find him standing over her. He had returned unexpectedly from a business trip to Victoria looking sad and depressed. As the two friends made small talk, Dawn mentioned that she felt stiff. Patrick rolled back the covers and started giving her a massage. His strong hands felt good on her tense shoulders, pressing and kneading at first until her muscles relaxed, and then stroking her warm flesh until she could feel his need.

"One thing led to another and we had intercourse. This was the first time we had a sexual encounter. Pat told me at this time that he had always loved me from the first time he met me because I never got upset and could handle the situation and could understand his situation with the RCMP. I was infatuated with Pat; I idolized him because he was always very kind to me. He seemed to be very much alive and an entrepreneur and I admired these qualities. We made plans to meet secretly in Montreal but we never did. Pat told me that he loved Jeannette but that she just could not handle situations and was never willing to take a chance on anything."

Shortly after their brief affair began, Patrick and Dawn were alone in the apartment again and he asked her to look at the life insurance policies he and Jeannette then had with London Life. Although the policies seemed more than adequate to cover the Kellys' needs, he asked Dawn to draw up an application for a much higher cash value. When she asked why he needed $500,000 worth of life insurance on each of them, he said that he had several business interests to protect. There was just one thing; Jeannette was not to know about any policies he might decide to purchase from Dawn. When she told him Jeannette would have to sign the application, Patrick smiled and said that that wouldn't be a problem.

Dawn spent a month drawing up proposals in varying amounts: $100,000, $250,000, and $500,000, with a double indemnity in the event of accidental death. The proposals showed the costs per year, the cash value, and the terms of acceptance. When she took them to John Edwards, the sales manager at Citadel Life, she asked if the owner of the insurance policy could also be the beneficiary. Edwards told her that under the law, anyone over the age of sixteen had to give their written consent to have insurance taken out on their life, a procedure that the insurance agent had to witness. When he asked her which of the Kellys wanted to buy insurance on the other's life, Dawn simply replied that she was having difficulty getting the couple together and would talk to him later when she had more information.

A few days after Dawn showed Kelly the proposals, they went up to the rooftop club at the Palace Pier, where he extended a stunning invitation. Telling her again that he could not face going to prison, he asked if she would run away with him. If she would, he could get her a false passport and driver's licence, and they could leave the country under one identity, and then assume another at their first international port of entry. Although she could never contact her family again, Victor Simpson would anonymously call her mother to let her know that Dawn was alive and well. Before leaving, he wanted her to apply for several Visa cards and take out a series of loans at the bank. She would repay a small loan and then take out a bigger one which she would not repay after changing her identity. Once they had run away, they would start a family and experience life the way it was meant to be lived.

"We talked about living on a sailboat in the south of France, travelling, skiing, and never having to work. Then he asked me if I ever heard about the man who had either fallen or jumped from some apartment in the Palace Pier when it was first opened. He told me that it was not known whether the man jumped, committed suicide, or was pushed because of the state of the body after it hit the ground."

Patrick never spoke about what would happen to Jeannette after he and Dawn disappeared, other than to say that she would be "well taken care of." Although the whole thing seemed fantastic to Dawn, like so many things Patrick did, she drew up the insurance proposals, applied for the loan and credit cards he asked her to get, and even opened a joint bank account with him.

Then, on the day before she and Jeannette had set out for Europe, Patrick awakened her at 5:30 A.M. and asked her to drive to Jimmy Culbert's place in Bradford. He wanted Dawn to talk with Culbert, who was set to testify against him at his arson trial, so she could tell the court that he had recanted the story he had given police about Patrick and his insurance claim. Dawn did as she was told, but found out when she got to Bradford that Culbert was away on a camping trip. When she reported this to Patrick, he said that it didn't matter; the important thing was that she had made the trip. Finally, on the day Jeannette and Dawn were leaving for Europe, Patrick had dictated the letter to Austin Cooper that Dawn signed and mailed.

Now that they had been apart for nearly two months, these events seemed like a dream, and Dawn wondered what it would be like to see him again. Had he meant what he said on the roof of the Palace Pier or was it all part of the beguiling spell he could cast over a person when he exploded into their humdrum lives, turning everything upside down?

After a few days back at the apartment, Dawn had the feeling that her relationship with Patrick was over. He treated her well enough, but there was a new aloofness in his demeanour. What she didn't know was that Jeannette had told her husband that Dawn had gone wild in Europe, taking up with men of "all sizes, colours, and nationalities, rich and poor" during their lengthy vacation.

When Dawn told Kelly that the Citadel insurance proposals would not pay the beneficiary if the insured party committed suicide during the first two years that the policy was in force, he dropped the subject of running away with her and never renewed their romantic involvement. The fact was that Citadel executives had already decided that writing such a large policy for a couple who were already adequately insured wasn't a good idea, particularly after they found out that Kelly had criminal charges pending against him and was no longer with the RCMP.

If the romance between Dawn and Patrick had cooled, it was nothing compared to the chill that had come over the Kellys' rapidly deteriorating marriage. They fought about the fact that Patrick had apparently sold apartment 1907 in Jeannette's absence, and even forged her signature to cash in a spousal RRSP without his wife's permission or knowledge. But the principal trouble between the unhappy couple remained what it had always been: the arson charges against Patrick and the pending court case. They sniped at each other in Dawn's presence over who was to blame for their legal problems, and the atmosphere in the apartment was uncomfortably tense. More than once, Dawn had to leave the living room because she couldn't bear to see the people whose deepest secrets she knew turning on each other.

Two days after Dawn's arrival, the three of them were having a glass of wine in the den when the inevitable explosion took place. Jeannette got up and began swaying to the Greek music they were playing on the stereo, while they reminisced about their recent holiday. Suddenly Patrick jumped up and "hit her with his forearm," spitting out the words that "she wasn't in Greece anymore." It was the first time that Dawn had ever seen him assault his wife, but it wasn't the last. Shortly afterwards, during an argument over money, she witnessed an attack that convinced her that it was time to move out.

"Pat had a wicked temper, an awesome temper. When he picked her up by the neck, he had a wild, crazy look in his eyes. It looked like he wanted to hit her, but he just dropped her and turned around and got his gym bag and went downstairs . . . Jeannette pulled herself together, cried a little bit and didn't say a word." Two hours later Patrick returned with a squash ball he had exploded from driving it so hard against the wall.

Although Dawn continued to see Jeannette through the late summer and early autumn of 1980, their friendship gradually soured until their only point of contact became a bitter squabble over the $4,000 Patrick had lent Dawn for the trip to Europe. Jeannette badmouthed Dawn to their mutual friends, and Patrick left a dunning letter under the door of her Mississauga apartment. It was the last straw.

Two days later, with a money order in the amount of $4,000 tucked in her purse drawn against the proceeds of her house sale, Dawn used the key she had been given while living with the Kellys to enter the back door of the Palace Pier and took the elevator to the seventeenth floor. After leaving the money on the kitchen counter, she went out to the balcony with Patrick and Jeannette and tried her best to melt some of the frost that had come over their friendship. Whether it was because Jeannette was still bitter about the tardy loan or had found out about Dawn's affair with her husband, she gave the unmistakable impression that bridges had been burned between them. She was as cold as the grey-green expanse of the lake that stretched before them.

"She was so cool, I finally said, 'Your money is on the counter,' and I got up and left and I returned to my apartment. I did not talk to either of them anymore."

Or at least not until March 29, 1981.

A few days after Jeannette broke off her friendship with Dawn, the Kellys started seeing Dr. Howard Irving, a marriage counsellor recommended to them by Dr. Joseph Allen. Patrick's approaching arson trial had created such tension between them that they both realized that they had to do something. Patrick struck Dr. Irving as being paranoid and distant, obsessed with the idea that the RCMP was trying to "set him up," but Jeannette was forthcoming about their personal situation. She told Irving that she felt guilty about leaving Patrick for the two-month vacation in Europe, even though she had been unable to handle the pressure of his pending trial and needed to get away to preserve her own sanity. She complained that Patrick ignored her emotional needs and kept her in the dark about the case that was ruining their lives. Not once mentioning that Patrick had hit her or that they had financial problems, she told the counsellor that the solution to their marital troubles rested with her husband.

Patricia Miller also believed that Patrick was the key to Jeannette's problems, albeit for very different reasons. For several years, Jeannette had been paying monthly visits to the Aesthetic Skin Care Salon, where Miller had been her beautician. Jeannette was universally popular with the staff as she was the kind of person who "loved life" and liked to look her best. She seemed keenly aware that her husband set a high personal standard for her appearance, one that she desperately tried to meet.

But by the late fall of 1980, Miller noticed a change in her formerly vivacious client. Her hair had to be dyed more frequently to cover the solid grey beneath, and she constantly complained of internal problems and other physical ailments. When Miller asked if anything was bothering her, Jeannette explained that the RCMP was unjustly harassing her husband over a fire at their Cookstown home, an official hounding that was putting a tremendous strain on their marriage. When Jeannette then began showing up at the salon with bruises on her body, which she attributed to falls at the apartment, Miller started to worry. She suspected that Patrick was beating his wife and that Jeannette was too proud or protective to admit it. But the best she could do was refer her friend to a nutritionist she knew in the hopes that he might be able to suggest a diet that would help Jeannette with some of her other physical problems.

Miller's friendly advice inadvertently led Jeannette Kelly back into her friendship with Abby Latter, who as it turned out was also seeing Dr. James D'Amano. Although Dr. D'Amano charged $140 for a consultation and $50 per subsequent visit, Jeannette booked at least two appointments a week, hoping that his treatment might ease the depression, headaches, and digestive problems that had been plaguing her ever since her husband's charges.

After the sessions, she and Abby would go to a little vegetarian restaurant not far from the doctor's St. George Street clinic, where they talked about old times and the latest goings-on in each other's lives. Abby couldn't believe how withdrawn her friend had become and the extent to which she appeared to have lost her confidence. One thing she was pleased to hear was that Dawn Taber was out of the Kellys' lives, since she had always believed that Dawn had used Jeannette's friendship to get close to Patrick. In fact, the Kellys' cleaning lady, Dora, had told Abby that she had seen Patrick and Dawn in bed together when Mrs. Kelly was away, painful information that Abby had decided to keep from her friend.

Jeannette insisted that everything was fine in her marriage and told Abby that even though she was often alone, that was only because Patrick had worked out an agreement with his lawyer, Austin Cooper, to reduce his legal bill by half in return for conducting his own investigations for his upcoming fraud and arson case. When the two women returned to the Palace Pier after dinner, the concierge would often deliver messages from Patrick saying that he was working late. Abby felt sure that Jeannette knew that he was having an affair, but refused to admit it because part of her still loved Patrick and all of her wanted to keep the lifestyle he had given her. Like Joanne MacLean, Abby felt powerless to help the friend whom she couldn't help thinking was heading towards something terrible.

As the striking woman with the long, dark hair helped a friend set up furniture at Toronto's Harbourfront antique market in November 1980, the last person she expected to see was Patrick Kelly, or as she knew him, Patrick MacLean. Although they had kept up a casual friendship ever since the day they had met in a flower shop in the Bridlewood Mall, where Jan Bradley worked as a librarian, she hadn't seen him since the previous May. Looking tanned and relaxed, Patrick explained that he had been away in Mexico on business and asked her if she had time for a coffee to ward off the cold wind blowing in from the lake. As they were standing in line at a kiosk, he leaned over and whispered in her ear, "Bradley, you have a great ass."

To his surprised companion, the words marked a watershed in their relationship, which until then had been platonic. After their first, chance meeting a few years back, this mysterious man had quickly gained Bradley's trust, listening sympathetically as she confided the details of her unhappy personal life to him. She was in love with a wealthy but insensitive man who took her for granted, ignored her emotional needs, and didn't want to marry her, despite a lengthy live-in relationship. Her new friend had been such a good listener that she hadn't asked anything about his personal life, including whether he was married. The extent of her knowledge was that his name was Patrick MacLean and that he worked as a consultant to Toronto's best antique stores, a profession in which he did a great deal of travelling and appeared to make a lot of money.

What she didn't know was that their initial meeting in the flower shop hadn't been accidental. At the time, Kelly had been watching her for weeks as part of an intelligence gathering operation for a high-level drug case he was working on. Bradley was associated with a suspected marijuana importer, and Kelly was trying to get close to her to see if she could provide him with any compromising information about the target. The investigation fizzled out but not his interest in the beautiful librarian with the unappreciative boyfriend.

As they sat sipping coffee and catching up on the news, Bradley told him that she had finally moved out on her inattentive lover and was now living alone in an apartment in the Beaches. Although she had expected to be tormented by the breakup of her five-year love affair, at age twenty-nine she was finding life on her own surprisingly agreeable. Before Kelly left, Bradley invited him to stop by the Bridlewood library for lunch. Kelly took her up on the invitation and they started meeting more regularly for coffee or lunch, and then a few intimate dinners. Their tantalizing encounters reinforced Bradley's impression that her low-key friend was a wealthy and worldly businessman. The relationship remained platonic, but with new and exciting possibilities as far as she was concerned, now that her boyfriend was no longer in the picture and Patrick MacLean seemed so available.

That Christmas, Kelly gave Bradley a bottle of L'Air du Temps. A few weeks later he decided to take their relationship to the next level, asking her to spend the weekend with him at the Briars at Jackson's Point on Lake Simcoe. On the morning of Saturday, January 24, 1981, the couple arrived at the resort and checked in as Mr. and Mrs. MacLean. Over dinner that night, Kelly began to reveal who he really was. He told Bradley that he had been an undercover RCMP officer up until the previous summer when he had quit the force over a matter of principle. Back in their room, he put some birch junks on the fire and told her about the marijuana investigation involving one of her former boyfriends.

The revelations made for a restless night. The couple made love but it was not a memorable occasion and both of them slept poorly. The next morning Bradley was full of questions about Kelly's undercover career and was visibly shaken when he admitted that he had had her under surveillance as part of the marijuana investigation he had already told her about. Sensing that Bradley wanted to be alone, Kelly went for a walk while his companion read a book. When he came back, Bradley was still upset. That night at dinner, the conversation was stilted and the couple didn't share a single dance. The drive back to Toronto passed in awkward silence, and when he pulled up in front of Bradley's apartment, Kelly asked if he could call her, expecting her to say no. To his surprise, she kissed him goodbye and said yes. Although he didn't know it yet, Jan Bradley was falling head over heels in love with the enigmatic Patrick Kelly.

As he drove away through a gentle fall of snow, Kelly's own emotions were also in turmoil. After living under the long shadow of the Cookstown fire for over two years, his trial for fraud and arson was just four days away. Very soon now he would know if he would need the passport that Victor Simpson had locked away in K&V's safety deposit box. It would be such a pity to leave behind the beautiful woman who had so unexpectedly come into his life.

Austin Cooper was entitled to feel optimistic about his client's chances in his upcoming arson trial, and not least of all because he had a stunning answer to one of the Crown's key witnesses against Patrick Kelly, the furniture doctor, Jimmy Culbert. The rebuttal came in the form of a June 6, 1980, letter from Dawn Taber, a young insurance agent who had provided Cooper with information that completely undercut what the Crown no doubt hoped would be Culbert's devastating testimony against the accused. The information took the form of an account of a meeting between Taber and Culbert, both of whom knew the Kellys:

"As I am sure you can appreciate, with my job I am constantly seeking out new prospects. Approximately two weeks ago, I went to Mr. Culbert's house with the intention of perhaps discussing insurance with Mr. Culbert. The conversation started with Mr. Culbert asking how the Kellys were doing. I mentioned they were both very upset. Mr. Culbert seemed to get very pensive and upset with my reply to the point where he started sobbing. He started telling me that he had been interviewed by two guys from the RCMP and they were asking questions in relation to the letters which he signed for Mr. Kelly. He stated that at the time of the interview, he was having difficulties with his wife and was very upset and was on medication. Apparently he was very depressed as he felt his marriage was falling apart. He said on thinking back, he must have just felt a little vindictive towards Mr. Kelly, knowing his marriage was very steady, because when he was asked the questions, he replied that the entire contents of the two letters were untrue and supplied by Kelly. When, in fact, at the time of the letters, Kelly was so upset about both the fire and the insurance problems that he had to discuss the contents with Culbert, as around that time, Kelly was having trouble remembering anything.

"Apparently, the officers also asked Culbert if Kelly received any funds from the sale of any salvaged items from the house. Culbert told them that he did, when actually, apparently Kelly didn't receive any funds, even when they were offered to him by Culbert, as Kelly stated he didn't want any problems with the insurance company.

"Culbert also mentioned that he told the police that Kelly had a chair which was claimed from the house, when actually, apparently, Culbert refinished and rebuilt this chair and gave it to Kelly as a gift. Kelly had a bunch of furniture redone by Culbert after the fire. Culbert simply included the cost of repairing the chair in with other bills, knowing Kelly would trust him and not check the invoices.

"By the end of our conversation, Culbert was in tears and almost uncontrollable. He told me that the wanted this conversation held in confidence and I assured him that it would be. However, I feel the details are too important not to be brought to your attention.

"I have not discussed this with Mr. Kelly and I am concerned as to what his reaction might be if he were to talk to Culbert and no one else was there. If Culbert told him what he told me, I think Kelly would blow up and there would be problems, after all he has been through since the fire.

"I wanted you to have this information and was going to talk to you personally, but this trip came up suddenly and I had to leave. I will contact you when I return."

Taber kept her word, but not in the way that Austin Cooper had anticipated. Since leaving the Palace Pier, the young woman's life had fallen apart. She had lost her job at Citadel Life Insurance and then her car, and later became entangled in a tumultuous relationship with the owner of a Toronto construction company. Fleeing the unhealthy relationship, she returned to her mother's house in the state of Maine shortly after New Year's in 1981. As the date for the trial approached, she grew more and more unnerved and finally contacted Richard Anisio, a lawyer she had know when she worked in the litigation department of the Toronto law firm of Harries Housser. She told Anisio that she had prepared a false document pertaining to a criminal matter and then sent it to the lawyer of the accused in the case. She was now worried that the false information would be used in Patrick Kelly's arson trial and wanted to know what she could do to stop that from happening.

Anisio gave her Austin Cooper's telephone number and instructed her to call the eminent lawyer and tell him that the letter was a fraud. On January 27, 1981 Taber made the call, telling Cooper that Kelly had dictated the letter and made her sign it. The astonished lawyer told her that he had planned to subpoena her, but would take the matter up with his client. Kelly denied any knowledge of the letter, and Cooper struck Taber from his witness list and prepared to head into court without one of his strongest weapons to attack the Crown's case.

As it turned out, he didn't need it. One of the first Crown witnesses, Gil Coates, the senior claims examiner for Waterloo Mutual, testified on behalf of both insurance companies that neither had been defrauded, since the Kellys claimed a content loss of $71,000, but only had $55,000 in coverage. In other words, the couple had sustained an actual loss of $16,000, which Coates testified allowed them to salvage an equal amount of goods without committing a fraud on the companies. And although Crown witness Jimmy Culbert testified that the letters he signed for Kelly substantiating part of his claims were false, Austin Cooper extracted the admission under cross-examination that the accused did, in fact, own the items in question – contrary to what the witness had told the RCMP. The presiding justice, Judge D. Inch, found that the evidence of fraud wasn't "more than a suspicion," and the entire case was thrown out. A terse RCMP internal memo signed by Insp. Will Stefureak, which noted that Jimmy Culbert had changed his testimony from the statement he had given investigators, summed up the stunning end of the curious affair: "As the committal on the arson charge was contingent on the fraud charges, the arson charge also had to be dismissed."

Instead of hearing evidence about the two gas cans, the time it took to drive from the Calders' lodge to Cookstown, or Kelly's alleged forgeries in the Donnelly notebooks, the court was treated to a victory celebration by Patrick and Jeannette Kelly. The happy couple embraced each other and their counsel with tears streaming down their cheeks.

Later that night, Kelly held a private celebration of his own. Exultant to be free at last of the arson charges that had ruined his career in the RCMP and shaken his wife's faith in him, he took Jan Bradley to

Simpson's on the Strand for "a very romantic dinner." Afterwards he dropped the clearly infatuated woman off at the Royal York Hotel, where she joined friends who were attending an event at the Imperial Room.

When Kelly realized that Bradley had his car keys in her purse, he rushed back to the hotel, where he found her standing in line with the Davidsons, the couple she had come to meet. They had heard a lot about Patrick, but he didn't stop to chat. After retrieving his keys and saying a quick hello, he ran back to his Porsche and sped towards the Palace Pier. He and Jeannette were about to leave on a dream vacation to Mexico, and he had lingered so long with his lover, he was now running late for his wife.

10

THE LAST BOUQUET

It was the perfect holiday. After flying to Mexico City on January 31, 1981, the day after Patrick's criminal charges were thrown out, the Kellys rented a car and meandered south, happy to be alone, free, and away from Toronto. Although the weather was wet, even the rain seemed to be a blessing, washing away the memory of the last two years and reminding them of their first meeting all those years ago in Acapulco. They stayed in out-of-the-way places, enjoying each other's company and the beautiful Mexican countryside.

Eventually tiring of the sweet, warm rain, they jogged west and drove along the Pacific coast towards Manzanillo, sunbathing along the way and taking their meals in small restaurants on endless golden beaches. At one seaside cantina, the old man who served them was so delighted that they both spoke Spanish that he advised them to change their order and take the fish selection. While they sipped wine and watched the play of the tropical sun on the turquoise water, they saw him row out into the harbour, returning half an hour later with grouper to cook for them. Sitting on a bench out of the scorching heat, he played his guitar while they ate their dinner and listened to his wife singing softly from the kitchen.

Hours later, after giving them fresh fruit for their journey, the old man told them of a place up the coast that God had made for sweethearts such as themselves to watch the sun go down. Following his directions to a breathtaking cove, they made love as they once had under the wooden cross overlooking Acapulco's harbour. The next day they drove to Manzanillo, finishing their holiday with a stay at Los Hadas, the luxury hotel made famous in the movie *10*. The time of their lives had cost $10,000, but to Patrick Kelly it had been worth every penny. "We deserved this time together," he later said, "and I could always do another money trip."

When the Kellys returned to Toronto on February 13, Patrick told Jeannette that he had to go to New York on business the very next day. With his wife aglow after their romantic interlude in Mexico, it was time to turn his attention to his lover. On Valentine's Day, he jetted off to New York City for three days with Jan Bradley. They spent the first two nights at the Algonquin, where the librarian soaked up the atmosphere of the hotel made famous for its literary round table, as Kelly had suspected she would. Knowing that Jan had a special fondness for unicorns, Kelly had even called ahead to have a painting of the mythical creature hung in their room. After two nights at the Algonquin, they moved to the Plaza; as Kelly put it, you couldn't go to New York without staying at least one night in the great, old hotel.

Bradley's favourite saying was "power is acting impeccably," and during their romantic weekend, Kelly did his best to live up to her maxim. The happy couple caught some Broadway plays, dined out in a chic French restaurant off 5th Avenue, and took a ride in an open calèche through Central Park. At Bradley's suggestion, they spent hours at the Metropolitan Museum of Art. As Kelly watched her admiring the stunning exhibits, he felt his feelings towards her beginning to change. A sexual convenience during the stressful period leading up to his day in court, she now struck him as a complete person in her own right, "a great lady" who had suddenly become powerfully attractive.

As for Bradley, the weekend in New York made her even more anxious to get away with Kelly on the April holiday they had been planning for months. In fact, things had been going so well between them since Christmas, she thought that she and Patrick might even get married when they were away – a possibility she had mentioned to her boss, Carol Silverberg, when she booked her vacation time shortly after New Year's. Although she didn't know for sure if that would happen, she was more convinced than ever that Patrick was exactly the kind of sensitive and sophisticated man that any woman would be proud to call her husband. There was only one problem; she still knew virtually nothing about him. She hadn't visited his home or met any of his friends or business associates, so she didn't really know what kind of financial stability he could bring to a marriage. Having been "thrown out" by her well-heeled boyfriend, the beautiful woman with the high standards and lofty expectations wanted to know a little more about Prince Charming before climbing on his steed.

A month after their return to Toronto, she finally got a closer look at her lover's private life. With Jeannette away, Kelly invited Bradley to spend the weekend with him at the Palace Pier. The tasteful seventeenth-storey apartment looked so austere, it made Bradley think of a model suite rather than someone's actual home. Kelly ordered up dinner from the Palace Pier's gourmet restaurant and after sharing a bottle of wine they made love. Afterwards, Bradley found a lady's gold-coloured bath-robe in the master bedroom and slipped it on to keep off the chill.

Although it was clear that a woman also lived there, Bradley was surprised by the scant evidence of her daily presence. There was no shower cap, shampoo, or makeup, and apart from a dried flower arrangement in the en suite bathroom and several bottles of perfume, it looked as though the place was shared by "two people who were never there."

The observant guest noticed that there was a pullout couch in the den with a blanket folded over it. Bradley concluded that someone regularly slept there, and after seeing that all of his toiletries were in a second, smaller bathroom, away from the master bedroom, she decided that the someone must be Patrick.

When Bradley went into the kitchen to make coffee, she noticed that the receiver was off the hook, dangling almost to the floor at the end of its cord, a position it remained in all weekend. When she asked Patrick about it, he smiled and said, "It gives them something to play with." Although he didn't explain what he meant, she concluded that the RCMP or others were trying to listen in on his calls and this was his way of frustrating them.

Then she found the bill from Nethercott Motors addressed to Mrs. Jeannette Kelly. When she showed it to him, Patrick's features darkened, the way they always did when he didn't want to talk about something.

Making clear that further questions weren't welcome without actually saying it, he offered the terse explanation that it was an RCMP arranged marriage and that things were not what they seemed. His relationship with his "wife" was strictly platonic.

As uncomfortable as she had been in "Mrs. Kelly's" apartment (she never returned), Bradley counted the weekend a success. Patrick was as charming and attentive as ever, and judging from the tasteful antiques and the high-quality carpeting and drapes, there wasn't much doubt that he was a man of means. So when they met at the Great Escape restaurant in late March to discuss their upcoming holiday, she wasn't surprised when Patrick told her that he still hadn't decided whether to take her to Europe, Hawaii, or some other exotic location. Their delicious problem apparently came down to choosing the most beautiful place on earth, and money, it seemed, was no object.

For the time being, that was true, but Kelly had Victor Simpson to thank for it. On February 25, 1981, the lawyer had advanced his friend $40,000 from the trust fund of his very first client, an old and infirm woman named Mina McIntosh, who had no relatives and who lived alone in a cheap hotel in downtown Victoria. A few months later, Simpson sent his colleague in K&V Enterprises another $20,000 from the McIntosh estate. Kelly said he needed the money for "high-yield investments" and offered a second mortgage on his Palace Pier apartment as collateral for the short-term loan.

Although Simpson had the power to conduct the transaction as the trustee of the McIntosh estate, he advanced the funds without arranging any fixed security. He had seen enough private examples of Kelly's affluence to assure himself that the paper work was a mere formality. Besides, his well-connected friend only wanted the money for four months.

Jeannette Kelly's last bouquet was delivered on March 27, 1981, by a clown with tufts of orange hair sprouting from the sides of his head and a red nose that looked like a swollen cherry tomato. His arrival at Anesty's restaurant, where a few of Jeannette's friends had arranged a going-away party before her trip to Italy in two days' time, brought the festivities to a temporary halt. After reciting a few lines of doggerel in a lilting, falsetto voice, the clown presented her with a white box tied with a ribbon. Inside, she found a dozen long-stemmed roses and a card from Patrick: "I'll miss you when you're away."

It was obvious to Jeannette's friends that she was "ticked off" rather than touched by her husband's romantic gesture. She handed out the roses to her girlfriends around the table almost as if she knew that their sender was at The Great Escape restaurant in the Beaches having dinner with Jan Bradley. In fact, earlier that afternoon, Kelly had personally delivered a bunch of yellow and orange helium balloons to Bradley at the Bridlewood library when he had asked her out.

It was common knowledge in Jeannette's circle that the Kellys had hit a rocky patch in their marriage. Although everyone thought that Patrick's criminal charges had been the main source of the couple's unhappiness, they reconsidered that view when their bitter arguments continued even after the case was thrown out of court and the Kellys returned from their dream vacation in Mexico.

Just the day before the going-away party, her colleague, Judy Seres, had overheard Jeannette "screaming" into the phone after calling Patrick from work. Seres would never forget how upset Jeannette had been on January 20, 1981, the day she had turned thirty-three, when she called in sick because Patrick had forgotten her birthday. Saddest of all, she seemed to attribute her husband's flagging interest in her to the fact that she was gaining weight and her looks were beginning to fade, things she knew were beyond the powers of designer clothes and the most artful wiles of her beautician.

As Brenda Rodine took a rose from Jeannette, she remembered the night in the Kelly apartment when Patrick had talked about going into business with her. Rodine, who knew the Kellys from her days as a bartender at the Palace Pier, had started a greeting and message company called Hullaballoon. In fact, it had been one of Rodine's clowns who delivered Jeannette's roses at Anesty's. Patrick had been so taken with the idea that when he paid Austin Cooper the last instalment on his legal bill for the arson case, $2,971.35, he had had the cheque delivered to the lawyer's office by a clown. Anxious to get in on the action, Patrick had offered Rodine $20,000 for a 49 per cent interest in the company.

While they were discussing his proposal, Jeannette had returned from a night out with the girls. Although she was "pretty sloshed," she seemed delighted to have company at the apartment and took out the Kellys' wedding pictures to show Brenda. At first Patrick had been embarrassed, but he became increasingly sentimental as Jeannette flipped through the album and gave a humorous commentary on the people in each picture. When she got to Dawn, standing on the steps beside the bride in a pale-blue dress, she ran out of funny things to say.

Brenda wasn't surprised. Over dinner one night, Jeannette had told Rodine and Seres that she knew that Patrick had had an affair with Dawn. Despite the infidelity, though, it was Rodine's impression that Jeannette wanted to remain in her marriage, if for no other reason than to maintain her lifestyle. As excited as Jeannette purported to be about the trip to Italy to see Marcello, Brenda had the feeling that what she really wanted was for Patrick to ask her not to go. "She was very confused at this time. I feel she was depressed over her relationship and I think she was down [because] she wasn't happy with her appearance. I think she even wanted Pat to get jealous over her."

If he had known that Marcello Rodocanachi had been with his wife in their apartment just the week before, perhaps he might have been. But Jeannette had been very discreet about seeing her Italian lover, who had been in Toronto buying skins for his wife's mink coat when he visited her at the Palace Pier. It was ultimately a sad reunion. To Jeannette's dismay, Marcello had ever so tactfully backed away from a deeper relationship with her, making it clear that he intended to move closer to his wife. She had taken elaborate precautions to hide the relationship from Patrick, including, at one point, charging her overseas calls to Marcello to a friend's telephone number.

And that was the problem, Jeannette explained to Brenda, as the women drove back to the Palace Pier after the party at Anesty's. Patrick was so indiscreet, throwing his affairs in her face by staying out every night under the transparently false pretence of working late. What kind of a fool did he take her for? There was no more court case to investigate, and they hadn't even made love since their return from Mexico. Depressed and lonely, Jeannette invited Brenda up for a drink.

As it got later and later and Patrick still didn't show up, Jeannette "let loose" the frustrations that his philandering was causing her. She told Brenda that when she had found out about the affair with Dawn, she had chased Patrick with a knife, threatening to make good on a long-standing promise that if she ever caught him with another woman, she would "cut it off and put it in a pizza."

When Rodine started for home at around 1:30 A.M., leaving Jeannette to keep a lonely vigil for her husband, she was frightened by the thoughts that were going through her mind. Jeannette was so unhappy and depressed that Rodine worried she might commit suicide.

On Saturday, March 28, the day before she was scheduled to leave for Florence, Italy, Jeannette Kelly called Judy Seres to go downtown for a day's shopping. Like Brenda Rodine, Seres was worried about her friend and agreed to go.

Seres had first met Jeannette when she came to work at CP Air in the spring of 1979, but had only got to know her after she returned from a vacation to Europe in August 1980. Seres knew that Jeannette had gone away on medical leave, suffering from stress brought on by her husband's legal problems. Although Jeannette stuck to the story that their Cookstown house had been burned as a reprisal against her husband and his undercover police work, Seres always had the feeling that she was tormented by something she just couldn't talk about. When she came back from her sick leave, Jeannette seemed even more like a "lost soul," and Seres had gone out of her way to be kind to her.

Like Sheree Brown, Seres had spent time with both of the Kellys, inviting them to her home and occasionally going out with them to the expensive restaurants they enjoyed. But unlike Sheree, Seres didn't like Patrick, finding him to be "a real braggart" who played "the hero routine" to the hilt and passed himself off as an expert on everything and who knew all "the right people." She had always had the feeling that the fancy apartment, the Porsche, the trips, and the $10,000 mink coat Jeannette was so proud of all rested on a dark foundation connected to Patrick's work on the drug squad. That Christmas, when he had given Jeannette a box containing $1,000 to buy a fox coat, Seres couldn't help thinking that Patrick's dealings would some day catch up with them, especially now that he was no longer wearing a badge.

When Jeannette began showing up at work with injuries, Seres suspected that Patrick had been beating her. It was just too much to believe that she had fallen in the apartment, been struck by the dog, and got her finger caught in the car door, all in such a short space of time. But Seres hadn't had a chance to talk to Jeannette about the state of her marriage until after she had stayed at the apartment while the Kellys were vacationing in Mexico. Every night at 11:30 P.M., the phone would ring, but when Seres answered, the caller would hang up. On the last night of her stay, a female asked if "Mr. Kelly" was home, but refused to leave her name. When Seres mentioned the calls to Jeannette, her eyes had filled with tears and she replied, "It must be Pat's girlfriend." Then she had told Seres about her unhappiness in the marriage and her relationship with Marcello. When Seres asked why she just didn't get a divorce, Jeannette said she was too old to start all over and didn't want to give up the things she now had.

On the Saturday that they went shopping, it was obvious that Jeannette was still in a bad mood from the previous night. She told Seres that when Patrick had finally come home, he wasn't wearing the clothes he had gone out in and she asked him where he had been. He said that he had driven up to Cookstown to look at the place where their house had once been. She accused him of being with another woman, he denied it, and they had quarrelled.

One of the day's events didn't leave Jeannette any more kindly disposed towards her wayward husband. When she and Seres had gone to Expo Furs on Spadina Avenue to pick up Seres's fur jacket, on a whim Jeannette asked the owner what he thought of her mink coat. After examining the garment, he asked her if she really wanted to know, and then told her that it was not, in fact, a North American mink, as the Black Diamond Label indicated, but a vastly inferior Russian mink. If her husband had indeed paid the price she indicated ($10,000), he had been badly overcharged. The coat was worth no more than $3,000. Infuriated by what she had been told, Jeannette vowed to take the mink back to the shop where Patrick had bought it.

The incident at Expo Furs cast a shadow over the rest of the day, and when the two women parted, Seres told Jeannette to give her a call at the airport in the morning, where she was scheduled to work the 10 A.M. to 6 P.M. shift on the ticket counter. On Sunday, March 29, Jeannette called at around noon and Seres confirmed her seat number on the flight to Florence. Jeannette wanted to talk but the counter suddenly got busy, and Seres told her she would call back when things slacked off. At around 3 P.M., she called the apartment, and this time it was Jeannette's turn to say she couldn't talk and would call back. A little concerned by how faint her friend's voice seemed, Seres told her that she would be leaving work early at 4 P.M. so to be sure to call before then.

After waiting around several minutes for Jeannette's call, Seres headed home. When she arrived, she decided to call the Palace Pier apartment to say goodbye, hoping that Jeannette had not already left to catch her 6 P.M. flight. To her surprise, a police officer answered and told her that Jeannette couldn't come to the phone. Before Seres hung up, the sergeant took down her name and number and told her she would be called.

With her heart suddenly pounding, Seres thought that Patrick Kelly had finally been arrested for drug dealing, and that he had sent Jeannette away to avoid embarrassment. She had gotten up the nerve once to ask Jeannette where all their money came from and she had simply replied, "I don't know." Seres couldn't sleep that night worrying about her friend and wondering where she was. When she got to work the next morning, she checked the computer on Jeannette's flight to Florence; "No Show" flashed on the screen.

A few moments later, her supervisor took Judy Seres aside and told her that Jeannette Kelly was dead. She had apparently committed suicide by jumping from the balcony of her luxury apartment on the seventeenth storey of the Palace Pier.

11

AS COLD AS ICE

On Monday, March 30, 1981, Jimmy Hanlon got the visit that every parent dreads. He had been dozing in a chair with the newspaper folded in his lap, when just after midnight Glasgow time there was a knock at his apartment door. Blinking at his watch as he bent down to put on his slippers, he wondered who could be calling at this hour. The last person he expected to see was his old friend, Jack Dempster, a sergeant in the Glasgow constabulary. Smoothing his dishevelled shock of silver hair, Hanlon smiled and waved him in.

"You're a long way from Pitt Street. What is it then, Jack, a traffic ticket?"

Dempster, who usually appreciated Hanlon's sense of humour, remained sombre.

"I've got bad news for you this time, James. The CID got a call from Canada. There's been an accident." The officer hesitated when he came to what is the worst moment in every notification. "I'm afraid Jeannette is gone."

Hanlon heard the words, but they somehow didn't register. It just couldn't be. Hadn't he talked to Jeannette just the previous day about her trip to Italy? Hadn't she promised to call him on Monday from Florence, which was why he hadn't placed his usual Sunday call to her in Toronto? The recent past and the awful present collided in his spinning head. When he finally came to grips with what Dempster had told him, he could only think of one thing: telling his ex-wife about Jeannette before she found out from strangers.

Pulling on his clothes, he drove over to the Arbuckle residence and rang the bell. When no one answered, he banged on the door with both fists. Lottie, who had been peeking through the curtains, thought Jimmy was drunk and wouldn't let him in. They had parted as bitter enemies after the divorce and, even though she had remarried, he had been an irritation to her ever since. When he began shouting something about Jeannette being dead, Lottie thought he was trying to "act" his way into her house to cause mischief and sent for the police.

By the time she confirmed that her former husband was telling the truth, her personal agenda had come down to a single, dread item: getting to North America in time for her younger daughter's funeral. In keeping with their soured relationship, Jeannette's parents arrived in Toronto on separate flights, both wondering why they hadn't received the tragic news from their son-in-law.

John and Winnifred Kelly might well have wondered the same thing. Patrick's sister, Candi, had been at home in Port Alberni, when Dave Wright called to tell her about Jeannette. Wright, a former dogmaster in the RCMP and a friend of Patrick, had heard about the accident on the radio. Not wanting to deliver the shattering news to her parents over the telephone, Candi and a friend drove to Nanoose Bay, where the Kellys had just moved to a hillside trailer park overlooking the mountains. Patrick's sister barely got the words out before she and her mother "went to pieces" on the doorstep of the Kelly home.

John Kelly, Sr., was on his way back to his job in the interior when Candi arrived in Nanoose Bay. Winnifred immediately worried that her emotional husband might have a heart attack if he heard about Jeannette on the radio. Knowing that he always stopped at his eldest son's for Sunday dinner to break up the long drive back to the construction site at Campbell River, she phoned John, Jr., and told him what had happened. John broke the news to his father, and the two men immediately set out for Nanoose Bay.

When they still hadn't heard from Patrick by the next morning, the Kellys called to see if he wanted them to come east. Citing the expense and the fact that there was nothing anyone could do, he said no. They decided to come anyway. Having passed up Jeannette's wedding, they weren't about to miss her funeral because of the cost of airfare.

Word of Jeannette Kelly's death sent a shock wave through her circle of friends. Abby Latter, who had used an inheritance from her father to buy her own condominium at the Palace Pier, was awakened at 7 A.M. on Monday, March 30, by a knock at her apartment door. When fellow resident Linda Mallette told her what had happened, Latter immediately recalled the stern warning Jeannette had once given her about going out on her own balcony. No, she grimly thought, Jeannette had not fallen; she had been pushed by Patrick.

Shortly after Mallette left Latter's apartment, Dennis Morris called. He said he had visited Kelly in hospital the night before and was looking for a telephone number for Jeannette's father. Unconvinced by Kelly's explanation of events that Morris related to her, Latter voiced her own dark suspicion.

"She couldn't have fallen over the balcony," she declared.

"What do you mean?" Morris asked.

"She never went near the balcony."

"Do you know what you're saying?"

"I know it. I hear myself. I know what I'm saying."

"Don't say another word," Morris snapped. "Just don't say it."

When Ian MacLean heard about Jeannette's death from a friend at the television production company where he worked, he went out to get a copy of the *Toronto Star* to read the terse report for himself:

"A 33-year-old woman fell to her death from the 17th floor of a luxurious condominium apartment building in Etobicoke yesterday. Police say they are investigating the death of Jeanette [*sic*] Kelly who lived . . . with her husband Patrick, 30, a former RCMP officer. Officers said Kelly told them his wife was standing on a wooden stool on the balcony when she lost her balance and fell backwards over the railing. Kelly, who told police he was also on the balcony, said he tried to grab his wife, but failed. He was taken to St. Joseph's Health Centre for treatment of shock."

Holding the grim confirmation in his hands, MacLean called his wife and then went home to comfort her. Although they were grief-stricken by the death of their friend, the MacLeans weren't "deeply shocked," having personally witnessed the pressures that had been building in the Kelly marriage ever since the Cookstown fire.

"Months prior to this, Joanne and I had commented to one another that Pat and Jeannette in an apartment, seventeen floors up . . . one day, one or the other of them was going to go over the edge. I made some statement that Pat was responsible for Jeannette going over the balcony to her death," MacLean recalls.

Like Jeannette's other friends, Luanne Rowbotham, whose husband was with the RCMP, was dumbfounded when she read her newspaper that day. After going over the article three times, and noting that the *Star* had misspelled Jeannette's name, she grasped at the only straw she had: could the dead woman be someone other than the Jeannette Kelly that she knew? If anyone could answer that question, she thought it would be Dawn Taber, who used to live with the Kellys at the Palace Pier and who at one time had been closer to Jeannette than almost anyone else. Taber had recently come back from the United States to resume a stormy relationship with boyfriend John Nascimento, with whom she now lived in an apartment on Sherbourne Street.

Deciding that the most diplomatic way of raising the subject was to ask Taber if she had seen or talked to Jeannette recently, Rowbotham quickly concluded after their first few moments of conversation that Taber couldn't have heard the news. She was too much her usual cheerful self to know about the death, but that changed dramatically when Rowbotham brought up the newspaper story. Taber fell silent, then asked exactly what the article said. Rowbotham read it to her and Taber "just fell to pieces," crying so hard she could barely talk. Rowbotham got the impression that she didn't want to go into the details of the story. After making sure that the distraught woman wasn't alone and promising to call back later, Rowbotham hung up.

As soon as John Nascimento found out from Taber what had happened, he hurried out to a nearby Becker's store and bought a copy of the newspaper. Taber read the four-paragraph story, then dropped the paper from her hands and mumbled, "he did it." Not knowing what she was talking about, Nascimento tried unsuccessfully to calm her down. Taber insisted on calling Joanne MacLean, asking her friend if the story in the paper was true. As distressed as Taber obviously was over Jeannette, MacLean got the impression that her overriding concern was for Kelly. She repeatedly asked how he was doing and said that she had to talk to him. Taber called the MacLeans twice more that evening, the last time to report that she had reached a Dr. Paul Stewart at the Palace Pier, who was apparently looking after Kelly. Although he had taken her number, the doctor explained that his charge was still too much in shock to take any supportive calls from friends.

As the day wore on, Taber became so emotionally unhinged that a desperate Nascimento even called his wife, Maria, who had just returned from Portugal after the couple's separation. Complaining that he didn't know what to do, he begged her to come over and look after his hysterical girlfriend. When the kindly woman arrived at 8 P.M., she did her best to comfort Taber, who was still crying uncontrollably, her face covered in red blotches.

"She was really bad news," Maria remembered. "Dawn seemed very sick about it all. She was really sick about it."

Deep in shock over her friend's death, and racked by a debilitating flu that had kept her bedridden for days, Abby Latter was wondering how she could face Jeannette's parents when Taber telephoned her late that night. Bordering on hysterics, Taber told Latter that the various injuries Jeannette had sustained in the months leading up to her death had been inflicted by Kelly. Already feeling guilty that she had not been more vigilant about the interests of her now dead friend, Latter exploded.

"She had phoned me many times before, asking me to see Jeannette. It was almost like she was appealing to me to intervene. And now she is telling me this story. I was so upset and angry with her. I just remember saying to her, 'What good is it now? Why are you telling me this now?'"

After advising Taber to tell the police what she knew, Latter hung up. Then, to make sure that the detectives working on the case found out about Kelly's abusiveness, she called the homicide squad herself and reported what Taber had told her.

By then, though, the police already had reasons of their own to suspect that things hadn't happened in quite the way Patrick Kelly had told them.

Nineteen hours after falling to her death, Jeannette Kelly's body was wheeled into the city morgue, where Dr. John Deck performed an autopsy. Sceptical as any homicide detective, the experienced coroner lived by the morgue's grim but heroic motto: "We speak for the dead, to protect the living." As homicide detectives Stewart and Hill watched him work, carefully probing Jeannette Kelly's body, they hoped the subtle communications of the dead might be able to tell them if they had an accident on their hands, or a murder.

An hour later, Dr. Deck turned to the detectives and told them that the cause of death was transection of the brain stem and the rupture of several bodily organs, including the heart, lungs, and liver. Based on the nature of her injuries, Deck concluded that Jeannette had struck the loading dock in a semi-sitting position, with her legs parallel to the ground and her hips partially flexed. The fracture of her upper spine indicated the upward transmission of a tremendous force through the backbone to the head, accounting for the fact that the skull itself had not been fractured. When she hit the cement, her head had snapped back violently, the resulting whiplash causing extensive fracturing of the spine just below her skull. Death would have been instantaneous, one of the possible explanations for the fact that there had been so little bleeding; Jeannette's heart had simply exploded on impact and stopped pumping blood. The other possibility was that it hadn't been beating when she went over the balcony.

Although Deck found most of Jeannette's injuries to be consistent with a fall from a great height, there were other wounds on her body that could not be so explained. The fourth and fifth fingernails of her left hand were broken at the tips, as were all the fingernails on her right hand. In addition, the right middle fingernail had been lifted from its bed, a phenomenon Deck had seen in homicides when no fall had been involved, but where the victim had desperately clawed at their murderer. The same injuries could be self-inflicted if the victim had used her hands in a clawing motion to prevent a fall.

There were three other wounds on Jeannette's body that in the coroner's view had not been caused by the fall. Although her scalp was externally unmarked, there had been recent bleeding into the subcutaneous tissue on the top of her head towards the back, a part of Jeannette's body that had never made contact with the ground. Given that there was so little bleeding elsewhere, this could mean that the fresh wound had been sustained before the fall.

There were also blotchy discolourations on the left side of Jeannette's face and eye, as well as her left jaw. Although the marks did not correspond to an identifiable object, the position of the woman's body on impact did not account for their presence. Finally, Dr. Deck found a laceration to the inside upper lip on the left side of Jeannette's face that corresponded to an underlying tooth. Stewart looked at Hill and wondered if he was thinking the same thing: had the victim been punched prior to going off the balcony?

After taking a sample of head hair, fingernail clippings from both hands, various biological samples, and some articles of clothing for the biology and chemistry section of the Centre of Forensic Sciences, the detectives drove to the Palace Pier to follow up on the previous night's interview with Patrick Kelly. The suspect wasn't home, so Stewart and Hill headed back to the station.

Searching for a motive for the potential murder, Sergeant Stewart called the offices of London Life and spoke with the Kellys' insurance agent, John Atkinson. It turned out that Patrick had held a meeting with Atkinson just ten days before Jeannette's death to review his personal insurance. Stewart confirmed with Atkinson that the surviving partner of the marriage would receive approximately $220,000 on the death of their spouse.

Stewart wasn't the only person that day who was thinking about life insurance. Around noon, just before the detectives had come looking for him after Jeannette's autopsy, Patrick Kelly and Dr. Paul Stewart left the Palace Pier in the Porsche to take care of a few items of business. With Kelly driving, they stopped first at a bank, where he returned $1,800 of the $2,000 he had withdrawn on his Visa card for Jeannette's trip to Italy. Then they paid a visit to the law offices of Austin Cooper, where Kelly complained that his phone was bugged, his car was under surveillance, and he himself appeared to be a suspect in his wife's tragic death. Finally, they drove to Dennis Morris's law office, where Kelly left

Stewart in the foyer while he and Morris began the formal process of applying for his wife's life insurance.

For a man who was so incapacitated with grief that he needed the twenty-four-hour care of Dr. Paul Stewart, Patrick Kelly's first day as a widower was surprisingly productive.

The next morning, detectives Stewart and Hill were on the job at 6:55 A.M., arranging the day's interviews and gathering as much information as they could on Kelly. RCMP Internal Affairs told the detectives about the $3,500 the force believed Kelly had stolen from informant fees, although he had never been criminally charged for the alleged offence. Just before leaving for the Palace Pier to reinterview Kelly, Stewart double-checked with John Atkinson on the details of the Kellys' insurance. All told, there were three life insurance policies on Jeannette with London Life paid for by Kelly, and a fourth that she held as an employee of CP Air.

When the detectives arrived at apartment 1705, Kelly invited them in and seated them around an antique table in the dining room. While members of the Identification Branch snapped pictures and removed the kitchen stools for expert examination, Stewart and Hill questioned the former RCMP officer about the state of his marriage, the nature of his work since leaving the force, and the details of Jeannette's accidental death. Kelly was co-operative and gracious, serving the officers tea, while he told them about his job with K&V Enterprises and the various businesses he was involved with in Toronto. He gave a candid description of the arson charge that had been laid against him, and a detailed account of his career with the RCMP. All the while the detectives questioned him, he sipped at a glass of water, remaining clearheaded and composed for most of the five-hour session.

Kelly painted the picture of a marriage that had been excellent until the Cookstown fire, had hit a few bumps during the police investigation and subsequent charges, and had been improving until the events of March 29 so tragically intervened. When asked if he had ever assaulted his wife, Kelly told them about Jeannette's anger over the proposed separation agreement and how he had thrown her to the floor only after she "went for my balls." He insisted that was the one and only time he had ever used force on his wife and that the marriage had become stronger than ever after the charges against him were dismissed and the spectre of his going to jail was removed. "We were very much in love," he said.

When the time came to describe the events of March 29, Kelly broke down and cried, and the statement-taking had to be suspended until he regained his composure. The story he told was essentially the same one he had already given them. The day before the accident, the Kellys had been sitting on the yellow director's chairs on their balcony when they heard a persistent rattle. Kelly, who had never heard the rattle before and attributed it to a loose metal flashing above the balcony that was vibrating in the wind, made a mental note to call maintenance about it.

The next day, just before Jeannette was set to leave for the airport on her four-week trip to Italy, Kelly had asked her if she wanted a cup of tea. While he was busy preparing it, his wife had come into the kitchen and picked up a wooden stool, remarking that she could again hear the annoying rattle. A few moments later, he heard an alarming noise and "ran like hell" towards the balcony. When he reached the living room, he could see that his wife was already falling backwards over the railing.

"I ran to the balcony and all the way over to the railing and I reached over and I had her, I had my arms around her . . . I had my arms around her legs, almost around her waist, but I couldn't hang on. She was trying to reach me, but she couldn't hang on. She was gasping, she fell right out of my hands. I even had her arm at one point but I couldn't hang on. She just slipped away."

"Can you tell us how you got that cut on the left side of your nose?" Stewart asked.

"I have no idea," Kelly answered. "I noticed the cut this morning when I was shaving."

While Kelly spent the next half-hour going over his statement line by line before signing it, the detectives were making mental notes of the distance between the kitchen and the balcony and coming to the same tentative conclusion. If Kelly had indeed seen his wife already falling over the balcony railing by the time he reached the living room, there was no possible way he could cover the distance to the balcony in time to get his hands on her.

They were also troubled by his claim that he had been busy making tea when Jeannette had come into the kitchen complaining of the rattle. When police had arrived on the afternoon of Jeannette's death, there were no teacups, milk, or sugar in sight, only the boiling kettle. What had Kelly been so busy with that he "didn't pay much attention" when Jeannette mentioned the rattle and left the kitchen with the stool?

After Kelly signed his statement, the detectives cleared up another matter that had been bothering them. Ever since the accident, Dr. Paul Stewart had apparently taken personal charge of Kelly's every movement, ostensibly because he was a doctor. The police had been told that the two men had been virtual strangers before the accident and wondered why Stewart was now taking such a deep personal interest in Kelly.

They decided to interview Stewart to find out more about his background. They knew that he had previously told other residents of the building that he was a forensic pathologist who held the rank of lieutenant-commander in U.S. Naval Intelligence and that there was a Lear jet standing by at a Toronto military base to whisk him anywhere in the world in the event of a political assassination. After talking to him, the detectives checked his story with the FBI and found out that it was a total fabrication, as was his claim to ambulance attendants on the afternoon of Jeannette's death that he was a doctor. As Sergeant Stewart soon discovered, Paul Stewart's actual occupation was considerably less glamorous than the ones he so blatantly assumed; he was, in fact, a mortician at Jerrett's Funeral Home.

Like so many things in the case, nothing was quite what it seemed.

After the police left, Patrick Kelly and Paul Stewart visited the Turner & Porter Funeral Chapel on Bloor Street to make arrangements for Jeannette's burial. Kelly's instructions to the funeral director were precise and austere: there were to be no pre-funeral visits, no graveside service or visits, and the casket was to remain closed at all times. He wanted the simplest, and by implication, speediest service that the chapel could provide.

On their way back to the Palace Pier, they stopped to put the mink coat Jeannette had planned to take to Italy back into storage. They also visited Yolles Antiques, where Kelly spoke to proprietor Graham Gordon about selling his Palace Pier furniture while Stewart admired a twelve-place setting of English bone china that had caught his eye. Before they left, Gordon told Patrick that the china had been in storage for forty years and was worth $7,500.

Ten minutes after the two men got back to the Palace Pier, Stewart received a call from Jeannette's mother, who had arrived earlier in the day from Scotland. Understandably, she wanted to see her son-in-law to get an explanation of what had happened to her daughter. In keeping with Kelly's instructions, Stewart told her that he was too heavily sedated to receive visitors.

When she inquired about the funeral arrangements, Stewart informed her that the coffin would be closed, a decision that greatly upset the grieving mother. She couldn't even go through Jeannette's personal things, since John and Winnifred Kelly were now firmly ensconced in apartment 1705. For some reason, Kelly apparently preferred to stay with his newfound friend, Dr. Stewart, rather than with his own parents.

The only person who would talk to Lottie Arbuckle about the "accident" was Abby Latter. But the heartsick young woman was too afraid of upsetting Lottie more than she already was to mention her suspicions about Patrick. Abby needn't have worried; Lottie's every instinct as a mother told her that her son-in-law was responsible for Jeannette's death, an intuition that was reinforced by his refusal to see her, ostensibly for medical reasons.

"Now if he had nothing to hide, I'm Jeannette's mother and her father is here. How ill can a person be?" she thought.

A few minutes after Stewart finished talking to Mrs. Arbuckle, he received a call from Jimmy Hanlon, who had arrived in Toronto at 5 P.M. to attend his daughter's funeral the next morning. It became obvious that there would be no putting off the grieving father. But instead of inviting his father-in-law up to the apartment, Kelly met him in the hall outside one of the Palace Pier's ground-floor guest suites. Like his ex-wife, Hanlon had only one thing on his mind: finding out what had happened to his daughter. Sullen, and hanging his head as he spoke, Kelly told him that Jeannette had been fixing something on the balcony when she had accidentally fallen over the railing.

"I knew myself at that point, it was nonsense. It never happened the way he said for sure. Immediately I knew there was something wrong someplace," Hanlon recalled.

When Lottie Arbuckle had a chance to speak to her ex-husband, she told him "it was not right" that she couldn't see Jeannette. Hanlon agreed. Later that night, he spoke to Stewart and insisted that the casket be opened for him and Lottie. He would not take no for an answer from the man he thought of as a "flitting fairy." Hanlon's demand tripped off a desperate search for a photograph of Jeannette, so that the funeral director could prepare her face for a viewing.

Dreading the morning's grim finale to his relationship with the daughter he had loved so much, Hanlon spent a sleepless night running over the spare facts of the story Kelly had given him during their five-minute talk. None of it added up, including the manner in which his son-in-law had related the details of Jeannette's death. A lover would have cried, the old man thought. Kelly had been "as cold as ice."

The same day that the former Mountie was painting the portrait of his essentially happy marriage for detectives Stewart and Hill, Sgt. Michael Duchak was getting a different story from one of Jeannette's co-workers at CP Air. Barbara Newar told the CID investigator that just the night before Jeannette's death, the Kellys had visited her home for wine and cheese, staying until approximately 1 A.M. When they were alone in the kitchen, Jeannette had told Newar that she had had "a terrible fight with her husband that morning."

It didn't strike Newar as surprising, since everyone in her circle knew that the Kellys' marriage had been in trouble for the past two years. She knew, for example, that Jeannette had gone to dinner with her Italian lover just ten days earlier, telling her husband that she had been "out shopping" when he asked where she'd been.

Newar told Duchak that Jeannette had also admitted to her that the knee injury that put her leg in a Jones Splint had not been caused by a fall, as she had told everyone at the time, but by Patrick. When Newar had asked Jeannette why she stayed with him, she got the same answer Jeannette had given to her other friends who knew her real situation. Now she told Duchak, "Jeannette continued to live with her husband because she had no desire to be single and start all over again."

As for the story that Jeannette had climbed up on a stool seventeen storeys above a cement loading dock to fix a rattle on her balcony on a windy day, Newar was even more sceptical than the homicide detectives.

"That's completely erroneous. You would have to know Jeannette. If something was wrong, she'd call down and get someone to fix it. She wouldn't do it herself. She wouldn't even go and mail a letter, she'd leave it at the front desk for them to mail it. She was basically lazy. She liked the idea of living in the Palace Pier, the doorman, being wealthy. Fixing noises was beneath her. It wouldn't cross her mind to do that. She was leaving in an hour for the airport. She wouldn't be concerned with a noise. She was leaving the country for a month."

Even for an April 1, it was the strangest funeral that the Kellys' neighbours, David and Linda Mallette, ever attended. The first surprise of the day came when Paul Stewart asked the couple to ride to the chapel with him and Kelly. Wondering why Kelly wasn't going with his or Jeannette's parents, they reluctantly agreed, even helping Stewart to assist the grief-stricken man into the limousine at the front door of the Palace Pier. Linda offered her condolences, but the embrace Kelly gave her seemed curiously inappropriate to her husband. "It appeared more like an amorous hug than [sic] a bereaved husband who had just lost his wife."

On the way to the chapel, Kelly sat in the backseat between the Mallettes, while Stewart rode in front with the driver. Kelly whispered to Linda that he thought it would be a good idea if he took a trip to France or Spain to put everything behind him. Although she agreed, Linda was not really paying attention to what he was saying; she was more concerned with the way that Stewart kept turning around and rubbing Kelly's knee, a gesture that seemed more affectionate than sympathetic.

David Mallette shared his wife's uneasiness. The truth was, he didn't particularly care for either Stewart or Kelly. They weren't the only people at the Palace Pier to wonder about the relationship between Stewart and his elderly wife, a cousin of Roland Michener, who was twenty-five years his senior. Nor did Mallette believe Stewart's story about the Lear jet that was supposedly on standby for him at Downsview airbase. When Mallette, a licensed pilot, had asked questions about the aircraft, Stewart's uninformed answers had proven that he didn't know what he was talking about.

As for Kelly, he had once told David that he liked the idea of having a valet service for his car, since he worried that someone might wire a bomb to his ignition; the fact that an innocent teenager would be blown up in his place didn't seem to bother him. And then there was Kelly's curious view of the law. After a squash game at the Palace Pier, Mallette remembered Kelly saying that it didn't matter if a person actually committed a crime; what mattered was whether or not the authorities could prove it.

When they reached the chapel, the Mallettes tried to get out of the limousine, but Stewart told them that Kelly needed them for "support" during the service. They helped him inside, although Linda Mallette thought that his extreme grief was more theatrical than heartfelt. "It just didn't look real. He didn't appear to be in a state of shock. He had to make a special effort to convince people."

Kelly was engulfed by a crowd of mourners, including Dawn Taber. Although she clearly wanted to talk to him, Kelly never once looked at her, turning instead to Stewart, who led him into the room reserved for next of kin. Word began to circulate that Kelly was heavily sedated and couldn't talk to anyone because he had lost his voice.

Taber was disappointed. Earlier that morning, she had called Joanne MacLean to say that the Metro police had picked up her boyfriend, John Nascimento, on an unrelated matter and she had no way of getting to the funeral. What she didn't say was that when the plainclothes detectives had come to her door, she thought it was her they had come to arrest. When the MacLeans found out that she didn't have any money, they offered to pay her cab fare, and Taber agreed to meet Joanne outside the chapel and attend the service with her. Ian MacLean declined to join them and watched the proceedings from his car across the street, fearing what he might say or do if he met Kelly face-to-face.

Before going into the chapel, Dawn and Joanne spoke with some of Jeannette's friends from CP Air. Knowing that Dawn and Jeannette had had a serious falling out in the fall of 1980, Judy Seres was surprised to see her there at all. The women commiserated with each other and then exchanged telephone numbers so that they could arrange a private dinner in a few days' time. Dawn also spoke to Dennis Morris and Harry Morozowich. Morozowich told her that the police had been looking for her because she had been such a close friend of the Kellys and advised her to talk to them. Both men would later remember Dawn telling them that she had been in the United States at the time of Jeannette's accident.

Abby Latter attended the service with Jeannette's mother and father. Although Jimmy Hanlon and Lottie Arbuckle had never met Patrick's parents, no one introduced the two families. Clearly devastated, Lottie was the first person to take her place in the pew in front of her daughter's casket. Kelly briefly appeared and placed his hand on her head. Convinced more than ever that he had murdered Jeannette, a strange fear swept over the grieving mother. "I thought he was going to bash my brains in. You know, it just came over me. Ooh, I thought, my head, my head."

After appearing in the chapel before the service started, Kelly went outside, where Ian MacLean watched him pacing the sidewalk and greeting latecomers, including half a dozen RCMP officers who had worked with Kelly on the Toronto Drug Section. Paul Stewart finally had to come out and usher Kelly back inside. The service itself was so brief Abby Latter wondered who had given the clergyman his information about Jeannette; his eulogy was impersonal to the point that they might have been burying a stranger. But his pro forma remarks had an effect on at least one of the mourners.

"Dawn was just shrieking, crying hysterically," Judy Seres recalls. "We figured the reason she was so hysterical was because Dawn and Jeannette had had this argument, and Dawn was feeling guilty about not having made amends over it earlier."

After the formal service, which lasted just over half an hour, the casket was opened so that Jeannette's parents could see their daughter one last time. They were accompanied by Abby Latter, whose last memory of Jeannette had been a casual wave from her car as she drove past Abby in the parking lot of the Palace Pier five days before her death. It was a gruesome sight.

Because of the terrible damage done to her neck, Jeannette's head appeared to be resting on the top of her body. Despite heavy makeup, the bruises on her left cheek were still visible and there was a curious cross-shaped smudge on her face. Lottie Arbuckle took out her handkerchief, and in a last motherly gesture, tried to wipe the mark away. As the casket was being closed, she turned to Abby and sighed, "Oh, she's beautiful" while Jimmy Hanlon clenched his fists and fought back the tears. When the hearse delivered Jeannette Kelly's body to Mount Pleasant Cemetery, the only people at her grave were her estranged parents and Abby Latter.

Just when they thought that their semi-official duties were over, David and Linda Mallette found themselves imposed on for the second time that day. Explaining that Kelly's apartment was too small for the number of people expected to attend the reception, Paul Stewart asked the Mallettes if he could shift the event to their much larger suite on the forty-second floor. They agreed, and a few moments later, Stewart showed up with sandwiches and tea that Maureen McGuigan had already had waiting in apartment 1705. Although Kelly attended the wake, he spent so much time in the Mallette's den making telephone calls that some of the guests actually thought he wasn't there.

All day long, Linda Mallette had been resisting terrible thoughts about Kelly. She sensed that there was no real feeling behind his show of grief and she was bothered by the fact that no one, including Kelly, would tell her what had actually happened to Jeannette. But it wasn't until she caught him in an unguarded moment during the wake that she finally made up her mind.

"As I was bringing coffee to him, he was in the den making a phone call. As I approached the den, I overheard the following conversation: 'I put the furs and the jewellery in storage.'"

In the circumstances, it was not the kind of thing a grieving husband would be thinking about, and Mallette concluded with a shudder that Kelly had murdered his wife.

After returning to his own apartment to get ready for a private dinner that night with a few close friends and family members, Kelly finally encountered some people he could not avoid: sergeants Roy Yacynuk and Michael Duchak of the Metropolitan Toronto Police. The detectives asked Kelly if they could check his body for marks that they suspected may have been inflicted by his wife. Leading them into the den and closing the door, Kelly took off his shirt and allowed the two sergeants to examine him. His chest, back, and arms were unblemished. Before leaving, the detectives asked Kelly to demonstrate on one of them where he had taken hold of Jeannette as she was falling over the railing.

"We stood face-to-face," Sergeant Duchak remembers. "He lunged at me and grabbed me by the waist, his head against the right side of my chest. His arms were completely around me. While demonstrating this hold to me, he stated: 'She was already over the balcony, we were face-to-face. I remember looking into her face. I was leaning over the rail. I was too weak to hold onto her and she fell.'"

Kelly told them one more thing before they left to interview Abby Latter. He had spotted the detectives at the funeral, and now he said that the reason he hadn't attended Jeannette's interment at Mount Pleasant Cemetery was because the couple had previously agreed that if either of them died, the survivor would remember the other as they had been in life rather than death. The detectives nodded politely and wished him goodnight.

The last official event of the day was the dinner at Percy House on Bloor Street put on by Paul Stewart for the Kellys, the Arbuckles, Mr. Hanlon, the Mallettes, Abby Latter, Paul Stewart, and Kelly. If Lottie Arbuckle thought she was finally going to get a chance to speak to Kelly about what had happened to her daughter, she was wrong. Just as he had at the wake in the Mallette's apartment, he spent most of the dinner on the telephone. Lottie became so upset that she left the table and went to the washroom, where she poured her heart out to Abby Latter.

"Abigail," she said, with a stitch in her voice, "he's done that to my daughter."

"Come on, love, come on now," Abby said, trying to comfort her. Winnifred Kelly walked in and saw Lottie crying.

"Are you all right?" she asked.

"No," Lottie replied. "I'll never be all right until I get justice done."

In fact, Lottie was already fantasizing about acting as Patrick's judge, jury, and executioner, if only he would join her for lunch on the rooftop patio of the Palace Pier.

"I'd have went on that terrace and I'd have put him over. That was my intentions because I knew he done that to my daughter."

Lottie Arbuckle never got the chance. When she boarded the plane back to Glasgow the next day, she still hadn't talked to her son-in-law and would never hear from him again. But she didn't go home entirely without hope. Before leaving, Sergeant Stewart told the heartbroken woman that justice would be done. It was a promise she would live on in the long, difficult months ahead.

For several days, Jan Bradley had been worried sick about Patrick Kelly. The last time she had seen him was Friday, March 27, when they had dined at the Great Escape restaurant. He told her then that he was going to New York for the weekend but would keep in touch. Although he did call the next day at the library, telling Jan he expected to be home by Monday, it was the last she heard from him until he called on the evening of April Fool's Day.

He had sounded terrible, but when Bradley asked him what was wrong, he would only say that he couldn't talk about it at the moment. She invited him over to her apartment, but he told her he couldn't come because of "social obligations." Instead, he promised to pick her up the next day for lunch. After the call, Kelly returned to the table at Percy House where the other mourners were waiting impatiently for him to resume his seat at the head of the table.

By the time he showed up at the library the next day, Bradley's stomach was in knots wondering what on earth could have happened. As they walked to his car, she noticed that Kelly was shaking and asked again what was wrong. It was no use. All she could get out of him was a one-word answer: "later." Even though it was a grey, overcast day, Kelly was wearing sunglasses, and she made him take them off so she could get a good look at him. His face was chalk white and his eyes looked sore and red. Whatever was bothering him, she thought, it had certainly left him "looking like hell."

Bradley began questioning him in the car, but Kelly put his finger to his lips and shook his head. By now she was used to his extreme caution and got the message that he didn't want to talk in the Porsche because of possible police bugs. Kelly drove to a dead-end street in a nearby suburb and the couple got out for a walk. He could see that she was looking at him strangely and in a nervous voice whispered, "I'm on medication."

Knowing that Patrick didn't even take Aspirin, Bradley was now convinced that very bad news was on the way. As they strolled arm in arm down the deserted street, Kelly told her that his RCMP wife, Jeannette, had died on Sunday, which was why he hadn't kept his promise to call her. He explained that he had been taken to hospital in the same ambulance as Jeannette, suffering from shock over the woman's death.

An astonished Bradley asked the question that Kelly had so effectively avoided answering during the days following Jeannette's death with everyone but the police. Appearing to be "almost angry," he told Bradley that "the stupid broad" had fallen off their apartment balcony trying to fix a rattle. Bradley was nearly as stunned by Patrick's uncharacteristically crude way of putting the news as she was by the news itself. Afterwards, he continued, he had run down seventeen flights of stairs to Jeannette's body, covering her face with his own shirt. Bradley found that strange, but concluded that he must have been so anxious to get to Jeannette that he hadn't been able to wait for the elevator.

Bradley asked her trembling lover if he wanted to stay with her, but he declined. He was temporarily living with a doctor at the Palace Pier who had sat up with him all night after the accident, Patrick told her, and the man had been looking after him ever since. Bradley got the impression that Patrick and Paul Stewart were "definitely old friends" and was thankful that there had been a qualified person on hand to look after him.

Patrick gradually relaxed. It felt good to be back with Jan. That night, he took her out for an elegant dinner at the expensive Three Small Rooms restaurant in the Windsor Arms Hotel. The next night, he picked her up at 8 P.M. and they drove to the Corner House restaurant on Davenport Road for dinner with Jan's best friends, Jill and Roger Davidson. Shortly after Jill arrived from a shower for one of her girl-friend's, a waiter appeared with a bottle of wine. Roger Davidson was tied up at his car dealership and the wine was his apology for being late. Although she did her best to be cheerful for Jan's sake, Jill Davidson could think of people she would rather sip wine with than Patrick Kelly.

Ever since Jan had started talking about the "international business-man" she was seeing, Jill had wondered about some of the stories he had apparently told her. Did he really own a chalet in France or a gold mine in British Columbia, or, as Jill suspected, was he just trying to impress Jan? After meeting him for the first time, both she and Roger doubted that he was the "genius level" entrepreneur that Jan believed he was. But it was only after Jan had called to warn Jill that Patrick might be upset at dinner because his "undercover wife" had just fallen to her death from their balcony that she really began to worry that her friend might be getting mixed up with the wrong sort of person.

The Davidsons' suspicions about Patrick weren't diminished by the stories he told that night. First he talked about the various businesses he owned, including a Rolls-Royce dealership in London, England, and a travelling Rolls-Royce service trailer based in Los Angeles. It was a great sideline, Kelly said, explaining that he charged his wealthy customers $220 an hour. Personally, though, he preferred sports cars, like the two Porsches and the Ferrari he owned. Then he boasted about his properties: several luxury condominiums in Toronto, two houses in Europe, and a country estate north of the city, which he rented out while he lived alone in the coach house. For a man who had just lost his wife, whether she was of the undercover variety or not, Patrick was in a very festive mood, or so it seemed to Jill. "Pat was laughing and joking and appeared to be having a good time."

Kelly told the Davidsons that he had bought his first car, a Jaguar, when he was just sixteen. Already a black belt in judo at that age, he bragged, he had bought it with the proceeds of his $100-an-hour job teaching hand-to-hand combat to the Armed Forces. When he told them that his face had been rebuilt after a fight with eight attackers, (Kelly vanquished them all) Roger wondered how he would get through the dessert course. "It was beyond me to see Jan swallowed up by all this nonsense."

After dinner, the foursome went to Bradley's apartment for a night-cap. Kelly became ill and decided to spend the night with Bradley. On the way home, Jill asked her husband if there was any way they could check out Patrick MacLean before their friend got hurt. There was some urgency to her question, since Jan had already told her that she and Patrick might even get married on their upcoming holiday together. They had already talked about Jan resigning from her library job by telegram. Roger shook his head and promised to see what he could do.

Back at the Palace Pier, Paul Stewart was beside himself wondering what had happened to his errant charge. When Kelly telephoned the next day, telling Stewart that he had spent the night at the Sutton Place Hotel, the man who had become his doting, emotional custodian was angry. "I made it quite clear to Pat that this wasn't to happen again."

But as Stewart explained in a complaining phone call to Abby Latter, even though Kelly had behaved badly, he still loved him and enjoyed taking care of him.

Just to make sure that there was no repeat of Kelly's truant behaviour of the night before, Stewart decided to take him to his cottage for a weekend away from demanding relatives and the meddlesome detectives and all their annoying questions. But even on the lonely stretches of Highway 11, the police crossed their path again, pulling Kelly over for speeding on the way to Mary Lake.

From the morning that the MacLeans had driven her home from Jeannette's funeral, Dawn Taber had been a self-admitted basket-case. She had tried again to reach Kelly at the Palace Pier to see how he was holding up, but he didn't respond to the message she left with Winnifred Kelly requesting a return call. She then phoned her estranged husband, John Hastey, and in a near-hysterical state asked him why police officers had been at the funeral. Hastey, who had once shared his suspicion with Jeannette that Dawn and Patrick "had something going," told her that he didn't know. John Nascimento could only watch helplessly as his girlfriend became more obsessed with her friend's death. The very day she got back from the funeral, Taber had told a perplexed Nascimento that she would do everything in her power to put Kelly in jail.

By Saturday, April 4, the distraught young woman began to make good on her grim vow. She voluntarily appeared at the Homicide Division of the Metropolitan Toronto Police, deciding it was better if she went to them rather than waiting for the detectives to come to her. She was so nervous when she met with detectives Stewart and Hill, she refused to sit down and began by telling them that she didn't know what to say. When she said, "You start, okay?" Stewart smiled and gently asked if there was something troubling her.

"Yeah, oh yeah. There's a lot troubling me. A lot."

He urged her to start from her first meeting with the Kellys and to just take it from there. After Taber told the detectives that Kelly was an "actor" who used people and who enjoyed taking chances, unlike his security-conscious wife, Stewart interrupted her vague generalities with another question. He sensed that Taber had a point to make but was having trouble coming to it.

"What is it that's really troubling you? Something you want to tell us?"

"Yes, yes," she replied. "I think we all know what it is."

If the detectives thought that the woman standing in front of them was about to deliver a bombshell that would help them break the case, they were about to be disappointed. Still, what the strangely reluctant witness had to say to them was very important. In a halting voice, Taber confessed to having had an affair with Patrick after moving in with the Kellys in the spring of 1980, explaining that "this is how everything got started."

With the detectives listening hard, Taber said that Kelly had often told her that the two of them could change their identities and leave the country to escape from the arson charges hanging over him. They would live in the south of France on a sailboat and Jeannette would be well provided for by the bonds and shares he had entrusted to his lawyer in Victoria, Victor Simpson. As for the Cookstown fire, she told the detectives about the false letter she had written to Austin Cooper at Kelly's request. She admitted that Kelly himself had never confessed to her, but said that she believed he had burned down his own house for the insurance money.

The atmosphere in the interview room was heating up. So there had been a love triangle, the detectives thought. Anticipating where the conversation might be going, one of them asked Taber how she felt about Jeannette's death.

"I am still not quite over it. I'll never be over her death and whether he did it or not. I don't know, but I think eventually it should be found out. But my concern is that – where is he now? Does anyone know where he is now?"

Sensing that Taber had once again backed away from what she really wanted to say, Stewart said that they didn't know Kelly's precise whereabouts. Was she implying that he planned to skip the country? Like so many of her answers that day, her reply was both suggestive and evasive.

"Because of my relationship with him and knowing him, I have questions . . . I don't know if people realize what he is capable of, what he can do, you know, what he *could* do."

"We know a bit about him," Hill said. "And, of course, where he worked before, they gave us some information as to what he was involved in and what he was capable of." It was a circumspect way of saying that the RCMP had told the detectives to treat the case as a homicide, given who was involved.

With Taber talking in circles, jumping from one part of the puzzle to another, Hill brought the interview back to her affair with Kelly. It was clear that it bothered her to talk about it, and she tried to explain to the detectives that it was "not like a mad love thing," but rather the way that Kelly needed to be supported at the time. They understood one another, she said, and in a way, she was like Kelly in that she was prepared to "take a chance to get ahead." But they had only had intercourse three or four times, and the affair had quickly ended with both of them realizing that Taber's friendship with Jeannette meant much more to her than an affair of convenience with Patrick. From the looks on the detectives' faces, Taber could tell that they didn't believe her.

"This is what I was afraid of. I don't know how to explain it because I know the implications if I am saying, 'Yeah, yeah, I was madly in love with him,'" she said.

Hill didn't disagree, but offered what he hoped would be a helpful qualifier.

"You certainly had some feeling for him."

"And I do."

"And still do?"

"Yes."

Taber then described for the detectives Kelly's abusive behaviour towards his wife, telling them that he had kicked her in the tailbone and on another occasion threw her to the floor and sprained her leg. Wondering if she was trying to lead up to the thing that was really bothering her, Hill asked the most trenchant question of the interview.

"Did he ever threaten her life?"

"I – I, he talked to me, okay. I don't want to say – because at the time I never thought of it, that if you – initially, sometimes in the heat of an argument you say, like, 'If you weren't here, you know, life would be so much better. If you weren't here, I'd have all this insurance money.' And he said things like that, and he spoke about her insurance."

Suddenly the case was taking on a sharper focus, as the second of the two classic motives for murder was put on the table by Taber: not only was there a love triangle, but now there was talk of life insurance. The detectives found it interesting that Kelly's former lover had also been an insurance agent and probed more deeply into her latest revelation. Taber explained how Kelly had wanted her to increase the amount of coverage on his wife and structure the policy so that the payout would be in a lump sum rather than an annuity. But when Hill asked if Kelly had ever explained why he wanted so much life insurance, Taber's answer washed out the picture that had been emerging throughout her statement: that Kelly may have killed his wife for the money.

"If he left the country, it would have been . . . he said to me, 'If I leave, she will get all this insurance money because I'll be dead.' And I said, 'Well Pat, they are not ready to give Jeannette the insurance money without a body. What are you going to do for a body?' . . . But he is smart. I'm sure that something was going to be thought up."

"When was the last time you saw either Pat or Jeannette?" Hill asked.

"About November 4, 1980."

"Have you spoken with them since?"

"I haven't personally. The person that I am living with did."

After more than three hours, the interview ended and Taber left the station. The detectives were ultimately puzzled rather than enlightened by what she had told them. Although they had learned many valuable details about the suspect and the state of his marriage, they wondered how far they could trust Taber's story about running off to the south of France under a new identity and living on a sailboat with Kelly, while Jeannette apparently remained behind in Toronto living off the proceeds of his life insurance. It might be true, although the insurance angle didn't add up, or it might be a jilted lover's way of settling an old score.

Two days after her session with detectives Hill and Stewart, Dawn Taber finally got a call from Patrick Kelly. He explained that he hadn't phoned earlier because his mother hadn't given him her message until Thursday and he had then gone up north for a few days with a friend to unwind. Unfortunately, he didn't have time to see her right now because he was on his way to Los Angeles to get away from the crushing events of the past few days.

Dawn told him that Jeannette's friends had been devastated by the news and then asked if he was all right. In an apparent reference to the arson charges, Patrick replied that "the other thing turned out OK," and that, as Dawn put it, "he didn't need this because he had recently started to get it together again." Now he just planned to relax, play some tennis, get a tan, and walk on the beach. When Dawn asked him if he was going away by himself, he said that he was and that she shouldn't be surprised if she got a long distance call asking her to join him. She impressed on him that if he needed to talk, all he had to do was call. Patrick thanked her and said that he had, in fact, been depressed a few times and wanted to call but hadn't had her new number.

When Dawn found out that he intended to be away for five or six weeks, she asked if there was anything she could do. Patrick thanked her again and said no, explaining that Kelly was in a kennel, the apartment was being looked after by Palace Pier staff, and Dennis Morris had power of attorney to take care of his business affairs while he was away. Before saying goodbye, he called her "Babe" and told her that he loved her.

As soon as Kelly hung up, Taber called Homicide. Sergeant Stewart was in need of some good news, since the Centre of Forensic Sciences had just reported that the laser equipment had been unable to find any prints on the stool Jeannette Kelly had allegedly fallen from on the day she died. But he quickly forgot that dead-end in the investigation when a breathless Taber told him that Kelly had just called her and was about to leave the country. Remembering that Kelly himself had told detectives the day before that he might be going away for a while, Stewart called the Palace Pier and discovered that apartment 1705 was vacant and under the supervision of building staff.

Stewart immediately called Sgt. Lou Nave of the RCMP's Special Squad at Pearson airport and asked him to check all airlines to see if Kelly was indeed scheduled to leave the country. Stewart then received a call from Hill saying that he couldn't reach Taber at her home. Was it possible they were leaving together, just as she had told police they had once planned to do? Could that have been what was bothering her so much during her interview? The detectives raced over to her apartment on Sherbourne Street, but no one was home, or so they thought. In fact, Taber had seen the car pull up and decided for reasons of her own not to answer the door.

While the detectives returned to the office, wondering if Taber was about to abscond with the prime suspect in their murder investigation,

Kelly was already in the process of buying a second airline ticket. After leaving the pay phone from which he had called Taber, he had driven to the airport alone and left the Porsche in the long-term parking area. He then walked to the American Airlines counter, where he verbally identified himself to ticket agent Valerie White as Patrick Kelly, producing a prepaid ticket to Honolulu.

White pulled up his reservation, and read the note on the file: "V. Simpson and a second party of Patrick Kelly." Kelly told White that he wanted to pay for the second ticket in cash, but change the name from V. Simpson to J. Bradley. She told him that it was against company policy to change names on a reservation, but when Kelly insisted that the American Airlines office where he had purchased his own ticket earlier that morning had okayed the transaction, she relented.

"What happened, are you taking a different girl?" White joked.

"Yeah," Kelly replied, leaving the ticket agent with the impression that he hadn't appreciated her quip. But the last laugh belonged to Kelly. After he had gone, White recounted the $738.85 he had given her for the second ticket to Honolulu and found that she was short. "Somehow, someway, he shortchanged me a hundred dollars." White was so upset that she called ahead to L. A. International Airport to leave a message for Kelly to call Toronto. He never answered the page.

Working the same airport detail as Kelly had been assigned to early in his own career with the force, RCMP constables T. McLaren and P. O'Brien watched Kelly while he completed his business with White. He was alone and dressed casually in a white, open-necked shirt and blue jeans. Judging from his body language, he was extremely wary. "Subject Kelly, while waiting in the line, appeared to be constantly looking around, giving me the impression that he was surveillance conscious."

Since McLaren actually knew Kelly and was afraid of being recognized, O'Brien took up the observation post and watched the subject as he walked thirty feet towards the front of the terminal and began talking to a female with long, dark hair. By now, Const. Michael Ambrosio of the Peel Regional Police had joined the surveillance team and took several surreptitious photos of Kelly and his female companion as they checked in, cleared U.S. customs hand in hand, and headed for Lounge T before boarding flight 35 to Los Angeles en route to Honolulu.

When detectives Hill and Stewart found out from the Special Squad that Kelly and a woman named Jan Bradley were at the airport and on their way to Hawaii, they rushed to 361 University Avenue and spoke to Frank Armstrong in the Crown Attorney's Office. It was decided that the couple would be permitted to board the aircraft and that the FBI would be asked to provide surveillance when flight 35 landed in Los Angeles four hours later. But Hill and Stewart had few doubts left about what had happened to Jeannette Kelly. After all, only a week had passed since her horrific and suspicious death and her grieving husband was now headed for Hawaii with his girlfriend.

Back at the Palace Pier, Paul Stewart broke into tears when he read the letter that Kelly left for him in the bedroom that they had so briefly shared. He couldn't believe that Kelly had left without saying goodbye, despite the tender words:

"Have gone away south. I just need some time. I don't know how long, probably a few weeks. Please understand that I won't call or write directly to you but [will] call Jerrett's every now and then for a message. I've left Jeannette's jewellery in the cabinet. Put it in your safe. My passport is also there. Just to ensure the police that my trip is not one way, please leave it there. . . . Thank you for the last week. Without you, it would have been impossible. We've become very close, very quickly. . . . We have something most people only read about between two people and it can never be taken away. It will only grow. . . . With all my heart and soul, go well. . . . Soon we'll walk together again.

"Your Brother – Pat"

Stewart was adrift in a rush of emotions, feeling reassured and betrayed all in the same moment. Had Kelly taken advantage of him in the days after Jeannette's death, using him as a barrier against anyone he didn't want to speak to? And when Kelly had called one night to say that he could hear the rattle again and asked Paul to make an entry to that effect in his diary, had he been telling the truth or was he only trying to use him to create evidence to back up the version of events that he had given to police?

In the middle of these distressing thoughts, a knock came at the door. It was a delivery man with a number of boxes. When the mortician protested that he hadn't ordered anything from an antique store, the man told him that the shipment had already been paid for and was definitely for him. Stewart was stunned when he looked inside one of the carefully wrapped boxes and saw what it contained: the bone china that he and Kelly had admired in Yolles just a few days before. Judging from the number of boxes, it was the complete set.

"Please accept my little gift in the manner in which it is given," Kelly wrote, "from the heart to the heart."

Paul Stewart's pleasure at reading this sentiment evaporated when he found out the next day during an interview with police that Kelly had left the country with a woman.

12

THE GREAT ESCAPE

Despite her vertigo, when the small plane suddenly banked left and circled back towards Honolulu, Jan Bradley smiled at her quiet companion, then craned her neck towards the porthole and gazed down at the sea. Below them, a pod of whales was sounding in the emerald waters off the island of Molokai and the pilot had backtracked to give his passengers a better look. Bradley turned and said something to Patrick Kelly, but her words were lost in the drone of the plane's engines.

As subdued as he had been during their first few days in Honolulu, Patrick couldn't help admiring the way that Jan responded to the beauty around her. Watching the whales, she was "like a child with a new toy," just as she'd been at the Metropolitan Museum of Art in New York while marvelling at the man-made masterpieces. He savoured her enjoyment, and found himself thinking yet again that he was in the company of "a very special lady."

It had taken an unusual woman to get through the first four days they had spent at the Hawaiian Regency Hotel after flying in from Los Angeles, where their arrival from Toronto had been secretly observed by the FBI. Kelly had warned Bradley that the police might be following them as part of the routine homicide investigation that took place whenever someone died suddenly the way Jeannette had. But there had been no way to anticipate the incident with Sheree Brown, the attractive blonde who had been "adopted" by the Kellys when she first came to Toronto to work for CP Air until Jeannette accused her of having an affair with her husband.

Brown had been vacationing with her mother at the Hawaiian Regency, where Patrick and Jan were registered as "Mr. and Mrs. Bradley," when she was stunned to see Patrick at poolside with a young woman with long, dark hair. Disgusted by their "kissy-face, huggy-cheek" intimacy just days after Jeannette's death, Brown decided to confront Kelly when his female friend got up and walked back towards the hotel. Although he was surprised by Brown's sudden appearance, Kelly did his best to be his usual open and friendly self.

"Hi, I guess you haven't heard," he said glumly.

"Oh yes, I know," Brown replied, looking steadily into his eyes.

With the unspoken question hanging in the air, Kelly finally explained that his companion was a friend of his and Jeannette's who was helping him deal with his grief by doing some of the things that he and his wife used to do. Sheree Brown was not persuaded. In contrast to the supremely confident man Brown remembered from the Palace Pier, she found Kelly to be "very tense and awkward"; when Bradley returned, the couple picked up their beach bags without any introductions and "left in a rush."

As they returned to the hotel, Patrick told Jan that the woman he'd been talking to was an old friend and that she'd been surprised to see him with another woman so soon after Jeannette's death. Believing what Patrick had told her about the nature of his marriage, Jan wasn't bothered in the least.

"It was our feeling that it was unfortunate that Jeannette was dead, but she was just a friend who had died and it was just a natural thing for him to do to turn to his lover, which was me."

During the day, Patrick and Jan looked like every other vacationing couple at the hotel, holding hands as they walked the beach and whispering to one another over romantic, candlelit dinners. The afternoon sailing had already given both of them a ruddy glow that would soon turn to a nut-brown tan under the heavy Hawaiian sun. But after the lovemaking, when the sun slipped into the ocean, and the yellow-green palm fronds rustled against their balcony in the tropical breeze, the demons came. As Patrick screamed and thrashed and cried out in his sleep, Jan didn't know how to help him. She tried to make out what he was saying, but his words were stifled by the mouth guard he still wore to keep from grinding his teeth. In the end, all she could do was hold him the way a mother comforts a nightmare-drenched child.

"The nights were bad, the same dream all the time," Kelly later said. "The run from the kitchen, the try, the falling, the finding, the confusion, the hurt. God the dreams were shitty. Helpless. The most vivid part is the inability to hold on and the falling forward – knowing she was gone."

A few days after their arrival, Bradley had had enough of the commercial overkill of Honolulu and suggested they would be more comfortable in a quieter place. After the chance meeting with Sheree Brown, Kelly was just as happy to leave the Hawaiian Regency and fly to Molokai. Three days later, they were in the air again on the way to Maui, where they stayed at the Kanapaali Beach Hotel, a famous playground for couples and honeymooners. There Bradley noticed a lone man who stood out from the other guests; every time she looked up, he seemed to be watching. Uneasy with the ubiquitous stranger she believed was a police officer, Bradley persuaded Kelly to return to Molokai, where they spent the last three weeks of their vacation in glorious privacy. "I wanted him to myself, so we booked out and stayed the rest of the month in Molokai. . . . It was a refuge from the world."

After a week on Molokai, Kelly began to feel better. During the day, the lovers talked and read, sunbathed, played tennis, and walked the empty beaches. One night they went dancing and talked about getting married in France. Kelly also wrote a few letters, including one to the proprietor of Hullaballoon, Brenda Rodine.

"Brenda,

Well even after only a few days away I feel much better. The headaches are gone and my stomach is keeping things down. The evenings are rough. (Too much time to think.) The nights are terrible still – I keep seeing the same things and having the same dreams – I hope they stop soon. I'm trying to fill the time by swimming and playing tennis. I'm dining out a lot and have even managed to talk to a few ladies, but it doesn't somehow seem right and doesn't take long before I must leave. Even here I'm running into people who know! I'm not taking any medication but if I can't stop the hard nights, I might try them for awhile again . . . I love you dearly and hope that soon we can be together again to laugh and play as before – Your Friend, Pat"

In the blistering afternoons, while Bradley read or dozed in the cool of their room, Kelly made long distance telephone calls to business partners and various lawyers. Dennis Morris told him about a letter from Jimmy Hanlon asking for Kelly's assistance in recovering $15,000 in cash that Hanlon had given Jeannette to deposit for him in a Canadian bank. Morris felt sorry for the shattered, old man and Kelly promised to pay him back when Jeannette's estate was finally settled.

During one of the calls, Kelly found out that the homicide detectives knew that he had gone on vacation with Jan Bradley. He was "very quiet" after getting off the telephone and explained to Jan that he wouldn't be returning to Toronto with her after all. Instead, he would now be going to Victoria for business meetings with his West Coast lawyer, Victor Simpson. The police might put pressure on her when she got back to Toronto, but that was to be expected, and she wasn't to let them rattle her.

Although Kelly's nights were still restless, by holiday's end the nightmares had ceased. In his new dream, he saw himself slipping out of bed before dawn and walking across the cool sand until he found a path that led up from the beach through a stand of palm trees. He followed it for miles, floating above the tobacco-brown earth, until the path opened onto a lagoon where the water was dark and calm and the trees shimmered in a soothing, hypnotic dance. A familiar face called to him from the golden sand.

"Jeannette was there, she was real and soft and warm," Patrick remembered. "We made love on the beach and talked and walked hand in hand. The beach was real but Jeannette was not – she'd been gone for a long time now, years, no months, no, it's only been days. SHIT – am I losing it? How could she be so real? . . . How could the touching, the holding, the love have been so real? As she walked away, she said, 'It's okay – I know you tried.'"

Tanned and beautiful, Jan Bradley arrived back in Toronto on the afternoon of May 6, 1981, bursting to share her news: she and Patrick were going to be married in France, maybe as early as July. After dropping her bags at her apartment, she drove over to the Davidsons, intending to invite them to Europe for her wedding. But when the nervous couple opened their front door, they greeted her with more urgent news of their own.

A few days after she had left for Hawaii with Patrick, detectives Hill and Stewart had paid an official visit to the Davidsons, wanting to speak to Jan Bradley. They had already talked to Carol Silverberg at the library and were "furious" that Bradley had left the country with Kelly. The police told the Davidsons that they had reason to believe that Kelly had murdered his wife and that Jan's life might also be in danger. The unsettling news reminded Jan of the question Patrick had asked her again and again when they were away together: "If it were you, Jan, I wonder if I could have held on to you and not let you fall."

When Jill began recounting what the police had said, Jan abruptly brought her finger to her lips and motioned her friend outside. Sitting on the Davidsons' front steps, she explained to Jill that Patrick had told her that their house and telephone had been bugged for two years as part of the same RCMP undercover drug operation during which he had first seen Jan.

Brushing Kelly's story off as "silly," Jill returned to what the detectives had told her, including the fact that Jeannette had been Kelly's real wife, not a piece of RCMP window-dressing. The detectives had even considered talking to Jan's mother, Ruth Bradley, but decided it might be too upsetting for her to find out that her daughter had gone abroad with a suspected wife-killer.

To Jill's surprise, Jan said that she had known that Patrick was married, but that the relationship had been strictly platonic for some time before the tragedy. She explained that Jeannette's death had been "a terrible, unfortunate accident" that gave Patrick nightmares, despite the fact that he had done his best to save her. As for the fact that Patrick was being investigated by the police, he himself had told Jan about that before they went away on vacation. As she listened to Jan's stout defence of Patrick, Jill realized that everything she had told her had run into a solid, emotional wall that wouldn't soon be breached by allegations from homicide detectives or mere friends. "I think she was really in love with him and desperately wanted to believe him and not us," Jill recalled.

After a few moments, their conversation was interrupted by the telephone. Roger Davidson covered the receiver and whispered that it was the police. They wanted to talk to Jan and offered to meet her at the Scarborough Detachment, just around the corner from the Davidsons, to save her the trip downtown. Jan shook her head and Roger made an excuse. After talking things over, Jan and the Davidsons decided that they would all speak to the detectives in two days' time. Roger called the station at 11:30 P.M. that night and arranged to meet detectives Stewart and Hill at 43 Division in Scarborough on the afternoon of May 8.

Sergeant Stewart was looking forward to the interview. Ever since he learned that Patrick Kelly was not on American Airlines flight 50 from Los Angeles with Jan Bradley, but had flown instead to Vancouver, the detective had concluded that Kelly would never voluntarily return to Toronto. And that, as his chief suspect undoubtedly knew, would make the detective work a lot more difficult – unless the young woman who had accompanied Kelly to Hawaii could supply him and Hill with a reason to make an arrest.

During Kelly's absence in Hawaii, the two detectives had been quietly building a more complete picture of the man with whom they were playing a high-stakes game of cat and mouse. Both Paul Stewart and Brenda Rodine had provided copies of the letters Kelly had written them, which if nothing else, revealed his manipulative and deceitful side. Insp. Will Stefureak supplied more details of the suspect's shady RCMP career, and through Dawn Taber and Jeannette's medical records, they learned even more about the true state of the Kelly marriage. They even arranged for Marcello Rodocanachi to fly in from Italy to confirm that he and Jeannette had been seeing each other for several months prior to her death, though the married man played down the intensity of the relationship in his police statement. Everything the detectives had learned about the Kellys' marriage was at odds with the loving relationship Patrick had painted for them during his lengthy interview.

But the detail that stuck out in Stewart's mind was one he had learned when he and his partner had revisited the Palace Pier while the "Bradleys" were vacationing in Hawaii. First, the detectives had visited

John and Karen Kennedy, the owners of apartment 1805, whose balcony had allegedly produced the rattle that Kelly claimed led to Jeannette's death. The couple told Stewart and Hill that they had not heard a rattle, or any other noise on their balcony, since they had moved into the apartment in February.

The detectives next visited the precise spot where Jeannette's body had hit the cement on March 29. They noted that a small canopy protruded from the building, covering a portion of the loading dock. Hill climbed a ladder to measure how far it was from the railing of one of the building's balconies to the edge of the canopy – a distance, it turned out, of six feet, five inches. Since Jeannette had apparently landed without first striking the canopy, Hill's measurement carried a grim implication: her body had apparently been projected six and a half feet out from the balcony of apartment 1705 before it had started to fall.

Stewart realized that experts could argue endlessly about the physics involved, but the condition and resting place of the body, coupled with the distance that the canopy extended from the building, cast grave doubt on Kelly's story that his wife had tumbled directly over the balcony from the stool he claimed she had been standing on. But as the detective knew, there was only so far you could go with circumstantial evidence in a homicide investigation; to get a conviction for murder in the first degree, the Crown normally needed a witness, a co-conspirator, or direct physical evidence of an accused's guilt.

Since forensics had produced no damning physical evidence against the only suspect, and there was no witness to what the detectives believed had been a cold-blooded murder, Stewart was left with little to go on. Perhaps Jan Bradley could be persuaded to turn against Patrick Kelly. On May 8, as arranged, Bradley sat in the staff inspector's office at 43 Division with a tape recorder whirring, and related the history of her relationship with the ex-Mountie. Her account was detailed and truthful, and the detectives noted several inconsistencies, a few of them serious, between what Kelly had told his girlfriend and what he had said in his statement to police.

Bradley described how her slowly developing friendship with Kelly had taken a romantic turn in the fall of 1980. She told them that her lover had concealed his true identity from her until their tryst at the Briars, and said that she hadn't known that he was married until she spent a weekend with him at the Palace Pier just two weeks before the accident. During that weekend, Kelly had talked about getting married sometime that summer, a revelation that Stewart carefully recorded in his notebook: the laws may have changed, the detective thought, but nobody could get a divorce that quickly.

In certain difficult homicides, detectives occasionally furnish information to a potentially important witness to enlist their help in solving the crime. Hoping to persuade Bradley to visit Kelly again, this time wearing a wire, Stewart and Hill told her that the man she had fallen in love with must have been selling drugs in order to support the Porsche, the luxury apartment, and the jet-setter lifestyle. When Jan protested that he had several legitimate business interests in Canada and abroad, the detectives reminded her that Kelly's affluence had shown up while he was still an RCMP undercover agent and that police officers weren't allowed to have outside business interests.

They raised the matter of his strange relationship with Paul Stewart, a man whom the detectives were sure was a homosexual and a fraud, and told her that the RCMP believed that Kelly had burned down his Cookstown home to collect the insurance money. And did Bradley realize that she wasn't the only other woman in Kelly's life? They told her about Kelly's affair with Dawn Taber and the call she had received from Kelly on the day he left for Hawaii. The detectives left the impression with Bradley that Taber "thought she was going to Mexico with him and she was going to meet him at the airport." Angry about the betrayal, it had been Taber who called police and tipped them off that Kelly was on his way out of the country.

Although Bradley was "freaked out," as she put it, by the possibility that her fiance was a murderer, a drug dealer, and a bisexual two-timer rather than a wealthy and brilliant businessman, she tried not to show it. Nor did she reveal the stab of fear she felt when the detectives told her that the only reason she hadn't been picked up in Los Angeles by the FBI was that Canadian authorities weren't prepared to lay murder charges at that point.

As hard as the detectives tried to turn the librarian against her lover, and impress upon her the seriousness of the situation she found herself in, Bradley was not about to give up on the man she hoped to marry. She refused to spy on Kelly for the police. Stewart and Hill were visibly annoyed. "They were rolling their eyes a lot during my interview, as if to say, 'Boy, is this broad dumb,'" Bradley remembered.

When the interview was over, Bradley promised to keep in touch with the detectives and then left with the Davidsons. Upset by what the police had told her, and angry that her friends had been innocently drawn into a murder investigation, she called Kelly and demanded that he come back to Toronto to answer her many questions and to rescue her. "I said to him, 'I love you, but you are leaving me in front of the firing squad alone.'"

Shortly after the interview with Bradley, Stewart set the wheels in motion to intercept the uncooperative woman's private communications, as well as those of Paul Stewart and Patrick Kelly.

Victor Simpson was the first person Patrick Kelly met when he returned from Hawaii on May 6, 1981. He rode the airport bus into Victoria and joined Simpson in a coffee shop across the street from the courthouse where the young lawyer had just finished trying a case. It was their first meeting since Jeannette's death, and Kelly explained in detail how the accident had happened. Sergeant Stewart would have found his description very interesting.

"He told me that she was . . . watering plants on the balcony and was standing on a stool and fell over and yelled and he had run to her and tried to grab her," Simpson recalls.

Simpson had never seen Kelly cry before and was overcome with pity for his grieving friend, whose shoulders shook as he spoke of his wife's death. Composing himself, Kelly then asked Simpson to tell his wife and parents how Jeannette had died, since Kelly himself was still too upset to talk about it. Simpson wanted to raise the issue of the mortgage security for the $40,000 loan from the estate of Mina McIntosh that Patrick had still not provided, but after Patrick's display of grief decided that it wasn't the appropriate time to discuss business – particularly after Patrick showed him the probate papers from Jeannette's will. With more than $250,000 coming in from her life insurance policies, security for the short-term loan was a mere technicality.

When Simpson learned that Kelly had taken a woman with him on his month-long trip to Hawaii and that the police knew about it, he was dismayed. Despite Kelly's assurance that she had only been there to help him through his grief, Simpson thought that the authorities might easily draw a different conclusion and advised him not to follow her to Toronto. In fact, he thought it would be best for all concerned if Kelly simply put an end to the ill-timed and, if the matter ever got to court, potentially compromising relationship.

"Any involvement with her would only look suspicious in the eyes of the police and in the eyes of the general public. . . . It was unfortunate that he went away with her. . . . It was a bad choice for him to make. It was in bad taste. But it was something he wasn't hiding."

Kelly took his friend's advice and stayed in Victoria, but he pursued his liaison with Bradley in daily telephone calls made from the office he kept at Simpson's law firm. Furious and upset, Bradley repeatedly begged him to return to Toronto to help her through her ongoing ordeal with the detectives, who never missed a chance to tell her that they were investigating Jeannette Kelly's "murder." The pressure had become so intense that she had been forced to take a leave of absence from work and couldn't eat or sleep. She needed Patrick by her side, and she wanted answers to some of the things the police had confronted her with about her fiancé's mysterious past.

Kelly replied that he was experiencing "severe chest pains" and was unable to travel because of medication prescribed for him by Dr. Michael Greenwood, the doctor who was, in fact, treating him for bad nerves and muscle spasms. Besides, he said, the homicide investigators were "big boys with big budgets"; if they wanted to interview him, all they had to do was catch a flight to Vancouver. As for Bradley, he told her that the police were only using her to get to him, as he had predicted they would, and that if she had any questions, she was more than welcome to visit him in Victoria and ask them. But under no circumstances would he be returning to Toronto.

The memories were just too painful.

On May 15, at 3:30 P.M., Sgt. Ed Stewart called Const. Bill Noseworthy, a member of the Special Squad at Pearson airport, and asked him to confirm that Jan Bradley had taken a 3 P.M. Air Canada flight to Vancouver. A friend of Bradley's had called Stewart and told him that he had given her the money for the trip so that she could confront Kelly with his many lies and get out of the destructive relationship before it was too late. The same friend had even called ahead to Bradley's brother, a commercial fishermen who lived in Pemberton, British Columbia, and instructed him to follow his sister and protect her during her meeting with Kelly.

Noseworthy confirmed that Bradley was on the Air Canada flight, which had been delayed until 4 P.M. He then made his way to gate 79 in Terminal 2 to observe the passengers as they boarded the aircraft. He and his partner located Bradley standing by herself at the gate and photographed her as she boarded the jet at 4:05 P.M. Sergeant Stewart then phoned Vancouver to request that the Special Squad at the airport meet her plane and photograph anyone who picked her up.

Kelly did not meet the flight, and Bradley travelled on to Whistler, where she joined her brother. After spending a few days together, the Bradleys drove to Stanley Park in Vancouver, where they met Kelly, who had flown in from Victoria. With James Bradley trailing the couple just out of earshot, Jan confronted Patrick with the allegations made against him by the police.

As they walked the park's paths, surrounded by mountain vistas, towering trees, and the serene waters of English Bay, he again told her that certain elements in the police force were out to get him because of things he had learned about them as an RCMP undercover agent. If she would only accompany him to Victoria, he would prove that everything he had told her about himself was true, including the fact that he made his money by seeking investment opportunities for a legitimate, Victoria-based firm owned by a wealthy lawyer. Kelly was able to persuade at least one of the Bradleys to trust him. After Patrick lent Jan's brother $2,500 in cash, James Bradley returned home and allowed his sister to proceed to Victoria in the company of the man he had been warned might be a killer.

Kelly and Jan stayed at the Empress Hotel, with its magnificent tea room and stunning view of the B.C. legislature and Victoria Harbour. Kelly introduced her to his mother and then escorted her to Victor Simpson's law office, where his friend confirmed that Kelly was, in fact, in charge of investments for K&V Enterprises, and had a considerable personal net worth.

Bradley didn't particularly care for either Kay or Victor Simpson (the feeling was mutual) and confronted Kelly with bitter allegations in their presence. She eventually calmed down and began to believe in him again, especially when she found out that he intended to set up a trust fund for Jimmy Hanlon with Jeannette's insurance moneys. It was not all that much, he explained, "only" $250,000, yet if properly handled, could make a big difference to the broken man's life.

By the time she returned to Toronto, protected from further police harassment by the lawyer Kelly had hired for her on Simpson's advice, Bradley was back in her lover's corner. Once again, she seriously considered marrying him and moving to the south of France, snubbing friends who persisted in questioning his character.

With his love life straightened out, Kelly turned to other more pressing matters. Increasingly preoccupied with the prospect of being charged with his wife's murder, he sent a $1,500 retainer to his former criminal counsel, Austin Cooper, to represent him "should some unforeseen action be taken" by the Metropolitan Toronto Police. He also informed Cooper that he had decided not to come back to Toronto and had given instructions to another lawyer to either rent or sell his apartment at the Palace Pier and ship his clothes, dog, and Porsche to Vancouver.

It was a decision, Kelly explained, that was prompted by "unpleasant memories" of Toronto and one that was heartily supported by his doctor, friends, and family in British Columbia. In fact, he was now contemplating a permanent move to the United States or France in the near future. Since he was still entitled to several months of discount flying with CP Air because of Jeannette's previous employment, he would be travelling extensively in the South Pacific, South America, and Europe for the next several months – a fact that Cooper might want to pass on to the police.

Disturbed by reports from Bradley and others that homicide detectives had been openly accusing him of arson, theft, insurance fraud, drug trafficking, adultery, and murder, Kelly also wanted advice from Cooper on the legal remedies available to him. He told Cooper he realized that the detectives had every right to inquire into the circumstances of Jeannette's death, but that police smear campaigns violated proper procedure and were beginning to hurt him in his personal and professional life. "I am getting very annoyed and I wonder at what point do I take some form of formal action, whether it be a simple letter through your

office advising the police of my annoyance at their investigative procedures, or other formal legal action re: liable [*sic*] and slander?"

The seasoned lawyer's reply was frank: Suing the police was not a
good idea. As for Kelly's travel plans, they would do little to improve his
image with the homicide squad. "As our office has previously indicated
to you, your absence from the country may be misconstrued by the
police authorities who are investigating your wife's death. I feel an
obligation to reiterate this advice to you, although, of course, based
upon what you have told me, you have nothing to hide and have
attempted to be fully co-operative with the authorities."

As the summer of 1981 approached, the detectives of the homicide
squad weren't the only people who were getting on Kelly's nerves. Since
coming to Victoria, he had already personally contacted London Life to
find out the exact amount of Jeannette's life insurance, to check on
whether any of her three policies had double indemnity or accident
provisions, and to confirm that interest was payable on the amounts
owing to him from the date that his claim was submitted. After ten
weeks, he was tired of waiting for his money and wanted Dennis Morris
to do something about it, just as he had when the insurance companies
had been reluctant to settle after the Cookstown fire.

"The simple fact that a) interest will be paid from the time of the
claims; b) the police are conducting an investigation (should that be
the case); or c) that they (the insurance company) may be conducting
an investigation – does not concern me. I am now trying to start a new
life, and I want all matters cleared up ASAP – not at the convenience of
an insurance company," he wrote to Morris.

Kelly instructed the lawyer to contact London Life on a weekly basis
to ask when the moneys would be paid. Since he didn't want any delays,
Morris should use couriers rather than the mail. He left no doubt about
what he wanted done if payment was held up for any reason.

"Should you encounter any flack [*sic*], please institute whatever legal
proceedings are necessary. I had a budding business starting in Toronto,
and any possible future income from it is now not applicable. I have bills
as well as Mr. Hanlon to look after . . . I want to finish with this matter
now!!! . . . I am certainly not now (especially with not having Jeannette's
support) prepared to put up with, or take, any flack [*sic*]."

He also instructed Morris to go after the insurance agency that held Jeannette's company policy, telling him to use the employees' union representative to increase the pressure if he met with any resistance. He needed funds to rebuild his life, particularly now that he had just invested $50,000 in a luxury yacht that would soon be placing this advertisement in a Canadian magazine called *The Antiques and Travellers Journal*:

"Cruise the beautiful Caribbean, skin dive in the crystal waters at Cozumel amongst the wrecks of adventurers from ages past . . . Six generations of Navy experience have gone into outfitting this magnificent motor yacht which is now at your disposal . . . Carefully planned to meet every whim, fulfil every promise, follow your dream. Call Commander Paul Stewart."

A set of antique china was apparently not enough to express Kelly's appreciation for the timely assistance of the mortician turned sea captain.

Kay Simpson was relieved when Patrick Kelly finally moved out of her house towards the end of July 1981 to take an apartment of his own – an entire floor of a posh home on Beach Drive for $1,400 a month. It wasn't that she didn't feel sorry for him. She and Victor had often talked the night away with Kelly after he woke up screaming in the spare bedroom they had prepared for him after he arrived in Victoria from Hawaii. It was obvious that Jeannette's death was something he could barely endure. His appetite was poor, he drank Neo-Citran to get to sleep at night, and he would often break into tears when something reminded him of his dead wife.

But despite her compassion for her husband's best friend, Kay neither liked nor trusted Kelly. She hadn't approved of Victor lending Patrick $40,000 from one of his client's trust funds, and another $20,000 from the same source a few months later, nor had she liked the idea of mortgaging their home to invest in a Toronto restaurant with Kelly, especially after the first cheques due on the loan came back NSF. She thought that Patrick was commanding too much of her husband's valuable time with business ventures that seemed to her at best unfeasible, at worst, shady.

The Kenyan gold deal was a case in point. Using a Kenyan doctor as a contact, Kelly and Simpson planned to apply to the Kenyan government for a permit to export eight hundred ounces of gold, which they would carry to London or Zurich and sell at a 30 per cent profit. In addition to sharing in the mark up, Simpson expected to get substantial fees from doing the legal work for the deal. He would also travel to Kenya with Kelly to help carry the gold bullion to Europe and the money back to Canada.

Although the Trade Commission in Ottawa had still not confirmed that the venture was legal, Simpson put his passport in order, converted his expense money into U.S. funds, got all the necessary shots, and even arranged for another lawyer to look after his practice so that he could make the trip. But the day before he and Kelly were to depart, tragedy struck. A telegram arrived at Simpson's law office bearing the news that Wayne Humby, Patrick's closest friend and former roommate in the RCMP, had just been killed in a car accident along with his wife, orphaning the couple's two young children. The sender of the telegram advised that the news should be broken to Kelly gently, since he had recently lost his wife in a terrible accident.

Simpson did his best to treat his friend tenderly, but Kelly was inconsolable at word of Humby's death, weeping, swearing, and grinding his teeth. In fact, to Simpson he seemed more distraught than he'd been when he first related the circumstances of Jeannette's death. Given this latest catastrophe, the two men agreed that the Kenyan trip would have to be put on hold until Kelly had a chance to come to terms with this latest cruel blow. By coincidence, Kelly would now be able to pick up Jan Bradley at the airport when she arrived the next day.

And that was what bothered Kay Simpson most: the contradiction between the grief-stricken husband and friend and the insensitive playboy and lover, who had taken another woman on holidays just a few days after his wife's death. In the circumstances, it just wasn't right for Kelly to be involved with anyone right now, and as Kay Simpson knew, his lover from Toronto wasn't the only one.

Leslie Holmes wondered who had sent the dozen red roses until she read the unsigned card tucked inside the box. "From me. You still look great." The day before, Holmes had been standing at an intersection on

Douglas Street waiting for the light to change on her way to do some banking when she heard a man say, "You look great." The former flight attendant of Trans Australian Airlines looked up at the slender, dark-haired stranger and found herself nervously thanking him for the compliment – a reaction that her tutors at the private girls' school she had attended in Bournemouth, England, would never have condoned. A few moments later, she saw him again in the bank, where he repeated the same compliment: "You sure look great."

That afternoon, someone left a single red rose with the manageress of Tweedy Clothes, where Holmes worked as a salesperson. The next day, the dozen roses arrived, and the day after that, a dozen more, accompanied by a note asking her for coffee, drinks, dinner, or a weekend in San Francisco. After conferring with her boss, who thought Holmes's secret admirer must be a responsible sort of person with a sense of playfulness, she agreed to meet him for drinks. The stranger took her to the Delta Hotel, and then to dinner. He told her that he liked her Scottish accent and behaved like a perfect gentleman. "He walked me to the door and didn't even kiss me goodnight," she said of her first date with Patrick Kelly.

As the relationship developed, Holmes found herself intrigued by the mysterious stranger who had entered her life so romantically. And he was very generous. Although he barely knew her, Kelly offered her the use of his Porsche and his luxury apartment while he was away on business and even said he would deposit a few thousand dollars in a bank account for her if she agreed to go on holidays with him. Kelly told her about his life as a secret agent with the RCMP and said that someone associated with the Black Donnellys had burned down his house as a reprisal for his successful undercover work.

When Holmes asked him about his personal life, Kelly explained that his wife had recently died, and that Holmes was the only person he had been able to relate to since the accident. When she asked for more details, Kelly told her that Jeannette had fallen off a stool trying to fix a noise on their balcony. "He heard either a scream or a scream afterwards. . . . He was not near her when she fell," Holmes later said.

Hanna Kirkham didn't quite know what to do when the dozen red roses arrived. The self-employed interior designer was even more disconcerted when the original delivery was followed by two more. But she decided to go out with their sender when a friend told her that Patrick Kelly had lost his wife in a dreadful accident. Barbara Wilburn, Kelly's land-lady in Victoria, must have known that the information would strike a deeply personal chord. A few years earlier, Kirkham's husband had been killed in a car accident and she had had a terrible time coming to grips with his loss. Wilburn was worried about her lonely friend and was delighted when Kirkham and Kelly began playing racquetball together and going out to dinner.

Despite the tragedies they had in common, Kirkham was wary; there was something about Kelly that she found "a little too smooth." But after meeting his sister, Candi, who clearly idolized Kelly, she decided that he couldn't be "all that bad." They continued to date, and Kelly told her that he owned a villa in France and a pasta restaurant in Toronto. During one of their tête-à-têtes, he said that his wife had been killed in a domestic accident. Kirkham wanted to know more and asked him exactly how the former Mrs. Kelly had died. Kelly told her that he had not actually been there when it happened, and only found out that Jeannette had fallen from their seventeenth-storey balcony when he drove up to their apartment building and saw the ambulance that had come to take her away. In recounting the story, Kelly exhibited no signs of grief, and Kirkham was left with the impression that the accident had happened a long time ago.

When Tracey Charlish received the expensive sweater from Tweedy Clothes, it reinforced her impression that Patrick Kelly was a wealthy and generous man. When the flowers started coming, Charlish realized he was interested in her. She had first met him at the bank on Douglas Street where she worked, when he came in wearing an expensive suit and asking for the rate on a $250,000 term deposit. When she gave him the information, he told her that he could do better with a private place-ment, but asked if she would like to have lunch. Charlish agreed, and they continued to see one another for dinner, bike rides, and drinks, even attending a Nylons concert together.

One evening over dinner, Charlish asked Kelly what he did for a living. He said that he owned an interior design company and a restau-rant in Montreal, although most of his time was taken up with rescuing failing businesses. Before that, he had been an undercover agent in the RCMP. To demonstrate his acting ability, which he told her had been an indispensable tool in his police work, he placed his hand over his smiling face; when he removed it, Charlish shuddered – the smile was gone and Kelly's expression had turned to "stone."

The couple dated frequently, often dining at Kelly's apartment. Although he never said as much, Charlish had the feeling that their relationship was headed towards marriage, even though she had rebuffed his physical advances. He told her that he had been married once, but that his wife had died in a domestic accident. Charlish never asked for details, and Kelly never volunteered any.

One day in the late summer of 1981, Charlish had encountered Kelly on the street looking pale and drawn. Over coffee, he explained to her that he had just received a telegram informing him that a very dear friend and his wife had been killed in a traffic accident. Fortunately for their two young children, there was an uncle who was willing to take them in. Although he loved his friend dearly, Kelly himself would not be going to the funeral because his doctor had advised him that he couldn't handle the emotional stress.

Charlish felt so sorry for him that she bought a sympathy card later that day and decided to deliver it personally to Kelly's apartment that night. Looking anything but grief-stricken, he came to the door in his housecoat, holding a glass of wine, and invited her in to meet a friend he had just picked up at the airport. To Charlish's surprise, there was a woman curled up on the chesterfield wearing a housecoat.

"Tracey, I'd like you to meet Jan Bradley."

All through the spring and summer of 1981, Joanne MacLean, Abby Latter, Judy Seres, and Dawn Taber stayed in touch, trying to help one another come to terms with Jeannette Kelly's horrifying death. From their first private dinner, held in a Front Street restaurant on April 6, 1981, the other women felt that there was something strange about Dawn. Abby could barely recognize the girl sitting across the table from her as the same person she had known through the Kellys.

During the dinner, she found Dawn unresponsive and "very uncomfortable," as if she was "playing a role" rather than being herself. Try as she might, Abby couldn't get her to elaborate on her previous story about Patrick beating Jeannette prior to the accident. Behind Dawn's curious evasiveness, Abby sensed that she was deeply troubled, and not just by the nagging suspicion they all had that Jeannette had been murdered by her husband. "It was almost like she was wanting to tell us something . . . and that she wasn't telling us the truth."

However taciturn she may have been with Abby, Dawn was considerably more forthcoming with another of the dinner guests. Joanne MacLean was shocked when Dawn leaned over and whispered to her under cover of the general conversation that she had talked to Patrick since Jeannette's death and that he was leaving the country and would soon be sending for her. Given the nature of the gathering, Dawn asked Joanne not to tell the others. "So here I have the confirmation of the relationship between Pat and Dawn. [It] sort of hit me in the face, but I wasn't allowed to show it at the table."

Although Dawn skipped the group's next dinner and dropped out of sight for almost a week, she spent a lot of time with Joanne that summer, much of it talking about the momentous event that seemed to eclipse everything else. Her conversation was a filigree of obfuscations, contradictions, and surprising admissions that left Joanne wondering what Dawn really knew about Jeannette's death. Dawn told Joanne that Patrick hadn't been such "hot stuff" in bed, and that sex hadn't been the motivating factor in their relationship. She also told her about a disturbing conversation she and Patrick had held on the dog run behind the Palace Pier. Sitting on the grass and looking up at the apartment building, they had wondered what it would be like to fall from one of the upper floors, and in particular, whether a person would die of a heart attack on the way down, or still be conscious when they hit the ground.

The story chilled Joanne, but the thing she found hardest to understand that summer was Dawn's ambivalence towards the man they both believed was a murderer. "Although Dawn believed that Pat had done it, she did not condemn him for this, but had a great deal of compassion for him and was constantly concerned with his feelings . . . I could never be a hundred per cent sure, but she gave me the impression that she could be in touch with Pat," Joanne remembered.

Even Dawn's tempestuous relationship with John Nascimento, which ended early that July when she permanently returned to the United

States, seemed blighted by Jeannette's death. Dawn would often show up in a taxi with her clothes and dog and stay with the MacLeans for a few days because of Nascimento's alleged brutalities. Given the horror stories she told about beatings and bondage, Joanne began to wonder if her tales were either blown out of proportion or downright false; after all, Dawn kept returning to her tormentor. When Joanne pressed her for the root of the problem with Nascimento, she found herself once again in a conversation about the events of March 29. "His problem was that he accused Dawn of being in cahoots with Pat on this murder, and he was on her about that all the way along," Joanne said.

Like Joanne MacLean, Sgt. Ed Stewart was of two minds about Dawn Taber; either she was more involved with Kelly than anyone realized, as Abby Latter had frequently told him, or her story about running away with Kelly to the south of France after faking his death was the fanciful product of an ex-lover's vindictive imagination. Either way, she was a difficult subject to read. On the one hand, she seemed anxious to co-operate in the investigation, contacting the police several times that summer with information about Kelly; on the other, she was almost protective of him, refusing to commit what she knew about the case to a signed statement. It was as if she was being pulled in different directions at the same time by equally powerful forces.

By late August, because the wiretaps had provided no firm evidence against Kelly, and the insurance companies were ready to settle if the police failed to lay a charge, the detectives started to play long shots. On Tuesday, August 24, Stewart and Hill interviewed John Nascimento about his relationship with the woman he had lived with for five stormy months, until she moved back to the United States. Nascimento explained that when he first started dating Taber in October 1980, she had told him that she was still seeing Patrick Kelly. Kelly, in fact, visited the couple five or six times at their Sherbourne Street apartment, and Taber and Nascimento had been invited to the Palace Pier once for drinks with Patrick and Jeannette.

Then, in the spring of 1981, Nascimento had gone to apartment 1705 on his own to retrieve a key to Taber's Mississauga apartment from Jeannette Kelly. They shared a glass of wine, and during their hour-long conversation, Nascimento asked if she knew that her husband had had an affair with Dawn. "At this time, Jeannette told me that she had come home and caught Dawn and Pat in bed. I believe this date to be November of 1980," he told the detectives.

If true, it raised some interesting possibilities. Taber had already told police that her relationship with the Kellys had come to an end in November 1980 over the $4,000 she had borrowed for the trip to Europe. But if money had indeed been the cause of the rift between the former best friends, why would Jeannette cut Taber off at the very time she repaid the debt? Had Jeannette's dismissiveness, as Nascimento claimed, been the cold fury of a wife who had caught her best friend in bed with her husband? If that was true, then the romantic liaison between Taber and Kelly had gone on for much longer than Taber had led police to believe. Why would she lie about that?

To the detectives' surprise, Nascimento confirmed Taber's story that she and Kelly had planned to run off to France using new identities, and that Kelly had wanted to increase the insurance on his wife and forge her signature on the application. Nascimento claimed that she had told him that Kelly was supposed to get her a false passport and driver's licence when Dawn and Jeannette were away in Europe. But why, the detectives wondered, would a woman living with one man tell him about her secret plans to run off with someone else?

Nascimento was also able to shed some light on what he believed were Taber's real feelings about the police effort to prove that Kelly had murdered his wife. He said that she told him that if the detectives ever asked her to talk to Kelly wearing a body-pack, she would take it off before meeting him. Reminding the detectives that one of them had called Kelly "a smart cookie" during a conversation with Taber and Nascimento early in the investigation, he now gave them the delayed punch line. "After you left, Dawn said to me that he, Pat, was smarter than you sons of bitches."

When Stewart brought the conversation around to the events of March 29, Nascimento told the detectives that Taber had been at home and in good spirits when he returned from delivering flyers for his construction business. The next day, when they learned about the accident, Taber had once again acted like a person being pulled in two directions at once, mumbling that Kelly had done it, and later telling Nascimento that Jeannette had fallen off the balcony while watering plants. Since such a version of the accident had never been reported in the media, where had the false detail come from?

After mulling over Nascimento's provocative interview, the detectives returned three days later to "clarify" certain points. He repeated Taber's story that her friend had fallen over the balcony while watering plants, and claimed that she'd also told him that the Kellys had been quarrelling on the day of Jeannette's death. This new detail left the detectives wondering where the truth ended and fiction began. If, as Taber claimed, she hadn't seen the Kellys since November 4, how could she know that they had been fighting on March 29, 1981? Then Nascimento added another detail that raised even more sinister possibilities; he claimed that Taber had also told him that "the best way to cover up marks from a fight was to toss her over the balcony."

Just as Joanne MacLean suspected that Taber was in contact with Kelly from the nuggets of information she dropped in their conversations about the case, the detectives began to wonder the same thing. Did Taber somehow know that Kelly had beaten his wife and then thrown her off the balcony to cover up the marks from the assault?

When they asked Nascimento if Taber and Kelly had ever communicated since Jeannette's death, he told them that he had been present on two occasions when they had: the day that Kelly called Taber on his way out of the country, which the police knew about, and again when Taber called Kelly from the United States while Nascimento was helping her move back to Maine. "I heard her tell him she was back in the States. She said if Pat comes to her, she would go back to him. We had a fight and I came home."

To back up what he told them, Nascimento handed Stewart a telephone bill showing two other calls to Kelly that had been made that summer from their apartment. As they headed out the door, Nascimento stopped the detectives and gave them a final piece of information. Shortly before she left for the United States, Taber and a friend had visited Jeannette's grave. That night she had had a nightmare and Nascimento heard her cry out, "Not over the balcony."

The detectives' quandary deepened. From what Nascimento had told them, Taber knew more about the events of March 29 than she had admitted to the police. From her anger when they had informed her that Kelly had left the country with another woman, they suspected a lingering romantic interest. But was she a conspirator, a jilted lover, or just a woman who had read too many Harlequin novels? It was all very interesting, but the seasoned homicide investigators didn't know how far they could trust Nascimento. After all, he himself was a spurned lover who may have an axe of his own to grind. And that wasn't all. When the detectives did a background check, they discovered that Taber's ex-lover had had some trouble of his own with the law. At the time of their interview with him, Nascimento was on probation for fraud.

Since the death of his daughter, Jimmy Hanlon's life had been a dark tunnel of heartbreaking memories and awful suspicions. Every time he passed a high-rise apartment building, he found himself counting up the storeys until he got to seventeen, and then saw his Jeannette "falling and being smashed like a doll on the concrete." Kelly never called either Hanlon or Lottie Arbuckle after they returned to Scotland, hardening their belief that their son-in-law was a murderer. One of Hanlon's nephews who lived in British Columbia even volunteered to go after Kelly with a 44 magnum "to shove it down his throat because he had killed Jeannette." Jimmy stopped him, telling the young man that Kelly was best left to the law.

In the meantime, Hanlon's disastrous financial situation left him no alternative but to appeal to Kelly's sense of fairness to return the $15,000 he had given his daughter to deposit for him in Canada. On June 28, 1981, he wrote to Kelly and asked him to wire the money to the same Glasgow bank that Hanlon had used to send the Kellys money in their hour of need. But even in the act of requesting repayment, Hanlon was impelled to write about the terrible loss of his daughter:

"Here in Scotland, it is worse than bad and I am in a very depressed state of mind. Sundays I nearly go mad. I have lost all will to do anything and I will never get over this. I only wish it had been me instead of her. I can't stop thinking about her. She was all I had left in this life."

When his letter was greeted with silence, Hanlon spent the rest of the summer and early autumn trying to contact Kelly by letter and telephone. After learning from Abby Latter that Kelly had sold the Palace Pier apartment in September, Hanlon called Victor Simpson's law office looking for his money. Simpson advised him that Kelly's address and phone number were private, and that he was not authorized to release them to anyone. He would, however, pass along Hanlon's request that Kelly contact him. The old man waited up half the night for the return call, but it never came.

A week later, though, Hanlon received a call from a distraught woman who, tipsy as she was, revealed details of his daughter's death that confirmed his worst suspicions about Kelly. In anger and frustration Hanlon once again wrote to his elusive son-in-law.

"This was some woman in Toronto who certainly knows you, and all about you, for sure. And she had a drink, for sure, but what she did not know about you is not worth talking about. And from her conversation regarding myself and Jeannette, it would appear I have met her, but no names would she give me. She went on to say that you were responsible for my daughter's death in no uncertain terms, and on the Sunday Jeannette died, she spoke to her, and Jeannette told her that she would phone her from the airport, *if she made it*. What did that mean? And that there was murder in the flat that Sunday morning, shouting and bawling.

"Also that Jeannette was leaving you over some woman that you were messing around with. This is the same one she told me that was with you in Hawaii and is now staying with you in Victoria. . . . She told me all about the house being set on fire at Cookstown. How much you got and how Jeannette was afraid for you in case you got caught. That is why you sent her over to Scotland during this time. And how much you got for the flat on the Lakeshore and how much you were awaiting the insurance money from Jeannette's policy and her firm, amounting to over $200,000. . . . Well, it's a story and a half, and I know for sure she was with some guy in a house, for he kept saying, 'no more,' and she kept saying, 'I'll tell all – should have long ago to the police anyway.' So what's it all about?"

Patrick Kelly finally broke his silence. After telling his father-in-law that he had not yet completed his financial dealings in Toronto, and therefore could not repay him, he turned his attention to Hanlon's anonymous female caller:

"I was rather distressed to hear of the phone call which you received from the unknown female. Unfortunately, I do not know who she might have been, but I do feel she is, perhaps, more than a little sick. After discussion with my friend and lawyer, Mr. Simpson, I was advised to tell you that if she should perhaps call again, you should advise her of my lawyer's name and address and she can contact him directly and we can deal with the matter in a proper fashion. Your other option, of course, is that you could just hang up, so as not to expose yourself to such gibberish, which is clearly and understandably upsetting you."

Just as she had been when she called Jimmy Hanlon, Dawn Taber had been drinking so heavily when she called Patrick Kelly about the newspaper reporter that she would later forget making the call. Bob Graham of the *Toronto Star*, the same reporter Kelly had once considered collaborating with on a book about the RCMP, had called her several times about Jeannette's death. After his calls, someone had smeared blood on the patio doors of the house where Taber was living in Maine. The intruder had also left a chilling note: "Happy Birthday. It might be your last one."

After hearing what Taber had to say about her relationship with Kelly in Toronto, her new boyfriend and future second husband, Victor Bragg, urged her to call Kelly in Victoria. The idea was to tell him that she was not co-operating with Graham in any way and "that he could go on with the rest of his life, and as long as he didn't bother me, I wasn't going to bother him."

The trouble was, Taber couldn't be certain that her nocturnal intruder hadn't been John Nascimento. Things had become so bad in their relationship by the summer of 1981 that Taber had called her mother, Starr Foster, and told her that the man she was living with had beaten and raped her. She wanted to come home, but Nascimento kept her under such tight scrutiny, Taber claimed she couldn't get away. Her mother suggested that she tell Nascimento that he could move to the United States with her, and then when he crossed the border, they would have him arrested if he wouldn't leave Taber alone.

After overhearing Taber on the telephone with Kelly after they reached Maine, Nascimento had quarrelled with her and returned to Canada on his own. Shortly afterwards, he had come back to Maine to claim the furniture he had helped Taber load into a Ryder truck when their plan had been to set up house together in the United States. When Taber refused to return the furniture, Nascimento went to Northwestern

Mutual, the life insurance company where she now worked, and told them about her involvement in Jeannette Kelly's death. But when he showed up at her sister's house telling the same story, the bitter relationship exploded in violence: "My sister and my brother are standing there and he is saying, 'You know your sister is a murderer?' I hit him. I hit him so hard there, I think I broke his teeth. He had a bloody mouth," Taber recalls.

Even though Nascimento eventually left, never to see her again, and nothing ever came of the macabre visit in which her life had been threatened, her past in Toronto was a nightmare from which Dawn Taber couldn't seem to awaken. She floated from job to job and just couldn't bring herself to do the things she knew she had to do.

"It just ate me up . . . I couldn't function. I couldn't be me. I just felt like I was a prisoner of what I knew and nobody would listen."

On the September afternoon that Dennis Morris wired a cheque from London Life for $210,250 to the Victoria law offices of Victor Simpson, Patrick Kelly ordered six red roses to be placed on his dead wife's grave. The money had come in just two days shy of what would have been their sixth wedding anniversary. He also paid Morris $19,000 for nearly five and a half months of priority treatment of his file, primarily for the almost daily dealings with the insurance companies and the sale of Kelly's Palace Pier apartment.

Morris explained to him that there hadn't been enough money in Jeannette's estate to pay her creditors, but that he was under no legal obligation to pay them unless that was his wish; it wasn't. The lawyer also pleaded with him to give Jimmy Hanlon a straight answer about whether he would be paid. Kelly promised to take care of the matter, but he never repaid the money to his father-in-law or set up the trust fund for him that he had mentioned to Jan Bradley. A month later, Confederation Life sent a cheque for $49,324.80 to Kelly representing his claim on Jeannette's policy with CP Air. Together with the proceeds of the apartment sale and the other insurance settlement, Kelly had $350,000 with which to start his new life.

In early November 1981, Jan Bradley packed all her worldly belongings and took them to the cargo depot of Air France for shipment to Nice.

On November 8, she flew alone to Dorval airport, where she met Patrick Kelly, who arrived within the hour from Victoria. The couple then drove to Mirabel airport, where they boarded an Air France flight to Paris, touching down at Charles de Gaulle airport at 9:30 A.M. on November 9.

Two hours later they were on a domestic flight to Nice, where they had arranged to meet a real estate agent, Jo Simon. Using La Perouse, an oceanfront hotel on the Nice boardwalk, as their base, the couple looked at twenty-one houses over the next ten days before they took possession of 6 Golf Residence de Valbonne, Opio. The rent for the four-bedroom, four-bathroom house was $2,200 a month, which included all furnishings, a pool, and a gardener to look after the three-and-a-half-acre grounds. At last Kelly was where he wanted to be – in a mountainside villa in the south of France a few kilometres from the dazzling Mediterranean.

When Sgt. Ed Stewart found out, he couldn't believe it. Dawn Taber had been telling the truth after all.

13

THE KELLYS OF VALBONNE

The Moulin de Mougins was the perfect finale to the elegant wedding at Holy Trinity Church on rue du Canada in Cannes. It was Jean-Claude "Baby Doc" Duvalier's favourite restaurant on the Côte d'Azur, and the deposed dictator with "the passion for the table" would have approved of the seven-course gourmet meal that master chef Roger Vergé had prepared for the wedding party, not to mention the two vintage wines and the Perriet Jouet "Belle Époque" for the champagne toast to the bride and groom.

As the sommelier poured Pichon Lalonde 1973 into his crystal wine glass, Victor Simpson considered asking exactly what Le Poupeton de Fleur de Courgette aux Truffles du Vaucluse was, but decided against it. He already felt sufficiently out of place in one of the great restaurants of the world without making it obvious to the waiter that he had no idea what he was about to eat. Sipping a little of his wife's Blanc de Blanc de Chardonnay, Simpson's head was soon pleasantly spinning from the latest of the fairy-tale events that swirled around his friend's second wedding day in two weeks.

Patrick Kelly had first married Jan Bradley in Victoria on May 7, 1982, a little over a year after the death of his first wife. Simpson and his office manager, Connie Jeffrey, had acted as the couple's witnesses. The purpose of the Victoria wedding had been to circumvent the exacting French law governing foreigners who want to marry in a religious ceremony, including the requirement that both parties produce the original birth certificates of their parents and grandparents. By presenting a civil marriage certificate from their country of origin, it was a relatively straightforward matter to remarry in a French church ceremony.

The wedding in Victoria had been as austere as the municipal office in which it took place. After leaving city hall, the wedding party spent the afternoon in the famous Butchart Gardens, gathering that evening for a reception in one of the Tudor-style private dining rooms of the Oak Bay Beach Hotel. The hotel provided a chicken dinner with the trimmings, the butter was presented in square, frozen pats in a dishwasher-proof crock, and the waitress who poured the Canadian champagne knew even less about wine than Simpson. It had been a comfortable family affair, attended by John and Winnifred Kelly, Bert and Pat Simpson, Patrick's sister, Candi, and Victor and Kay. The bride's family didn't attend, since they were planning a trip to France around Jan's "real" wedding in Cannes on May 22.

Although they did their best to make their new daughter-in-law welcome, the Kellys were not favourably impressed by Jan Bradley. Winnifred didn't like the way she constantly corrected Patrick's grammar, and John concluded that the bride's chief asset was her beauty. Neither parent had the feeling that Bradley loved their son; rather, both suspected that she was more interested in Patrick's money, and the chance to live in a villa in the south of France, than she was in him. Compared to the warm and spontaneous Jeannette, Jan came across as a condescending snob who made her working-class in-laws uncomfortable.

"It was like meeting Joan Collins," John remembers. "I thought she was a bitch. I'm sorry to say that, but I thought she was a bitch. Her attitude was that she was from the other side of the tracks. She was hoity-toity. She didn't fit in our family."

When Victor Simpson got off the plane in Cannes to find Kelly waiting for him in a pearl-grey Mercedes-Benz, it was his turn to feel uncomfortable. The opulence of his friend's lifestyle was reaching dizzying heights, and the lawyer knew better than anyone else just how much of it was being paid for these days by credit of one kind or another.

Kelly still had not paid a cent of interest or principal on the $60,000 he had borrowed from the Mina McIntosh trust fund that Simpson administered, even though the original four-month term had expired more than a year earlier. The deadline was also fast approaching for another $50,000 Simpson had arranged for him to borrow from a childhood friend, Victoria dentist Cameron Croll. Making the financial picture even shakier, Kelly had taken out yet another hefty loan that would come due in four months' time, and Simpson just hoped he had done the right thing in helping him get it.

In early May 1982, Kelly had flown to Victoria and "begged" Simpson to help him borrow $50,000 to finance his Cannes wedding, explaining that he didn't want to touch his other investments and needed the money right away. Believing that he was covered by the "assets" he controlled on his friend's behalf, Simpson approached the Toronto–Dominion Bank for a loan for Kelly that he would guarantee. He told the bank that his firm had power of attorney over Kelly's $750,000 worth of investments, including a $500,000 term deposit and $125,000 in stocks.

After confirming with the RCMP that Kelly had been a member of the force for ten years, the bank manager authorized the loan, but only after Simpson signed an undertaking that his law firm would repay the moneys by September 1, 1982, if Kelly defaulted. Despite Kelly's real purpose for borrowing the money, the authorization form showed that the loan was to be used for purchasing an option on a villa in France.

As uneasy as his friend's expensive tastes made him, once he arrived in France, Simpson was soon beguiled by Kelly's charm and unstinting hospitality. The groom had arranged his wedding date around the nearby Cannes Film Festival and Simpson got a firsthand glimpse of some of the world's most famous movie stars. Afterwards, the two men visited a casino, and Kelly, an avid gambler, shared his system for beating the roulette wheel with his old friend. "You wait and see how many times it comes up black, and then when it has gone on black a number of times, you bet on red. . . . If the colour comes up black and you've bet red, you double your bet on red, and you just keep doubling your bet until red comes in," Simpson recalled. Simpson was so excited by winning 25,000 francs ($5,000 Cdn), he forgot that the same system lost him 24,000 francs ($4,800 Cdn) before the night was over.

His fears that Kelly might be living beyond his means were further allayed by a visit to the office of a Cannes lawyer with whom Kelly was negotiating for up to $3 million to finance the Kenyan gold deal he had already broached to Simpson. It was clear that the man wanted to invest in Kelly's scheme, and Simpson made a mental note to remember that what was big money to him was not necessarily big money to Kelly. The previous year, for example, Kelly had loaned the Simpsons $10,000; a few months later, during a dinner party at his Beach Drive apartment, Kelly had thrown their loan agreement into the fire as a Christmas present to Victor and Kay.

In better spirits after Kelly's personal attentions, Simpson soon found himself caught up in *la dolce vita*. A week before the wedding, the guests began arriving from North America, some of them on tickets paid by Kelly. Bobby Rapson, a musician friend of Jan's, flew in from Los Angeles. Ruth and John Bradley arrived from Canada, and Candi jetted in from Victoria to represent the Kelly clan.

On her way back from Victoria, Jan had stopped in Toronto to pick up her matron of honour, Jill Davidson, who accompanied her on the flight back to France. Jill came alone because she and Roger Davidson were now separated. Patrick took a separate flight back to France from Victoria, travelling via London, where he picked up Jan's wedding dress and a few more of the Saville Row shirts that he had taken to wearing.

For a solid week, the wedding party enjoyed the sun-drenched pleasures of the Riviera, with Kelly picking up the bill in a string of chic restaurants from Nice to Cannes. Most of the guests stayed at the Kellys' villa, but Rapson and his wife were put up in the nearby Hôtellerie du Golf at Kelly's expense.

On the day of the wedding, the women festooned the bride and groom's Mercedes with fresh daisies, affixing a yellow rose to its trademark hood ornament. Pink ribbons were tied around the necks of Jan's Irish setter, Shanty, and Patrick's sheepdog, Kelly, before they were photographed with their owners by the old ruins that had been expertly incorporated into the villa's breathtaking gardens. During the church service, Rapson and a professional musician from the Côte d'Azur symphony played a duet on flute and harp, tape-recording their performance as a present for Patrick and Jan.

After the sumptuous dinner at the Moulin de Mougins, the newly-weds stayed in Mougins for the night, while the wedding party returned to the villa, which Kelly had stocked with wine so that the revelry could continue in their absence. In the morning, he and Jan were jetting off to Ireland for a month-long honeymoon, and he had invited his guests to stay at the villa for as long as they wished. But a pall had fallen over the wedding party and Simpson thought he knew why. "Everyone knew the background of Pat, I guess, about what happened to his wife. Pat was tense. Jan was tense. Everybody was tense. It wasn't a jovial occasion."

With the candles guttering down and everyone feeling suddenly awkward now that their hosts were gone, Rapson suggested that they listen to the duet he had recorded. Everyone enthusiastically agreed, and one of the guests uncorked another bottle of wine while Rapson slipped the tape into Kelly's stereo. After a long silence, broken only by the metallic thrum of insects from beyond the open patio doors, it became obvious that the tape was blank. Simpson shivered. "We all looked at each other and said, 'Is this an omen?'"

The tension that Victor Simpson observed in Jan Bradley had nothing to do with her believing that the avenging spirit of Jeannette Kelly was hovering over her wedding. In fact, she had been in "a major depression" a full two months before she married Patrick over the perilous state of their finances and her discovery that living in paradise with an international entrepreneur was a very lonely proposition.

When they had first arrived in France in November 1981, money seemed to be the last of their worries. Fearing that their dogs might be lost during the change of aircraft in Paris if they were shipped out on their own, the couple had returned to Canada to accompany their pets back to Nice. Patrick bought Jan a Renault "Le Car" and a stereo, and gave her a monthly allowance of $1,000 for her personal needs. Not long after they arrived, Jan fell in love with a seventeenth-century *maison* that had once belonged to the American playwright Arthur Miller. Patrick immediately engaged the same real estate agent who had helped them find the villa in Valbonne to negotiate its purchase, while he worked on the financing.

The newlyweds set up a joint chequing account at the Banque de l'Indochine et de Suez in Cannes, where they also kept a safety deposit box. To facilitate wiring money in and out of France, they also opened a chequing account at the Banque Nationale de Paris in Valbonne. Victor Simpson would pay Kelly's bills from Victoria, either with money that Kelly transferred to him from France, or, on instruction, by cashing in stocks from Kelly's investment portfolio using his power of attorney.

In the fall of 1981, Kelly had deposited $115,000 with Pemberton Securities and $100,000 with Richardson Securities from the proceeds of Jeannette's life insurance. Simpson then deposited money from these brokerage accounts into Kelly's Royal Bank account in Victoria as his client needed it. On December 21, 1981, $20,000 was deposited, with a further $25,000 going in just over two weeks later on January 7, 1982. As Kelly had once told Simpson, "I like going first class."

But by February 12, 1982, the Victoria account was overdrawn and a cheque for $1,793.67 to pay Kelly's American Express account was returned NSF. Since Patrick kept his business dealings to himself, Jan was at first unaware of their financial difficulties. When Patrick was at the villa, they went to the casinos once or twice a week at Cannes, Beaulieu-sur-Mer, and Monaco, where foreign patrons were required to show their passports and pay a 100,000-franc ($20,000 Cdn) "tuition" every time they played. Kelly was a heavy gambler and often began his games with bets of $2,000. Although the most popular games in France were baccarat and *trente-et-quarante*, he preferred blackjack, even when there were five or six decks in use at the same time. The former undercover agent's near total recall was put to good use in the casinos of the Riviera. "He had an excellent memory and would win often, playing odds, by remembering what cards were gone already," Bradley recalled.

Kelly continued to play squash, but since the game was not then popular in the south of France, he had to make an hour-long drive to Monaco to play at the Monte Carlo Country Club. Most of his social contacts were made on the squash court, and the Kellys settled into a quiet social life of poolside barbecues and dinners out with people like English squash pro Howard Smith and German squash star Uwe Fenz and his girlfriend, Marlene Lee.

To vary the pleasant routines of Valbonne, they travelled frequently, making the short drive down the autoroute to lunch in Italy, or catching a flight to London or Paris to dine, shop, or sightsee. Just two months after they settled into their villa, they vacationed in the Bahamas, staying at the Nassau Beach Hotel, where Shirley Shaw, a CP reservations clerk who had worked with Jeannette, saw them signing a bill. It was high season, and Shaw noted that the exclusive resort was not on the airline's discount list.

Tiring of Nassau, the couple took a charter flight to Eleuthera, where they stayed at the Pink Sands Hotel on nearby Harbour Island. After ten days of wandering the luxury resort's world famous pink beaches, they flew back to Nassau for a few more days in the casino. Kelly quickly attracted a crowd of goggle-eyed tourists with the size of his wagers. On their last day, he disappeared from the pool, leaving Jan wondering where he'd gone. When he returned, he presented her with an 18-carat gold Cartier watch that she had admired at a duty-free store. "He told me to thank the casino when he gave it to me, and looked quite pleased with himself."

The storybook interlude in the sun extended all the way to the last event of their vacation. When they boarded the jet that would take them back to France via London on February 27, they discovered that Prince Charles and Lady Diana were on the same flight, returning from the disastrous Bahamian vacation during which a photographer had managed to snap a picture of the bikini-clad and very pregnant princess that was instant front-page news around the world.

Less than a month after they returned from the Bahamas, the couple flew to London so that Jan could be fitted for her wedding dress. They stayed at their favourite London hotel, the Athenaeum on Piccadilly, where they were known by name by the desk clerks and concierge because of their frequent visits. While in London, they enjoyed some theatre and dance, catching Elizabeth Taylor in *Little Foxes* and the Ballet Rambert and the Royal Festival Ballet before returning to France.

In Paris they stayed in a suite at the Hotel Lancaster on rue de Berri and spent their days wandering the Left Bank and dining in some of the famous little restaurants Jan had read about. She got a chance to use some of the French she had been learning in a Berlitz course in Cannes,

and the couple was delighted with a mall of antique dealers they discovered just across the road from the Louvre called "La Louvre des
Antiquaires."

But Jan's personal Camelot was short-lived. After their wedding and
Irish honeymoon, Patrick virtually vanished. Jan passed her time
reading, knitting, puttering in the villa's gardens, and walking the dogs.
As beautiful as the south of France was, she found herself growing bored
and lonely. She certainly hadn't counted on Patrick being away so much
on business and sorely missed Toronto and the active social life she had
enjoyed there for nearly ten years as a working woman. But most of all,
she was worried about money. Haunted by memories of the extreme
unhappiness her financially irresponsible father had caused her own
family, she began to think that the same thing was in store for her. "I
began to feel a nightmare repeating itself – financial insecurity terrifies
me. I was in a strange country, with no security, I didn't have a clue
about our bank accounts, and many bills seemed to go unpaid."

Although Jan had no detailed knowledge of Patrick's financial affairs,
she believed that the money they were living on in France was coming
from several businesses in which Patrick held a stake in Toronto and
Victoria. She also thought that he was taking a percentage of the profits
from various investment projects he had negotiated on behalf of K&V
Enterprises. There was Ange Gold, for one, a defunct mine on north
Vancouver Island that had been closed since the thirties. Thanks to a
new technology for reprocessing the original tailings from the mine, it
had been made viable again, and there was even talk of newly discovered veins of gold on the old property. And then there was the exotic
deal Patrick had worked out with Princess Emma of the Kingdom of
Tonga, in which he had planned to ship a large quantity of timber
through Seattle to the South Seas in exchange for copra. More recently,
she believed he was negotiating for a squash club and wine bar in
London.

With all these sources of income and exciting investments, Jan wondered, why was Victor Simpson hounding Patrick for money to pay off
a mountain of unpaid bills? Suspecting that the Victoria lawyer was to
blame for mismanaging their funds, she "nagged and nagged" her
husband to cancel Simpson's all-powerful control over their finances

and to take charge of their own affairs. In defending Simpson from Jan's angry accusations, Kelly kept repeating a famous line from *To Kill a Mockingbird*: "It's not time to worry yet, Scout."

Victor Simpson aged ten years in the summer of 1982.

By July 21, he was sufficiently worried about his friend's mounting financial obligations that he flew to France to discuss the situation with Kelly in person. Kelly told him that he would shortly have $250,000 from a shipment of jewellery that had recently been sold in Miami, and invited Simpson to wait in France for the courier to arrive with the money. A few days later, Kelly informed the worried lawyer that the man had been picked up at the Paris airport and that the money had been confiscated. After making a flurry of phone calls, Kelly reported that the funds would be released in a few days. In any case, Simpson was not to worry because he was also expecting another $100,000 to be delivered to the villa in Valbonne from a second courier, who would shortly be en route to France from Ireland, where Kelly had recently done a job for the CIA.

Time was very much of the essence, so Simpson instructed his Victoria office manager, Connie Jeffrey, to fly to London. He planned to have her personally transport $100,000 back to Victoria to pay off some of the more pressing debts, while he remained in France awaiting the release of the other funds Kelly was expecting.

After four days of waiting for the telephone to ring in London, Jeffrey flew back to Victoria empty-handed. Simpson remained in France, but after a few days Kelly informed him that the courier they were waiting for was tied up in other matters and was unable to complete his delivery. But since Kelly had "insured" the transaction, they were guaranteed to get their money in a few days. Desperately overdrawn on his own credit card after nearly three futile weeks in Europe waiting for Kelly's elusive cash to appear, Simpson decided to fly home, telling his friend to bring the money to Victoria himself as soon as it arrived.

For the first time in months, Simpson felt reassured when Kelly called him a few days later in Victoria and said that he now had over $200,000 in his possession. As soon as he sent off another shipment of jewellery, from which he expected to realize $300,000, he would fly to Victoria and turn over $100,000 to Victor so that all outstanding accounts could be paid off. A few hours later, Kelly called again to say that he was in London and would be leaving for Canada on the next flight.

But when Kelly called twenty-four hours later, it was from Los Angeles, not Vancouver. He told Simpson that everything was fine, but that he had an ear infection and couldn't fly; someone else would now be meeting Simpson in Victoria. The courier would be Bobby Rapson, the musician Simpson had met at Kelly's Cannes wedding. Not caring who brought the funds as long as they arrived, Simpson breathed a sigh of relief when Rapson appeared on his doorstep on August 19, or at least he did until he found out that Kelly's friend didn't have the money.

Instead, Rapson gave Simpson a series of cheques drawn on his own account in Los Angeles, explaining that Kelly had in turn written cheques to Rapson on his accounts in France. The nervous lawyer was so upset with the arrangement that he flew back to Los Angeles with Rapson the next day and confronted Kelly. His unflappable friend calmly advised him that the moneys he had brought from France to repay the Mina McIntosh and Cameron Croll loans had been seized by U.S. customs authorities because it was against American law to bring more than $5,000 in cash into the country. He assured Simpson that the French cheques would be honoured and that the seized cash would soon be returned.

After the cheque Rapson had made out to Croll for $11,400 was returned NSF, Kelly invited Simpson to join him in London in late August, explaining that all was now clear for them to proceed with the African gold deal, and that a courier would be arriving shortly in London with $100,000. Simpson and his office manager flew to London, so that she could take the $100,000 Kelly had promised back to Victoria to repay loans that were about to come due. From August 31 to September 10, Simpson and Connie Jeffrey hobnobbed with Patrick and Jan in London, waiting for the courier to show up with the money. After taking in a performance of *Cats*, Kelly invited them all to an exclusive restaurant for dinner. They had a wonderful time until the bill came. "You ever see that commercial where they take the meat cleaver and they chop the guy's American Express card in half? Well, they did that to Kelly. And I thought, 'Oh, shit,'" Simpson remembered.

After paying Kelly's hotel bill and lending him his credit card,

Simpson and Jeffrey flew to Valbonne, where, Kelly had assured them, a large amount of cash would be delivered shortly. But he forgot to give Simpson the key to his villa, so the lawyer and his office manager had to check into the Hôtellerie du Golf to wait for the courier. After several days of running up their hotel bill without receiving any money, Simpson sent Jeffrey back to Victoria and pondered his next move.

Kelly called from London and told Simpson that he was on his way back to France and that a new gem deal had been arranged for Geneva, because there was no duty on such transactions in Switzerland. Simpson would be contacted at his hotel after the deal was completed and paid $100,000 to apply against Kelly's debts. Simpson's wife, Kay, was flying in from Victoria the next day, and he called to tell her that they would now be meeting in Geneva. Kelly arrived back in Valbonne just in time to take Simpson to the airport. As they waited for Simpson's flight to be called, Kelly jokingly suggested another way out of their tangled affairs:

"If we had to disappear, he knew this place in South America where there was a priest who ran a village and for a certain sum of cash, one could live there very comfortably without any problems," Simpson remembered. "He further advised me that he was fluent in Spanish and that there would be no problems for him in getting to this country and living there."

As Simpson waved goodbye to his friend, he wondered if Kelly had really been joking about his plan to abscond. After all, the lawyer had found out that the package Kelly had asked him to put in K&V's safety deposit box in Victoria had contained a false passport, a false passport that Simpson had carried into France on Kelly's instructions and handed over to his client during one of his many European junkets.

After the Simpsons had checked into their Geneva hotel, Kelly called to say that one of the principals in the gem deal had missed his plane in Los Angeles and that the transaction would now be delayed for a few days. Rather than waiting for him to arrive, he suggested it would be better if Simpson and his wife drove to Italy to check out an exciting investment opportunity Kelly was exploring in Venice. Grasping at straws, the Simpsons rented a car and headed south.

"The plan had been for the company to buy lumber from B.C. to sell to the Italians and to buy ceramic tiles from Italy to sell in southern California through Bobby Rapson's friend. It sounded like a really good deal because the tile manufacturers had a deal with the Italian government — for every tile they exported, they got a kickback from the government," Simpson recalled.

Fate did not smile on the lumber-for-tile caper. Just before Simpson contacted Cameron Croll in Victoria to negotiate the deal's financing, Bobby Rapson's cheque to pay back the dentist for moneys he had loaned Kelly bounced. Croll threatened to sue Simpson and hung up on him before he had a chance to explain the new project. When the lawyer tried to call him back, he couldn't get through. Princess Grace of Monaco had just been killed in a car accident and for days the telephone lines to North America were jammed.

Kelly meanwhile called Simpson with more bad news. The man who was to meet Simpson in Geneva with the proceeds of the gem transaction turned out to have been involved in a bank fraud in Germany, so Kelly had cancelled the whole deal. Instead, Kelly told Simpson to fly back to London, where he had arranged for $50,000 in cash to be delivered to the front desk of his hotel. Wearily, Victor and Kay made their way to the airport and set out for London. Nothing happened the first night, but on the second, Simpson was summoned to the front desk to pick up a package. Smiling hopefully at his wife, be bolted out of the room and raced to the front desk. With his heart pounding and beads of sweat glistening on his forehead, he introduced himself to the night clerk and was handed a hotel envelope that appeared to be bulging with currency.

He could barely wait to get back to the room. But when he tore open the envelope, he discovered that it contained 50,000 francs in crisp new 500-franc notes ($10,000 Cdn), not the $50,000 Kelly had promised. Kay Simpson had had enough. The next day, September 21, she flew back to Victoria.

Her husband, meanwhile, had one more country to visit before his clandestine globetrotting was over. When he called Kelly to say that the delivery at his hotel wasn't satisfactory, Kelly told him that everything was finally cleared up on the jewellery deal and that he could now pick up the cash in Miami. Kelly supplied him with the name of a hotel and the exact time when a man would meet him with the $100,000. "I go there and there is no hotel by that name," Simpson recalled.

In the final stages of credulous desperation, Simpson called Kelly yet again, only to be told that he must have misunderstood the name of the hotel. He was given the name of another hotel, a new time for the meeting, and assured that everything was under control. With time to kill before he met the phantom courier, Simpson decided to take in a Miami Dolphins game, only to discover that the National Football League was on strike. He had just hit the beach to get a little sun when a lifeguard informed him that there was a hurricane warning and he had to return to his hotel room, where Simpson spent the longest three days of his life. The courier never appeared, and when he tried to contact Kelly in France, he couldn't get through. Terrified of what was waiting for him at home, but unable to wait any longer, Simpson boarded a flight back to Victoria, wondering who had ever said that Miami was nice in September.

When he arrived in his office, he found his world going over a Niagara Falls of unpaid bills and lawsuits. The power company was even threatening to cut off his electricity. Since Kelly had never provided any security for the Mina McIntosh loans, Simpson owed her trust fund $60,000 plus interest. Kelly was also three weeks late in paying back Cameron Croll $50,000, most of which had been lent at the astonishing interest rate of 100 per cent per year! And then there was the $50,000 cheque to the Toronto–Dominion Bank drawn on one of Kelly's French accounts that had been returned marked *Compte Sans Provision*. It was the loan for Kelly's Cannes wedding that Simpson's firm had given its "absolute and irrevocable" undertaking to pay. Finally, there was the havoc Simpson's travelling had wreaked on his American Express account. In a single month, the lawyer whose annual salary was $30,000 had racked up $35,000 in charges.

It was a bleak picture, but at least Simpson still had power of attorney over $30,000 worth of securities that Kelly had pledged as partial collateral for the Cameron Croll loan. But when he attempted to convert the securities into cash, one of the brokers at Richardson Securities told him that there must be some mistake. The account had been liquidated on August 28, 1982, and the money handed over to a Jan Bradley. Simpson suddenly found himself looking down the barrel of over $160,000 worth of Kelly's bad debts.

The despondent man doggedly tried to reach his client in France, but for days none of his calls were returned. Then Kelly himself finally picked up the telephone at the villa in Valbonne, and the lawyer from Victoria held a short and unhappy conversation with his boyhood friend.

"Patrick, what's going on?"

It would take Simpson a long moment to appreciate the grim humour of Kelly's cold reply.

"Speak to my lawyer."

14

FAST AND LOOSE

From the moment he walked into the Toronto–Dominion bank on December 1, 1982, teller Diana Ross thought that Patrick Kelly was one of the most attractive men she had ever seen. Tanned and expensively dressed in a grey Italian suit with a pink shirt and burgundy tie, he sauntered up to her wicket and placed his expensive briefcase on the counter. In a voice exuding a commanding mix of confidence and worldliness, he explained that he wanted to deposit $24,600 in his Visa account. Reaching into his briefcase, he produced a cheque in that amount drawn on the Banque Nationale de Paris in Valbonne, France.

The perplexity of the inexperienced teller, who had worked at the branch for only a month, must have registered on her face as she examined the unfamiliar cheque because her suave customer offered an unsolicited explanation. He did a great deal of international travelling and found these particular instruments drawn on his French account extremely useful because they were honoured all over the world. They were certainly more convenient than standing in line to convert currency at the foreign exchange or fumbling about with a pen and traveller's cheques. "All you simply do is write in the currency that you are using, in this case Canadian funds, and the amount, and then they go through to the head office to be, I guess, rated and cleared," she remembered him saying.

Still unsure of what to do, Ross took the cheque to her supervisor, who told her to pull Kelly's account card with the branch. In a rush to get to lunch, the supervisor glanced at the card, and seeing that everything was in order, told Ross to follow standard procedure, since the cheque was made out to Visa. When the transaction was completed, Kelly continued talking with Ross for a few minutes before walking out of the bank, leaving the young woman wondering what foreign destination her handsome customer was headed for that day.

The fact was that Patrick Kelly had more banking to do before he went to the airport. Carol Quaite, a teller at a Bloor Street West branch of the Bank of Nova Scotia, was as taken with her tastefully dressed customer as Ross had been. While she was helping him open a chequing account with the branch, he explained that he was in the process of moving back to Canada from France. Since he had a lot of travelling to do in the interim, he also wanted to deposit $14,000 on his Bank of Nova Scotia Visa account with a cheque drawn on his French bank in Valbonne. Unfamiliar with the bank's clearing regulations for foreign cheques (the process usually took three to four weeks), the teller accepted the cheque and immediately posted the credit to Kelly's Visa account. After talking with Quaite for half an hour, Kelly said goodbye. Outside the bank, he hailed a cab to the airport and caught a flight to London.

He checked into the Athenaeum Hotel and the next day visited Barclay's Bank, where he withdrew $13,000 in cash from his Bank of Nova Scotia Visa account. After spending a few more days in London in business meetings with a Toronto antique and art dealer, he flew back to France, where he withdrew $20,796.19 from his TD Visa account: $9,939.19 from his account at the Banque Nationale de Paris in Valbonne, and another $10,857 from Barclay's Bank in Cannes. Both Canadian banks had obviously credited his Visa accounts before the French cheques used to make the deposits in Toronto had been sent out for collection. The transactions had left him with an apparent credit on the two cards of $38,600, against which he had just drawn almost $34,000.

Just over a week later, on December 10, Kelly appeared in the Toronto–Dominion Bank at King and Bay streets in Toronto and deposited

$24,284 in his TD Visa account, once again using a cheque drawn on his account with the Banque Nationale de Paris. The teller, Linda Dove, got the approval of her supervisor before completing the transaction. Just before closing time, the well-dressed businessman returned to the same branch to make a second deposit, this time of $36,000, in his TD Visa account. Although Dove had been free to serve him, Kelly presented this second cheque to the teller in the wicket beside her. When Dove saw Joanne Noftall puzzling over the strange instrument, she leaned over and told her that she had processed an identical cheque earlier in the day after consulting with their supervisor and that it was all right to put it through.

The transaction took only a couple of moments, but Kelly lingered to chat with Noftall, explaining to her that he bought and sold small businesses around the world and didn't like using cash or traveller's cheques, particularly since Visa had given him an unlimited line of credit. He patiently answered all her questions about his travels and the young teller was impressed. "He was very well dressed and clean-shaven, and I really had no doubt. I believed him," Noftall says.

Kelly immediately returned to Nice, where he requested a $250 cash advance on his TD Visa account at Barclay's Bank in Cannes. When the transaction went through without a hitch, he made a second request the same day for $28,543 U.S. from the same Visa account. This time permission was denied, although he did get authorization to withdraw $5,000 U.S.

Kelly was puzzled. To find out why he hadn't been able to draw against the paper balance he had created with his December 10 deposits in Toronto, he made a long distance call to the TD's security officer, who told him that the only thing he could think of was that there had been a computer malfunction. Kelly instructed Keith Kerr to either freeze or cancel his Visa card until the matter was investigated, adding that he would call him again when he returned to Toronto for Christmas. He wanted Kerr to make absolutely sure that no one else had been taking money out of his account. Kerr froze Kelly's Visa card and promised to get to the bottom of the computer glitch before his client came to Toronto.

Had Kelly called a day later, Kerr would have been able to explain what the trouble was. On December 15, 1982, the $24,600 cheque that

Kelly deposited to his Visa account on December 1 in Toronto was returned to the TD Bank by the Banque Nationale de Paris marked *Compte Sans Provision*. The security officer called Kelly's bank in Valbonne, where he found out from the manager that several cheques drawn on the same account had recently been returned NSF. Kerr's next call was to Kelly's villa. In a calm and reassuring voice, Kelly admitted that he had made the NSF transactions and arranged to meet Kerr in his Toronto office on December 20 to straighten out these honest mistakes.

By the fall of 1982, officials at American Express must have been wishing that Patrick Kelly had left home without it. By late November, the outstanding balance on his gold card was $43,763.61. Two large cheques to American Express, one for $18,666.77 Cdn drawn on Kelly's TD bank account in Victoria, and another for $21,168.71 U.S. drawn on Bobby Rapson's account at the Security Pacific National Bank in California, were both returned marked NSF. Meanwhile, based on the fleeting paper credit showing on his American Express account at the time of the deposits, Kelly had obtained nine cash advances from the American Express office in Cannes. Before his deposit cheques bounced, he had collected $21,658.34.

Although the company had immediately "hot-listed" Kelly's card with its international data centre and managed to find and destroy it in a London restaurant before further expenses could be incurred, they wanted restitution for the outstanding balance and interest and began dunning him at his villa. On October 29, Kelly finally returned their calls, explaining that he was in the process of liquidating assets to clear his American Express balance. Toronto lawyer Howard Saginur was now handling his affairs, and they should speak to him about the matter. The collection agent on the other end of the line would never forget Kelly's answer when he informed him that any repayment schedule hinged on the approval of American Express. "He said it would be very hard to collect from overseas. Then he hung up."

Spending at the rate of $25,000 a month, Patrick Kelly had all but exhausted his dead wife's insurance money by the time of his remarriage in the spring of 1982, forcing him to arrange a series of loans from private individuals and banks to maintain his lifestyle. The fund-raising attempts were occasionally on the unorthodox side.

During the same trip to Victoria in which he persuaded Victor Simpson to co-sign for the $50,000 loan from the Toronto–Dominion Bank to pay for his Cannes wedding, he approached the Royal Bank for a $500,000 loan to buy Arthur Miller's French country house that Jan Bradley so admired. Kelly offered to secure the loan by pledging $600,000 worth of Roymor Certificates that he wanted to buy with the proceeds of a pending property sale in Ontario. Although he said he expected the $590,000 sale to go through imminently (the last of his Ontario property had been sold in 1981), Kelly wanted the bank to advance funds against his intended purchase of the Roymor Certificates. To any champion of capitalism in a three-piece suit, his explanation had an agreeable, ideological ring. Because of the anti-business policies of France's socialist government, the present owner of the French country house was being forced to liquidate at fire-sale prices; as a shrewd businessman, Kelly didn't want to miss the real estate opportunity of a lifetime.

Whether it was the fact that Kelly's account was overdrawn to the tune of $19,000 at the time of his loan request, or that in subsequent talks local solicitors representing Kelly told the bank that *they* wanted to borrow $500,000 secured by the deposit of Roymor Certificates to be held in the name of Patrick Kelly, the Royal Bank decided not to get involved. The whole encounter had created "some doubt as to Kelly's integrity," and in a May 12, 1982, internal memo, one bank official wrote: "Further dealings with Mr. Kelly will need detailed investigation."

Kelly's finances had become so strained by October of that year that Jan decided to leave her husband and return to Canada. During the domestic flight from Nice to Paris to make her international connection, Jan berated Patrick about Victor Simpson's alleged mishandling of their affairs, telling him in no uncertain terms that she wasn't prepared to put up with the kind of financial insecurity she had recently been forced to live with. "I'm going to Canada while you get this mess that I've been nagging about for the past eight months cleared up – and I'm staying there while you do."

The couple separated at Charles de Gaulle airport, with Jan flying on to Toronto and Patrick proceeding to London "on business." Unaware that he viewed her ultimatum as a major betrayal, Jan expected Patrick to get in touch with her soon at either Jill Davidson's or her mother's, as he always did whenever they were separated. When he still hadn't called by Thanksgiving weekend, Jan telephoned Valbonne to see if her husband was at the villa, only to learn from one of the couple's squash friends, Uwe Fenz, that Patrick had given instructions to pack up all their belongings and ship them back to Canada. "We were apparently moving," Jan recalled. "I was frightened and furious at the same time."

Instructing Fenz not to touch a thing, she decided on the spur of the moment to return to Valbonne. That same day, she boarded a plane for France, passing her husband in the air somewhere over the Atlantic as he made his way back to Toronto for the first time since he and Jan had set out for Hawaii nineteen months before. People there owed him money and the time had come to collect.

When Patrick Kelly showed up at Yolles in downtown Toronto to get the money from the sale of the antiques that had once furnished his Palace Pier apartment, he must have been disappointed with what proprietor Graham Gordon had to report. Thanks to the recession, the antique dealer had only been able to sell about $10,000 worth of the lot; after deductions for the china setting that Kelly had purchased for Paul Stewart at the time of Jeannette's death, and Gordon's 25 per cent commission for selling the furniture, all that Kelly had coming to him was a paltry $2,500.

Unperturbed, Kelly said that he had $500,000 in cash that would be available for a suitable investment by November 15. He explained that he was in the process of liquidating his business in France and moving back to Canada, where he planned to buy, and, of course, furnish a house. To reinforce the point that he was a man of means, Kelly opened his briefcase, allowing Gordon to see that it was filled with several thousand dollars and large amounts of various other currencies. Kelly explained that it was necessary to carry so many different currencies because he could never be certain where his travels would take him, leaving it to Gordon's imagination to decide what business he was in.

Over the next few days, the two men continued talking and Kelly made the antique dealer an ambitious proposition. He was looking for a safe, long-term investment and if Gordon would put together a package of art and antiques worth approximately $1 million, Kelly was prepared to pay him 50 per cent of the insured value of the goods for the entire lot. Yolles had been battered by the recession and Gordon found it a tempting offer, especially since he would have been willing to accept just 30 per cent of the insured value to make the sale.

But as attractive as he found Kelly's proposal, the experienced dealer knew that it was also fraught with danger, given the conditions his prospective buyer had set. All of the items on the list of goods he had agreed to sell to Kelly were subject to a Registered Security Agreement with Gordon's bank, which he knew would have to be discharged at the time of the sale. And that was the catch. Kelly wanted to move the goods to a humidity-controlled storage facility right away and pay Gordon for the shipment on November 15.

It left the antique dealer in a tantalizing dilemma. If the proposal was a straight deal with no unusual features, Kelly was a great benefactor at a particularly difficult time for his business and his offer should be snapped up. But if the deal was a fraud, as Gordon vaguely suspected, he would need to protect himself. Putting Kelly off for a few days, Gordon decided to seek some expert advice, and he knew of no better place to get it than the Investigative Support Squad of the Metropolitan Toronto Police.

It was an odd reversal of roles. As an expert in his field, Gordon had often helped the police with thefts and frauds involving art and antiques, which statistically comprise the second biggest international crime category after drug trafficking. He told Sgt. Walter Korchuck of the ISS that he was considering a very substantial offer from a man named Patrick Kelly and wanted to know if the police knew anything about him.

After a quick check, Korchuck told Gordon that the Metro homicide squad was still investigating the suspicious death of Kelly's wife in 1981. Although Kelly had no criminal record, the sergeant advised the antique dealer to proceed with caution, and, in the event that he went ahead with the deal, to make sure that he maintained control of his property until he had actually been paid for it. In return for the information, Gordon agreed to keep a diary of his dealings with the former Mountie and even to tape-record their conversations whenever possible.

Gordon's scepticism about the deal eased a little when Kelly produced a $450,000 security bond apparently drawn up by a lawyer in Victoria named Victor Simpson. The bond cleared the way for Kelly to take possession of five valuable items from the lot of art and antiques he was interested in buying and to deliver them personally to Sotheby's in New York to be authenticated and appraised. Since Kelly's uncle, "Michael Kelly," would be advancing the $75,000 downpayment Gordon required, he had also flown in an expert of his own from London to examine the pieces at a cost of $8,000, or so Kelly claimed.

On the long drive to New York in a vehicle from Rent-A-Wreck, in which he was transporting a Boulle bracket clock signed by René Bodin and a "Gainsborough" painting, Kelly was accompanied by Bobby Rapson, who had played the flute at Kelly's wedding in France. For someone who had lost $10,000 of his own money when the cheques Kelly had given him to pay Victor Simpson in August had bounced, Rapson was remarkably forgiving. If he held any grudge against Kelly, his feelings were softened on the journey by Kelly's reminiscences of his dead wife and the tears they inspired.

"He told me she was up on a stool watering plants on the balcony and he came into the room and saw her slip and he ran to help her, but he just couldn't hang on to her," Rapson remembers. "He was holding her by the ankles. He was then really crying, troubled, but quiet crying. I felt sorry for him. He then suggested we sing a song."

After they had sung themselves hoarse, the subject of Judge Walter Rapson, Bobby Rapson's father, making a short-term loan to Kelly came up, and Rapson promised to see what he could do. (Shortly afterwards, the judge lent Kelly $20,000 secured by a promissory note signed in front of Howard Saginur.) Kelly then pulled over to call Jan in France, explaining to Rapson that he had to patch up some trouble he was having with his wife over a temporary shortage of funds. "He told me he needed to get money over to her as she needed it to live in the manner to which she was accustomed."

When Kelly next spoke to Graham Gordon, it was to tell him that both Sotheby's and his uncle's expert were concerned about the authenticity of the "Gainsborough" and questioned the assigned value of a Robert LeFévre painting. Although Gordon told him to send the two paintings back if he doubted their value, Kelly said he had a better idea. If Gordon would agree to have the other 122 pieces of merchandise included in their deal shipped to New York at Kelly's expense, "Uncle Michael" would arrange for a new insurance appraisal at Sotheby's. Afterwards, if the valuations were in line, Kelly would pay Gordon for the entire lot, and the shipment could be sent to a climate-controlled warehouse for storage. Kelly sent him $6,000 worth of cheques drawn on his French bank to have the consignment of valuables shipped to New York by Fine Arts Transport, and Gordon cautiously agreed.

Kelly arrived in Toronto from France on November 19 and met with Gordon at the Nag's Head restaurant in the Eaton Centre, where the antique dealer confirmed that the shipment had been received at Sotheby's. The two men decided that they would fly to New York together on Monday, November 22, where, if all was in order, their deal would be consummated. After they toasted the arrangement over a glass of wine, Kelly made out a cheque for $8,500 and offhandedly asked Gordon if he could get it cashed at his bank, explaining that he needed $8,000 for the weekend; the other $500 was for Gordon and his wife to go out to dinner. When the Continental Bank refused to honour the foreign cheque, Kelly said his goodbyes and told Gordon he would make other arrangements.

When Kelly didn't call or show up for their Monday morning trip to New York, Gordon decided to go ahead on his own to keep an eye on his merchandise. When he arrived at Sotheby's for what he thought was going to be an insurance appraisal, he was introduced to Sarah Coffin, the employee of the auction house who was in charge of all incoming consignments. Gordon told Coffin that he had not heard from Patrick Kelly, the man who was interested in buying the antiques, but that Kelly's "uncle," Michael Kelly, would be arranging the appraisal. When they compared notes, Gordon discovered to his dismay that Michael Kelly and Patrick Kelly were one and the same person. But the biggest surprise came when Coffin told him what was about to happen to the shipment that Kelly had told Sotheby's had come from his own house. "Sotheby's told me very, very clearly that they had clear instructions from Mr. Kelly that everything was to be sold now. He wasn't particularly concerned about the individual items, just sell it," Gordon later told police.

Gordon returned to Toronto and reported the details of his New York trip to the ISS, who encouraged him to find out how far Kelly was prepared to go in his attempt to gain control of the shipment of antiques and art. On Friday, November 26, Kelly called from New York to say that because the Sotheby's appraisal came in at just half of the insured value that Gordon had given him, he was now having problems coming up with the downpayment. But he suggested a way of expediting the deal. If Gordon would fly to London and meet him on November 30 at the Athenaeum Hotel, Kelly would pay him the full amount of money they had originally agreed to; he was not concerned about Sotheby's lower appraisal because he had since learned that it was based on liquidation value in a deflated market, rather than the value of the goods as a long-term investment. Since their deal would now be done in London, Kelly also asked that Gordon bring along the $450,000 security bond that would act as Kelly's receipt for the cash transaction.

When Gordon checked in to the Athenaeum Hotel at the appointed hour, he was given a message from Kelly saying that he had been delayed by fog in France and would be flying in from Nice the following day. In fact, Kelly was on his way to Toronto to make the two deposits on his Visa card that he would later withdraw in Europe before his cheques bounced. On December 1, after doing his banking in Canada, he flew to London and met Gordon at the Athenaeum, assuring him that his lawyer, Marcel Delmontine, would be flying in from Geneva the next day with the money.

The next morning while they were waiting for Delmontine to arrive, Kelly asked Gordon to show him the security bond. The antique dealer handed him a double-sealed envelope and Kelly opened it and examined the document inside. Expressing some concern over the amount of the bond relative to the appraised value of the antiques and art he was about to buy, Kelly suggested that they reseal the bond in fresh envelopes, and place it in the safety deposit box in the hotel. Although the box was in Kelly's name, he handed Gordon the key after both men had initialled the flaps of the envelopes containing the bond. "You have the key," he said reassuringly, "so you have control over it."

When Delmontine had still not arrived by lunchtime, they went to the Four Seasons Hotel, where the lawyer was planning to stay, only to discover that he hadn't shown up for his reservation. That night, the two men went to dinner and the theatre, and it wasn't until the next day that Kelly got the bad news, which he relayed to Gordon over breakfast. A drug dealer on the same flight as Kelly's lawyer had been arrested when the plane landed in Paris with a large quantity of heroin and cocaine in his possession, and in the subsequent search of the aircraft, it was discovered that Delmontine was carrying a great deal of cash in his briefcase. Thinking that the funds were related to the drug deal, authorities had impounded Kelly's funds. They had also taken Delmontine into custody, since the Swiss lawyer was clearly in violation of France's Draconian currency laws.

In Gordon's presence, Kelly made numerous phone calls in both English and French to the Public Prosecutor's Office in Paris, trying to explain that Delmontine was a lawyer simply trying to conduct a legal business transaction that required him to travel from Geneva to London with a large amount of cash. But from Kelly's frustrated tone, it was obvious that the French authorities were being difficult; Gordon wasn't surprised when Kelly got off the phone and told him that he would now have to go to Paris to straighten the whole mess out. The setback, he explained, was merely temporary. As soon as the French authorities discovered that the money was part of a legitimate business transaction, and not a drug deal, it would be released and he would fly back to London with the funds to complete their deal.

After Kelly left, Gordon went to the safety deposit box to make sure that the security bond was still there. He looked at the brown manila envelope a long moment before he decided to open it. Inside, he found a few pieces of hotel note paper and nothing more.

Ever since Jan Bradley walked out on him in October 1982 over the chaotic state of their finances, Patrick Kelly had been cool towards his wife. But by December, after a few days of theatre and fine dining in London, the couple had worked out a reconciliation of sorts. On December 19, they flew to Toronto, where they planned to spend Christmas with Ruth Bradley before flying to Aspen, Colorado, for a week's skiing. They were to fly to Toronto on January 3 and return to France a few days later, hoping to put their troubled marriage back together. But the Christmas trip wasn't all pleasure. While in Toronto, Kelly had set aside time to deal with his mountain of unpaid Visa bills and his angry bankers.

Although he had made an appointment with the security officer of the Toronto–Dominion Bank to meet on December 20, Kelly called from the office of Toronto lawyer Howard Saginur and rescheduled the appointment for the following day. It was a mistake. The bank had already decided that it had been defrauded, and uncertain about whether

Kelly would ever show up after cancelling his original appointment, Keith Kerr called the police.

On the morning of December 21, Kerr was sitting in his office at 68 Yonge Street, nervously awaiting Kelly's arrival. With the former police officer were Sgt. Norman Brosseau and Const. Dave Donald of the Metropolitan Toronto Police Fraud Squad, who had taken up a position in a nearby office. Even if Kelly now made full restitution of the moneys they believed he had fraudulently obtained through his Visa card, the bank had decided to press charges against him anyway and it wanted the police on hand just in case he kept his appointment.

Shortly after 9 A.M., Kelly arrived for what turned out to be a very short meeting. After seizing Kelly's charge card, Keith Kerr produced photocopies of the French cheques Kelly had used to deposit nonexistent funds into his TD Visa account. Kelly agreed that he had written and deposited the cheques and confirmed that he had also made seven cash withdrawals with his Visa card based on those deposits. When Kerr asked when the bank could expect repayment of the money it was owed, Kelly told him that he had no cash at the moment, but that he was expecting funds to be wired in shortly from California that would more than cover his Visa bill.

It had better be a lot of money, my friend, Kerr thought. Between American Express and his Visa accounts at the TD Bank and the Bank of Nova Scotia, Kelly had withdrawn $87,244.93 against bogus deposits. Kelly also owed an estimated $30,000 to various other creditors, including MasterCard, Air Canada, CP Airlines, Eaton's, Simpson's, The Bay, Harry Rosen, and the agency from which he rented his French villa. Kerr made a mental note to call Malcolm Douglas, the chief security officer at the Bank of Nova Scotia, to inform him of Kelly's imminent arrest.

Having finished with business, Kerr picked up the telephone and told Sergeant Brosseau that Kelly was in his office. Unaware of who Kerr was speaking to, Kelly was surprised when Brosseau and Donald appeared, identified themselves as police officers, and placed him under arrest for fraud. After reading him his rights, they frisked the suspect and found $10,950 in cash in the breast pocket of his suit jacket, along with Kelly's passport.

"I'm really surprised you were stupid enough to come back," one of the officers said.

"Why?"

"You knew this was fraud."

"What's the fraud? I was of the understanding the funds were coming in to cover the cheques."

"Where from?"

"A friend in California." When the officers asked for the name of the friend, Kelly fell silent.

After Kelly made a brief call to his lawyer at 9:25 A.M., the officers were preparing to take the prisoner to 52 Division of the Metropolitan Toronto Police when he asked if he could stop at his hotel to talk to his wife. Brosseau and Donald escorted Kelly to suite 1519 of the Westin Harbour Castle and searched the premises while Kelly spoke to a distraught Jan Bradley.

"What's this all about Patrick?" Bradley asked.

"You got me. I have no idea at all. They're talking about something to do with fraud."

The officers then took Kelly to 52 Division. Suspecting that other banks wanted to recover their credit cards from Kelly and perhaps press charges, the police took him to a small interview room and waited for their representatives to arrive.

While Kelly was on the telephone with his lawyer, Ronald Riddell of the Royal Bank arrived and seized two Royal Bank client cards and two Visa cards from him. At 12:15 P.M., Robert Pierce of the Canadian Imperial Bank of Commerce appeared and cut Kelly's Visa card from his bank in half. Shortly before 1 P.M., Malcolm Douglas walked into the room to seize Kelly's Bank of Nova Scotia Visa card and to press fraud charges. In the twenty years he had worked as a security officer, Douglas had never seen a fraud quite like this one.

After the bank officials had stripped Kelly of his credit cards, the officers took him to police headquarters on Jarvis Street, where he was photographed and fingerprinted. No court time was available that day to arraign Kelly on the fraud charges, so he was taken back to 52 Division and lodged in Cell No. 1. While Kelly had been talking to his bankers, police had been searching the bag he had picked up from his hotel, removing what appeared to be a key to a safety deposit box. After Kelly signed the record of his arrest and was about to be locked in his cell, Sergeant Brosseau asked him for the bank branch where they could find the safety deposit box.

"You must be kidding," Kelly replied.

Sgt. Ed Stewart of the homicide squad had been waiting a long time to see Patrick Kelly again, and when the prisoner was led into Insp. William Urie's office at 52 Division at 7:20 P.M. that night, he had to admit that he was looking good. Impeccably dressed in grey flannel trousers, black loafers, and a grey sports jacket, whose wine stripe subtly picked up the hue of his maroon turtleneck, the former undercover operator still knew how to make an impression. Stewart shook his hand and directed him to take a seat in the yellow chair on the other side of the desk beside Staff Sgt. William Fordham.

After advising Kelly that he was still investigating the 1981 death of his wife, Stewart asked about his relationship with Jan Bradley. Kelly said that he'd met the librarian in the mid-1970s and had been dating her ever since. He couldn't recall if Jan had ever stayed with him in apartment 1705 of the Palace Pier or whether she knew that he was married before Jeannette Kelly's death. Asked why he hadn't told police about Jan during the March 1981 interview in which he claimed that his marriage was solid, Kelly replied, "It is certainly nothing to do with the death of my wife."

Stewart turned his attention to Kelly's relationship with Dawn Taber. Kelly denied ever having an affair with her, and explained that Taber had come to live with the Kellys at the Palace Pier in the spring of 1981 because her husband was abusing her. Kelly also denied discussing his wife's life insurance with Taber while she was an agent for Citadel Life, and openly chortled when Stewart inquired if they had been planning to fake his death and run off to the south of France together. Asked why he was laughing, Kelly replied, "Because I don't know where you are coming from or where you are going to. I find your questions odd."

For nearly two years, Stewart had been troubled by the trauma to the top of Jeannette Kelly's head, a wound that the coroner didn't believe had been caused by the fall that killed her. Kelly told him that his wife had never mentioned anything to him about hitting her head on March 29 and suggested that her injury had probably been inflicted when she hit the ground. When asked if Jeannette had been afraid of heights, a fact the detective had already confirmed with people like Abby Latter, Kelly replied, "I believe I was more scared of heights than she was. I remember papering the house, she would be the one on the ladder."

Recalling Kelly's show of grief at the time of his wife's death, Stewart asked him why he had been so upset, since he had everything to gain from Jeannette's demise, including a lot of money and the freedom to marry his sweetheart. Kelly looked straight into the detective's eyes and answered in a cold, calm voice, "I loved my wife. It was a tragic accident. It was very traumatic to me. And all the money in the world is not enough to gain. If I wanted to marry Jan at that time, I wouldn't kill to do it."

Stewart nodded his head and asked if Kelly would submit to a police polygraph. Kelly declined, telling Stewart that in his opinion "the matter was finished" two years ago and there was no reason even to consider taking such a test now. When Stewart asked Kelly to sign his statement after the two-hour session was over, the dapper young man held up both hands and exclaimed, "No need to sign it." The detective did his best to interpret the strangely unreadable eyes of his subject as he delivered his final words of the interview; as one of the investigating officers on the case, he had to tell Kelly that he found his actions at the time of his first wife's death "troubling."

Kelly looked silently back at Stewart and smiled at the man who was trying so hard to peer into his soul. When the detectives escorted Kelly back to his cell, Stewart noted that he was reading a fantasy classic by T. H. White, *The Once and Future King*. Before Stewart and Fordham left, Kelly asked each of them for their business cards.

Patrick Kelly spent the morning of December 22, his thirty-third birthday, in jail. But he wasn't there for long. Mark Sandler of Austin Cooper's office arranged for his release after Ruth Bradley put her house up as surety for his $50,000 bail. Under the terms of his bail, Kelly had to reside at his mother-in-law's house in Dunsford, Ontario, and remain in the jurisdiction until the charges against him were adjudicated.

As he was leaving the courthouse that day, investigators from the Metropolitan Toronto Police were executing a search warrant for Kelly's safety deposit box, which they had traced to the Toronto–Dominion Bank branch in the TD Centre. Inside, they found another passport in the name of Patrick Kelly, a third passport bearing his picture and the name Patrick Shannon Ryan, and a Social Insurance card and birth certificate, also in the name of Patrick Shannon Ryan. Since the laws governing such offences were federal, the incriminating material was turned over to the RCMP.

A few weeks later, Kelly was hit with another legal thunderbolt on the courtroom steps. When Victor Simpson heard of his former client's arrest for fraud, he realized that his last hope of collecting on any of the debts Kelly had left him with was gone. He had already mortgaged his house to pay off $25,000 of Kelly's $50,000 wedding loan from the Toronto–Dominion Bank, and had taken out a personal loan to cover the rest. Cameron Croll had followed through on his threat to sue Simpson over his $50,000 loan to Kelly, and had also formally asked the B.C. Law Society to investigate Simpson for misrepresenting assets purportedly under his control that had been used to secure the loan. By December, Simpson hadn't known what else to do other than write to Kelly and make an appeal to his conscience. "As you are aware, there is no translation in French for fair play. I hope there is still fair play in your vocabulary." There was no reply.

Once Simpson found out that Kelly had been charged, he knew that he had no other option than to launch some immediate actions of his own, if only because the law required him to provide a paper trail to show where the outstanding moneys had actually gone. Simpson and his uncle flew to Toronto, where they personally served Kelly with three writs; one for the $50,000 TD loan that Simpson had co-signed for Kelly's wedding in France, one for the $60,000 from the trust fund of Mina McIntosh that he had loaned to Kelly without security, and the third for the $50,000 loan from Cameron Croll that Simpson had guaranteed.

Kelly was "cool and unemotional" when he was served, telling Simpson and his uncle that he would meet them at another time and place to discuss the situation. Nor would Kelly discuss the $168,258.07 legal bill Simpson handed him at the same time, the first professional invoice that the lawyer had ever presented him with during their lengthy business association.

Deciding to deal with one problem at a time, Kelly hired Michael Moldaver of the firm Greenspan, Moldaver to represent him on the fraud charges brought against him by the banks. He told his lawyer that he had unwittingly written the bad cheques to the various credit card companies in the belief that one of his own creditors had deposited $100,000 into his French account. In fact, the creditor in question, Californian Lois Perry, had so advised him personally. Taking her at her word, Kelly said he had simply issued his cheques believing they were more than covered by the loan repayment from Perry. To back up his story, he even produced a telegram from her admitting the facts of the matter: "Confirmed that I did advise you that funds in the amount of $100,000 U.S. were sent during November and December 1982. However, this was an error on my part and this indebtedness to you will be forthcoming ASAP. – Lois Perry."

Persuaded that the whole matter was a misunderstanding, Moldaver convened a meeting of all the complainants in the fraud case, as well as the Metro police's investigating officer, in his law office. He told them about Perry's $100,000 debt to Kelly, and said that she was prepared to fly up from California to testify on his client's behalf if the matter went to court. The fact was Kelly had no criminal intent to defraud anybody when he wrote the bad cheques on his French account, and the whole matter could either be amicably cleared up with a simple exchange of cheques in the privacy of Moldaver's law office or fought out in open court – whichever venue the complainants and police preferred. In either instance, thanks to Perry, Kelly would be vindicated.

After further negotiations with the Attorney General's Office and the police, Moldaver worked out an excellent settlement on behalf of his client. If Kelly made full restitution of the $100,000 he owed to the banks, presumably by collecting from his American creditor, and Lois Perry would agree to tell her story to the Toronto police in person, the charges against Kelly would be dropped.

A few days later, Perry flew to Toronto, where she was interviewed by Sgt. Norman Brosseau of the fraud squad. Perry told the sergeant that Kelly had indeed lent her $100,000 in 1979 and that he had requested repayment of the debt in the fall of 1982. Although she told Kelly that she had transferred the funds to his French account, the truth was she had not; she had made up the story on the spur of the moment to buy herself more time to raise the money, which she was having difficulty putting together.

In light of Perry's disclosures, Brosseau concluded that Kelly had a good defence to the fraud charges and perhaps a civil suit for damages as well. When the Attorney General's Office requested Perry's bank records to verify the $100,000 loan as one of the conditions of dropping the charges against Kelly, she immediately complied, sending them an August 28, 1979, bank statement showing a deposit into her account of $99,500.

With all the elements of Moldaver's deal with the Crown in place, Kelly had reduced his immediate agenda to a single problem: coming up with a quick $100,000.

Lois Perry was proving to be quite an understanding person. When Kelly had called her in California and asked her to send a telegram admitting to owing him $100,000 she had never borrowed, she had been confused but nevertheless glad to help out her young friend. And when he picked her up at the airport on the day she arrived from California to talk to Sergeant Brosseau at the Crown Attorney's Office, she hadn't been offended when Kelly asked her to tell the false story to the authorities, including the detail that she had personally advised him that the $100,000 she had never borrowed had been deposited in his bank account in France.

The accommodating Perry accepted Kelly's story that he had the money to pay all his creditors in a super-restricted bank account in London that could only be accessed by his fingerprint. But since the conditions of his bail prohibited him from leaving the country, he couldn't get at his funds unless he could somehow arrange to have the fraud charges against him dropped. Without Perry's help, there was a good chance he would go to jail and no one would be paid.

If Perry had only remembered the events of 1981, when she had first met Kelly through Bobby Rapson, she would have seen the irony in his request. It had been Kelly, in fact, who had asked Perry for $100,000 that year for an unspecified European investment he promised would pay the middle-aged divorcée 5 per cent per month. Although he never went into detail at the time, it would have been the most unusual investment Perry had ever made, if she had been able to sell one of her Arabian horses to raise the money. "I was planning to utilize the funds to gamble and build my funds back up. My gambling would easily bring in 100 per cent per month on limited exposure," Kelly said later.

Perry had been so ready to help Kelly out of his predicament that she not only lied to Sergeant Brosseau, but even produced an old bank statement to verify Kelly's claim that he had, in fact, lent her $100,000 in 1979. In fact, the $99,500 deposit slip she sent to Canadian authorities at the request of the Attorney General's Office was the record of an old real estate transaction in Connecticut. Not satisfied by merely covering for her young friend, Perry borrowed $25,000 against a property she owned in northern Ontario and lent it to Kelly until March 5, 1983, as part of the $100,000 he needed to raise to get his charges dropped. She set only one condition: the money was for the specific purpose of repaying the complainants in the original fraud case, until he could get to his own funds in the London bank.

After using $10,000 of Lois Perry's money to pay Michael Moldaver's retainer, and splitting the rest between Bobby Rapson, Jan Bradley, and himself, Patrick Kelly played a long shot. He found out Paul Stewart's address from lawyer Howard Saginur and drove to Grimsby, Ontario, where his old friend had returned to the funeral business after running aground in his new career as a charter-cruise captain in the Caribbean. Stewart still owed Kelly $50,000 for the loan he had given him to buy the ill-fated *Carol Ann III*, and Kelly was hoping that the man who had been so useful to him at the time of Jeannette's death would be in a position to repay it.

The mortician gave Kelly a warm welcome. Over tea, Kelly noted that Stewart looked ten years older, twenty pounds overweight, and decidedly unprosperous. After Stewart's elderly wife, Marjorie, left the room, Kelly asked about his money. As he had half-expected, Stewart said that he was penniless and couldn't raise any money to repay his friend. He fully intended to repay the loan, it was just that he didn't know how to do it. As Kelly got up to go, Stewart stopped him and said that he had a confession to make. "He began to tell me that he loved me and had since he first saw me at the Palace Pier with Jeannette. He longed to be with me."

But Kelly didn't need warm sentiments, he needed cold, hard cash.

As the days crawled by, and Kelly seemed unable to extricate himself from his legal problems (on January 17, additional charges of false pretences arising out of the frauds were laid against him in Moldaver's office), Jan Bradley began thinking of returning to France alone. They had been able to spend the occasional night at the Harbour Castle, where an old girlfriend of Patrick's managed to arrange a 50 per cent discount for them, but between the police and the banks, their cash and credit cards had been seized, so they ended up spending most nights at Ruth Bradley's. Jan found it a difficult arrangement, and she welcomed any opportunity to escape to the city with her husband, however banal the reason.

As part of getting their financial house in order, the couple decided to take out life insurance, settling on mutual policies with a cash value of $1 million apiece. But even during a meeting with their insurance agent at the Harbour Castle, the shadow of Kelly's difficulties with the police fell across their luncheon table. Kelly and Bradley both had the feeling they were under surveillance during the meeting and were certain that Keith McNab of London Life was wearing a wire.

When McNab asked who the beneficiary was going to be on Bradley's policy, he was astonished when she named her brother, John Bradley. Bradley explained that her husband would not need the money in the event that something happened to her, and that her brother had always been the beneficiary on her life insurance policy when she worked at the library. Kelly had also found the choice of her beneficiary "a little odd" when she had first mentioned it to him, prompting Bradley to quip, "Just consider it one of the perks of being your wife."

The policies were never taken out.

To relieve the tension of living in close quarters with her mother, Bradley spent the occasional night with the Davidsons, who were back together, but she chafed under Roger's unwillingness to extend their hospitality to Kelly. Breaking with her former friends, and unable to live at home with her mother, she suggested to Patrick that it might be best for all concerned if she went back to France to await his return.

Kelly agreed, and on January 21, he drove her to the airport for her flight to Nice.

Returning to France turned out to have been a better idea in Toronto than it was in Valbonne. Bradley arrived to a bankrupt household, where she learned from Uwe Fenz that there hadn't even been enough money to buy food for the dogs, let alone run the villa. There was a stack of unpaid bills and a notice from their bank in Valbonne that unless Kelly explained and made good his raft of bad cheques, his banking privileges would be cancelled. Driven by her worst nightmare, financial insecurity, Bradley sent a terse ultimatum to her embattled husband just two days after returning to France. "Please straighten out this account <u>immediately</u> so as not to further jeopardize our financial security in this country. This is a top-priority item as it is our <u>only</u> contact with a transfer method – let's not lose it okay?"

With Jan "waiting and waiting and waiting" for Patrick to resolve his legal problems and get their finances back under control, the marriage began to show signs of coming unglued. Their daily long distance telephone conversations turned into bitter sparring matches that left both parties feeling hurt and hard done by. On February 14, Kelly had had enough and sent his wife a Valentine's letter that looked more like the first salvo in a divorce settlement.

"Jan,

"5:45 P.M. I spoke to you at 4:45 P.M. today, again the conversation ended on a sour note, or as I said, it was a 'shit' conversation. I haven't been keeping track, but I would estimate that 9 out of 10 have been ending that way lately. . . . My days lately are filled with running around trying to solve the present situation and also hopefully building a lot of protection so that you, we, are never exposed to this again. I'm not in control. In fact, I'm quite out of control. I'm working, trying, begging, crawling – I'm really not used to this but each day I rise and continue. . . . I don't have to continue like this. My choices are:

"I could leave now, and say to hell with everything, including you, your mother, my family.

"I could leave and hope you would join me and I could still say to hell with your mother.

"I could leave and hope you would join me and I could send your mother the surety funds.

"I could steal the required funds and your mother would be home free and you and I would continue our lives and hopefully regain whatever we have perhaps lost.

"I could commit suicide, your mother would be relieved of her surety position, you would have some funds, you would probably return to Canada and resume a <u>normal</u> life.

"I could do what I'm doing, letting the charges take their course, obtain the funds, have your mother properly released of her position and hope my wife is still home when I return. . . .

"I see the situation as one of choices, like the kind we always discuss. . . . You can stay or go, your feet are not nailed to the floor . . . if you decide to pack it in, I'll have between 10 and 25 thousand Canadian dollars to you immediately. Other funds will be to you as I liquidate things. I never screwed you and I never would, but I don't need <u>shit</u>. If you're going to stay, and I truly hope you do, then let's have no <u>shit</u>. . . . Black or white – you stay and we'll work through it or you'll go and we won't. . . . If it sounds cold, it's because it is cold. . . . My facts are – you're beautiful, you're bright, you're personable, you're loving (most of the time), you can be a true bitch (usually for just cause but fact none the same) – you want a lot and I want to give it! . . . <u>Choices.</u> LOVE & STAY & ASSIST & REBUILD & LIVE NO SHIT! <u>OR</u> GO WELL & I'LL LOVE YOU FOREVER & START AGAIN & I'LL ASSIST YOU FOREVER – WANTED OR UNWANTED. NO BLAME EITHER WAY. <u>JUST FACTS.</u>

"All my love, Pat. Please don't flounder, decide."

Two days after sending his own ultimatum to Jan, the RCMP added to Kelly's problems by charging him with passport fraud. The noose was getting tighter.

In the course of his frantic attempts to put together the money to satisfy his creditors and win back the trust of his fretting wife, Kelly was having a coffee with Howard Saginur, when the man he described as his "corporate lawyer" mentioned that perhaps an undertaking from another party might help him attract some capital.

Kelly must have agreed that it was a good idea. After Saginur left his office to attend a meeting, Kelly noticed that he had left some of his letterhead on the table where they had been having coffee. Seizing the chance, he typed up a letter to Lygoe & Co., a British law firm and investment house Kelly had previously dealt with, asking for an immediate advance of £30,000. The moneys were to be secured by an undertaking from Howard Saginur to remit to the British firm £30,000 plus interest on or before May 30. The moneys for the undertaking were to come from the sale of goods worth $200,000 U.S. at a Sotheby's auction in New York that were being disposed of "on behalf of Mr. Kelly." When he'd finished the letter, Kelly signed Saginur's name to it and put it in the mail. In later explaining this "naughty" deed, Kelly claimed that when Saginur laid the letterhead on the table after talking about getting an undertaking, he was tacitly sanctioning his client's action.

"I read between the lines and certainly understood what he was trying to say and I took advantage of it. . . . Can't say he agreed, but can't say he didn't know or didn't agree, but the unspoken was a presented opportunity."

When Lygoe & Co. responded to the terms of Howard Saginur's apparent undertaking a few days later, Saginur was so upset that he called its London office twice, and when no one responded, he fired off a registered, special-delivery letter to J. P. Lygoe. Unaware of who had written the phony letter, the frustrated lawyer informed the British company that his files showed no record of any correspondence between their two firms. He asked for the immediate return of all documents referred to in their reply to his alleged proposal for raising £30,000 on behalf of his client. But someone knew exactly what had happened. "This was a little bit of my past coming out, where I just got my back up and thought, screw you guys . . . and I ripped them. I ripped them for fifty thousand dollars. It was really no big deal," Kelly later said.

With his forged undertaking to Lygoe & Co. in the works, Kelly went back to Graham Gordon of Yolles with yet another proposition to swing a deal on some valuable paintings the antique dealer was anxious to sell. Although Gordon claimed the paintings were worth $300,000, Kelly offered to pay $125,000 U.S., explaining that in order to mask the title to the works, the money would be placed in a lawyer's trust account and not identified in the buyer's name. Once he got out of the country, Kelly would pay 10 per cent down on the paintings and the balance in ninety days. A Toronto dentist and art collector, Norman Rasky, was interested in participating in the deal, and would sign a promissory note guaranteeing the transaction.

Gordon told Kelly that he would require the physical possession of the paintings to secure the note, as well as a registered chattels mortgage against them until they were paid off in full. To transfer title, the moneys would have to be paid to Gordon's bank. Kelly agreed, and said that he would be meeting Rasky on Wednesday, March 2, to get the promissory note.

On March 3, Graham Gordon received two urgent telephone calls. The first was from Norman Rasky, who was "quite upset" because Kelly hadn't shown up for their morning meeting, the second from Howard Saginur, who told Gordon that his client, Patrick Kelly, would appreciate a visit at the Metro Toronto West Detention Centre.

Something unexpected had happened.

15

THE RELUCTANT WITNESS

Patrick Kelly rose early on the morning of Wednesday, March 2, shivering when his bare feet hit the cold bathroom floor. He slipped a new blade into his razor and thought ahead to his meeting with Norman Rasky. The "Gainsborough" was already wrapped in protective blankets in the trunk of his rental car, and he hoped that when the dentist saw the painting, he would be convinced that there was big money to be made by getting in on his deal with Graham Gordon.

Kelly stepped into the shower and gasped at the cold water, but the momentary discomfort was soon replaced by a familiar exhilaration, and he focused again on the crucial task of getting funds to Bradley in France. With Rasky's promissory note guaranteeing the $125,000 U.S. he had promised Gordon for the paintings, Kelly would be a big step closer to taking possession of $300,000 worth of art. Even if he couldn't sell the works because of Gordon's security conditions, there was a good chance that the paintings could be used as collateral for a substantial loan. God knew how badly he needed the money.

Stepping out of the shower, he dried himself briskly, and then began to shave slowly and carefully before getting into the clothes he had laid out the night before. He moved quietly through the house so as not to disturb Ruth Bradley and stepped outside into the chilly March sunshine.

Years of undercover work had left him constantly on "yellow," a perpetual state of caution that had saved his life on more than one occasion over the course of hundreds of encounters with drug dealers and other criminals. He scanned the street. Off to his right, almost out of his peripheral vision, Kelly noticed a car back up, dipping its lights as it disappeared out of sight. A typical surveillance move, he thought, glancing quickly to his left. No one was in sight, but then they wouldn't be if they were any good. Putting on his aviator sunglasses, he got into his car and headed south on Highway 36 towards Lindsay, Ontario, and the 401, frequently checking his rearview mirror to see if he had company.

Detectives Ed Stewart and Joe Cziraky had also risen early that morning, reporting for duty at 6:10 A.M. Cziraky arranged for the Lindsay OPP to send a surveillance team to Ruth Bradley's house, and at 6:30 A.M. Stewart awakened a startled Roger Davidson to verify that Kelly was still driving a grey Dodge Aries he had rented from the car dealer. The detectives then drove to Dunsford, spotting Kelly's car at 7:35 A.M. as he drove southbound on Highway 36, followed by an unmarked car from the OPP. Making a U-turn, they headed back towards Lindsay and radioed instructions for the cavalry to move in.

When the OPP cruiser behind him began flashing its lights, Kelly reacted like an undercover agent. Having been trained never to pull over in a remote area, he kept driving at the same rate of speed past the flaxen stubble of the late winter fields until he reached the outskirts of Lindsay, where he stopped directly in front of the nearest house. That way, he thought, if anything happened, there would be people around to see it. Noticing in his mirror that the OPP officer was getting out of his vehicle, Kelly decided to get out and meet him.

"I open the door of the car and go to step out, and this guy draws a gun and he points it at me. And he's shaking. He is just a-vibrating, and I said, 'Whoa!' I remember saying to this guy when I see him with this gun, 'I don't know what this is about, but take it easy. I'm going to turn around *real* slow here and put my hands on the roof and spread my legs.' And then all of a sudden, cops all over the place."

The official report of events made no reference to the gunpoint confrontation that Kelly so vividly remembers. After the suspect had been pulled over by the OPP, backup units from the Lindsay police arrived. Sgt. Ed Stewart got out of his car on the west shoulder of the highway, and walked over to the slender, well-dressed figure standing beside the grey rental car. It was a long way from that midnight in the morgue and Stewart had been thinking about this moment for almost two years. "I went up to him and took him by the left arm and I placed him under arrest for the first degree murder of his wife."

After advising Kelly of his rights and wishing him good luck, Stewart cuffed Kelly's hands behind his back and placed him in the backseat of his police cruiser. He then searched Kelly's car, finding the Gainsborough painting, a green bag containing a diamond cluster ring and other jewellery, six parking tickets, a library book on the art of Richard Wilson, a bill from Applied Polygraph Sciences Inc. for $350 (Kelly had taken and passed a private lie detector test over the fraud charges), and a Goudie squash racquet.

Stewart also came across a letter to a woman in England that had been written just two days earlier. From the text of the letter to Vicky Hill, it was clear that the correspondents hadn't known each other for very long.

"Dear Vicky,

"I really must apologize for not arriving yet, but this project is turning into a complete crusade and one I'm not enjoying very much. However, I'm in a position for the first time in my life that I've committed so much time and money to the project that I must now see it through. The only consolation is that when (not if) the project is completed, the returns are really quite incredible. Once it's done, I think it's time for a little time away for Patrick in the sun . . . (maybe with a truly lovely lady – hint, hint). I could really use the relaxation, the tan, the company. How do long nights, soft lights, stars, moon, fine wines, soft music, hot sun, warm beaches, white sand and no wake-up calls sound to you?

"Now, how about a little about me? I'm 33 years old, 5'10", 155 pounds, widowed, no children, Canadian, residing between Canada (Toronto and Victoria, B.C.) France, (the South) and Hawaii, self-employed, comfortable, come from a family of 5 kids, raised in Canada, high-school graduate, multi-lingual, (7 languages fluent, 4 passable) I love my sheepdog, I'm truly romantic . . . I think you are beautiful!!!"

Stewart smiled; it was his man all right. He placed the letter in a plastic evidence bag, got into the cruiser, and drove to the Lindsay

Detachment of the OPP, where he and Cziraky took Kelly to the basement canteen. At Kelly's request, Stewart removed his sunglasses and recuffed him with his hands to the front. The detectives then allowed Kelly the standard call to his lawyer, taking the telephone from him when he was finished to advise Michael Moldaver that his client would be appearing in the East Mall court later that day to be arraigned on a charge of first degree murder.

Stewart then interrogated Kelly at length on his previous statements to police, reading from a long list of prepared questions. Seated comfortably on one of the canteen's orange plastic chairs with his legs crossed and his cuffed hands folded in his lap, Kelly answered every one of them the same way: on the advice of counsel, he did not wish to make any statements to police. With the formal charade of the interview complete, Stewart called Crown attorney Lloyd Budzinsky to advise him of Kelly's arrest, then the three men returned to Toronto.

"How are you feeling, Pat?" Stewart asked, as the nondescript countryside that flanked the highway rolled by.

"Fine," he replied.

If Kelly thought he was going straight to jail when they got to Toronto, Stewart had a surprise in store for him. He headed west on Lakeshore Boulevard until the distinctive cruciform silhouette of the Palace Pier loomed up on their left.

"How are you feeling, Pat?" Stewart again asked as they drew near the high-rise complex where Jeannette Kelly had died.

"Fine, thank you. And you?"

Stewart didn't bother to answer. He stopped a few feet from the southwest corner of the building, got out of the cruiser, and took Kelly out of the backseat. Escorting him to the cement loading dock, he pointed to a precise spot by the steps and delivered his next words standing face-to-face with his rigid prisoner.

"Your wife's body was found right here," Stewart said. "And that was your apartment up there," he continued, pointing a thick finger towards the seventeenth storey. "Do you wish to make a comment?"

"I have no comment to make on the advice of my lawyer," Kelly said softly.

As they took the prisoner back to the cruiser, Stewart thought he detected some physical signs that his calculated shock treatment had had its effect on the man he believed had murdered Jeannette Kelly. Noting that Kelly "was very flushed in the face, neck and his hands," Stewart asked for the third time how Kelly was feeling.

"I'm okay."

"Are you crying, Pat?" Stewart probed, suspecting that he was, but unable to know for sure because he couldn't see Kelly's eyes.

Removing his dark glasses and looking directly at the detective, Kelly answered in a calm and confident tone.

"No, I'm not."

On the ride downtown to the police station Kelly found out why he had been arrested. The detectives apparently had an eyewitness who claimed to have been in apartment 1705 when Patrick Kelly threw his wife over the balcony.

The ranger station on Mount Pisgah stood straight and tall against the encircling forest, and Victor Bragg thought it would be the ideal place to take in the perfection of the May morning. Bragg, his girlfriend, Dawn Taber, and a younger couple had been "four-wheeling" in the remote area of central Maine when they came across the fire-tower and decided to climb to the top. Although Taber hadn't liked the idea from the moment Bragg suggested it, she went along with the others.

By the time the group mounted the last set of stairs, cooled by a mild spring breeze, it was obvious that something terrible was happening to Taber. Panic-stricken and short of breath, she looked completely terrified, almost as if she were having a heart attack. What the others did not understand was that their companion's difficulties had nothing to do with overexertion or vertigo: she was looking down the fire-tower of memory at a landscape of horror and murder, of blood and Jeannette Kelly's broken body lying on the ground below.

A few days after her frightening vision on the fire-tower, Taber turned to Rena McAllister for help. It wasn't the first time. She had met the University of Maine graduate in the fall of 1981 through her new job at Cycil Kettle General Insurance Agency in Portland, Maine, where she had been hired as a salesperson. McAllister worked as an industrial psychologist for the agency and also taught courses in business insurance and client-building to Kettle's new agents.

Taber attended McAllister's classes three Fridays a month and began arriving early and leaving late so that the two women could talk about personal matters. It was obvious to McAllister that something was bothering Taber, and when the classes ended in late January 1982, she wasn't surprised when Taber asked if she could start seeing her on a regular basis to discuss her personal life. Convinced that she needed someone to talk to, McAllister obliged.

"During these meetings, she related problems relating to her husband, Pinkie [John Hastey], and her mother, and being abandoned and abused as a child," McAllister remembers.

When Taber brought up Jeannette Kelly's murder, a subject she talked about in a flat, emotionless fashion, McAllister grew concerned. She wasn't certain about her rights and responsibilities as a citizen, but continued talking to her informal client (McAllister never charged for the Tuesday morning sessions) because she was sceptical about the whole story. More than anything else, Taber seemed to afraid "of being found," possibly by the man she said had committed the murder, Patrick Kelly. "She was a witness," McAllister later explained, "and she was afraid of him for that reason."

After the experience in the fire-tower, Taber became animated and emotional in their conversations about Jeannette's death. From the way that Taber cried and trembled when she talked about the vision, McAllister believed that she had come to a "crisis point" in her life, and asked the troubled woman if she saw any link between coming down the tower and her friend's violent death. "She said, 'Yes, Jeannette is dead. Her body is there. . . .'" McAllister recalled being told.

As the two women delved more deeply into Taber's complex emotional predicament, McAllister got a clearer picture of what had apparently happened. Kelly had planned his wife's murder in order to collect her life insurance money. Though Taber somehow knew of the plan, she had not been a conspirator in the crime. She had merely been in the apartment that day to patch up her friendship with Jeannette and had the bad luck of walking in on an argument and a homicide. After the victim had been disposed of, Taber had talked with Kelly on the balcony and then looked over the railing, where she saw the murdered woman on the ground below.

Taber's graphic account convinced McAllister that she really had witnessed a murder after all, and that during her ordeal on the fire-tower,

Taber had had "whole, unusual recall" of that terrible day. As the psychologist later observed, "She would never have had that reaction from the tower unless she had witnessed the homicide."

McAllister advised Taber to go to the police and to seek professional psychiatric assistance to help her cope with the event that was totally consuming her. Taber was grateful for the advice, but said that it was no use going to the police. She had already done that and they hadn't believed her.

From the day he found out that Patrick Kelly had remarried and moved to the south of France after collecting his dead wife's insurance money, Sgt. Ed Stewart had regretted not believing the story Dawn Taber had given him just days after Jeannette Kelly's death. At the time, it had all seemed like the stuff of soap operas, but after Kelly essentially carried out the plan Taber had described in her April 1981 police interview, albeit with a different woman, the detective had a change of heart. Maybe this woman knew more about what had happened after all.

Remembering how angry Taber had been when she found out that Kelly had left the country with Jan Bradley, Stewart decided to call her again after the fraud squad informed him that Kelly had been arrested. If Taber had been expecting to go away with Kelly, as both she and John Nascimento claimed, Stewart thought she might be ready to reveal more details about how Jeannette Kelly had died, especially now that the prime suspect was behind bars.

Stewart tried to reach her at her sister's house in Maine, where she was expected for a pre-Christmas family visit, and left a message for Taber to call him at the homicide squad. When she returned his call, he explained that Kelly had been arrested for fraud and was now in jail in Toronto. The homicide squad was still looking into the Kelly case, he said, and would appreciate it if Taber would jot down the information she had given them in 1981 that had never been committed to a formal statement. Taber asked when Kelly's fraud trial would be held, then promised to send the detective three pages of notes she'd made about the things she and Kelly had talked about in the year before Jeannette's death.

When the notes still hadn't arrived three weeks later, Stewart called Taber on January 10, 1983, at the Portsmouth, New Hampshire, law office where she now worked as a legal secretary. When he asked about the notes, she said that they had just been returned to her after apparently going to the wrong address. It was a lie: Taber had never mailed them and had no intentions of mailing them.

Unaware that the call was being taped, Taber went over the ground she had already covered with police, including Kelly's plan to increase Jeannette's life insurance without her knowledge, the letter to Austin Cooper about the Cookstown fire that Kelly had dictated to her, and the scheme to obtain credit cards and loans that would never be repaid after she and Kelly had disappeared into France with false identities – a detail that carried new authority with Stewart now that the fraud squad had recovered false identification from Kelly's safety deposit box.

The more Taber talked, the more Stewart realized that she may, in fact, have been part of a plot to murder Jeannette Kelly. Could that be why her loyalties in the matter were so strangely divided between Kelly and the police, and why she hadn't sent Stewart the notes she had promised? Was a fierce battle raging inside her between two of the most elemental psychic forces on earth – conscience and the instinct for self-preservation? Deciding that there was only way to find out, Stewart asked, point-blank, if she had been part of a conspiracy to commit murder without perhaps realizing it.

"I think so, yes I do. I certainly do," she answered

Before hanging up, Stewart played the card that he hoped might help him catch him a killer. If Taber had been involved, unwittingly or otherwise, in Jeannette Kelly's death, and was now afraid for herself, the only way he would ever get her to testify against Kelly would be to give her immunity from prosecution. Advising her that they could work out a deal in which nothing she said could be used against her, Stewart asked her to think about it and promised to call again.

A month later, on February 10, 1983, Stewart had been clearing up some paperwork in his office after a long day at a murder trial when he received the telephone call that would crack the Jeannette Kelly case. As soon as he recognized Dawn Taber's voice on the other end of the line, he activated the tape recorder connected to his telephone and began one of the strangest conversations he would ever hold.

After a perfunctory exchange about the progress of Kelly's fraud case, Stewart asked Taber if she had anything to tell him that she hadn't already mentioned during their earlier conversation. She admitted that there were things that she wanted to talk about, but told him she didn't want to write anything down. He instantly grasped her dilemma.

"You're probably a bit concerned about a few things, ah, that might be used against you and this sort of thing. Is that not true?"

"Yes," she answered. "I am very concerned about it."

"If there is something that you're scared could incriminate you," Stewart replied, "you are protected anyway under the Charter [of Rights and Freedoms] here in Canada, and ah . . ."

"In what way?"

Stewart explained the Canadian constitutional equivalent of the Fifth Amendment and also promised that he would give her a written undertaking that nothing she told police about the case would ever be used in any proceeding against her. It was an offer that left the door wide open to charging Taber with murder if other evidence emerged linking her to the case. The operative word in Stewart's immunity deal was that nothing *she* said would come back to haunt her. Still, he made it sound quite attractive.

"It would be in writing . . . it will have to be done up in legal terms. You would have to read it yourself to be satisfied with it. Do you understand?"

"Yes."

"If that was the case, there would never be any problem. . . . It would have to be done up front, and if you wanted to have a lawyer or something like that here, we could, but I don't think it would be advisable for you to have the same counsel as Pat Kelly."

"Oh God, no!" she exclaimed, realizing that Stewart might be thinking she had somehow taken part in Jeannette Kelly's murder. Nothing could be further from the truth, but it was that very impression that was causing her such anxiety, as she tried to explain.

"You see the problem is, I never realized just exactly how much the finger was pointed at me and how circumstances have put me in, really, I mean, as, as, you know, an accomplice in this whole thing . . ."

After a long pause, Taber asked the detective if they could continue the interview in the United States. Stewart asked if there was more that she wanted to tell him about Jeannette Kelly's death.

"A lot more."

"There is?"

"Not a lot more, but probably the one thing . . ."

"That we need?" he suggested.

"Yes."

"Okay. And why would you not tell me now?"

"On the phone?"

"Yeah."

"I don't know what the consequences are for me. . . . I have to save my skin too, in the sense that, you know, it looks pretty bad for me, when the fact [is] it is totally innocent and there is no way that I can explain it."

The experienced detective was on dangerous ground, since it was imperative to the case he was trying to build against Patrick Kelly that he not be seen as in any way prompting a response from a potentially crucial witness. Desperately wanting to hear what Taber was so afraid to tell him, Stewart had to make sure that the rules were clearly understood, without discouraging her from coming forward. It was a tightrope that every homicide investigator has to walk at one time or another in pursuit of the people who break the Sixth Commandment.

"I am pretty sure I know what you are going to say, but I do not want to put words into your mouth. I want to hear it from yourself, you know," he told her. "I can assure you right now that you can give it to me on the understanding that it will not be used against you at any future proceeding. You understand that?

"Yes, I do understand."

"Okay. Just give me an idea what it is you have to say," Stewart prompted. "Go ahead, spit it out."

"The day that . . ."

"Go ahead."

"I was in the Palace Pier the day that Jeannette was killed."

"You were?" the astonished detective replied. At most, he had theorized that Dawn might have had conversations with Kelly about the murder plan.

"Yes."

By the time they had finished talking, Taber had given Stewart a virtual eyewitness account of Jeannette Kelly's last doomed moments on earth. Taber told him that she had gone over to the Palace Pier that Sunday afternoon to make amends with Jeannette for an old falling out. When she arrived, the couple were quarrelling and she retreated to the den. A few moments later, the yelling and shouting abruptly stopped after she heard what she believed was the sound of Kelly striking his wife. When she walked back into the living room to see what had happened, Kelly was standing on the balcony, and she joined him outside.

"He was just looking in the air with a big, you know, look, I can't explain the look on his face, you know, a desperate look and I, I looked over."

"What did you see?" Stewart asked.

"Jeannette."

"You saw her?"

"Yeah."

Taber explained that Kelly had then escorted her to the express elevator on an upper floor, told her to leave through the basement parking garage and say nothing to anyone. Towards the end of the interview, Stewart posed a question that summed up the essential elements of her story.

"You were there, they were fighting, and you walked out onto the balcony and you saw him there and you saw her, down below?"

"Yes."

It was an explosive account, but one that had come so long after the event it claimed to describe that there was bound to be doubt about its truthfulness. After all, Taber had had every opportunity to tell her story to police from the day Jeannette Kelly had died. Given the added incentive that it was her best friend who had been murdered while she was in the apartment, why had she taken nearly two years to come forward? When Stewart asked that question, Taber's answer was not very convincing. It had been "a difficult situation" and she had felt "devastated." The more likely explanation, Stewart thought, was the desire to keep as far away as possible from the police.

There were also a few factual inconsistencies that bothered him. For example, Taber said Jeannette had been wearing a T-shirt that day in the apartment, when, in fact, the victim's body had been found in a long-sleeved, navy-blue cashmere sweater. But these were the worries of another day. The first item on his agenda was to get Taber's story down in statement form.

When Stewart asked her to come to Canada under the general terms of the immunity he had already outlined, Taber suggested that he come to the United States. Sensing that she still thought he was trying to trick her into returning to the jurisdiction so that he could arrest her for Jeannette Kelly's murder, Stewart pointed out that it was hardly necessary given the nature of the crime they were discussing.

"Well, the thing is, if we were going to charge you with something, you could be extradited from the United States. You know that?" he asked.

"Yes."

"So I'm talking to you honestly, if it's possible for you to come up, you've got nothing to fear. Now if that's difficult for you, I'll arrange to go down and see you, and talk to you down there. Would you prefer that, or would you prefer to come here?"

"I think it would be easier for you to come here," she replied.

"Okay. We'll do it that way."

Before hanging up, Taber made one more admission to Stewart that she had previously made to Rena McAllister: she was "terrified" of Patrick Kelly and wondered if people realized what he was capable of doing.

"Just leave it with us and we'll deal with that problem ourselves," Stewart said. "We're well equipped to, ah, look after your safety."

On February 21, 1983, Sgt. Ed Stewart flew to Boston and made the one and a half hour drive to Portsmouth, New Hampshire, to meet Dawn Taber. It was a Monday, and after Taber got off work, she and her boyfriend, Victor Bragg, drove to the local police station, where they met Stewart and Det. Don Clark of the Portsmouth police at 5:15 P.M. Before beginning the five-hour interview, which Stewart recorded on foolscap as Taber talked, he showed her the immunity agreement drawn up on February 18 by Crown attorney Lloyd Budzinsky.

Satisfied that it was in order, Taber once again described her relationship with Patrick Kelly and what she knew about his wife's murder. Protected by her immunity agreement, Taber cleared up one of the puzzles of her April 4, 1981, interview with police, in which she had claimed that Kelly planned to fake his own death, give Jeannette the proceeds of his life insurance, and then run off with Taber. The plan had made no sense to Stewart and was one of the reasons he had tended not to believe the rest of her story at the time.

Taber now admitted that what she had first told police about the insurance angle had been a "fabrication" because she was "afraid of going to jail" if she told the true story. Given what she was now saying, her fear had not been unreasonable. The real plan she and Kelly had talked about in the spring of 1980 when she was living at the Palace Pier had been to murder Jeannette and live in France on the proceeds of her life insurance, which would be sent to them by Victor Simpson.

"He told me after he killed her, I was to go to the airport in Toronto, and we would leave as the people we were, but we would have to make a stopover flight in order to change our identities and get rid of [our] old identification . . . I did not ask Pat how he was going to do it, but I assumed he was going to hit her and knock her unconscious before he threw her over. . . . In my mind, I felt Patrick was serious and that he would carry the plan through to kill Jeannette, collect the insurance through Victor, and move away with me, and live happily ever after."

It was that previous plan, which was never again discussed after Taber and Jeannette returned from their trip to Europe in the summer of 1980, that was now causing Taber all her problems. She claimed that on the day of Jeannette's death nearly a year later, she had been at the apartment by sheer accident to discuss some personal matters with her friend. But when the chain of events that led to Jeannette's murder began to unfold, she knew from their earlier scheme what Kelly was going to do. The guilt she was now feeling was for keeping that knowledge from Jeannette until it was too late. "I knew what Pat was planning to do, and I never told her and I never stopped him . . . I did not know it was going to happen that day, but I was part of a plan to kill her in the same manner."

Stewart terminated the interview at 11:30 P.M., when it became obvious that the witness was exhausted and that they wouldn't be able to get through everything they needed to talk about in one sitting. He drove Taber back to her home and told her that they would continue with her statement the following morning. All through the sleepless night, Stewart kept thinking about Taber's professed guilt for not stopping Kelly from killing his wife. But how, he wondered, could she be expected to stop him, when she hadn't actually seen him commit the crime? The answer to that question would provide the bombshell of Taber's statement, and the most damning evidence yet gathered against Kelly in the continuing investigation into his wife's death.

The next morning when the interview turned to the ghastly details of Jeannette Kelly's murder, Taber was "very emotional" and cried. Noticing that she appeared to be gasping for breath, Det. Don Clark opened the window of the interview room to make her more comfortable. Just as she had during the earlier telephone interview with Stewart, she described hearing the sound of flesh striking flesh, and then joining Kelly on the balcony, where she looked down and saw Jeannette on the ground. In the act of retelling the story, it seemed to the detectives as if the witness was reliving it.

"I looked at Pat and he said something like, 'Oh my God, what have I done?'" Taber said, explaining that she had fallen to her knees at the realization that her friend had just been killed.

"I kept seeing Pat throwing Jeannette over the balcony, but I am having trouble accepting that he did it. I keep seeing it over and over in my mind. It has been tormenting me ever since it happened. I keep having nightmares, I keep seeing him throwing her over. She was not moving when he fired her over, she was doing nothing. I was in the den when she went over, you can see the balcony from the den. I had no idea he was going to do it. I have been trying to block it out of my mind as I do not want to believe it. I do not want to believe that Jeannette is dead."

Taber began to weep softly and steadily, completing her chilling account through her tears. "I don't hate Pat. I pity him. I saw him throw her over. . . . I think I need a shrink, this whole thing is driving me crazy."

When the interview was over, Stewart gave Taber the thick pile of foolscap he had used to record her statement, and asked her to read it and to make any corrections or additions she saw fit. When she was finished, he had her read the whole document into a tape recorder, then sign the written version.

"Tell me now that you are going to arrest me," the emotionally drained woman said. Stewart replied that he had no intentions of arresting her, provided she had told him the "truth."

She assured him she had.

When he returned to Toronto, Ed Stewart met with Crown attorney Lloyd Budzinsky to discuss the latest development in the Kelly case. Everyone agreed that Taber's statement was precisely the piece of evidence they needed to charge Kelly with his wife's murder. But there was a big problem that came down to a single word: credibility.

Stewart had officially spoken to Taber on four separate occasions and each time she had told a different story. If what she was now saying in her signed statement was true, she had lied to police in her April 1981 interview by concealing the fact that she had been in apartment 1705 on the day of the murder. During the taped telephone conversation with Stewart on January 10, 1983, she had admitted that she had been an unwitting party to a conspiracy to murder Jeannette Kelly, but still made no mention of having been in the apartment on March 29, 1981. A month later, during their second taped interview, she had acknowledged for the first time that she had been there on the day of the murder, but swore that she definitely did not see Patrick Kelly either strike his wife or throw her over the balcony. But by the time Stewart took her formal statement in Portsmouth eleven days later, she was claiming that she had actually witnessed Kelly throw his wife off the balcony from her vantage point in the den, though her emotion-charged words had alternated between the language of fact and imagination.

Making her evidence even shakier was the fact that Stewart had repeatedly asked Taber during their February 10 telephone conversation if what she was telling him — that she had been in the apartment but had seen nothing — was the truth. It had been the one condition he set on his offer of immunity. Her answer that day had been categorical: "To the best of my knowledge, yes." Then, just over a week later, her story had changed dramatically with the claim that she had witnessed Kelly throw Jeannette over the balcony at the Palace Pier.

There had, of course, been a major difference between Taber's February 21 interview and all her previous conversations with police —

in Portsmouth, she had been presented with a written immunity deal. Since she had previously expressed fear of being charged if she told police everything she knew, it was altogether possible that she had been waiting for that document before relating the most damaging aspects of her story. And although she had changed that story on several occasions, there had been a definite progression from general information to very precise detail in each of her interviews, as if the higher her comfort levels, the more truth she was willing to tell.

But Stewart also remembered Taber's alleged vow to John Nascimento after returning from Jeannette Kelly's funeral that she would do everything possible to put Kelly in jail. Was she now taking her revenge on the man who may have jilted her? As devastating as her evidence against Kelly was, Stewart and Budzinsky knew that unless this witness was absolutely solid, their case could be blown over like a house of cards in a single, effective cross-examination. They agreed that before they took any dramatic steps based on her damning statement, Taber should come to Toronto for a final interview with Stewart and Cziraky. But this time, there would also be a medical expert on hand to assess her emotional state and, if necessary, to assist in removing any psychological obstacles that might be preventing her from articulating everything she knew.

Stewart arranged for Dawn Taber and Victor Bragg to fly to Toronto on February 27, where they were met at the airport by police and escorted to their hotel. Bearing in mind Taber's fear of Kelly, Stewart made sure security was tight.

At 10:30 A.M. on the first day of March 1983, Ed Stewart and Joe Cziraky introduced Dawn Taber to Dr. Peter Rowsell, the forensic psychiatrist who had been retained to help them with their problematic witness. Earlier that morning, Stewart had briefed Rowsell for an hour and a half on the case. When he was finished, Taber joined the two detectives and the psychiatrist in a room in the Ramada Inn at Dixie Road and Highway 401, where the session was held.

After introductions, Stewart, Rowsell, and Taber sat at a table by the window, while Cziraky propped himself up on the bed and took notes. According to Rowsell's usual practice, the two-part session was taped. The first session, which lasted for several hours, was spent trying to establish rapport between doctor and subject. They talked about Taber's early life in Maine, where she had endured "considerable suffering . . . usually the victim of some man." The painful accounts were in keeping with what she had previously told Rena McAllister about being abandoned and abused as a child. In the psychiatrist's opinion, Taber had consequently developed a deep empathy for anyone who was either helpless or in emotional turmoil, becoming their "great rescuer and protector."

Rowsell noted that this may have been one of the reasons she was so ambivalent about Patrick Kelly. On the one hand, she was well aware of his manipulative nature, but on the other, he had also shown her his vulnerable side. "This is one of the ways that Pat can look at her, apparently helpless and hurt, even to the point [where] he can cry like a little boy, so that her heart can, so to speak, melt towards him," Rowsell noted.

For his part, the psychiatrist did his best to explain to Taber how he intended to help her overcome her memory lapses concerning the events of March 29, 1981. It was not an easy task. Rowsell was a neurolinguistic programmer, an exotic specialty within psychiatry whose practitioners attempt to communicate directly with the unconscious side of a subject while that subject is in a state of full consciousness – relaxation therapy rather than hypnotism.

Rowsell told Taber that the competent side of her brain was well aware of what had happened that day, but that the incompetent side was preventing her from speaking the words because it was trying to protect her from Kelly and the potential legal consequences of telling the whole truth. She later remembered him illustrating his point by asking her to place her hands on her lap and observe that one was pink, the other, white. When she was at mental peace with herself over this matter, both hands would be the same colour, he assured her. Towards the end of their first session, although Taber was still in considerable turmoil, Rowsell thought he detected the beginnings of a change.

"In the interview time prior to lunch, when the events themselves in the condominium had not even been discussed, but we were really talking about Dawn [and] her fear of what she did not want to remember in that apartment, eventually she came to a decision that the competent side of her wanted to know what the truth really was and the fearful, weak side of her might have to give way, and it was suggested that she think it over during the lunch hour, and we took an hour break for lunch."

Rowsell was right, and Ed Stewart was the first to find out that his intervention had apparently led to a breakthrough. After a brief conversation with Taber and Victor Bragg in the lounge of the hotel, Stewart took out his notebook and scratched down a hurried but crucial entry: "Miss Taber [is] now afraid of her involvement because the time has come to tell us more. She told me, 'I was there, I saw him do it.'"

When Taber returned to the hotel room to continue her conversation with Rowsell, she seemed very different than the evasive and anxious woman of their earlier session. Brimming with confidence and making solid eye contact with the psychiatrist, she began giving clear and competent descriptions of things she had previously been unable to remember. Rowsell observed three distinct states in his subject as Taber revealed the details of Jeannette Kelly's death.

As she described the actual murder, she was clearly in the grip of a palpable fear. Her breathing grew shallow, her face grew pale, and her entire body began to shake, just as it had in the sessions with Rena McAllister after the vision in the fire-tower.

"What I saw was Pat picking her up. He had both arms underneath and bent over. He had her head in his left arm. I knew she was limp; in my opinion, unconscious. He was walking over. I watched as he opened the door with the hand that was holding her head. He slid the door open. He walked out and threw her over. When he was picking her up, he had looked at me. He knew I was watching him. There were no words spoken – nothing was said. He then threw her over. I was standing about where he had picked her up when he threw her over. I went out on the balcony and looked down after he'd thrown her over. I didn't stare, I just looked over. I didn't tell you before – the reason I couldn't make myself tell you before is because I was afraid. I didn't know what it meant. I didn't trust you. I thought about preventing it, but I did nothing to stop Pat and I knew when he was picking her up, I knew what he was going to do. I knew. It's God awful."

Rowsell noted that when Taber started to describe how tenderly Kelly had treated her in the aftermath of the murder, she fell into a very different state, a deep sadness in which her eyes welled up with tears and a red flush appeared on her face and neck.

"He kept telling me how much he loved me. He kissed me. He said there'd be no problems. He was holding me very lovingly. He took me out to the elevator. He kept telling me, 'Don't let anybody see me.' He told me to go down the back stairs. I took the opposite elevators as they don't stop on the way down . . . I went to the [Sherbourne St.] apartment. I didn't say anything. I stayed packed at all times . . . Pat was to call me. He didn't call me that day or the next."

By the time Taber reached the third state, in which she began to clearly relate what else had happened that day and answer his questions crisply, the psychiatrist's presence was no longer required and the police took over. Stewart asked if she had been in love with Kelly at the time of the murder, and she told him that she had been and perhaps still was. She also admitted that she had been angry with Jeannette at the time of her death. When he inquired what would have happened if Kelly had asked her to go with him when he left the country, her answer confirmed what Stewart had suspected all along about their relationship.

"If he had phoned me, I would have gone with him. I would have done anything he told me to do."

Stewart asked her if Kelly had struck Jeannette with anything other than his fists that day.

"I don't know. The way she was screaming, someone must have heard her screams. I was in the den. It was right in the doorway. He was first bent over her, picking her up, when I saw her. Her head was on his left arm. I walked out and saw everything. He saw me as he carried her out. I had thoughts – STOP, don't stop. She deserves it. This is my way out. . . ."

Stewart showed her a copy of her February 21 statement and invited her to make any necessary revisions and to initial every page. For the fifth time, Taber's story had changed. No longer observing events from the den, she now claimed that after hearing Jeannette's terrible scream she had entered the living room, where she saw Kelly lifting his unconscious wife from the floor.

"It was terrifying. Her voice was blood-curdling. I went out. Pat was picking Jeannette up off the floor of the living room just inside the doorway. When he picked her up, he turned and looked at me. His expression was nothing. He went over to the balcony doors. He opened the outside door. He was holding her. I just stood there. I watched him just dump her."

Turning to Stewart, Taber expressed relief that her awful secret was finally out.

"I can handle this in court. I feel better now."

Taber agreed to swear an affidavit attesting to the truthfulness of her final statement, including a clause that read: "I understand that any **intentional** omissions, lies, or misstatements may subject me to criminal prosecution." She also signed consent forms giving police access to her medical records and the false letter Kelly had her write to Austin Cooper on the subject of the Cookstown fire.

Comforted by Dr. Rowsell's impression that their star witness was not in any way mentally ill and appeared to be in command of the facts, the police and the Crown attorney agreed that the time had come to apprehend the man they believed was a murderer. Just fifteen hours after Taber told detectives that she had watched Kelly throw his wife off the balcony, he was arrested for first degree murder.

After Stewart and Cziraky made their brief stop at the Palace Pier with Patrick Kelly, they transported him to 22 Division of the Metropolitan Toronto Police, where he was fingerprinted and locked up. The detectives were careful to alert court security to the fact that Kelly was a former RCMP officer whose life might be at risk in either the general population or even protective custody. For his own safety, Kelly was later segregated in "the hole" at the Don Jail after making his court appearance on the day of his arrest.

The Metro police issued a brief press release to confirm the news that had already broken, that Patrick Michael Kelly, "the unemployed husband of the deceased," had been arrested for the first degree murder of Jeannette Kelly, as a result of an extensive homicide investigation. For his "night and day" work on the case, Ed Stewart would later be made Metro police officer of the month.

After discharging their official duties in court, Stewart and Cziraky picked up Dawn Taber from her hotel and returned to the Palace Pier. Although she had adamantly refused to visit apartment 1705 to participate in a re-enactment of the crime, she did show them where she had parked her car on the day of Jeannette's death. They then drove to the restaurant where Taber had written the phony letter to Austin Cooper, and the bank where Kelly had withdrawn the money he gave Taber for the 1980 trip to Europe with Jeannette.

After dropping Taber off at her hotel, the detectives returned to the Palace Pier to conduct further investigations. Late that night, Stewart performed a task he had been looking forward to from the moment he had arrested Kelly. He didn't think the person he was calling would mind the fact that it was 3 A.M. in Scotland.

"I'm sorry to get you this time in the morning," he said to the woman on the other end of the line. "But I've got some good news."

"What is that?" she asked.

"Well, we've got Pat Kelly."

"You're not joking?"

"No," Stewart replied. "I said that you would get justice. I've got him, and this time he won't get out."

Lottie Arbuckle was still thinking about her daughter when the grey wash of dawn showed at her window.

16

A REFUGEE OF LOVE

Jan Bradley spent the weekend before her husband's preliminary hearing in the quiet countryside of Dunsford, Ontario, contemplating the tatters of her life. Her belongings had just arrived from France, a modest piece of good fortune for which she was grateful. The wet, dreary spring of 1983 had turned warm at last, and she badly needed her summer clothes. Even her dog, Shanty, seemed happy when the boxes arrived, claiming a sheepskin from the villa as his new bed. Unpacking Patrick's things, Jan was unexpectedly transported back to France on the lingering fragrance of her husband's cologne. For five bittersweet minutes, she buried her face in his towel, trying to convince herself that there had once been a life in Valbonne.

Jan had been waiting in France for Patrick to resolve his fraud charges when Eddie Greenspan's office called with the news that her husband had been arrested for the murder of her predecessor. Until the court made a bail ruling, Jan was advised to stay in Valbonne, a request that was easier to make than comply with. For months there had been no money to pay bills, and the power and telephone at the villa had already been cut off. Although Jan bravely tried to hang on without heat and light, the nights finally grew too cold, and she flew back to Canada in late March, returning to the home where she had grown up.

Ruth Bradley welcomed her daughter with open arms. Although both women were convinced of Patrick's innocence, Ruth could see that the events of the last few months had already taken their toll on Jan. She had lost weight and had the haunted look of the dispossessed. Although she felt bitter, Jan did her best to be philosophical about the cruel turn her life had taken. "It certainly gives you a rather blunt revelation about just what exactly the essentials are," she wrote to Kelly's parents. "A bit like a war refugee I would think." The pampered bride who had savoured Europe's most sophisticated charms now couldn't afford to go to a movie. Her once frenetic life slowed to a lonely, contemplative crawl. "I could only go one better," she wrote to Patrick, "by becoming a recluse in a mountain hut."

Luckily, she had the dogs, Kelly and Shanty, to keep her company. But even the sheepdog was a living reminder of her reversal of fortune. The beautiful creature of their wedding photos, with her fluffy coat and pink ribbon, had become a shabby, matted mess. It had been three months since Jan had last been able to afford a grooming session for Kelly, and the dog's appearance wasn't improved by her habit of sleeping outdoors on her back, preferably in mud puddles.

In April, Jan moved to Toronto to take a job as a script-typist with the television series "The Littlest Hobo," renting a small apartment in the house on Crown Park Road where she had lived when she and Patrick began dating in 1980. In a letter to her husband, she joked that the place had a lot of good memories, especially now that she was living like an old maid. She had no social life, partly by choice, but also because Greenspan had advised her to keep to herself for the good of her husband's case.

For company, Jan brought Shanty to the apartment (Kelly stayed with Ruth Bradley) and filled in the lonely hours after work jogging along the boardwalk by Lake Ontario. Late at night, she sipped hot chocolate and wrote letters to her husband. She usually avoided her own problems and included little things that might buoy his spirits – Shanty's latest adventure or the fact that her white African violet, a variety she had never been able to find in France, had finally bloomed. But one night when the radio played the love theme from *The Deer Hunter*, music that had been popular when she and Patrick had been on their idyllic Irish honeymoon, she couldn't resist pouring out her lonely heart to the man she knew was even lonelier. "I don't think I'll ever be able to hear it without remembering all that green, all those mountains, all that laughter, all that love, and all of you – mine, totally mine, for an entire month."

Twice a week, she and her husband spoke to each other by telephone through two panes of bulletproof glass at the Metro West Detention Centre, a provincial jail hidden away in an industrial park in the west end of Toronto. Jan was Patrick's only visitor. Since the sessions were routinely taped, their conversations were guarded. Jan could never be sure if Patrick's words were for her benefit or that of the eavesdropping authorities. Although he lived for Jan's visits, it hurt Patrick to see his wife so depressed. As for Jan, there was something surreal about these antiseptic and closely watched sessions that passed for human contact. "It felt as though we were two strangers, yelling things of great personal importance back and forth across a great chasm."

Their face-to-face meetings were dominated by a single subject: how to raise the money to pay Greenspan's hefty legal fees. The defence wanted a minimum of $20,000 up front before they would begin working on the case. Greenspan had even agreed to deduct $5,000 from his usual retainer because he felt that this was such an unusual case. Beyond making the first payment, Jan didn't even want to think about his final bill – depending on how long it lasted, the estimated cost of the defence was between $50,000 and $100,000.

Kelly had attempted to use Graham Gordon's paintings to raise $200,000 to $300,000 from Norman Rasky, the dentist and art collector he had been negotiating with just before his arrest. But it soon became obvious to Rasky that, contrary to Kelly's claims, the paintings in question belonged to Gordon and not the ex-Mountie. Their deal fell through, and Kelly was left without any money for either bail or his lawyer.

In a burst of optimism, Kelly provided Greenspan with a list of thirty-eight people he believed would contribute to the cost of his defence. Twenty-five of them were former police colleagues or contacts, including OPP officer Harry Morozowich and his lawyer-brother Dennis Morris. He even listed his grandmother in British Columbia as a possible contributor because Grandpa Locke had died the previous year and Kelly thought he may have left some money. Although the list included the allegedly dead Wayne Humby and even Dawn Taber's former husband, John Hastey, the names of Kelly's parents were notably missing.

When not a single person whose name he had given Greenspan came through with cash, Kelly resorted to personal appeals, writing to Staff Sgt. Wayne Horrocks of the RCMP for a $10,000 contribution. Horrocks had been Kelly's immediate superior in the force for longer than anyone else, and had also worked as his partner in several undercover operations. Undeterred by the fact that he hadn't spoken to his onetime colleague for years, Kelly told Greenspan that Horrocks would be "extremely co-operative," because their work together "was often of a rather intimate nature." His appeal to Horrocks read more like a demand than a request:

"You know as well as I, mistakes do happen in our court system and everyone should have the very best counsel in order to avoid mistakes and miscarriages of justice. I am writing to you for old times' sake, as a friend, a close friend: I realise that by now you are getting ready for retirement and are probably very well settled and I do not wish to disturb your situation in any way, however assistance is required – NOW."

Horrocks never responded to Kelly's letter, and only one former RCMP colleague made a contribution to his legal defence fund – Dogmaster Dave Wright, who sent a cheque for $2,000.

By mid-April, Jan was beginning to panic. The couple had no money and even the $10,950 Patrick had with him when he was initially arrested in Toronto was being held as evidence in his international fraud charges. To make matters worse, Lois Perry had come forward after Kelly's arrest for murder and admitted that her story about owing him $100,000 had been a lie told at Kelly's behest. The authorities gave Perry immunity in exchange for her promise to testify against Kelly and added obstruction of justice charges to his long list of legal woes.

But these were minor matters compared to what Jan was now facing on behalf of her beleaguered husband. She had two weeks to raise $10,000 or Greenspan would be off the case, a turn of events that both she and Patrick agreed would be a disaster. Jan knew exactly how supportive

Greenspan's office had already been to her, and Patrick was adamant on the question of counsel: "Only Greenspan will do. When you are looking at 25 years, he seems <u>cheap</u>."

When her husband's fund-raising efforts came up empty, Jan begged John and Winnifred Kelly to see if any of their friends or relatives could contribute $1,000 or even $500 towards his defence. Trying to give them some idea of what she was going through, she told them that she struggled to get through each day "as sane and un-embittered as I can, knowing with an ache deep in my heart that there is a man I love a very great deal who is having to 'get through' an even more devastating day . . . Greenspan's the best, but you have to pay for the best always."

Jan was aware that Kelly's parents were in a difficult financial position, but the agreed-upon downpayment for Greenspan's fees was already weeks overdue and Patrick badly needed the money. Jan explained that her own mother had already put her house up for surety on the fraud charges and lent Patrick a substantial sum of money besides. "She doesn't have any more," Jan pleaded. But when their reply arrived, the Kellys had sent prayers not money, triggering an angry and frustrated note from Jan to Patrick's sister, Candi. "Please do not send me any more prayers – that's all I've received from the Kelly family and although I find the sentiment touching, and I, too, pray often (when I'm not busy pounding the pavement trying to come up with some financial assistance for your brother), I am no longer appreciative."

With nowhere else to turn, Jan took out a $4,000 bank loan on May 14, 1983. Together with Dave Wright's contribution and another $5,000 loan from her mother, she was able to give Greenspan $10,000 towards her husband's defence. At $2,000-a-day for the crack lawyer's courtroom presence, it wouldn't go very far, but Kelly would now be represented at his preliminary hearing by a man who was arguably the best criminal lawyer in the country, even if they could only afford his blue-chip services for a single week.

As good as he was, not even Eddie Greenspan could mend a broken heart. To prepare Jan for a possible trip to the witness box at Kelly's trial, his office had been obliged to discuss with her the long list of women with whom her husband had had affairs during their marriage. The day before he was arrested, Kelly had taken a Toronto secretary to the Magic

Pan restaurant, where he and Jeannette had brunched on the day of her death. With the help of a friend at the Palace Pier, Kelly had taken the same woman to the condominium's guest suite for a late-night dalliance.

When Greenspan's legal assistant, Francesca Briggs, asked Jan if she could handle talking about such matters, she bravely replied that her husband's affairs were a "non-issue"; after all, he was charged with murder not adultery. Behind her bravado, however, her marriage to Kelly was starting to crumble, although her commitment to seeing him through the trial remained rock solid.

The beginning of the end had come quietly one afternoon shortly after Jan's return from France, when she stopped at their Toronto drop-box to pick up the mail. Among the other correspondence was a per-fumed envelope from England bearing a return address she didn't recognize. Inside, she found a love letter to her husband from a woman named Vicky Hill. "I want to touch you so much it's painful. That's not all, but it will do for starters; come to me my darling, come to me, I want you so bloody much."

The infidelity cut deep. Jan's romance with Patrick had started when she was nearly thirty years old and on the rebound from a man she had expected to marry, but who had thrown her out. She had waited a long time to trust someone completely, and when she found Patrick, her passion had swept away every obstacle in its path, including the doubts of her closest friends and her own instinct for self-preservation. Despite her stoic answer to Francesca Briggs, she confided to Jamie Emerson, a friend from high-school days, that there wasn't much left of her marriage because of Patrick's infidelities. She passed along the same sentiment to her imprisoned husband with a poignant card listing three things that a person should never break: toys, hearts, and promises.

Kelly would later say that his indiscretions had been carefully designed to be discovered in order to drive Jan away from him and the dangerous situation in which he found himself. He compared his attempts to spare his wife further suffering on his behalf to a mother's concern for her young, a priest's for his church, or a martyr's for his cause. "I went about setting the stage for what I could feel was taking place. I set up the meeting and late evening with Saginur's secretary at the Palace Pier . . . I left the note in the jacket. I made sure at one point that a young lady would be writing to the [mail] box office. I just felt that things were coming to a head. If Jan was around, she too would be fished into whatever it was. I was not about to let that happen."

Ruth Bradley was the only person to remember the couple's first anniversary, giving her daughter a traditional gift of paper on May 22 – cocktail napkins to go with the bottle of Dom Perignon champagne that was "sleeping" in Ruth's cupboard for the day that Kelly was acquitted. But behind her occasional romantic gesturing, Jan's relationship with her unfaithful husband was now a tidal proposition. With every ebb and flow of her contradictory feelings towards him, a little more of the empty beach of their marriage was left exposed.

As Kelly's June 6, 1983, preliminary hearing drew near, detectives Ed Stewart and Joe Cziraky continued to build their case against the man they had been patiently tracking for so long. On the second anniversary of Jeannette Kelly's death, they delivered a pile of Kelly's financial documents to the accounting firm of Lindquist & Holmes, hoping an audit would establish that part of his motive for killing his wife was his desperate financial situation in the spring of 1981.

In mid-May, Stewart flew to Victoria armed with a search warrant for Victor Simpson's law offices. While there, he interviewed Simpson's office manager, Connie Jeffrey, and his secretary, Karen Rutherford. Rutherford, who had done Kelly's typing when he worked out of the law office, had never cared for K&V's enigmatic employee. "I didn't like him, I didn't trust him. I saw him do things here when Victor was away that I knew were wrong."

Rutherford told Stewart that Kelly had once asked her to type up a loan agreement for $100 million from some Los Angeles business interests using the letterhead of one of Simpson's personal companies. Kelly told her to make sure that there were no mistakes in the document because the deal was worth $1 million to him. Rutherford had then witnessed Kelly sign the loan agreement with the name of a female lawyer who worked in Simpson's firm. "It had to be notarized," the secretary explained, "so he signed her name and affixed her seal to it." Once Kelly realized that Rutherford had been watching him, he glared at her and said, "You didn't see that, did you?" She didn't answer him and he repeated the same words, the second time "in a sort of threatening way."

Before their interview ended, Rutherford told Stewart about another incident that made his blood run cold. The young woman claimed to have overheard Simpson telling Jeffrey that Kelly wanted to take out a life insurance policy on his second wife, Jan Bradley, without her knowledge.

After returning to Toronto, Stewart, together with Joe Cziraky, drove to Collins Bay penitentiary, where they interviewed inmate David Warriner. The threetime rapist had been in protective custody at Metro West when a bearded and reeking Patrick Kelly had been brought in from the hole at the Don Jail. He and Kelly struck up a friendship before Warriner's transfer to Collins Bay two months later, and he told the detectives that he had kept detailed notes of their conversations.

Tainted though it was by its source, the story Warriner told the detectives was extremely damaging to Kelly. The inmate claimed that Kelly had asked him to arrange for a motorcycle gang to carry out the contract killings of Dawn Taber and Victor Simpson before they testified against him. He said that Kelly offered to pay for the hits by setting up a cocaine connection for the bikers, but ultimately withdrew his offer because he felt that Warriner's $25,000 price tag for the murders was too steep. Kelly later confirmed these conversations, with the significant difference that he said it had been Warriner who offered to have Taber and Simpson "dusted."

"I listened to these offers and went so far as to inquire into the price of these services – advised $25,000 for a hit. These could take any form desired and the price for one was basically the same for two or three hits," Kelly wrote in his notes for his lawyer. "Bodies could be disposed of via meat grinders, branch-eaters, or buried, or dumped in the ocean."

When Warriner said that he was prepared to testify against Kelly, the detectives decided that they would take his information to Crown attorney Lloyd Budzinsky for possible use in the upcoming preliminary hearing. Before leaving, they asked the inmate if he expected anything in return for helping the Crown with its case against Kelly. After insisting that he was only acting as a citizen concerned that justice be done, the inmate who stood convicted on three separate incidents of rape and buggery admitted that he wouldn't turn up his nose at a transfer to a protective custody institution, Kingston penitentiary.

The detectives agreed that his next decade might be more safely spent at Kingston, and thanked him for his continuing interest in the administration of justice.

A man of eclectic inspiration, William Moulton Marston created Wonder Woman and also invented the lie detector. His clever gadget translates such biological indicators as blood pressure and the rate of a subject's breathing and sweating into inky spikes on a roll of graph paper. The theory is that as these measurable factors increase during a question and answer session, the more pronounced the spikes on the paper will become, permitting a skilled operator to distinguish false assertions from truthful ones.

As every intelligence agency including the RCMP knows, there are a variety of self-administered stimuli that can confound a lie detector, including biting your tongue or pressing your foot on a nail concealed in a shoe during the interrogation. Former CIA director William Casey once told an interviewer that with some Valium and a sphincter muscle trick he had learned in the OSS, he could "flatten the spikes" on any polygraph. If the subject has amalgam teeth fillings (either gold or silver mixed with mercury), one of the most effective ways to beat the lie detector is to chew a piece of tinfoil. When the metals in the filling and the tinfoil come into contact with saliva, which is acidic, the result is an electric current that confuses Marston's ingenious machine. Psychopaths, however, need not resort to such painful stratagems, since lying is one of their most highly developed natural talents.

For all these reasons, a 1976 Ontario royal commission condemned the use of polygraph evidence, arguing that it was as unscientific as the superhuman exploits of Wonder Woman. The following year, lie detector evidence was disallowed in Canadian courts. The ban notwithstanding, the police still resorted to the work of skilled polygraph operators like Ben Silverberg as an investigative aid. So when detectives on the Kelly case learned that Silverberg had conducted a private polygraph examination of Kelly shortly after he was charged with murder, they were more than a little interested in the results. Lloyd Budzinsky asked staff from Eddie Greenspan's office about the rumoured test during a May 31 disclosure meeting, but the defence team declined to answer.

Although the Crown never found out about it, Silverberg had been hired to administer the test to Kelly on the events surrounding March 29, 1981, not by Eddie Greenspan, but by Howard Saginur. Silverberg was instructed to make a verbal report of the test results to Kelly through Howard Saginur, placing the accused man in a good strategic position. If the results were favourable, Kelly could request a written report from Silverberg; if they proved inculpatory, there would be no documented evidence that the incriminating session had ever taken place.

In Silverberg's opinion, Kelly was telling the truth when he denied that Dawn Taber had been in his apartment on the day of Jeannette Kelly's death. But he concluded that Kelly was lying when he denied having an ongoing affair with Taber while his wife was alive, and lying again when he said that he hadn't had any communication with Taber after April 1981. Silverberg discussed the results of the polygraph test with Saginur and wasn't asked to provide a written report. He would subsequently claim that the lies Kelly had told during the test "were later confirmed by partial admissions rendered by Mr. Kelly and recounted in our telephone conversations."

Greenspan's associates learned little that was new during the disclosure session, but they did take note of what had hitherto been a hidden part of the Crown's theory of Jeannette Kelly's murder. Budzinsky made it clear he believed that his own star witness, Dawn Taber, was still holding back possibly incriminating information about her own involvement in the murder. They told the defence team that they had made no deals with Taber, beyond the provisions of the Charter of Rights and Freedoms; that is, nothing she had told police about her involvement that day would be used against her in the event that she was later charged. But if Greenspan brought out additional facts in cross-examination that supported her guilt, she would be charged, a possibility of which she was aware. The defence team made note of the bizarre situation they were faced with after the session ended. "It is their [the Crown's] understanding that she still loves Patrick Kelly and in fact feels sorry for him."

Kelly's preliminary hearing was a dreary, sporadic affair heard by Mr. Justice J. J. Belobradic of the Ontario Court's criminal division. It stretched from the spring of 1983 to the first snowfall of that year, a judicial formality that ran its course despite the lack of doubt about the outcome.

The first casualty of the proceedings was Eddie Greenspan, who withdrew in July as counsel for Kelly after a masterful demolition of police-informant David Warriner during one of his trademark cross-examinations. But it had simply been impossible for Greenspan to continue. The issue was money, as the lawyer made clear in a letter to Kelly's parents in which he mentioned his legal fees with the same consideration that had allowed them to go unpaid well beyond the deadline Kelly had accepted.

"I know that Patrick is disappointed that his family will not come to his aid at this time when he needs the assistance the most," Greenspan wrote, "but that is obviously something for you and the rest of your family to decide."

When proceedings resumed in August, Earl J. Levy, a formidable QC in his own right, had taken over the Kelly brief as a legal-aid case. The situation he inherited was a lawyer's nightmare. The Crown and the police had investigated and analysed the complex case for more than two years. They had an eyewitness to the alleged murder, scientific evidence showing that Kelly's explanation of how his wife died was impossible, and a parade of witnesses who could attest to his client's lies, frauds, and infidelities. The Crown was even calling Toronto Blue Jay shortstop Alfredo Griffin, the current occupant of apartment 1705, to testify that he had never heard the rattle on the balcony that Kelly claimed had drawn his wife to her death. Levy spent most of the summer playing catch-up with a very well-prepared and aggressive Crown team.

The case for the prosecution got an unexpected boost when it called Victor Simpson to the hearing to testify about the contradictory descriptions Kelly had given him of how his wife had fallen to her death. Simpson had accidentally run into Wayne Humby in the corridor outside the courtroom, the man Kelly had so extravagantly mourned in front of Simpson, after the RCMP officer's "fatal" car accident. Humby was in excellent spirits for a dead man, and when Simpson took the stand he was able to vouch for another of his boyhood friend's many skills: the ability to cry at will.

Despite all these handicaps, Levy managed to score some points on his client's behalf, most of them with the Crown's eyewitness, Dawn Taber. From his first question on cross-examination, he seemed to have the young woman on the defensive. When Levy asked where she was born, Taber replied with an interesting Freudian slip: "Valbonne, Maine." But it was when he confronted her over her admission that she'd been willing to go away with Kelly after watching him murder his wife that he made Taber look like a deceitful and cold-blooded opportunist.

"I cared for Pat, but I was certainly not in love with him . . . not that I would have wanted to spend the rest of my life with him," Taber testified.

"You mean you would have gone off on just sort of a fling after your best friend's death with the man that killed her? Is that right?"

"No," the witness replied, but that was exactly the implication of her previous answers.

Besides Levy's effective cross-examination of Taber, the only moment of drama at the proceedings belonged to John Nascimento, who stunned the courtroom with his testimony that Taber had been with him at the time of Jeannette's death. Kelly burst into tears at hearing what he and Jan both considered to be a death blow to the Crown's case against him, and Levy briefly believed he might have been handed a witness who could neutralize the prosecution's strongest evidence against his client. Nascimento's bombshell evidence sent the Crown scurrying for the investigating detectives, but they were tied up in another court case and couldn't appear.

When Nascimento returned to the witness box in November, the sensation of his initial testimony turned out to be a tempest in a teapot. When reminded of what he had told Staff Sgt. Ed Hill during the early phases of the police investigation, he admitted that he couldn't be sure that Taber had been with him on the afternoon of March 29. With that qualification, Kelly's only hope of avoiding a trial vanished.

On the last day of the preliminary, Levy argued that his client should be committed to trial on the reduced charge of second degree murder on the grounds that the Crown's evidence showed that Jeannette Kelly had died after an argument, not as the result of a deliberate plan. The accused, who had been taking copious notes while the parade of witnesses testified against him, had a very different view.

"What we have are rumours, supposition, conjecture, absolutely nothing more besides a man having an affair on his wife, jealousy of life-styles, a mysterious, romantic job, and a man who perhaps acts and reacts in ways contrary to the norm, and of course we must add unexplained income (which I think most would agree is no one else's business.) If the above constitutes first degree murder, then I am guilty – the only neces-sary ingredient that I question strongly is that I never killed anyone," Kelly wrote.

Judge Belobradic disagreed with both the optimistic accused and his astute counsel. After pointing out that the evidence produced by the Crown to show that Kelly had deliberately planned to kill his wife was circumstantial, he ruled that a jury might well find it proof of a "think-ing process"; they were, therefore, entitled to consider it. To the sur-prise of no one, the judge committed the accused to stand trial for first degree murder.

The weekend after his preliminary, Kelly wrote a twenty-four-page letter to Earl Levy with various suggestions on how to prepare for the trial. It also included a novel theory to account for the fact that no one but Kelly had heard the rattle on the balcony that had led to his wife's accidental death: perhaps, he suggested, Jeannette's desperate clawing had actually fixed the rattle before she had plunged over the railing. But if that was true, something else had to be explained – if Jeannette had repaired the rattle, how then could Kelly have heard it after her death, as he had told Sgt. Michael Duchak?

By late fall, Jan Bradley was beginning to founder under her husband's seemingly interminable legal problems. All through the summer's muggy heat, which had made her insomnia even worse, she had done everything she could to help Patrick's cause, making phone calls, finding addresses, and even doing legal research at the library. When the loneli-ness bit too deeply, she wore his cologne and tried to take comfort in his frequent letters, which were written in a hand that had grown so minute that she could barely read them. Their sessions at the detention centre usually left her feeling hopeless and depressed, and she decided to cut back on her visits, wasting few words in explaining why: "Please don't feel I'm abandoning you in any way – it's just better for both us if I'm in better spirits."

After the murder preliminary, Kelly had had to attend preliminary hearings on the raft of other charges he was facing, including credit card fraud, passport fraud, false pretences, and obstruction of justice. After the hearing, the Crown decided to hold these charges in abeyance until Kelly's murder case had worked its way through the justice system. If he was acquitted, the Crown would proceed to trial with the outstanding charges as quickly as possible; if he was convicted and given a twenty-five-year sentence, there would be no prosecution on the other matters because of the costs involved. To Bradley it hardly mattered. Every day seemed to bring some new legal hurdle to overcome, and after a year of struggling to survive, she couldn't take much more pressure. "Oh God, Patrick," she wrote, "will anything ever work out right again – ever, ever, ever?"

In September, Bradley moved to London, Ontario, where she enrolled in the University of Western Ontario, hoping that a master's degree in library science would free her forever from having to depend on someone else for her economic security. It had been twelve years since she'd last written an essay and she barely passed her first assignment.

Bradley couldn't get over how young her classmates looked. On October 6, the day she turned thirty-three, Kelly sent her a flattering letter. But Jan was feeling even more depressed than she had on the day he'd been charged with murder, and his well-intentioned compliments only made her feel worse. She celebrated her birthday by taking Shanty for a long walk along the Thames, but the sprightly pup of 1971 no longer ran ahead of her poking into mischief of one sort or another. "Such is age," she wrote to Kelly. "As for me, all I seem to have is grey hair and teenage stress-related acne – wonderful combination! Feel a lot older than I did this time last year – I guess we all do."

Bradley cut back her visits to Kelly even further and apologized for not writing more often, blaming her heavy academic load. As the weeks rolled by, she began to feel more comfortable in university. By midterm, she had hit her intellectual stride, scoring 96 per cent in her American literature course and would later hand in the best essay on *Moby Dick* that her professor had ever read. Bradley had also heard that Marlene Lee, her closest friend from Valbonne, was travelling around the world and planned to visit her in London. It was a pleasure to have something to look forward to that wasn't going to take place in a courtroom.

One day as she huddled under an Irish shawl, reading about the Anglo-Saxons in eighth-century Europe, she could almost hear the dreamy harp music she and Patrick had enjoyed listening to after wandering through the ruins of ancient castles and monasteries on their honeymoon in Ireland. But these sentimental reminiscences were getting as rare as her visits to Metro West. After a particularly cold telephone conversation in late November, she had asked Patrick not to call her collect anymore. If he had to get her a message, he could reach her through her mother and then only if the news was pressing. Otherwise, she could get her information about his case out of any newspaper once the trial began. Their relationship had changed and so had Bradley's priorities.

"My principal concern MUST be with me – my health, my well-being, my studies . . . I must take care of my sanity, and do everything I can to enable me to walk out of university knowing that I have done right by myself as well as I can."

Bradley visited Kelly on December 22, his thirty-fourth birthday, but she didn't return at Christmas, choosing instead to write him a letter recalling their times in France, Hawaii, and the Bahamas. Behind the recollections, a new truth about their relationship was quietly asserting itself: their marriage was quickly fading to a memory. She saw him twice during reading week, noting the same change in him she was beginning to feel in herself. "How quickly you age my dear!!"

For a brief interval in February, Bradley was able to put down her sorrows and labours and enjoy life with Marlene Lee. The vivacious globetrotter seemed to know everyone in London, and Bradley's apartment was jammed for days with visitors. The two women went out every night, and talked until dawn over bottles of wine back at the apartment. Bradley felt cheered to be in the company of someone whose life was a celebration of the things that she loved so much: travel, friends, and worldly conversation. "It's more like the life I'm accustomed to," she wrote to Kelly, "rather than my past year spent as a hermit – recluse – almost – a nun."

One subject the two women didn't discuss was Kelly's arrest for murder. Since Lee would be in Hong Kong by the time the story hit the media again, Bradley couldn't see the point of laying a stone on her heart. Although Valbonne seemed "several years and at least a few countries away," it was better for her to remember the Kelly of happier times. "I just can't see the benefit of telling the whole lousy, dismal, waste-of-time story once again," she wrote to Patrick.

A few days before the trial, Patrick sent Jan a long-stemmed rose. Although she sent a thank-you note, she asked him not to do it again. The delivery to "Jan Kelly" had been addressed without an apartment number, and could have gone to any of the four units in her building. The trial, with its sensational newspaper headlines, would start soon enough, and Bradley didn't want to be swept away by the approaching tidal wave of notoriety. "I have struggled very, very hard, and at great psychological and emotional cost to myself, to keep my presence here in this city, and particularly in this house, anonymous. I must insist that you respect that, Patrick."

With an ulcer eating into her stomach, and her husband about to go on trial for murder, it was getting very hard to believe in unicorns.

17

THE RECKONING

The first witness in Patrick Kelly's much-heralded murder trial took the stand on Friday, April 13, 1984. Prosecutors Lloyd Budzinsky and Wade Nesmith had forewarned the eight men and four women of the jury that as many as 150 witnesses might be called to prove the Crown's contention that Kelly had carried out a deliberate plan to murder his wife.

According to the prosecution's theory, Kelly's chosen method had been as diabolical as it was deadly; he had thrown the unconscious woman over the balcony of their seventeenth-storey apartment to cover up bruises or wounds inflicted during a violent quarrel that preceded the drop. As for his motive, there had really been three: Jeannette's insurance money, the freedom to marry his lover, and preventing his wife from talking about his involvement in the Cookstown fire and other clandestine activities associated with his "moonlighting."

In their vigorous attempt to portray Kelly as a liar, an adulterer, an arsonist, and a murderer, the prosecution opened its case with a woman who could vouch for all four contentions. But before bringing on her damning testimony, the prosecution apologized, in effect, for its star witness. The issue was not so much Dawn Bragg's credibility (Taber had married Victor Bragg) as her character. Rather than have the jury start wondering about her "reprehensible" role in the Kelly murder on their own, Nesmith acknowledged up front that Taber was a sinister lady in her own right. "What this woman did, and what she is going to tell you she did is not pleasant. . . . They [Taber and the accused] conspired to kill Jeannette Kelly to collect the insurance and move to the south of France."

Taber was led through her examination-in-chief by Budzinsky, who had to contend with a nervous witness and a PA system that had died earlier in the day in a puff of smoke. Budzinsky brought out that Taber, like the accused, had once made her living betraying criminals as an undercover police officer. After getting her to describe her friendship with the Kellys, Budzinsky asked Taber about the events of March 29, 1981.

The witness described hearing an argument between the Kellys, Jeannette's horrifying screams, and the sound of a blow. When she came out of the den to investigate, she had been greeted with a macabre sight. "Jeannette was on the floor and Pat was bending over her." With Taber watching him, Kelly picked up his motionless wife, walked to the balcony, and opened the screen door with his left hand, which he had trouble doing while balancing the 132-pound deadweight he was carrying. When the witness told the court what happened next, her description was remarkably casual: "He took Jeannette out to the balcony and dropped her over the edge."

It was the heart of the prosecution's case, yet Taber's words had been so matter of fact that Budzinsky worried that the jurors might have missed their horrifying import. Wanting them to hear it again, this time with feeling, he asked her exactly how Kelly had put his wife over the railing. "Just dropped her," Taber answered blandly.

Knowing that she had told investigators that Kelly had "fired" his wife off the balcony, Budzinsky tried again, asking if Jeannette had gone over feet-first, head-first, or with her back towards the ground. This time his witness not only refused to elaborate, she weakened her original answer. "I don't know," she replied. "He just dropped her. I don't know."

Budzinsky was aware that Taber's account was almost as devastating to the witness as it was to the accused. Even if the Crown was mistaken in its belief that Taber had played a part in the murder, at the very least, she had silently watched as her closest friend was killed by her husband. Remembering Levy's effective cross-examination at the preliminary on this very point, the prosecutor tried to steal the defence counsel's thunder by demonstrating that the Crown was well aware that it had a cold-blooded voyeur on its hands. Why, he asked, had Dawn remained silent while her unconscious friend was thrown over the balcony?

"I didn't say anything for many reasons. I thought about it, but I didn't," she replied lamely.

As self-damaging as Taber's answer was, it was the events following Jeannette Kelly's gruesome end that pricked the defence's interest. Taber testified that she had collapsed after looking over the balcony and seeing her friend's dead body on the loading dock below. Afterwards, Kelly had comforted her for several minutes, telling her that he loved her and that he would look after everything. When she felt well enough to leave, the murderer had escorted his former lover to the express elevator eight storeys above apartment 1705, where he told her to go home and to keep quiet about what had happened. Levy calculated the approximate time that all these actions would have taken and made a note to confront Taber with his estimates during cross-examination.

When Taber returned for the afternoon session, the matron who was looking after her informed the judge that the witness would like to stand while she gave some of her testimony. With a new microphone in place, Taber's words were easier to hear, but just as difficult to listen to; point by point, the grim events of March 29, 1981, were put in context by the rest of her depressing testimony. Listening to herself answer, Taber felt oddly unreal and had trouble hearing the questions; it was almost as if the proceedings were taking place under water.

Taber testified about her brief affair with the accused in the spring of 1980, the time during which she and Kelly had made plans to kill Jeannette and live in the south of France, according to what she had told police. She described how Kelly wanted her to take out a large insurance policy through the company where she worked, explaining that he planned to forge his wife's signature on the application so that Jeannette wouldn't know about it. Taber admitted that they had talked about the fact that if a person fell from a great height, it would be impossible for authorities to determine exactly how he had died because his body would be "jelled."

Contrary to Kelly's claim that his marriage to Jeannette had been in good shape around the time of her death, Taber testified that the arson investigation had driven a wedge between the accused and his former wife. After Kelly had been forced out of the RCMP, Jeannette blamed him for their serious financial problems and the constant meddling of the police, including the humiliating search of their Palace Pier apartment. Things had become so tense by the late summer of 1980 that Taber had witnessed the accused grab his wife by the throat and lift her off the ground with one hand.

Budzinsky finally felt some satisfaction with the way Taber's testimony was going. This last detail was crucial, illustrating both Kelly's violent nature and his great strength. When the time came to consider Kelly's story that he had been too weak to hang on to his wife on the balcony, Budzinsky wanted the jury to remember Taber's words. Here was a man who was so strong that he could lift up an adult woman with one hand and explode squash balls by driving them against the wall.

Taber's evidence about the fire at Kelly's Cookstown home, which the defence viewed as outrageous hearsay, was nearly as devastating to the accused as her description of the murder. She described in detail how Kelly had dictated the phony letter to Austin Cooper that she retracted just before his arson trial. But she also claimed that Kelly had confessed to her that he, in fact, had set the fire to get the money to buy the condominium at the Palace Pier. Kelly had even gone so far as to take Taber to the lodge where he had been staying at the time of the fire. On the way back, he demonstrated how he had covered the ninety-three miles to Cookstown in record time, a driving feat that allowed him to torch his house and return to the lodge before he was missed in the morning. The one flaw in the operation had been that the fire started more quickly than he'd thought it would, forcing him to flee before he could retrieve the gas can that he'd used to set the blaze.

Levy could tell from the faces of the jurors how right he had been to try to exclude Taber's arson testimony. As powerfully as the defence lawyer had argued that such evidence was both irrelevant to the murder charge and highly prejudicial to his client, Mr. Justice John O'Driscoll saw it differently. Since there was evidence before the court that Jeannette Kelly may have been murdered in part to prevent her from talking about her husband's role in the Cookstown fire, the judge ruled that Taber's testimony about the arson went to motive and was therefore admissible.

Satisfied that Taber had given the jury a good sense of Kelly's dark side and a solid grounding in the circumstances leading up to Jeannette's murder, Budzinsky brought her back to the events of March 29. Knowing that the defence might well argue that Taber hadn't even been in the Kellys' apartment on the day in question (there was no evidence to corroborate her own testimony that she was there), Budzinsky set out to elicit the sort of telling details that only someone who had been at the scene could possibly know. It was one of the few times in the trial that the prosecution stubbed its evidentiary toe, since so many of Taber's answers didn't square with the known facts.

Taber placed her arrival at the apartment at around 1 P.M., two and a half hours before Jeannette had gone over the balcony. She also testified that while she was at the apartment, the only pieces of furniture on the balcony had been two yellow director's chairs, not the stool that police had found when they entered apartment 1705 fifteen minutes after the discovery of the victim's body.

Taber also remembered Jeannette's luggage having been in the Kellys' bedroom, not in the front hall where police had found it. Nor could she recall seeing the sheepdog, though police had found her there when they arrived to search the apartment. Most important of all, Taber claimed that Jeannette had been wearing a pair of jeans and a T-shirt, a description that was only half-correct. Jeannette had actually been found in a man's long-sleeved, navy-blue cashmere sweater, an item of clothing that could hardly be confused with a T-shirt. Disregarding these puzzling inconsistencies, Budzinsky wrapped up his devastating examination with the question that he suspected was on every juror's mind: "Why didn't you stop Mr. Kelly?" he again asked.

"It just didn't seem – I don't know why," she replied, leaving the jury with the grim and still unresolved puzzle of how Taber could permit her best friend to be murdered in front of her eyes without lifting a finger to help her.

On Saturday, April 14, 1984, the *Toronto Star* ran a front-page story about the opening of the sensational trial, accompanied by a three-column picture of the Crown's star witness looking stern and tight-lipped outside the courthouse. Jan Bradley, who had promised herself that she wouldn't read the papers until after her university exams, was

drawn in by Dawn's photo and the shocking headline: "EX-MOUNTIE
THREW WIFE OFF BALCONY, COURT TOLD." The story explained that
Patrick Kelly had murdered Jeannette Kelly in order to marry his girlfriend, Jan Bradley, the woman he had taken on a Hawaiian vacation
just five days after his wife was buried.

"Well, that's not quite the way I wanted to make it to the front-page
of the *Star*," Bradley wrote to Kelly. "So much for anonymity, huh?
Thank God classes are over – now I just have to muddle through
exams."

Bradley told her husband that she had been ensconced in the library
until late at night all week, unplugging her telephone after coming
home because of too many wrong numbers. She was following what
was happening through Kelly's Aunt Vi, who was attending the trial
daily. Trying her best to keep up Kelly's spirits, Jan told him that the
weather had been wonderful and that she had been able to go on some
long walks with Shanty, who was getting slower by the day. "Still, his
tail's still wagging and he's still grinning . . ." She even made an attempt
at humour, telling Patrick that she had just received their bank statement from Valbonne. They had 115 francs ($20.00 Cdn) in their account
and the manager had sent them a Christmas card thanking them for
being such good customers!

During his preparation for the case, Earl Levy had received plenty of
help from his industrious client, not all of it welcome. Kelly bombarded
him daily with lists of things to check, picky details that Levy found
distracting rather than helpful. Kelly thought he was too frequently
"brushed off" by his own lawyer, who cut him off in conversation when
he didn't agree with what his client was saying. In the end, Levy worked
out a system in which his law student, David McComb, dealt with Kelly
and he dealt with the case.

Occasionally though, lawyer and client still collided. A month before
the trial, Kelly developed what Levy scoffingly referred to as "the dog
theory"; the notion that the sheepdog, Kelly, had inadvertently knocked
Jeannette over the railing after bumping into the stool she had been
standing on trying to fix the phantom rattle. Kelly wanted Levy to
arrange a split-screen videotape of the sheepdog's possible movements

in the apartment in the moments before the accident, not exactly the kind of Hollywood-style venture that legal aid was famous for under-writing. During a session at the detention centre where his client raised the matter again, Levy told him that even if the court allowed such highly speculative evidence, the whole idea was so outlandish that it would tarnish the credibility of the defence. When Kelly pushed his theory with McComb, Levy drew the line. "If you feel strongly about proceeding with your dog theory because your innocence may depend on it," he wrote to Kelly, "then I regretfully must suggest that you obtain other counsel."

Although few people knew it, the prosecution had offered to reduce Kelly's charge in return for a guilty plea to second degree murder. It was the difference between ten years in prison or twenty-five, and Levy had recommended that his client accept. Miffed that his own lawyer seemed to believe that he was "automatically guilty," Kelly, heedless of how little room Levy had to stickhandle in the powerful case the Crown and police had built against him, turned down the offer and instructed his counsel to proceed to trial. Lloyd Budzinsky had held the offer open until the first witness took the stand, but after Taber's testimony, Kelly found himself in a legal game of winner take all.

In Levy's view, Kelly's only real hope lay with the jury, not the petty details that seemed to obsess him. The best defence tactic was to remind the jurors at every opportunity of the kind of person the Crown was using to anchor its case – a woman who had slept with the victim's husband after being given the hospitality of her home, who never told Jeannette that Kelly was planning to kill her, and who hadn't come forward with her damning evidence until nearly two years after her best friend's murder, and then only because the police had approached her. If Levy could use his powerful courtroom presence to portray Taber as an immoral schemer who lied whenever her self-interest was at stake, there was a fighting chance that the jury might acquit his client, since the rest of the Crown's case against Kelly was circumstan-tial. It was agreed that Levy would deal with the "blood and gore" aspects of the case, and his co-counsel, Irwin Koziebrocki, would deal with financial matters.

Levy began his attack on Taber's character by asking her how many times she had slept with Patrick Kelly while living under Jeannette

Kelly's roof. Whatever her answer, he knew that it was bound to bring her into disrepute with the jury. Even though she had testified at the preliminary that she and Kelly had made love every night while Jeannette was away, Taber's memory had suddenly clouded over. "I don't know," she said. "I mean I could say three times or say ten times."

Sensing her irritation with his question, Levy bored in. No one was looking for a precise number, he assured her, but since she was living in her best friend's house and having sex with her best friend's husband, surely she could make some sort of estimate.

"That was certainly not the most important thing in my life at that time, and no big deal, and not something that I kept track of," the witness replied, an answer at odds with her earlier statement to police that she thought during their brief affair that Patrick Kelly "walked on water" and that she had felt enormous guilt afterwards because she had betrayed the trust of her friend.

Levy led Taber through her parade of lies to the police, hammering away at the remarkable metamorphosis in her evidence since she had first spoken with them. In April 1981, she hadn't been at the apartment or witnessed the murder; in February 1983, with an immunity promise from Sgt. Ed Stewart, she had been at the apartment, but hadn't seen Kelly throw his wife over the balcony; two weeks later, she had been at the apartment and watched Kelly dump her friend's body over the railing; and a few weeks after that, she had not only been at the apartment and witnessed the murder, she had also seen Jeannette Kelly lying unconscious on the apartment floor with Kelly standing over her just before the fatal trip to the balcony.

And then there were the lies within lies. Levy brought out that Taber had lied to detectives when she told them that Kelly had intended to make financial provisions for Jeannette after he and Taber had run away to France. In fact, Kelly's promise that Jeannette would be "taken care of" really meant that she would be killed, and Taber acknowledged to police she had understood this at the time. And what about the lie to Stewart that she had mailed a written statement to him from the United States, when in fact she had purposely decided against doing that?

Taber explained that she hadn't realized that her April 4, 1981, conversation with him was being taped, and had no idea that she might one day be held accountable for what she'd said. It was an extraordinary answer that alerted the jury to how effortlessly this witness could lie if she believed she could get away with it. When Levy asked her why she hadn't given police a written statement based on her April 4 conversation with Stewart, Taber replied that it would have been "too incriminating" and "there was no way I could write the truth and give it to them" – admissions that once again made her look sinister and deceitful, though Levy was not interested in pursuing the issue of her possible involvement in the crime.

After lunch, Levy caught Taber in another major contradiction that led to a very damaging exchange for the Crown's star witness. He pointed out that although Taber had told authorities in March 1983 that she had been in love with Kelly, she had virtually reversed her testimony on the stand. Taber's attempt to explain away the discrepancy further besmirched her already tainted reputation in the eyes of the jury.

"I was not in love with him the same way I was in love with him at the time we had the relationship," she protested, reminding Levy that there were "different kinds of love."

Remembering that Taber had already testified that she still might have gone away with Kelly after witnessing Jeannette's murder, Levy seized the opportunity and went in for the kill.

"You tell me what kind of love you had for a man who you saw throw your best friend over a balcony?"

"He was a man I trusted, who I had a relationship with," came the hopelessly inadequate reply.

"That you hadn't seen for five months, is that right?"

"Yes," Taber answered, again contradicting herself. Either she loved him or she didn't, which was it?

Levy sensed that he had the witness on the run and reminded Taber that she had even lied to one of her friends, Joanne MacLean, whom she had phoned for more details about Jeannette's death. When he asked her why she would ask questions about something she now claimed she had witnessed, Taber's attempt to explain herself made her look like a co-conspirator to the murder.

"I don't recall what I said or did during that time," she answered. "The only reason I would say anything like that was to take any suspicion away from myself or Pat at the time."

"You are phoning around to these people to divest yourself of suspicion?" Levy asked incredulously, hoping that the jury wouldn't begin subscribing to the Crown's all but stated theory that this witness should be standing in the dock with his client. In one of the enduring ironies of the trial, no one pursued the evidence that suggested Taber might be an accomplice to Jeannette Kelly's murder; the Crown, because it would cost them their only eyewitness to the crime, the defence, because it would implicate their client in a crime he had denied committing.

After the noon recess, Levy opened a frontal attack on the credibility of Taber's testimony about the murder against the background of her propensity to lie, a character trait that he had tried to establish with his earlier line of questioning. He wondered why his client would commit murder in front of a woman who had refused to lie for him during the arson case? Taber agreed that it made no sense.

And how believable was it that after a five-month deep freeze in her relationship with the Kellys, she had just happened to show up unannounced at their door on the day that Kelly decided to murder his wife? Taber knew that the Kellys regularly went out for Sunday brunch, so why hadn't she at least called to see if they would be at home, let alone to find out whether she was welcome? And why didn't she go in the front door of the Palace Pier past the concierge, instead of sneaking in through the side door by the loading dock out of sight of the building's surveillance cameras and security personnel? Once again, Taber didn't have solid answers.

Levy then turned to a crucially important element of Taber's story, which he thought would again expose her as the "liar and flake" the defence believed her to be. According to Taber, she had been in the apartment for ten minutes after Jeannette went over the balcony, a time during which she claimed Kelly had comforted and counselled her. Adding another five minutes for the trip to the express elevator on the twenty-fifth floor, where she claimed Kelly had taken her after leaving the apartment, she had been in the building for at least fifteen, more likely twenty, minutes after Jeannette's fall.

But she testified that she hadn't seen anything unusual when she came out of the building. Since her route that day would have taken her directly past the loading dock where Jeannette was lying dead, being attended to by the first police and ambulance officials at the scene, why hadn't she seen any of this activity? And how could Kelly have spent so much time with Taber when two other witnesses placed him at his wife's body somewhere between three and five minutes after she hit the ground? Once again, the witness had no explanations.

That night, Jan Bradley wrote to her husband, telling him that between finishing her essay on *Moby Dick* and following his murder trial, she was strung "tighter than a piano wire." Even though she had three exams and two essays to complete in ten days, she had been reading everything she could about the case, in particular, the evidence of Dawn Taber, a woman she referred to as "Shirley Temple" because of her long, freshly coiffed hair. "You've got Shirley Temple, I've got *Moby Dick* – Do you suppose we could arrange a dating service? I mean after three name changes already [Taber, Hastey, Bragg] I kinda like the sound of Dawn Dick, don't you?"

Levy finished his cross-examination by reminding the jury of the many details in Taber's eyewitness account that didn't fit the known facts. She had claimed that Jeannette had screamed so loudly that day that "someone must have heard it"; no one had. (In fact, Taber had first told police there was no scream.) She had the details of the victim's clothing only half-right, and couldn't tell the court what Kelly himself had been wearing on the murder day. Finally, there was the matter of the large sheepdog, which Taber couldn't remember seeing in the apartment, even though police had found the animal there when they arrived to search the premises.

To Levy, it all added up to a lie, and he proceeded to suggest why Taber might have needed to tell it. Wasn't it true, he asked, that there were rumours that she herself had killed Jeannette and that these rumours had followed her from town to town in the United States, forcing her to leave several jobs? And hadn't she told Sgt. Ed Stewart that she was caught in a mess that would not go away unless she did something about it? "I was not aware that there were false rumours," she answered.

When defence counsel finished, Lloyd Budzinsky pounced on Levy's last point as he re-examined his witness, asking Taber what rumours, if any, she had heard concerning her possible involvement in Jeannette Kelly's murder. Taber testified that John Nascimento was the only person who had ever made such a claim. Budzinsky asked Taber exactly what her former lover had said.

"That I had been involved in Jeannette's death."

"Alone?" the Crown prosecutor asked, anticipating that the defence might turn the tables and try to blame the murder on the only other person who had been in the apartment that day with the Kellys.

"No," she replied. "With Pat Kelly."

Dawn Taber was followed to the stand by a parade of Crown witnesses who had little or nothing to say about Jeannette Kelly's murder, but a great deal to offer about the character of the man who was charged with committing it. Taken individually, these vignettes of Kelly's personality were more demeaning than incriminating, anecdotes about a man obsessed with self-gratification, who routinely deceived people to get what he wanted. Taken together, though, they served as a devastating backdrop for the Crown's contention that Kelly was lying about the circumstances of his wife's death to avoid going to prison for twenty-five years.

John Atkinson, the Kellys' insurance agent, testified that Kelly had told him that he was putting out the garbage when Jeannette fell off the balcony, and that he discovered what had happened only when he returned to the apartment. Brenda Rodine, the proprietor of Hullaballoon, read the letter Kelly had sent her from Hawaii talking about his grief for his dead wife. The jury, who knew that the accused had taken Jan Bradley on that trip, listened in stony silence to Kelly's hypocritical and self-serving lie that it just wasn't "right" to be around women so soon after Jeannette's death.

Judy Seres, who had sometimes looked after the Kelly apartment when the couple travelled, said that she had not heard a rattle on the balcony in all her time in apartment 1705. Don Bayliss, who had lived next door to the Kellys at the Palace Pier, testified that he, too, had never heard a rattle from his or any other balcony in the building. In fact, during his lengthy tenure as treasurer of the Palace Pier, an official capacity in which he paid any bills for the upkeep of the apartment tower, not once had he authorized a cheque for balcony repairs.

When the Crown asked if it could call Alfredo Griffin before it had finished with another witness because the shortstop of the Toronto Blue

Jays was about to depart with his team on an extended trip, Judge O'Driscoll revealed his interest in baseball, and his sense of humour.

"He is not here as a pinch hitter?" the judge asked.

"I suppose as long as Mr. Levy doesn't throw any curves at him," Budzinsky quipped.

When the judge asked defence counsel if he had any objections to calling Griffin, Levy responded in the spirit of the exchange.

"Since he has given me an autographed baseball, I don't see how I can."

With the levities out of the way, Griffin testified that in the six months he had lived in apartment 1705 after Kelly moved out, he had not heard any rattle from the balcony. Griffin's testimony was seconded by the current occupant of the former Kelly apartment, Dr. Owaid Alnowaiser.

The only person who might have backed up Kelly's story about the rattle was his brokenhearted guardian angel, "Dr." Paul Stewart. Stewart had written the words "heard rattle" in his diary, but under cross-examination by the prosecution testified that it had been Kelly who had heard the rattle, not him. "You son of a bitch," David McComb thought as the man who had told the defence privately that he had heard the rattle reversed himself on the stand.

Before Ian MacLean testified, Judge O'Driscoll excluded the public from the courtroom under subsection (1) of Section 442 of the Criminal Code, which allows for the protection of witnesses whose lives might be endangered if their identities are made public at trial. It was the first time in twelve years on the bench that the judge, a staunch proponent of open proceedings, had agreed to hearing such *in camera* testimony. But since MacLean was still a paid civilian informant of the RCMP's Security Service, he felt he had no choice, philosophically observing that there was "a first time for everything."

The prosecution had called MacLean to testify about Kelly's reaction to the news of the Cookstown fire. MacLean told the court that it had been his impression that Kelly hadn't known about the fire when he called from a resort near Bancroft the day after the blaze. If the jury believed Taber's evidence that Kelly himself had burned his house down, the informant's testimony would be powerful proof of the accused's ability to fake his emotions and manipulate events.

Sheree Brown's evidence was detrimental to Kelly in two ways. The airline employee's eyewitness account of Kelly and Bradley hugging and kissing during their Hawaiian vacation just days after Jeannette's funeral called into question the extravagant grief Kelly had displayed on March 29, 1981, and again three days later at Jeannette's funeral. Compounding the impression of gross insincerity, Brown also testified that Kelly had told her that Bradley was a friend of both him and Jeannette, a lie that Victor Simpson's office manager, Connie Jeffrey, would testify that she, too, had been told by the accused.

Simpson's turn in the witness box began with submissions about his ability to testify, since he was technically bound by the rule of solicitor-client privilege in discussing his past dealings with Kelly. Judge O'Driscoll instructed Simpson to proceed with his evidence, but to pause for the court's guidance if he felt that he was violating his professional responsibilities to his former client. For the record, Levy informed the court that Kelly was not waiving any privilege to facilitate Simpson's testimony.

The evidence of Kelly's former lawyer was extremely damaging, as it amounted to a catalogue of lies, dishonourable acts, and other crimes allegedly committed by the accused. First, there was the phony account of how Jeannette had died – watering plants on the balcony while standing on a wicker stool. Then there was all the money Kelly had borrowed and never repaid, including $60,000 from the trust fund of Simpson's client Mina McIntosh. Simpson also testified about the false passport Kelly had given him for safe-keeping, a document that the lawyer said he had eventually delivered to his client during a trip to France in the winter of 1982.

Finally there was the Wayne Humby episode. Simpson testified that Kelly had gone to pieces at the news that his former roommate in the RCMP had been killed, exhibiting even more grief than he had when he told Simpson about his wife's death. At first, Simpson had not known that Humby was the person who died in the accident, because the telegram named someone else as the victim. But Kelly explained that the other name was actually Humby's RCMP code name.

The prosecution brought the hail and hearty Humby into the courtroom, and Simpson identified him as the person Kelly said had been killed along with his wife in a car accident. The deception looked even more studied when Simpson testified that Kelly had even had a telephone conversation in his presence with the person who he said had sent the telegram.

Although they had a field day with much of the bizarre evidence led by the prosecution, the media took particular interest in the testimony of the bevy of women Kelly had been seeing in Victoria shortly after he returned from his trip to Hawaii with Jan Bradley. Quickly dubbed the "Kelly Girls," they added some crucial brush-strokes to the unflattering portrait emerging from the Crown's evidence – of Kelly as a philandering liar who kept several women on the string at the same time by convincing each one of them that they were his real love interest.

Tracey Charlish, the bank teller Kelly had sent flowers to and dated in the summer of 1981, testified about Kelly's pride in his acting ability, which allowed him to portray any emotion he chose. Leslie Holmes told the court that after showering her with roses, Kelly had told her that she was "a very easy lady to love," and invited her on several international trips. In December 1981, Kelly had told Holmes that he was going to France to spend his birthday and Christmas alone because he was still mourning his wife's death, when, in fact, he and Jan Bradley were returning to their villa in Valbonne. Finally, Hanna Kirkham, who also received flowers from Kelly, testified that he had told her that he hadn't even been home when his wife had fallen off the balcony trying to fix a rattle.

Obviously hoping to undermine Kelly's own version of Jeannette's death by showing the jury how he changed the facts to suit his purpose, the Crown failed to impress at least one observer. After reading about the testimony of the "Kelly Girls," Jan Bradley wrote a brief note to her husband on a card decorated with a horse from a carousel: "I move we reduce the charge to 'first-degree roses.'" In a postscript commenting on the carnival horse on the card, Bradley made a stinging reference to the way she saw justice unfolding: "I thought you'd appreciate the 'circus' motif."

Kelly's parents were unable to attend the trial, partly because of the costs and partly because they didn't know if they could "take it." But every evening in British Columbia they waited by the telephone to get the call from Kelly's Aunt Vi, who gave them nightly reports on how the case was going. Even though they were thousands of miles away, the

Kellys were living under siege. Every newspaper in the country wanted more information about Patrick's past, and his beleaguered parents eventually went to a psychiatrist to deal with the harassment.

"Everyone from the *Windsor Star* to the *Chatham Herald*, everybody was phoning us. The *Globe* was calling every day. . . . They wanted a statement about what happened that day. I guess they figured that I knew. 'Do you think your son did it?' What the hell am I going to say to them, 'Yes?' How do I know what happened? I don't know what happened. I wasn't there. I mean we were harassed," John Kelly recalled.

Don Holmes was one of reasons that Kelly's trial was one of the most expensive in Canadian history. The Crown paid Holmes, a partner in the accounting firm of Lindquist & Holmes, over $50,000 to delve into Kelly's finances, hoping to prove that by the spring of 1981 he was desperately short of money and needed his wife's insurance funds to maintain his extravagant lifestyle. Holmes was one of the best forensic accountants in the business, regularly lecturing the commercial crime units of police departments, government agencies, and law firms, and frequently appearing as an expert witness in complex court cases involving financial chicanery.

For months, Holmes had scrutinized Kelly's financial records, including his numerous bank accounts in Canada and abroad, twenty credit cards, and multiple brokerage accounts that police had seized from Kelly's apartment and Victor Simpson's law offices. The witness's accounting covered the period from January 1980 until the end of 1981 (although Holmes also brought his investigation forward to December 1982 to take in the accused's fraud charges).

In April 1980, Holmes found that Kelly was making $1,538.60 a month and spending $8,587.15. In the twenty-month period from January 1, 1980, to September 30, 1981, Kelly's employment income was $16,184.38 and his expenses were $151,235. Even though Holmes admitted on cross-examination by Irwin Koziebrocki that Kelly had made at least $67,000 in unreported income (a windfall that laid him open to further prosecution on income tax evasion), the accountant testified that the accused's net worth had nevertheless been in sharp decline until the autumn of 1981. In September and October of that year alone, Kelly had spent $40,000. When asked what his financial analysis meant, Holmes made the understatement of the trial: "Patrick Kelly is living beyond his means in relation to the income he is bringing in."

Although Levy and Koziebrocki characterized the forensic accountant's use of coloured courtroom charts to illustrate his numbers as "show-biz," the look on the jurors' faces at these figures was proof that Holmes had firmly established one of the main tenets of the Crown's theory – by the spring of 1981, Patrick Kelly had been desperate for money, perhaps desperate enough to kill.

Throughout the lengthy trial, it stood in the courtroom like a prop from an avant-garde play; a full-scale model of the balcony of apartment 1705, originally built at a cost of $189 to test Kelly's account of how his wife had died. The model became even more important after Judge O'Driscoll rejected a Crown request to move the proceedings to the Palace Pier. Although he agreed that the change in venue would assist the jury in understanding the Crown's evidence, the judge wasn't willing to risk weeks of testimony where something might happen outside the court to cause a mistrial. Lloyd Budzinsky would just have to rely on the model of the balcony and the results of certain tests conducted at the police academy and the Centre of Forensic Sciences to make his point that Jeannette Kelly could not have died the way her husband said she did.

The prosecution was so sure that Kelly's description of how he had tried to save his wife was demonstrably false that it offered to have Kelly himself participate in the re-enactment of the victim's fall from the stool. Budzinsky told Levy that the Crown was also willing to test any other explanation of the events of March 29, 1981, that the defence might have. Earl Levy was not impressed with his colleague's strategic generosity. "A first-year law student would regard your offer as a trap, I regard it as an insult," he wrote, though the offence would be forgiven if Budzinsky bought him lunch.

One of the key Crown tests involved Paul Malbeuf, a member of the Metropolitan Toronto Police, who played the part of Kelly in the re-creation of the balcony scene. Knowing that Kelly was in top physical condition, the Crown and police had selected Malbeuf with great care. A member of Metro's Emergency Task Force for the previous five years, he worked out for an hour and a half every day, including a five-mile run and weightlifting. If anything, Malbeuf was in even better shape than the accused and that was exactly how Budzinsky wanted it.

In an experiment at the police academy, Malbeuf waited for a police-woman to scream and then bolted, exactly the same distance Kelly would have dashed, towards the model of the balcony, where she simulated a fall from a stool. Malbeuf's instructions were to get to the balcony as quickly as possible and to catch his colleague before she went over the railing if he could. To document the experiment the police used a video monitor that had a timing device like the ones used at the Olympic Games. The fastest time Malbeuf recorded in his sprint to the balcony was 3.8 seconds.

It was devastating evidence if the jury accepted its implications, and the defence knew that it couldn't allow the tests to go unchallenged. Levy argued that the results shouldn't be admitted because the simulation was unscientific and didn't take human factors into account; Judge O'Driscoll disagreed. The defence was not surprised. Throughout the trial, it had seen the judge consistently rule in the prosecution's favour and now believed that Budzinsky had a *carte blanche* to present his case.

On cross-examination, Levy got Malbeuf to admit that his adrenalin might have been flowing at a higher level if it had been his wife on a real-life balcony instead of a colleague on a model. But the unspoken implication that Levy hoped the jury would take from his line of questioning, that Kelly had come up with a superhuman effort to get to his wife when the event was happening in real life, didn't stand up for long. On re-examination, Budzinsky asked Malbeuf if it had been his own wife on the balcony could he have saved her? "No," the officer calmly replied. "Impossible."

Malbeuf's evidence was supported by the testimony of Eric Kreuger, an engineer from the Centre of Forensic Sciences, who had tested Kelly's description of his wife's "accident" against the laws of physics. Kreuger's January 1984 tests had confirmed his theoretical conclusions: that Kelly's explanation of both his wife's fall and his own reaction that day as described to police were not consistent with the principles of physics.

Kreuger testified that there were with problems with Kelly's claim that Jeannette had been completely outside the balcony when he had grabbed her waist, just as there were with his assertion that for a horrible moment, the couple had been face-to-face before the victim had slipped away. The engineer explained that if Jeannette had been standing on the stool with her back to the lake and began to lose her balance, the first part of her body to go over the railing would be her centre of gravity, which is located in the area of the waist – the very part of his wife's body that Kelly said he had got his hands on.

Nor would a person who toppled from a stool fall straight down, feet-first, as Kelly claimed. In fact, once Jeannette toppled backwards from the stool and went over the railing, she would have first assumed a near horizontal position as she fell away from the building, until her head went down, her feet came up, and she began to rotate. Even if Kelly had been able to get to the balcony at the very moment that his wife went over the railing, it would not be her face that he would have seen, but the bottoms of her feet.

Kreuger also testified that, during the simulations, Malbeuf had never been able to get close to the policewoman on the balcony, let alone reach her before she toppled over the railing. In fact, since it took nearly four seconds for him to get to the balcony and just three seconds for a person of Jeannette's weight to fall seventeen storeys, the victim would have been on the ground by the time Kelly reached the balcony.

Levy tried to take the sting out of Kreuger's evidence by suggesting that Jeannette Kelly might have delayed her fall by grabbing the cuff of the balcony's flashing above her head after the stool went out from underneath her, causing her body to twist as she grimly hung on with one hand before falling to her death. Kreuger testified that such a hypothesis was not "terribly likely." The engineer pointed out that if a person were hanging from the flashing in such a fashion, they would still be completely inside the balcony; in order to have fallen over the balcony, straight down, "you would have to pull up your legs in order to get them outside the railing."

Levy then returned to his point that a re-enactment could never duplicate the reality of a real-life panic situation. Reading from the accused's statement to the police, he reminded the court that Kelly had already been running as he rounded the corner from the kitchen, unlike Malbeuf, who had only begun his sprint after the policewoman's scream. Kreuger agreed with Levy, but then made a telling point of his own. The test with Malbeuf had been based on the assumption that the accused had responded to the victim's cry; if that wasn't true, why would Kelly be running from the kitchen before he had heard the alarming noise from the balcony?

The last person to testify for the prosecution was Dr. John Deck, the coroner who performed the autopsy on Jeannette Kelly. Over the objections of the defence, Judge O'Driscoll ruled that the jury could see the gruesome autopsy photographs that documented the trauma to the victim's back and lower body. The damage had been so massive that the cause of death could have been any of five or six fatal injuries, including the one that Dr. Deck cited – the complete destruction of the brain stem at the point where it joined Jeannette Kelly's brain.

Deck also talked about the strange wound to the top of the victim's head that had only been detected after her scalp was peeled back during the autopsy. There was some bleeding into the tissue of the scalp beneath the skin that the coroner said could have been caused by "some kind of blow to the head by something that didn't leave a mark." Since Deck had already testified that there had been little or no bleeding in the victim because death had been instantaneous and her blood flow had stopped on impact, the fact that the victim's scalp had bled raised the likelihood that this wound was sustained before the fall.

The last photograph the jury saw showed the face of the deceased as she looked the day after plunging to her death. There was an irregular abrasion and bruising in the area of her left jaw and minor bleeding below her nostrils, with a greater concentration of blood on the left side. There were also recent injuries on her upper and lower lip. The inside of the victim's mouth was cut behind the upper lip at a point that corresponded with one of the external abrasions. In the coroner's opinion, these minor injuries had not been caused by the fall. When Wade Nesmith asked if Jeannette Kelly's minor facial injuries were consistent with a punch, the coroner replied, "I think they are quite consistent with more than one punch."

Dr. Deck was among the last of the Crown's witnesses. After calling ninety-two people to testify, the prosecution rested its elaborate case and passed the legal baton to Levy. Although he would call a total of eight people, including Dr. Frederick Jaffe, who quibbled with the coroner's opinion about the wounds to Jeannette Kelly's face, his only real witness was the man whose fate would soon be in the hands of the jury: Patrick Kelly.

Earl Levy had burned the midnight oil to prepare for the Kelly case, reaching deep down for a little of the old magic that had made his reputation as a formidable barrister. There were cases that a lawyer did for money and others where the coin was column inches; Kelly's trial was one of those you took for the ink. Levy had never seen a case as thoroughly investigated by the police as the one against Patrick Kelly, and when he'd received the full brief from Eddie Greenspan, he had quickly realized just how difficult it would be to win.

Levy believed the case against his client came down to a contest of credibility between the Crown's eyewitness and the accused, leaving him little choice but to put Kelly on the stand. Levy had spent many long hours in the detention centre coaching Kelly on how to give his evidence, and the lawyer hoped that his client's previous experience as a witness in drug cases might make his testimony more effective. Now, in court, Levy wasted no time in getting the bare essentials of Kelly's position on the record.

"Mr. Kelly, did you kill your wife?"

"No sir, I did not," he replied.

In rapid succession, Kelly denied that he had burned down his home in Cookstown, that Dawn Taber had been in his apartment on the day that Jeannette died, that he had arranged the bogus telegram concerning Wayne Humby's death, or that he had faked his grief for his dead wife. The RCMP had taught him how to "act" appropriately in the company of criminals, not to simulate grief by producing tears, blanching, or going into shock.

To counter the image of the Kellys' marriage presented by the Crown, Levy asked the witness to describe his relationship with Jeannette. Kelly testified that their only problem as a couple arose because of the continuing police investigation into his alleged part in the Cookstown fire. It was only after he and Jeannette stopped having sex because of the "stress" created by rumours and innuendoes against him that he had started seeing other women, including Jan Bradley. But he had never wanted to divorce his wife "and honestly felt once that stress was removed [the arson investigation], that the relationship would continue."

Why then had he written the letter to his wife that listed the assets of the marriage and talked about separate living arrangements? Kelly explained that he had done so at his wife's request, and that it had been his preference for them to start seeing a marriage counsellor or a psychiatrist. Even though he and Jeannette had had a platonic relationship from the time of the arson investigation to the day of his wife's accidental death, he insisted that their relationship had been "quite good and friendly" and "was well on the way to recovery."

If that was true, why then had he been out with Jan Bradley just a few nights before Jeannette's death? Referring once again to his platonic marriage, Kelly implied that Bradley was no more than a sexual convenience, although he certainly admired her as a person. As for previous testimony from witnesses like Abby Latter that the Kelly marriage was under great strain in the weeks immediately preceding Jeannette's death, the accused claimed that the tension had been caused by his wife's demand for a second $50,000 Porsche he hadn't wanted to buy. "She was a little unhappy about that. My wife was quite used to getting her own way."

When Levy raised the subject of his relationship with Dawn Taber, Kelly denied that he had ever had an affair with her, an answer contradicted the results of his privately commissioned lie detector test and his earlier statements to Eddie Greenspan. But Kelly did describe giving Dawn a backrub that he claimed she had tried to take further. "At one point, she turned over and reached up to me and pulled me toward her to kiss her, and I said I would make another cup of coffee and got up."

Asked about his statement to police that he had never discussed life insurance with Taber, Kelly testified that he remembered these discussions after seeing the proposals from Citadel Life at his preliminary trial. But Jeannette had been present when the discussions took place, and the only reason his handwriting was found on the proposals was that he had taken some notes as Taber explained the financial terms of the policy. As for the discussions between he and Taber involving much larger amounts of insurance, Kelly denied that they had ever taken place.

Denial was a tactic that could only be taken so far. When he was asked about the false passport police had found in his safety deposit box,

Kelly admitted that he had applied for the document at the time that the RCMP was investigating him for the Cookstown fire.

"I knew I was innocent in connection with the fire but at that time I was rather nervous about the entire situation and felt that I did not want to go to jail as an ex-policeman or as a policeman, and I was not familiar with the protective custody measures which are in institutions, and I simply obtained the passport as a precaution." It was a lot of words to say that he had been planning to run away.

The Crown had gone to great lengths to show that money had been one of the prime motives behind Jeannette Kelly's murder, and Levy now elicited from Kelly some astonishing evidence to show that cash had been the least of Kelly's worries. Kelly testified that he made approximately $400,000 from various freelance enterprises between 1976 and 1981 when he was member of the RCMP, including smuggling currency into the United States for clients in Colombia. On the advice of his then lawyer, Victor Simpson, he had funnelled these moneys through K&V Enterprises, where they mysteriously disappeared. Although Jeannette benefited from his moonlighting, Kelly said that she hadn't known how her husband subsidized their lavish lifestyle. "She simply turned a blind eye to where the money was coming from, and when she asked, I simply replied, 'The money is not being obtained illegally.'"

One of the deadliest pieces of character evidence against his client was the post-funeral trip to Hawaii with Jan Bradley. Levy asked Kelly why he had gone on vacation with another woman so soon after his wife's death. He explained that since he had asked Bradley to go on the trip several months before, he felt obliged to carry through with their plan. The reason he told certain people that she was a friend of the family was "simply to save embarrassment on both sides." The fact was, at the time of the Hawaiian vacation, Jan Bradley had been no more than "a good friend" he just happened to be sleeping with.

As for his various lies to people like Victor Simpson, Connie Jeffrey, and others about how Jeannette had died, Kelly said he was just going along with false press reports because he didn't want to discuss the details of his wife's death. "I was advised that the initial story was released by the press that my wife was checking or watering plants on the balcony when she fell, and it was simply my position at that point that I really didn't like talking about the subject to begin with, and if that is what the press has released to the newspapers and television then I was just going to say my wife fell off the balcony while watering flowers."

When asked to describe how his wife had actually met her death, Kelly demonstrated that he had been listening carefully to Eric Kreuger's evidence. He had previously told police that he had grabbed his wife around the waist, but he now made an alteration to his story that more closely matched what the engineer had testified he would have seen if he had been able to make it to the balcony that day. "I managed to get my arms around the upper part of her legs, but I was still basically in motion, I couldn't hang on with my hands and she was falling away, and at one point I recall grabbing for her arm and she slipped away."

The jury watched in silence as Lloyd Budzinsky rose to cross-examine the witness.

In the opinion of the Crown, Patrick Kelly had murdered his wife in exactly the same way he would have carried out any other assignment as a highly trained RCMP undercover operator, and Lloyd Budzinsky's witheringly effective cross-examination was devoted to expressing that theory rather than eliciting information from the accused. Kelly had developed a cover story for the murder based on cleverly "blending" truth with fiction, and had resorted to a variety of diversionary tactics and command performances to pull off his charade. What he didn't say was that the prosecution was privately convinced that Kelly was a victim of his former role-playing in the RCMP – a little man trying to be a somebody by living out his undercover identity as a high-rolling entrepreneur.

When Budzinsky asked Kelly if it was true that a criminal sometimes tested a suspected undercover agent by involving them in a crime, the ex-Mountie agreed that it sometimes happened.

"So if Dawn is correct and you are wrong, and she was present when your wife died and watched you beat and throw your wife over the balcony, it is logical she would feel implicated, isn't that right? That she would feel – implicated, involved, [a] co-conspirator?"

"I think if one drew the conclusion or assumed she was there, perhaps," Kelly replied. "But I think if one takes that one step further according to her evidence as I recall it, she did not see, for instance, my dog in the apartment."

"That is not the question," Budzinsky snapped. "If someone saw someone killing somebody and stood by and did nothing, it is not illogical to assume that the person who did the watching would feel involved?"

"I would say so, sir. But Dawn Bragg [Taber] was not in my apartment, and I did not commit murder," answered Kelly, who thought that Budzinsky was behaving like a "cocky kid" trying to get under his skin. He had no intention of accepting the lawyer's slurs sitting down.

"And certainly someone that was involved with someone killing someone by watching or discussing a plan or opening a screen door or whatever couldn't confide to the police about that without implicating themselves, isn't that right?"

"I would have to suppose so, sir."

Budzinsky suggested to Kelly that if he had been planning to kill his wife, Taber was the weak link because of their previous discussions on the same subject. Before the prosecutor could finish his supposition, Kelly tried to interrupt him, touching off a fiery exchange.

"Give me a chance to explain," Budzinsky said, "and you can add on and deal with [Taber's] evidence if you wish."

"I shall," Kelly angrily replied. "I am here to defend myself on a charge of first degree murder, and I am trying to defend myself, and you are right, I will stand up and defend myself, and you are trying to put me in jail for the rest of my life."

"Did you rehearse that?" Budzinsky calmly replied, realizing along with the defence that aggressive sparring almost always worked against the accused.

"No, I have been in custody for fourteen and a half months for something I didn't do."

"Do you want the jury to feel sorry for you?" Budzinsky needled, trying to turn Kelly's outburst into a live example of how he constantly tried to manipulate events.

"I think it is quite obvious I have been in custody for a long time," Kelly answered, "and the jury is very capable of assessing the facts, and I think the fact that Dawn Bragg was not in my apartment is very clear. I have finished and you can continue."

"That is my decision, Mr. Kelly, not yours," the judge sourly interjected.

"I apologize, my lord," Kelly said, returning to his former courtroom demeanour that made him look almost like a third party talking about someone else.

Budzinsky continued with his hypothesis that Taber had been in the apartment because Kelly had had to silence her about their previous plan to murder Jeannette. It was obvious that the Crown still believed that its star witness had not yet told the whole truth about her activities on the day of the murder.

"I am putting to you as a suggestion, whether she dropped in accidentally, or whether she has still withheld some information and was invited there by you, your plan to go ahead would gain force because she would be implicated with you."

"No, sir," Kelly replied.

Budzinsky then drew a tenuous but damaging parallel between Kelly's money-smuggling and his wife's murder, suggesting that if Kelly had ever threatened the people he had been working for in Colombia with exposure to the authorities, there was a good chance that he would have been killed. When Kelly agreed, Budzinsky explained the "Stockholm Effect" in which hostages begin to sympathize with their captors. In a related psychological process, wasn't it true, Budzinsky asked, that certain undercover operators begin to take on the psyche and thinking of the criminals they mix with? Kelly agreed and Budzinsky pounded his point home.

"And your wife knew too much, you were like the people you were running money for. If she knew too much and threatened your existence, you would have her killed, isn't that right?

"Sir, are you trying to suggest I would kill my wife because she knew I had undeclared income?" Kelly asked in disbelief.

"And the fire," Budzinsky added.

"No sir, I did not commit arson, and I hardly think I would commit murder for undeclared income."

Budzinsky then accused Kelly of buying the expensive china set for Paul Stewart, a virtual stranger to him at the time of Jeannette's death, so that he would write in his diary that he had heard a rattle from the balcony while in the Kellys' apartment.

"You discussed the accident with Stewart and you got him to write down the rattle in that notebook, didn't you?"

"No, sir."

"That is what you paid the $5,000 for wasn't it? . . . That is the problem with your plan, Mr. Kelly. You relied on too many people that didn't come through according to your plan."

The Crown prosecutor went on to mock much of Kelly's previous testimony with hard fact. How could he claim that at the time of Jeannette's death that their marriage was recovering, when in fact he was seeing Jan Bradley several times a week and, in his wife's absence, had even had her over to the Palace Pier for a romantic weekend? How could he complain in his letter to Brenda Rodine of the terrible nights in Hawaii, when he was spending every one of them in Jan Bradley's arms? And why would he lie about Bradley being a friend of the family if he didn't think he was doing anything wrong in taking her to Hawaii just five days after Jeannette's funeral?

By the time Budzinsky suggested to Kelly that the reason he had asked for a closed coffin during his wife's funeral was to hide the bruise his fist had left on the dead woman's face, he had done to Kelly what Levy had previously done to Dawn Taber, leaving the jury in front of the trial's essential dilemma: which liar would they choose to believe?

Earl Levy did his best to make sure the jury would believe Patrick Kelly. In his eloquent address to the jury, he ridiculed the Crown's case as a grand smear campaign against the accused that was long on salacious details about his personal life and short on incriminating evidence proving a charge of first degree murder. The testimony of forensic accountant Don Holmes, which the Crown was relying on to show that money was one of the motives behind Jeannette Kelly's murder, was flawed because it didn't take into account the large amounts of unde-clared income the accused had been making as a currency smuggler. The expert testimony of Eric Kreuger couldn't be trusted because the tests he had used to dismiss Kelly's account of his wife's accident couldn't possibly reproduce the real-life conditions of an actual emergency. And the parade of witnesses the Crown had produced to establish Kelly's bad character had virtually nothing to contribute to a judicious consideration of whether he had murdered his wife in cold blood.

The only direct evidence the prosecution produced had come from a woman who was a "compulsive liar." Levy reminded the jury that the police had known for years about the stool, the lack of a rattle on the balcony, Jeannette Kelly's life insurance policies, and the autopsy report, but hadn't arrested the accused for murder until Dawn Taber came forward with her alleged eyewitness testimony.

"They have gambled Patrick Kelly's future on the likes of Dawn [Taber], a woman who has more stories than Hans Christian Andersen."

None of Taber's story made sense. Why would Kelly, a trained under-cover agent, commit murder in front of a witness? Why would he argue with his wife for fifteen minutes, if he had indeed been planning to kill her that day? Why had Taber done nothing to save her best friend if she had really witnessed the crime? Why hadn't she seen the sheepdog in the apartment or correctly identified the clothes the deceased had been wearing if she was really there? Why hadn't she seen the police and ambulance attendants when she left the building that day? And why had she remained silent about the murder for nearly two years if she really had witnessed it?

Just before he finished, Levy reminded the jurors that they were not there to determine if Kelly was guilty of obtaining false passports, living beyond his means, romancing too many women, or not paying his income tax. "We may not think much of him for the way he has lived his life. . . . We are here to determine if he is guilty of murder."

When Lloyd Budzinsky told the jury that they could find Patrick Kelly guilty of first degree murder on Dawn Taber's eyewitness testimony, or on the separate case made by the Crown's powerful circumstantial evidence, he was indulging in a little professional exaggeration. If the jury really had such a choice, then why hadn't the police and Crown moved against Kelly years before when they already had most of the circumstantial evidence against him? The fact was, the Crown was relying on Taber to secure Kelly's conviction, just as the police had depended on her statement to arrest the accused in the first place. And that left Budzinsky with the problem of how to restore the credibility of a witness that the defence had so effectively made out to be a liar, and that he himself had suggested might even be an accomplice to murder? His answer was to tell the jury that Dawn Taber's day in court might come, but this day belonged to Patrick Kelly.

"She is not on trial. . . . There is no promise made not to prosecute

her . . . that is for another day and another time if [there is] sufficient
evidence. . . . There is no special deal or immunity to Mrs. Bragg. Maybe
Mrs. Bragg knows more, maybe she was involved to a greater extent,
maybe she assisted Kelly, but only Dawn Bragg and Mr. Kelly know,
and Mr. Kelly can't admit that because if he implicates Dawn Bragg, he
implicates himself."

Budzinsky pointed out that if Taber had wanted to commit perjury
against Kelly, there were far safer ways of doing it. She could, for
example, have accomplished the same objective and been "clean" by
simply saying that the accused had confessed that he had killed his wife.
Instead, she had chosen a course that left her an eyelash away from facing
a murder charge of her own.

"She implicates herself as a potential party to the offence. I mean
listen, if you wanted to – if you are bizarre, and you wanted to get
someone, frame someone, are you going to say, 'He and I killed someone
and dumped the body over the balcony?'"

Clearly worried that the jury might reject the Crown's case because
it was based on the testimony of an unsavoury witness, Budzinsky force-
fully reminded the jury that Taber might one day find herself charged
with murder if evidence other than her own testimony pointed to her
involvement. "Maybe she was there at one o'clock, and maybe she is
still holding back evidence. Maybe the beating in the apartment took
place earlier before the body went over." But although she was "not a
nice person" and her conduct on the day of Jeannette Kelly's death was
"reprehensible," the jury had to remember that it still didn't change the
truth of what she had to say.

After the morning recess, Levy asked for a mistrial based on the fact
that the Crown had put a theory to the jury during its summation that
hadn't been advanced in its examination of Taber: that she and his client
had jointly been involved in the murder of Jeannette Kelly, a new scenario that "hopelessly prejudiced" the accused. The judge dismissed
Levy's application and Budzinsky completed his speech, painting Kelly
as a man who couldn't wait to get out of his marriage so that he could
be with his lover.

According to Budzinsky, Kelly's account was totally unbelievable.
Why would Jeannette Kelly be up on a stool trying to fix a rattle on the
balcony when she had to leave for the airport to catch an international

flight in less than an hour and she still hadn't finished packing or even taken a shower? And if there really had been a rattle, why hadn't the Kellys complained about it? Why was Patrick Kelly the only person who had ever heard it? To demonstrate how ludicrous Kelly's rescue story was, Budzinsky twice dropped his pen as he spoke, reminding the jury of just how quickly things fall to the ground and how hard it would be for someone who was thirty-five-feet away to catch them before they did. The only reason Kelly had concocted his impossible story about getting his hands on Jeannette before she slipped from his grasp was to protect himself against the possibility that someone might have seen him when he carried his wife out to the balcony and threw her over.

To erode the accused's credibility further, Budzinsky listed all the witnesses that Kelly claimed were mistaken: Hanna Kirkham, John Atkinson, Tracey Charlish, Victor Simpson, Connie Jeffrey, Dawn Taber, and a host of others. Were all these people lying, and was Kelly the only honest man? He concluded by telling the jurors that the key to Kelly's heartless plan was his ability to control his emotions, "to act and thereby manipulate people to think what he wanted them to believe about himself and others," skills he had perfected as an undercover operator with the RCMP. Jeannette Kelly's murder had just been another mission.

Working from the thousand pages of notes he had made during the trial, Mr. Justice John O'Driscoll delivered a charge to the jury that reviewed the key evidence and explained a few matters of law before he sent them out to begin their deliberations.

One of the things he drew to their attention was an exchange between the accused and Lloyd Budzinsky, in which Kelly had claimed that he had been "exonerated" of any criminal responsibility for the Cookstown fire because the case had been thrown out at his preliminary hearing. The fact was, the judge said, that a discharge at the preliminary level does not equal an exoneration, as Budzinsky had correctly pointed out during his skirmish with the accused. Having said that, the judge directed the jury to use the arson testimony only as a possible motive for murder, not as proof in itself that Kelly had killed his wife.

The judge noted that no one other than Kelly had ever heard the rattle that supposedly lured his wife to her accidental death, and reminded jurors that Kelly's lack of money might have eventually cost him the love of a woman he had convinced of his great wealth. But like everyone else in the strange trial, Judge O'Driscoll finally turned to the witness who was at the heart of the Crown's case, Earl Levy's defence, and the jury's task, the inscrutable Dawn Taber.

The judge candidly admitted that he found Taber to be an "enigma" or a "riddle." He cautioned the jurors that unless they believed Eric Kreuger's evidence that Jeannette Kelly's death had not been an accident, it would be "unsafe" to base a conviction for first degree murder solely on Taber's evidence. He pointed out that there was no evidence confirming her presence in the apartment on the day that Jeannette Kelly died, and reminded them that the accused had earlier sworn that she was not there. His admonition notwithstanding, it was the jury's right to believe Taber's evidence on its own if they decided that it was credible.

At 3:33 P.M. on May 30, 1984, Patrick Kelly's fate passed into the hands of an electrician, two homemakers, a maintenance man, three business managers, a planning analyst, a cashier, an office supervisor, a steamfitter, and a chef. Jan Bradley, who had been attending the trial since finishing her exams at the end of April, was there to share the dramatic moment with her husband. Photographers from the *Toronto Sun* snapped a picture of her as she left the courtroom that day with Earl Levy, shielding her face from their cameras. The media weren't the only ones who watched the unhappy woman trying to protect what was left of her shattered privacy. Lottie Arbuckle hadn't even known that her former son-in-law had remarried until she had attended the trial and was taken aback by the appearance of his new wife.

"She was a wee bit small, wasn't any bigger than Jeannette I would think. Same sort of, you know, how Jeannette had her hair, parted in the centre. But I said to myself, 'That girl must have known.' She must have known what Pat Kelly done."

That first evening, the jury deliberated for seven hours before Judge O'Driscoll ordered that they be sequestered in a hotel for the night. They continued their discussions the next day, sending a message to the judge late in the afternoon of May 31 that they had reached a verdict. At 5:18 P.M., the jury trooped back into the packed and silent courtroom, and the foreman announced that they had found the accused guilty as charged. Jan Bradley, who was sitting directly behind her husband, closed her eyes as the verdict was pronounced, gasped once, and then swept out of the courtroom in tears. Judge O'Driscoll asked the red-faced prisoner if he had anything to say. Patrick Kelly stood and answered in a voice reporters would later say had the hard edge of defiance:

"I now know how Donald Marshall feels."

"Pardon me?" the judge said.

"I now know how Donald Marshall feels," Kelly repeated.

With the prisoner's twice-stated reference to the country's most famous victim of a miscarriage of justice ringing in his ears, Judge O'Driscoll pronounced the mandatory sentence then prescribed by law for a person convicted of first degree murder: life in prison with no eligibility for parole for twenty-five years. Kelly was whisked from the courtroom just eight minutes after the jury returned their verdict, sending the press scrambling outside to watch his departure.

On the steps of the courthouse Earl Levy told the press that his client's conviction would be appealed and that he would need special protection in prison because of his previous occupation. A group of Jeannette Kelly's friends told reporters that they would be throwing a party that night in honour of the verdict. Sgt. Ed Stewart, who had won two civic awards for his work on the case, confirmed that he would be investigating Dawn Taber with a view to charging her as an accomplice to Jeannette Kelly's murder. Shortly after the verdict, Taber herself heard from Stewart and the Crown prosecutor, who had painted her at every opportunity in the trial as having been Kelly's taciturn helper.

"Budzinsky and Stewart called and they both said to me that they had said things that were not nice about me but not to worry about them, that they had to say them . . . to keep the jury focused on their job of convicting Pat of first degree murder."

Enterprising reporters who called Kelly's parents' home in British Columbia to get their reaction to their son's conviction were to be disappointed. They had gone to Reno, Nevada, to avoid the media when the big moment came. John Kelly had just won two bottles of champagne on the slot machines when news of the verdict reached him and his wife.

"I decided to drink the champagne, and I think it was made in Sam's basement. It was so horrible. I think it was thirty-five cents a bottle. I was drunk for three days. I was devastated. Winnie, now she's a silent crier."

The next day the *Toronto Sun* announced Kelly's conviction in a front-page headline: "CONDO KILLER GETS LIFE." The accompanying article said that the story of Patrick Kelly "rivalled *Dynasty* for sex, life in the fast lane, greed and cunning."

One of the interested parties that had been following the trial was the police force that had given Kelly the training he had apparently applied with deadly consequences for his wife. Kelly's former handlers had already looked bad over his charges for passport fraud, because the false documents Kelly had used to get the phony Ryan passport had been supplied to him by the RCMP. During Kelly's murder trial, the Internal Affairs Branch had been quick to disavow any knowledge of the matter. As a secret RCMP memo to then Solicitor General Robert Kaplan made clear, the force believed that Patrick Kelly was somebody else's problem.

"As jurisdiction for this incident [the murder] fell within Metro Toronto Police Department and Kelly was not a member when the incident occurred, it is felt we could not press this matter but simply follow the events as they transpire, namely the trial itself. Insofar as keeping the Minister current on the events, we are in a similar position as he is and our source would be the news media."

The day after Kelly's murder conviction, Kaplan's office asked the RCMP for additional information to deal with the potentially explosive questions it believed might be asked in the House of Commons: "Was there ever an internal investigation of Patrick Kelly? If so, why was he not charged internally? If there was an ongoing inquiry, why was it halted? Was it stopped before or after he left? If after, why was it not continued?"

The point of the minister's query was clear: had the RCMP contributed in any way to the events that ended with Jeannette Kelly's murder by failing to uphold the law against one of its own for fear of public embarrassment to the force?

RCMP Comm. R. H. Simmonds smoothed Kaplan's ruffled political feathers. He reported that although there had been internal investigations into Kelly's activities as a member of the force, there had been insufficient evidence to proceed with either internal or criminal charges. The internal investigation stopped when Kelly resigned from the force, at which time any ongoing criminal investigation became the responsibility of the police departments having jurisdiction. As for unattributed media reports that Kelly had misappropriated money from a drug buy, Simmonds told Kaplan that "all cases involving Kelly were re-examined to ensure that all was above board and we are unaware of any cases as suggested by the *Toronto Star* newspaper article."

As soothing as it was, Simmonds's reply to the minister could not have been more misleading. After conducting an internal investigation into Kelly's activities, the RCMP had found several grounds for launching internal proceedings against him but had chosen not to act. Two senior RCMP investigators had read Kelly his rights and informed him that he might be charged with arson, the fabrication of evidence, defrauding his insurance companies, and "Disgraceful Conduct." The force had even provided key evidence subsequently used by the OPP to lay arson and fraud charges against Kelly arising out of the Cookstown fire.

But the most telling deception in the commissioner's report to the solicitor general was his assurance that allegations that Kelly had misappropriated drug funds had been investigated and found to be without foundation. RCMP Supt. D. H. Heaton and staff sergeants Norm Harvey-McKean and Wayne Horrocks knew better. But in the intelligence business, there is only so much you can tell the civilians.

"Badly shaken," Jan Bradley took her husband's conviction as well as could be expected. In a letter written the day after the verdict, she told him that she loved him and still believed that he was innocent: "you are simply incapable of that kind of violence." She knew that the road ahead would be long and frustrating as Kelly appealed his conviction, and she offered her assistance in any capacity but a financial one. Her husband's legal problems had left her owing a great deal of money to her mother, and the notoriety of the trial would make it difficult if not impossible for her to find a job in Toronto. As trying as things were, she promised to keep visiting him at the detention centre until the authorities moved him to a federal prison.

Throughout the ordeal, Bradley had always believed that the Kellys had let their son down, and she now wrote them "a not nice letter" to say so. Half-lecturing, half-pleading with them, she reminded the couple that she and her mother had been the only people to stand behind Patrick during the trial. Referring to a quote attributed to the Kellys in a newspaper article – "We do not know our son anymore" – she accused them of putting their own comfort levels ahead of Patrick's interests: "I write to you now because I left your son in tears and desperate . . . I don't think he deserves his parents stabbing him in the back and jeopardizing his chances at even getting an appeal heard."

The Kellys were so stung by their daughter-in-law's letter that they took it to a lawyer, who told them that it was libellous and harassing. They decided not to take any action and wrote to their son professing their love for him and their belief in his innocence. They complained to him about Bradley's "vicious letters," which Winnifred Kelly felt were aimed at sending them both to an early grave: "I honestly think that she is trying to cause your father and I to have a heart attack with her accusations about us. Let her keep the harassment up and you will be an orphan."

When her exam results came back, Bradley had made the dean's list and received 95 per cent for her essay on *Moby Dick*. Her professor's accompanying note meant even more than the mark: "You are the most intelligent, most imaginative, most accomplished student I have ever had the pleasure of teaching – or learning from. Also the strongest."

As the months slipped away, so too did Bradley's resolve to remain in Toronto near her imprisoned husband. "I do not want to be here," she wrote to Kelly. "I am worn out with hurting, worn out with being strong." She returned to graduate school in the fall, but by the spring term found herself depressed, bored, and exhausted. Shanty was ill and her mother could no longer care for Kelly's sheepdog. Reluctantly, Patrick gave her permission to give the animal away.

That summer Bradley was hired by the *Ottawa Citizen* but soon had her fill of the city's comfortable but suffocatingly bland charms. She started to think about leaving Canada and beginning a new life somewhere else. "There is nothing left here – it disappeared a year ago (if indeed it ever existed). The only people who still inhabit my world . . . serve only to remind, to reopen the wound."

Kelly was not surprised when Jan's card arrived from Singapore in early September 1985: "Although our paths have taken us in different directions, you are still part of my life – and I wish you much happiness." Shortly afterwards, the Ontario Supreme Court dismissed his first appeal. A few weeks later, Jan wrote from Jakarta to commiserate. By the time the Supreme Court of Canada turned down his appeal, Kelly's wife was half a world away in Indonesia, where it was rumoured she had taken a job with CUSO. When she got in touch again, it was to tell him that she was thinking about settling in Japan or England; wherever she went, she doubted that Canada would ever be her home again.

In the fall of 1986, her letters stopped, and Patrick Kelly felt like a castaway on a forsaken island.

18

THE LEPER

Patrick Kelly knew that the young prisoner spread-eagled on the garbage cart was dead when his right arm slipped from his side and swung limply to and fro as a guard wheeled him out of the prison kitchen. The inmate who had driven a shank into the young man's heart while he was standing in line for Sunday lunch was already facing charges for another murder at nearby Collins Bay penitentiary, and his latest victim was just another casualty of the nothing-to-lose attitude of a lifer.

The razor-sharp plexiglass knife used in the fatal attack was the weapon of choice at Kingston penitentiary because it could be turned out "like candy" in the prison workshops and didn't show up on the institution's ubiquitous metal detectors. Best of all, anyone with a carton of cigarettes could afford to buy one. Kelly had been close enough to the victim to see "a large gash near the sternum, and his shirt covered in blood." Just the day before, another prisoner, known as Downtown Brown, had hung himself in his cell. Authorities reacted to this second "incident" by locking down the prison for the afternoon.

"One hell of a weekend," Kelly wrote of his first experiences in Kingston after being transferred from Metro West Detention Centre, where he had served the first two years of his life sentence. "There is not a week that goes by when I either don't see blood or we don't hear of yet another murder or suicide at one of the area pens."

The facts backed up Kelly's observation. Between 1980 and 1986, sixty-three inmates were murdered by their peers in Canadian prisons. In 1984, the year Kelly was convicted of first degree murder, there were five hundred serious inmate attacks across the penal system, including scores of cases where survivors had been stabbed as many as thirty times. One of the more popular forms of assault at Kingston was to cover the victim's head with a sheet so that he couldn't identify his assailants and then beat him unconscious with bars of soap or cups tied in a pillowcase.

No matter how hard Kelly pushed himself during his five-hour daily workouts, sleep never came easily in the endless prison nights. He kept seeing that lifeless arm swinging in dead relax from the garbage cart in a room that smelled of macaroni and cheese and the coppery tartness of fresh blood. The image held special anguish for Kelly, blending prison horrors with dreams of the event that had put him behind bars for twenty-five years.

"The whole thing is so very reminiscent of the scene at the apartment in March 1981," recalled Kelly. "As the right hand falls off the cart – in my dream it happens in slow motion – I see Jeannette's right arm reaching up – I remember grabbing it and not being able to hold on and she slipped away. . . . My right hand is on the balcony rail and I'm squeezing tightly as I feel myself falling forward – off. I can actually feel my feet leaving the balcony floor . . . I can't hang on any longer, I'm looking straight into her face. There is no sound, only a knowing that she is falling. A helpless look."

It was not as if he needed anything else to trouble his anxious nights. As a former RCMP officer, he knew that death was only as far away as one ill-timed encounter with a con enjoying Her Majesty's hospitality as a result of Kelly's undercover work. Capital punishment may have been abolished, Kelly thought, but it had been brought back especially for him on the day that correctional authorities had decided to send him to a prison in the same jurisdiction where he had once worked as a narcotics agent.

Whether by accident or design, inmate 731505B had indeed been sent to the wrong prison. After Kelly's murder conviction, his lawyer, Earl Levy, had written to Crown prosecutor Lloyd Budzinsky, expressing concern for his client's safety once he was assigned to a federal penitentiary. Both Budzinsky and Metro Toronto police chief John Ackroyd agreed that the ex-RCMP officer's life would be at serious risk and recommended "that steps should be taken by the jail authorities to conceal Mr. Kelly's true identity and to place him in an institution where the appropriate security for his protection can be obtained."

Kelly himself applied for a name change and incarceration in an out-of-province institution when the time came to leave Metro West. Prison authorities agreed, because of his former employment as an undercover drug officer based in Toronto, he shouldn't be assigned to an Ontario penitentiary. Since his offence required that he be placed in "super-protective custody," there were only two institutions Kelly could go to: Kingston, or the federal penitentiary in Prince Albert, Saskatchewan. Since Kingston was in Ontario, Prince Albert would be his new home.

But when his transfer came through, he found himself travelling east. Despite the advice of Budzinsky and Ackroyd, and the recommendations of two placement reports prepared at Metro West, Kelly was sent to Kingston penitentiary in May 1986. Standard bureaucratic practice was to send a federal inmate to a prison in the jurisdiction where he'd been convicted first, and Kelly was no exception. He was admitted under his own name. Kingston's deputy warden gave Kelly a choice between living in the open population or complete segregation in the protective custody unit of the institution. Kelly chose limited freedom with all its dangers over the live burial of being locked in his cell for twenty-three hours a day.

The reports recommending that he go to Prince Albert went missing in the system until mid-1987, by which time Kelly had already spent a year at risk in Kingston. Although prison officials scratched their heads over how the reports had gone astray, there was no mystery as far as Kelly was concerned: the RCMP had both intervened in his institutional placement and turned down his request for a name change to make sure that he never got out of prison alive.

"What the fuck are you doing here?" the guard rasped, instantly recognizing Kelly's face from the saturation media coverage of his high-profile Toronto trial. "What the fuck am I going to do with you here at Kingston?"

"Beats me," Kelly replied, feeling awkward and more than a little nervous under the silent scrutiny of the other inmates.

Pointing down the range at a hulking man who was staring in Kelly's direction, the keeper offered the new inmate some jailhouse wisdom.

"My advice to you would be to align yourself with that man there. His name is Clifford Strong, Jr., and he is probably the toughest son of a bitch alive. If you are going to live here, I suggest you get real friendly with Clifford or I expect you won't last very long."

The keeper escorted Kelly to cell 4-1-A, where his first visitor was Strong, who brought him a welcoming cup of coffee. Following the keeper's advice, Kelly did his best to make friends with the convicted murderer whose massive frame and dark, piercing eyes created the impression of a powerful animal rather than of a man. Strong invited the new inmate to work out with him in the yard, and Kelly accepted, but not before warning him about his police past, describing it as his "particular brand of leprosy."

If Kelly was trying to tell his potential protector that he was a dangerous man to be seen with, Strong's slow smile made it clear that the warning had been unnecessary. He had faced far more menacing demons than the ones that might be unleashed from lifting weights in the yard of Kingston penitentiary with an ex-Mountie doing life. The inmates shook hands and Kelly was astounded by Strong's bear-like grip. When the big man turned to leave, Kelly noticed the "zipper" running up the back of his partially bald head, an eight-and-a-half-inch scar from an old "piping." He shuddered. If they would come after someone like Clifford Strong, what might they do to an ex-RCMP officer behind the thick and pitiless walls of the 150-year-old prison?

One of Kelly's first observations about life inside was that inmates respected physical prowess and were suspicious of intelligence. Through Strong, he hooked up with Kingston's most formidable iron-pumpers and kept his distance from other inmates. Although Kelly would never come close to Strong's feat of bench-pressing five hundred pounds, his own lift of three hundred was enough to serve notice on Kingston's cop-hating population that coming after him would not be without its hazards.

It didn't take long for the classic hatreds to emerge. On Kelly's first day in the general population, another prisoner screamed at him in the supper line, "I'm going to kill you, you fucking pig." Kelly was unnerved by the threat until Strong explained that it had been made by a "burn-out," the term inmates used to describe a prisoner who was not quite right, or "wired backwards." Usually they were semi-retarded or their brains had been damaged by drugs. Although they were capable of making a deadly, unprovoked attack, they weren't "planners" and normally reserved their worst savagery for themselves. Strong's point was soon illustrated. The inmate who threatened Kelly slashed his own wrists the next day and ended up in the hole.

Jackson Taylor was a different proposition. While Kelly was exercising in the yard on his second day, he noticed the same inmate scowling at him every time he looked up. Taylor knew that Kelly was an ex-police officer and immediately began organizing the other prisoners against him. Although Taylor was circumspect in his approach, Kelly noted that as the circle of prisoners Taylor stood talking to changed, he moved a little closer to the spot where his quarry was working out. Kelly followed the inmate's progress out of the corner of his eye as he continued to push weights, until the man came too close for comfort. When Kelly stood up, Jackson pulled a shank, making small circles in front of him with the homemade knife and edging closer to his intended victim.

"If you're going to try this, you better be prepared to kill or be killed," Kelly said. He was well aware that just because hundreds of inmates were watching them, it didn't mean that the man wouldn't attack. Everyone had heard on the jungle drums that on May 30, 1986, a prisoner at nearby Joyceville penitentiary was stabbed to death in front of four hundred inmates during an exercise period. But the confrontation with Taylor was settled without bloodshed by the timely arrival of Strong, who "talked" to Kelly's would-be assailant, telling him that it was not his wish to see the new inmate harmed. Even though nothing had happened, Kelly was sufficiently terrified by his initiation into Kingston pen that just four days after his arrival he applied for a transfer to British Columbia, ostensibly to be near his parents. Permission was denied.

Under Strong's protection, Kelly settled uneasily into the routines of the prison. Up every morning at 5 A.M., he made coffee and read the Bible, surrounded by the banal sounds and smells of the awakening prison. The smoke from someone's first cigarette of the day wafted into his cell, blending with the rhythmic wheeze of snoring and someone urinating. And then there was the sound like no other, the metallic double-click that came every morning at exactly 6 A.M. when the guard loaded his automatic shotgun.

The cell doors were unlocked an hour later when the inmates went downstairs for breakfast, a meal that was eaten in relative silence. The beginning of another day in prison, it seemed, was hardly cause for lively conversation. After breakfast, the inmates lined up for the first count of the day before filing out to their respective jobs, which in Kelly's case was the prison school, where he worked as a clerk and teaching assistant.

While the other prisoners ate lunch, Kelly worked out, a daily ritual he repeated after the evening meal, which was served at 5 P.M. Late at night, he studied for the psychology degree he was taking by correspondence from the University of Waterloo, until at 11 P.M. sharp, he heard the sound of the guard unloading his shotgun and knew that he'd put in another day behind bars. When he stretched out on his bunk, he closed his eyes and tried to imagine himself in some other place – walking a beach in the Bahamas or running by Grenadier Pond in High Park. But after a while, even his imagination seemed to be locked up, and he could only see the bars "as if they were burned into the underside of my eyelids." As the months and then the seasons melted into one another, he began feeling safe and warm when the guard came by at 11 P.M. to lock him in, realizing with a start what that meant; his tiny cell was the only place he felt truly secure.

"What I am very concerned about is that after years of being trained to see the signs of wear and tear on those under excess stress, I am starting to see these signs appearing in me – the edginess, the sleeplessness, the paranoia, the irritability, the sharpness, the tears, the loneliness, the want of support of any kind," he wrote in October 1986.

Kelly got a hint of how short his fuse had become from an unexpected encounter in the south passage that inmates used to make the daily walk from the dining hall to their work places. Next to the gymnasium, it was the most dangerous place in Kingston, a hundred yards of relative privacy where the guards had only a limited view from their security posts. One day, the south door had just closed behind Kelly when the north door opened and David Warriner entered the passage. It was the first time that the two men had been alone in a "free zone" since Warriner had testified at Kelly's preliminary that the accused had wanted to put out contracts on the lives of Victor Simpson and Dawn Taber. "Wild thoughts" raced through Kelly's head as Warriner drew nearer, smiling nervously and commenting on the nice weather. Wanting nothing more than to break his miserable neck, Kelly controlled his rage, smiled, and let the man pass.

"Mr. Warriner will never know how close he came to being a little (very little) piece of history," he later said.

But Kelly couldn't afford to forget the encounter just because nothing had come of it. He had seen the fear in Warriner's eyes, and knew that it was a dangerous emotion to arouse in a fellow inmate. After all, if a frightened man thought you were out to get him, his only recourse was to arrange for someone else to get you first. And where they were, there was no shortage of muscle willing to do the job for a price.

Although Kelly himself was pining for human companionship and understood the homosexual relationships in prison for that very reason, he could never quite get used to seeing men sitting hand-in-hand in front of the TV or hearing them squabble "like husband and wife" over some petty matter. And when a blanket was hung over the bars of one of the cells and the sounds made clear what was happening inside, he made a point of getting as far away as possible. Love triangles and jealousy sparked more violence inside than anything else except drugs.

If loneliness is one of prison's more refined torments, Kelly must have suffered exquisitely on the day that he was summoned to Kingston's admissions and discharge area. When he got there, he saw the usual prison personnel, one or two inmates, and an obviously uncomfortable man he had never seen before.

"You Kelly?" the stranger asked.

"Yeah."

"Well your old lady's left you, asshole," he replied, throwing the divorce papers from Jan Bradley on a pile of boxes. "Consider yourself served."

Humiliated in front of the staff and other prisoners, Kelly once again found himself on the edge of a volcanic explosion.

"He [the sheriff] has no idea of how close he came to not making it out of that building," Kelly said. "He's just real lucky that I have a certain amount of control. I was treated like crap . . . I wanted to climb all over his body."

Shortly after Bradley divorced him, other pressures began to mount on Kelly. His father had a serious heart attack and Kelly felt the full impotence of not being able to support John Kelly when he needed him most. In a letter to the author, who had begun looking into Kelly's claim of innocence in 1986, the frustrated inmate included copies of his divorce settlement and details of his parents' medical records, both of which he thought would make interesting reading for the woman he blamed for his wrongful murder conviction, Dawn Taber.

"Perhaps the next time you meet with Dawn, you might want to show this [the divorce papers] and the doctor's report on the physical condition of my mother and father and a picture of my dog, Kelly – let her know that even Kelly is dead now, and maybe tell her to imagine garbage carts with bodies on them and your neighbour after he's slit his own throat and some guy you spoke with only this afternoon – hanging now from his bars. Or, perhaps a copy of my warrant with the release date of 2008 – ask her to figure out how many days and better yet, how many nights that adds up to.

"You might just want to ask her what the hell she is gaining from this and maybe you will want to tell her that it is my most sincere hope that when she lays her head down at the end of each day that her thoughts are of butterflies, sailboats, old English sheep dogs and kids running through the park. I truly hope that she can think of these things and not of the SHIT in which I must walk – for NOBODY should think of this much SHIT."

Kelly's own health was deteriorating from the constant state of vigilance in which he was forced to live at Kingston, and tests showed that he now had an unusually high pulse and heart rate. His medical problem wasn't helped when Kingston's internal preventive security officer warned him of a possible attack by associates of David Warriner. When the RCMP arrested a visitor in Kingston's visiting area trying to smuggle drugs into the institution, inmate anger boiled over at the ex-cop in their midst. Twice that night, Kelly was confronted with shank-wielding attackers, but managed to talk his way out of trouble with the same vow he had made in the yard: if anyone attacked him, he would kill them on the spot if he could. But he knew he had won only a reprieve; living in Kingston as a former "narc" was ultimately a one-way ticket to the cemetery. Once again Kelly applied for a transfer to British Columbia.

His performance in the open population at Kingston had so far been exemplary; never once had he made the trip to the institution's protective custody units for disciplinary infractions. According to his case management team, Kelly was a "model prisoner," excelling in his work as a clerk in the prison school, where he displayed the progress and attitude of a medium-security inmate. But because he was a convicted wife-killer who was ineligible for parole until 2008, he would have to be kept in a maximum-security institution until more of his sentence had been served. Besides, there was his stubborn insistence that he was innocent of the charge that had landed him in prison in the first place. Permission to transfer was again denied.

Christmas for Kelly was the dreariest time of the year. Among the many cards he sent was one to the woman whose testimony had put him in prison. It depicted the Easter Bunny gazing up at Santa Claus under the caption, "I'll believe in you, if you believe in me." He spent New Year's Eve 1987 pushing himself through a particularly strenuous workout before returning to his cell to struggle with a statistics assignment that had been giving him trouble. His hard work on his university courses was not merely a matter of getting a degree. He was using his studies in psychology to gather sufficient evidence to reopen his case and prove his innocence, as he candidly admitted to one of his professors at Waterloo. "It is for this reason that I undertook a university education and registered in psychology courses and certainly the prize at the end of my quest is the worthwhile one of FREEDOM and TRUTH."

At the cold stroke of midnight, his New Year's prayer was for "a retraction from Dawn, quick action by authorities, an opening of the big North Gate, some sand, white wine, long walks, some hugs and a new life . . ."

Although 1988 didn't bring the answer to his prayers, it did bring about Kelly's desired move to the West Coast. On February 4, 1988, he was admitted to Mission Institution, a medium-security prison. Kelly thought he would be safer there because the inmates were on their way out of the system and had a vested interest in staying out of trouble. The correctional officials wore civilian clothes and, unlike their counterparts at Kingston, the guards didn't carry guns. Best of all, Kelly was able to have his first visit with his family since he was arrested for his wife's murder in early 1983.

During the two-day visit, Patrick, his sister, Candi, and his parents sat around the kitchen table of a house on the prison grounds and caught up on each other's news. It was wonderful to be around people who believed in his innocence. John Kelly marked the special occasion by saying grace over the meal of steak, potatoes, and peas that Patrick prepared for them. Revitalized by the companionship of people who loved him, Kelly wrote to Ross Toller, his case management officer at Kingston, to thank him for supporting his transfer: "My new home is quite delightful and a pleasant change after the walls of KP. The food is fantastic, the gym facilities are great, and the educational arrangements are first class and the lack of guns and uniforms most refreshing."

Two months later, things didn't look so rosy. An inmate returned to Mission from the Regional Psychiatric Centre, where he had spoken with a patient from Kingston pen, and spread the word that Kelly was an ex-RCMP officer. When Kelly woke up the next morning, there was a shank hanging above his door. Verbal threats followed the menacing appearance of the knife, and after only four months at Mission, Kelly applied to William Head, a light-medium-security institution on Vancouver Island, just outside Victoria and even closer to his parents. During his short stay at Mission, Kelly had impressed authorities with his daily routine of work, physical fitness, and academic study, and his transfer was approved.

It would be difficult to imagine a better place to do time than William Head Institution. Situated on a stunning peninsula on Vancouver Island overlooking the chilly waters of the Strait of Juan de Fuca, the eighty-five-acre facility was the former site of Western Canada's quarantine station for immigrants. Surrounded by Quarantine Cove to the north, Pedder Bay to the south, and heavily forested Department of National Defence lands to the west, the exposed volcanic rock of its rugged shoreline is unfenced. Escapees from this institution are officially classified as "walk-aways."

They could also be described as hard to please. In their recreational hours, inmates of William Head can watch whales, hand-feed the wild deer that freely roam the park-like grounds, play a few sets on the seaside tennis courts, golf, or cast for salmon from their own wharf. (The cover of the prison's Inmate Handbook features a leaping salmon trying to throw a fisherman's fly.)

The list of possessions inmates are allowed includes jewellery, watches, casual clothes, colour televisions, stereos, musical instruments, golf clubs, tennis racquets, computers, calculators, books, newspapers, magazines, and public documents. There are twice-weekly visits from the institutional doctor and dentist, and every three weeks the optometrist visits; if his patients need glasses, the institution bears the cost, unless the prisoner wants a designer frame, in which case he must buy his own.

Inmates are permitted to have their own bank accounts into which relatives or friends may make deposits. Although inmates are expected to save 25 per cent of their prison pay (rates range from a high of $6.45 a day for a general cook to $1.60 a day for the "unemployed"), hobby loans are available to prisoners who want to take up pottery or woodworking but have no money in their current accounts, where the other 75 per cent of their salaries must be deposited.

William Head's visiting facilities are the best in Canada, including a large lounge that opens onto an outdoor area featuring swings, teeter-totters, and a private beach. The prisoners can even order in their own health food, and once every three months they are entitled to weekend trailer visits with family, wives, or girlfriends. To its supporters, William Head is state-of-the-art correctional rehabilitation; to its detractors, it is a holiday resort for felons, the "Club Fed" of a penal system that is off the rails.

Like most of the two hundred hand-picked prisoners at the institution, Patrick Kelly worked full time at improving his education. In the fall of 1988, he earned his BA in psychology from the University of Waterloo, and immediately entered an honours program that would qualify him for graduate school. Once again, Kelly quickly established his reputation as a model inmate, helping test the aptitudes of incoming prisoners and donating hundreds of hours of his recreational time to volunteer work. He appreciated his new surroundings, but he concentrated on preparing himself for a battle with the system that he insisted had convicted an innocent man.

On his first New Year's Eve in William Head, Kelly attended a candlelit service at the prison chapel, passing most of it with his head bowed and tears streaming down his face. It reminded him of a similar service he and Jeannette had once attended in a small town in France. Even after he'd married Jan Bradley and moved to Valbonne, he used to go to a small church in nearby Menton to remember his first wife. "These were my times alone with Jeannette, my times to reflect and be at a special peace with myself."

After the service, he went outside, leaned against a tree, and gazed longingly at the lights of Victoria twinkling across the bay.

Although most of the staff at William Head was impressed with Patrick Kelly, John Costello had his doubts. Kelly's case management officer couldn't believe that in just three years in the federal system an inmate serving a life sentence for first degree murder had managed to transfer from a super-protective custody, maximum-security institution to a place where an escape-minded prisoner could simply walk away.

Equally astonishing to Costello was the fact that during Kelly's entire five and a half years in prison, he had never undergone a formal psychiatric evaluation. When he informed Kelly that an evaluation would have to be done for the National Parole Board, the inmate requested that Dr. John Jensen, a friend of his family, prepare the assessment. The institution declined, and psychologist Mel Strangeland completed the first psychological assessment of Kelly on January 17, 1989.

Strangeland prefaced his findings by noting that Kelly had taken a third-year course in psychopathology, a subtle reminder that the subject may know enough about the tests he was undergoing to skew the results. That reservation aside, Strangeland was struck by the degree to which the subject "idealized" all aspects of his life. In fact, Kelly presented himself in such a "Pollyanna" fashion during their interview that the psychologist was left wondering "how anybody outside of prison, let alone inside, could be that nice." Strangeland had an idea of what this "nice-guy" façade was designed to conceal.

"His calm, composed exterior is likely to effectively cover up his difficulties in dealing with his anger, the fashion in which he deals with this anger is considered to be characteristic of individuals who commit murder in response to relationship difficulties."

When Strangeland took into account the abyss between the evidence presented at Kelly's trial and the subject's own version of events as given during their interview, as well as the results of his psychological tests, he drew a very unflattering portrait of William Head's model prisoner. Assuming that the trial evidence was valid, Strangeland wrote that "one would be led to the conclusion that Patrick is a ruthless and calculating person who places gratification of his extravagant desires above all other considerations. His highly controlled and moralistic presentation could be consistent with his efforts to convince the public of his innocence and to win a re-trial."

In the same report, Strangeland also made note of the many positive attributes of the subject, including his intelligence and capacity for leadership: "Were he able to come to grips with those features of his personality that are troublesome – his dominance, denial, intense emotional control, and pathological suppression of anger, he has the capabilities of functioning very effectively in the community."

Kelly was outraged when he read the report and pounced on its every minor factual mistake. In citing the inmate's criminal past, Strangeland had mentioned a string of 1986 charges on Kelly's crime index file that were in fact laid in 1982 and 1983. Since then the charges had been either withdrawn, stayed, or discharged. Kelly was so furious at the psychologist's sloppiness that he lodged a complaint with the British Columbia Psychological Association. He also fired off a letter to the Regional National Parole Board, asking that all other criminal charges against him that had not gone to court be removed from his file at once.

"They are accusations and allegations that have not been substantiated in any way and thus there should not even be the most remote possibility that they 'may' be considered by those making decisions on an inmate," he wrote.

A second psychological assessment was done in the spring of 1989 after Kelly applied for Escorted Temporary Absences (ETAs) from William Head to further his graduate studies at the University of Victoria and to visit his parents. This time Kelly was sent to the Regional Psychiatric Centre from April 28 to May 26 for a thirty-day assessment. During his stay, he was co-operative and communicative, exuding an air of confidence and self-assurance, while emphasizing the fact that he was innocent of any criminal wrongdoing in his wife's tragic accident.

Dr. Myron Schimpf, the psychologist who interviewed Kelly, knew that he was facing a difficult clinical situation. For one thing, the subject had been selected and trained by the RCMP to present effortlessly whatever façade the situation required. His "smooth, suave, and urbane personal style" combined with a "soft-spoken demeanour" left the impression of a refined and gentle person who could never have committed such a gruesome crime as throwing his wife off a balcony. But was that impression the real thing or merely more acting?

Kelly's protestations of innocence created another problem. Since a record of undisputed behaviour is crucial in the diagnosis of psychopathy, and Kelly was denying any part in his wife's death, his calm, confident, and remorseless exterior was consistent with the reaction of an innocent man. "However," the doctor noted, "a similar presentation associated with heinous and egregious behaviour would represent a powerful indicator of psychopathy."

Schimpf found that Kelly had an IQ of 123, high enough to place him in the superior range of the general population. But Schimpf also discovered an odd discrepancy between the subject's verbal and nonverbal IQ, which he measured at 127 and 109 respectively. He concluded that Kelly successfully managed to put on a verbal front that was not backed up by an underlying IQ of the same high level. His superior intelligence, it appeared, was itself a kind of verbal conjuring trick.

Kelly vehemently rejected any suggestion that he had a deviant character, presenting himself instead in the same Pollyanna fashion that had so struck Mel Strangeland; he was not only innocent of murder, he was also in every other way "noble, honourable, magnanimous and well beyond the norm." Kelly told Schimpf, for example, that he had resigned from the RCMP because he could not take part in the force's unethical activities. As for his currency-running out of South America, he presented it as "an altruistic effort to assist Nuns and Priests within the Catholic Church."

In the end, Schimpf recommended that ETAs, or any other form of early release for Kelly, would be "highly inappropriate" – provided that the evidence at his trial had been well-founded. But because of the imponderables in the difficult case, including the subject's claims of innocence and his RCMP training, the doctor's clinical assessment was quite ambivalent.

"Based upon the features of this case, Mr. Kelly is either a crafty, cunning, and malevolent psychopath, capable of masterful and adroit manipulation and deception; or he is as he claims, an innocent man wrongly convicted. . . . We know that high-functioning psychopaths are intelligent, charming, and articulate with a calm, cool, and collected demeanour. However, while these traits do indeed describe Mr. Kelly, they also describe thousands of individuals who are by no means psychopathic."

It was not exactly the definitive diagnosis that Costello had been looking for, but correctional service officials nevertheless took Schimpf's advice and decided that, for the time being, the best place for Kelly was behind bars.

Before the doctors of the correctional service ever began to address the possibility that Patrick Kelly was a psychopath, the RCMP had undergone some soul-searching of its own after its former star agent's meteoric demise. In the wake of Kelly's arrest, Dr. Michael Girodo, a professor of psychology at the University of Ottawa, was given the green light to test and interview 155 Mounties who had either worked undercover or who had been accepted for that assignment.

Girodo found that one-third of the working agents needed medical treatment for stress-related conditions, and three or four of the active officers should be considered "psychiatric emergencies." Girodo advised the RCMP that it was recruiting the wrong kind of person for its undercover program, candidates who were "very highly talented, good role-players . . . good con artists." As Girodo later said in an interview about his work, "Unfortunately, what they were doing was attracting those who verge on being psychopaths. . . . If you attract people with good acting ability, then you inadvertently attract a certain segment of the population which dotes on neuroticism."

Girodo found that the stress of constant role-playing was so great that a handful of undercover officers had committed suicide and several others had suffered nervous breakdowns or serious marital problems. Alcohol and drug abuse were common, and agents often behaved violently towards other Mounties or their own wives. Still others enjoyed their undercover roles so much that they filed false activity reports so that their covert assignments would continue, refusing to cut their hair or turn over their expensive cars when the time came to return to regular police work. There were even cases of RCMP undercover agents refusing to testify against drug dealers who had become their friends.

When he published the results of his work in the periodical *Behavioural Sciences and the Law*, Girodo gave a thumbnail sketch of the psychic forces that sculpted the personalities of all undercover agents. Their greatest fear was the possibility of being harmed or killed if their target discovered their true identity. They also harboured deep fears of professional shame should the target discover that they were really police officers and their mission fail. Surprisingly, Girodo found that an agent's mental health was most at risk after the operation was over. The list of telltale symptoms included sleeplessness, obsessive-compulsive behaviour, stormy personal relationships, depression, anxiety, anger, hostility, phobias, paranoia, and psychotic impulses.

In high-level undercover operations, Girodo discovered, the agent often developed "an inflated ego, an exaggerated feeling of importance, [and] an idyllic but spurious sense of entitlement." Prolonged dealings with affluent targets made it difficult for some agents to give up their lives of pseudo-luxury and go back to regular duty – particularly when their fellow officers or supervisors didn't acknowledge the sacrifice and courage that such role-playing demanded. According to Girodo's paper, the psychological problems of some agents were not unlike those of prisoners of war or refugees.

While weaving the results of Girodo's research and his own inquiries into a feature article on the terrible toll undercover work takes on "super-cops," *Globe and Mail* reporter Peter Moon was astonished at the response he got when he brought up the case of Patrick Kelly with other Mounties. Even as they condemned Kelly for murdering his wife, they "still expressed a surprising degree of sympathy for him." Moon reported that the officers blamed the pressures he worked under as an undercover agent for the tragic turn his life had taken: "They say the RCMP had a responsibility to recognize his growing emotional problems and help him, instead of continuing to exploit him in the demanding role of an undercover operator."

The year 1989 was an eventful one for Patrick Kelly, as his bureaucratic skirmishes with the system began to escalate. Unexpectedly, his sixth year behind bars began with romance. Just after New Year's, Kelly met an attractive nurse who had come to the prison with a girlfriend to visit another inmate. The thirty-two-year-old woman began visiting Kelly and soon found herself swept up in a whirlwind love affair. The dashing lifer proposed to her, and the couple planned for a June 25 wedding. But after the woman's family found out that the man she was planning to marry was a convicted wife-killer serving a life sentence, they forced her to call off the wedding.

When he found out that he couldn't have trailer visits with his girl-friend because he hadn't had a common-law relationship with her for at least six months prior to his incarceration, Kelly launched a campaign to have the regulation changed. He submitted a grievance to the commissioner of the Correctional Service of Canada, filed a federal court writ, and wrote a total of sixty-three letters to various officials and politicians until the rule was changed and he and his new lover could have conjugal visits every three months.

Kelly immediately appealed the CSC's decision when it turned down his request to fund his master's program at the University of Victoria on the grounds that Canadian taxpayers had already made enough of a contribution to his education by paying for his honours BA. His appeal was denied. He also sued the CSC unsuccessfully when it turned down his request to transfer to Ferndale, a minimum-security institution on the mainland. He was upset that one of the main reasons cited for denying the transfer was Dr. Schimpf's report.

Incensed by the stigma of his criminal record, Kelly redoubled his efforts to dry-clean his file of everything but his conviction for first degree murder – false though he maintained it was. Although he agreed to remove media reports of Kelly's criminal history from his penitentiary file, John Costello resisted his request to have all small factual errors expunged from his psychological assessment by Mel Strangeland, reasoning that they were inconsequential anyway, since Kelly wasn't eligible for parole until 2008. Kelly didn't appreciate Costello's "cocky" attitude during their sessions, and in a reversal of roles consistent with a psychopath, the assessed suddenly became the assessor.

"Again it was quite obvious that he [Costello] is getting a little out of hand . . . I do get the distinct feeling that he is not happy with my wave-making. At one point during the conversation he indicated that as much as I might have lots of time to challenge things, he and others here have lots of other things to do besides answering my challenges," Kelly wrote. (Costello was right; an internal report prepared for the CSC found that its eleven hundred caseworkers were badly overburdened, deluged with paperwork, and demoralized.)

Not satisfied with Costello's response, Kelly pressed his demand with the solicitor general of Ontario, demanding that all other charges against him be removed from both his prison record and CPIC, the police intelligence computer. When he was informed that such records could only be amended under the Young Offenders Act, which obviously didn't apply in his case, Kelly expressed outrage that he had to live under "the cloud of suspicion," even though the charges in question had never proceeded to court. That being the case, he argued, they shouldn't form part of the deliberations of parole board members who would one day decide his fate. Turned down by Ontario's solicitor general, Kelly took his case to the Metropolitan Toronto Police and then to Canada's justice minister, in both cases without success.

When Costello wrote his progress report on the ex-Mountie at the end of 1989, it became a new battleground between the two men, largely because Costello continued to oppose Kelly's request for ETAs. Not long after Kelly arrived at William Head, Costello had received a call from Jimmy Hanlon, who explained that he was the father of Kelly's victim and said that her murderer should never be released. Whatever he may have thought of Hanlon's opinion, Costello's main reason for opposing the temporary absences was that Kelly simply wasn't far enough along in his sentence to enjoy a privilege that would regularly send him outside the prison walls.

After reading a detailed police report of the case provided by Sgt. Ed Stewart, Costello had also been openly sceptical when Kelly told him that he had been "framed" after his wife's accident. Costello pointed out that "the rationale for being 'framed' was never fully explained by the subject, except to imply that it related to the period of his life during which he worked as an RCMP officer. He indicated that he knew too much about illegal activities by fellow Police Officers. This behaviour by his colleagues, he claimed, was so morally repugnant that he resigned as a member. According to Kelly, his enemies were so fearful that he would expose their corruption that his wife's 'accident' was conveniently used as a way to discredit him and get him out of the way."

Furious about the assessment, Kelly took his complaints to the deputy warden, informing him that he was "most displeased with the general negativity of the reports" and some of "Costello's general comments." He insisted that Costello's offending report be rewritten and that he be replaced by another case management officer (CMO). What Costello wanted, Kelly claimed, was "a quiet little inmate who will lay [sic] down and lick his nuts. He is looking at the wrong inmate."

The deputy warden pointed out to Kelly that Costello wasn't the only correctional worker at William Head who viewed him as being a tad "manipulative," but nevertheless he agreed to revise the report and take Costello off his case. He also agreed to have Dr. Strangeland delete any mundane factual errors from his psychological assessment. But Alvin Kube, Kelly's new CMO, apparently shared his predecessor's shortcomings. "I find Mr. Kube's attitude and position unacceptable," Kelly bristled in a subsequent letter to the deputy warden. "I am not prepared to have my life controlled by this man."

This time officialdom stood its ground: Kube would remain in charge of Kelly's case. In handing down his decision, the deputy warden pointed out to Kelly his pattern of demanding a new caseworker whenever he didn't get his own way. Instead of making war on the correctional service, Kelly would be better advised to simply do his time, since he wouldn't be getting anything else out of the system until he had served more of his sentence.

But Kelly's biggest frustration in 1989 was the amount of time it took for the first official police reinvestigation of the Jeannette Kelly murder case to be called. On December 14 of the previous year, Kelly had written to Liberal MP John Nunziata about a cryptic message he claimed to have found in his jacket pocket that read: "Information sent to

Nunciata [*sic*], it could help." The trouble was, Kelly's inquiries about the mysterious information arrived before the information itself! The author of the anonymous letter laid out a scenario that was remarkably similar to Kelly's own theories about his wrongful conviction.

The gist of the typed letter was that there had been a massive conspiracy on the part of the police, the Crown, the judges, and even Kelly's own lawyer to frame him for his wife's murder. The RCMP and the Metro police had pushed the case to "get Kelly out of the way" because, as a former insider, he had a great deal of damaging information against senior police officials in both forces.

In the course of the conspiracy against Kelly, the rattle on the balcony, which he had honestly reported to investigators after his wife's death, had been located by police but repaired in order to discredit his story and lay him open to a murder charge. Ex-police security personnel at the banks had also manufactured his credit card problems to trump up fraud charges against him. As for the allegation that he had torched his own home in Cookstown, the fact was, he had been "hundreds of miles away" at the time of the fire and the charge was bogus, all of which the authorities knew.

Kelly's anonymous benefactor claimed to be a senior police officer who had been asked to review the Kelly situation because the independent investigations of this author were causing concerns on the part of those who had originally worked on the case. In fact, they were so concerned, according to the phantom police officer, that "there was some indication that the police involved might 'deal with' Kelly, the girl [Dawn Taber], or Harris."

When Nunziata still hadn't taken action more than two months after receiving the anonymous letter, Kelly wrote then Liberal leader John Turner to say that he was "not impressed whatsoever" with the MP's performance. He then persuaded Patrick Duffy, a former Crown attorney he had worked with in his glory days in the RCMP, to take a copy of the letter to Douglas Rutherford. Rutherford, an associate deputy minister in the federal Justice Department, later wrote to Duffy that there was nothing he could "responsibly do" with the anonymous document.

Undeterred, Kelly contacted another federal MP, John Brewin, as well as former solicitor general Robert Kaplan. He also organized a letter-writing campaign by his parents and sister to a number of other public officials. Almost a year after he first wrote to Nunziata, his frenetic efforts finally achieved the desired result. Det. Insp. David Crane of the OPP was given the task of investigating the allegations made in the anonymous letter, including the implied death threat against three people.

Kelly was euphoric at hearing the news, but later was absolutely furious when Crane reported at the end of a lengthy investigation that "No evidence of misconduct has been uncovered" and further investigation was not warranted. The only firm thing the OPP knew about the anonymous letter that so strikingly supported Kelly's claim of innocence was something it had known from the very beginning of its investigation. It bore the same postmark as other mail from William Head Institution.

On December 5, 1990, a nervous Patrick Kelly placed what was surely the strangest telephone call of his life. The day before, he had been handed a message by a correctional officer asking him to call Dawn Taber. As he listened to the telephone ringing in far-away New England, he was "curious, frightened, nervous, happy, and angry" all at the same time. When he heard the familiar voice accepting the charges for the call, he felt like he had been given an enormous present. His letter had worked, Kelly thought, praying that the institution's tape recorders would catch the conversation he hoped he was about to have with the woman whose testimony had sent him to prison for life.

In November 1989, Kelly had written to Taber, begging her to reconsider her testimony in light of what her lie had done to him: "We both know that what you testified to was false. You were not in the apartment and you witnessed no murder. You have my immediate future in your hands and I am praying that you will come forward with the truth . . . I don't want to see you dragged through the courts either. I do not pretend to understand why you have done this to me, but neither do I wish you any ill will."

Now, just over a year later, here was the voice that he hadn't heard in six years asking him how he was. When he replied that he had been better, Taber asked if he was ill. Kelly explained that the problem was with his address, not his health; she laughed nervously, then assured him she wasn't making light of his situation. But if Kelly thought that she had called to admit that she had lied at his trial, he was in for a disappointment.

Taber explained that she was writing a book about the events surrounding Jeannette's death from her perspective. It was tentatively entitled *Dancing in the Blender,* and she had already spoken with prospective publishers and travelled to Toronto to carry out some research. She was worried, though, about the consequences of saying certain things and wanted to visit Kelly at William Head to discuss matters that she didn't want to go into over the telephone.

In particular, Taber wanted to know whether Kelly had actually asked David Warriner to arrange a contract on her life. Scoffing at the whole idea, Kelly denied he had ever raised the subject with his former cellmate and explained that it was a commonplace of prison life for inmates to volunteer damning evidence against an accused in a high-profile case in exchange for favourable treatment from the Crown. In Warriner's case, he had wanted out of Collins Bay penitentiary, and his lies at Kelly's preliminary had earned him a transfer to Kingston, or so Kelly explained.

At the end of the conversation, Kelly realized that Taber had not called to recant her testimony, and his anger flared. When she asked if she could visit him, he agreed, but it would not be to pass the time of day. If Taber wanted to tell the truth about her lies on the stand, she was welcome; if not, there was no point in coming west.

"I was trying to work things out that had been bothering me for years," Taber later said of their conversation. "But he took it the wrong way, and things that I wanted to talk about I put away for a few more years."

Although Max Haines lived thousands of miles away, Patrick Kelly blamed the Toronto crime columnist when a shank was slipped under the curtain of his room at William Head on June 28, 1991. Haines had written a sketch of the Jeannette Kelly murder case in a crime digest called *True Crime Stories,* and the trial information it contained about Kelly's police past had clearly made its way into the prison. Kelly had several verbal confrontations with other inmates in the days after the appearance of the knife, and when he showed up in the prison classroom where he worked, there was a note on the chalkboard reading: "Hey pig, try sleeping at night. You can thank Max Haines for the confirmation."

Making the threat more unnerving was the fact that a $14-million expansion was underway to replace some of the prison's decrepit buildings with stylish condominium units: in the interim, inmates had been shifted from their trailer units to an open dormitory with only a curtain covering the entrance to each sleeping area. Kelly told his CMO that he was uneasy with his living arrangements because of Haines's book, and reported that two prisoners on his own range were threatening his life. The authorities gave Kelly the option of checking into William Head's segregation unit or transferring to another medium-security prison, such as Mission or Matsqui. Instead, Kelly reapplied for a transfer to Ferndale. Once again he was refused.

"I am feeling incredibly frustrated at this point," he wrote, "much like I am on a ship of fools and something to be treated with disdain and toyed with on a constant basis. It is a most unpleasant feeling."

Kelly would later say that the "Haines thing" led to his toughest time behind bars, a period of constant threats and harassment that forced the authorities to ship out three inmates who were threatening to kill the ex-Mountie. It was the high tide of Kelly's anger, as the people who had contributed to his misfortunes would soon find out.

One of the people to feel the sting of Kelly's bitterness was Eric Kreuger, the engineer who had testified at the trial that Jeannette Kelly could not have fallen from the balcony in the way her husband had described. On February 25, 1992, Kelly lodged a formal complaint against Kreuger with the Association of Professional Engineers, just as he had against Mel Strangeland with his governing body after the psychologist's unflattering assessment.

Kelly charged that Kreuger had overstepped his area of expertise in attempting a re-enactment of Jeannette's fall. To have done it properly, Kreuger would have required knowledge of kinesiology, physiology, biomechanics, biochemistry, psychology, and psychiatry – fields in which the mechanical engineer had no formal training. Affixed to Kelly's complaint was a list of experts in these fields who agreed with him that Kreuger had not followed scientific methodology in performing the various tests he had run for the Crown.

Determined to win exoneration from the justice system that he claimed had wrongfully convicted him, Kelly turned his attention next to the Correctional Service of Canada. In May 1992, he launched a lawsuit in the Federal Court of Canada, accusing the CSC of wrongful placement for the years he spent in Kingston penitentiary. In total, he was asking for $667,000, which included $200 for each day of the twenty months he spent in Kingston, and special damages of $328,000.

During pretrial discovery, Kelly said that he believed he had been placed in Kingston against the recommendations of other authorities because of his refusal to go along with certain practices within the RCMP when he had been a member. "It certainly is quite possible that people did not want me to talk and by placing me in Kingston Penitentiary it was quite possible I would have been silenced," he wrote.

In its defence, the CSC noted that there had been no evidence of physical assault or injury to Kelly during his time in Kingston and claimed that the reports recommending that he not be sent to a federal institution in Ontario were not binding on the service.

Kelly's lawyer in the action was Gary Botting, a writer, professor, and poet who saw all of the ingredients of a miscarriage of justice in Kelly's complex predicament. Not one to shrink from unpopular causes, Botting's passion for free speech had brought him some dubious clients, including Howard Pursley, an American white supremacist and self-styled "Aryan Warrior," and James Keegstra, the Alberta teacher who taught his students that the Holocaust was a hoax and that there was a Jewish conspiracy to dominate world business and politics. Botting also testified as an expert witness on behalf of anti-Jewish propagandist Ernst Zundel, arguing that Zundel's published denials of the Holocaust "balanced" existing literature on the same subject by providing an "alternative reality."

Not satisfied with Botting's *pro bono* participation on his behalf, Kelly appealed to superstar lawyer Clayton Ruby to take up his cause. After looking into the fact base, Ruby sent his personal assessment to Kelly that "there is nothing that is sufficient to justify making an application to the Minister of Justice that might be successful. . . . There would have to be some key evidence showing that Dawn [Taber] lied on the crucial question of her being there and witnessing your wife being thrown over the balcony."

Ruby's opinion was not the only bad news Kelly received in the second half of 1992. The Association of Professional Engineers dismissed his complaint against Eric Kreuger, finding no evidence of professional misconduct on his part. Kelly characterized its conclusion as "<u>unacceptable</u>" and immediately challenged the finding. "I ask that you review the complaint in its entirety, reverse the finding of the Complaints Committee, find Mr. Kreuger guilty of professional misconduct, and discipline him accordingly."

His request was denied, and Kelly flew into a towering rage. "I felt like ripping off heads and shitting down the hole."

19

THE LIE

Under the bright lights of the television studio high in Rockefeller Plaza, Phil Donahue's shock of white hair made him look almost magisterial, the presiding judge of one of America's most popular courts of public opinion. Wagging his trademark microphone like a teasing finger, he titillated his live audience with his introduction to the next item on his show of September 26, 1994 – an hour of television devoted to the cases of former convicted murderers and the false evidence that had sent them to prison.

In the first two segments, Donahue had interviewed Lawrencia "Bambi" Bambenek and William Evans-Smith, spouse-killers who had been released from prison after their original convictions were reviewed and overturned. Befitting the showman that he was, Donahue had saved his most dramatic interview for last, hoping to hook his huge viewing audience for the broadcast's finale.

"Is Patrick Kelly with us on the satellite? He will be?" he said, repeating his producer's answer.

"Well, he's doing time for – he is accused in Canada of having thrown his wife off the seventeenth-storey balcony of their apartment." Donahue turned to the well-dressed woman sitting on stage with her hands folded neatly in her lap. "Dawn Taber, a former police officer, *is* here. You were friends of the Kellys and you originally testified that you saw him do it."

Wheeling around, he completed his introduction in a voice freighted with the promise of the bizarre story to come – an apparently innocent ex-Mountie live-via-satellite from prison and the eyewitness who had put him there for life with a lie.

"And then she recanted and said, 'I didn't see him do it.' Kelly, a former member of the Royal Canadian Mounted Police, is doing time for the murder. Should he continue to be serving time? We'll be back to ask him and Dawn in just a moment."

The road to the "Phil Donahue Show," and a much less entertaining rendezvous with the Canadian justice system, stretched all the way back to the event that had dominated Dawn Taber's life for almost fifteen years, the death of Jeannette Kelly. Though the killer had apparently been punished and her friend's death avenged, Taber had been unable to put the murder and her own role in sending Kelly to prison for the crime behind her. In the years since Kelly's trial, her life had been a series of false starts and fresh beginnings that always foundered in an emotional quagmire of unanswered questions and nagging doubts.

Upset that his wife remained under the cloud of something that he believed had long since been resolved in the courts, Victor Bragg didn't take kindly to the caller from Canada who wanted to interview Dawn for an upcoming book about Kelly. Bragg said that no one could appreciate what the couple had been put through by the Jeannette Kelly murder, from having their phone tapped to being hounded by the press; besides, Dawn had kept extensive diaries from those days and intended to write a book of her own.

So the author was mildly surprised when a week later, on Easter Monday 1987, Taber herself called. For two hours, she talked about the case in general terms, praising Dr. Peter Rowsell for the "remarkable" way he helped her to talk about what she had seen in the apartment that day, and making clear that the police hadn't pressured her into giving her damning evidence against Kelly. When asked if she was satisfied that the truth had been told, she offered a curious qualifier about the role of detectives Stewart and Cziraky. "What they got out of me was what they wanted and nothing more."

Her words were even more provocative six weeks later when she called the author again with a fact that had never surfaced in the course of his research. On the day of the murder, Taber said, she had called a girlfriend and begged for a loan to leave the country. But March 29, 1981, had been a Sunday and the banks were closed. Since the woman in question didn't have the funds on hand, she hadn't been able to accommodate her friend's desperate request. Taber claimed that she told the police and Crown prosecutor about the incident at the time of Kelly's trial, but that they hadn't wanted her to talk about it because it would "complicate" things.

Several months after their telephone conversations, Taber and the author met in New Hampshire, where she ran a pet-food store near the small community of North Conway. Looking like a tomboy in jeans and a plaid shirt, her long hair falling just below her shoulders, she talked about the Kellys and the ordeal of the trial.

Taber's sense of what had happened to her in 1983 had undergone a host of subtle re-evaluations since she had testified at Kelly's murder trial. Although she still claimed that Dr. Rowsell had helped her come to grips with the horror she had witnessed in apartment 1705, she now believed that the police had arranged the session with the forensic psychiatrist, not because Taber was "confused and distraught over everything," as she had been told, but to elicit the eyewitness account that the detectives needed to arrest Patrick Kelly.

"Stewart said that they were going to have this Dr. Rowsell come over and talk to me and try to help me because I could not say what they wanted to hear, I could not speak these words. And now that I understand more, I think that I didn't speak, I *could* not speak the words – not because I could not remember, but there was a part of me that was scared to death of what my involvement was . . . I thought that he [Rowsell] was there to help me, when in fact he was there to help them, not me. . . . They weren't seeking what I knew. They had this man over here that they believed had committed first degree murder and they wanted the pieces to get them – the stones, the stepping stones – to get them to that point, and they didn't want any sidetracks from it . . . I didn't know what my rights were and I didn't know what I was doing."

Taber now wondered why the detectives had shown her a photograph of the balcony and asked her if the stool had been there when she was in the apartment that day. She had also concluded that the police had purposely denied her access to a lawyer during the Rowsell interview, and regretted that she had taken Stewart's word that Crown prosecutor Lloyd Budzinsky was there to take care of legal matters. How could a prosecutor have looked after her interests, she now asked, when the police made no secret of the fact that they suspected Taber herself of playing some part in Jeannette's murder? Hadn't they taken a strand of her hair to see if they could match it with other hair found on the balcony and listened to her advice to do forensic tests for Jeannette's blood in the apartment? She now believed that they had needed her eyewitness evidence for only one reason: to rule out the possible defence by Patrick Kelly that it had been Taber who threw Jeannette Kelly over the balcony.

"It was in their theory that he could say that I was the one who was there and did all of this . . . Kelly could say, 'Yes, she was there. I was not there. I came home – and I had been trying to protect her all this time by taking the rap for this.'"

Once again, Taber talked about calling a friend on the day of Jeannette's death to borrow money to flee the county. Concerned that her immunity agreement with the police would be cancelled unless she told the whole truth, she had tried to pass that information along to the authorities through the matron who looked after her during the trial. When no one contacted her, she had sought out Ed Stewart and Lloyd Budzinsky, but they wouldn't listen. She remembered the two men telling her, "Don't bring it up. If any question leads to that, do not address the issue because it's new evidence, and it's nowhere else."

And then there was the strange matter of the lie detector test the police had initially wanted Taber to take to verify her account of the murder day. When she finally agreed to a polygraph to "get it over with," the detectives suddenly changed their minds. Many years later, she claimed, Stewart, whom she called from time to time, had been very upset that she had voluntarily submitted to a polygraph examination in the United States as part of a job application – particularly after he found out that she had been asked about any involvement in a criminal act for which she had never been brought to justice. Looking back on how the detectives had not wanted her to talk about her request for a loan to leave the country on the murder day, Taber posed a question of her own to the author: "Do you think that they were afraid that they would find too much so that I would be charged and they would lose a witness?"

When the subject shifted to what Kelly had actually done in the apartment that day, Taber grew sad and silent. At first she said that she couldn't "see" anything anymore. After a long pause, she started talking again, until it almost seemed as if she were watching the terrible events of 1981 in a dark and private mirror.

"He just walked over there. It was almost like when you see somebody leave their body, I mean when you see these movies where the person leaves their body – and you notice how that person walks differently than the real person walks. . . . It was just like 'there goes Pat, but that's not Pat,' and I knew what he was going to do. . . . It was a final gesture. It was like a final gesture when you throw a rose on a grave."

In one of their previous conversations, Taber had described her time in court as an "out-of-body experience." Struck by the coincidence that she was now describing the murder in the same way, the author wondered if the dream language of her description suggested that her eyewitness account was not as solid as it appeared to be.

"Is there any possible way that these guys got from you what they wanted, but it didn't necessarily represent how it happened?"

"Yes."

"And are you comfortable with that?"

"No, I'm not. I've never been comfortable with that. . . . I know not all the truth was told."

Unhappy as she may have been with the public record as it stood, five years would pass before she tried to set it right.

Wells, Maine, is a postcard-pretty New England town that markets its wide, tawny beach and fresh salt-air to harassed city dwellers from New York and Philadelphia. In summer, you have to get up early to get a good spot on the beach, and in the evening, the lineups at Hurricane's, a popular restaurant on Perkin's Cove in tonier Ogunquit, seem as long as the summer days. But after the Labour Day weekend, when the wind shifts to the northeast and the tourists return to their cities, an older clientele arrives to take in the beauty of the landscape.

After the breakup of her marriage to Victor Bragg, Dawn Taber had eventually made her way to Wells, where she now lived with the man who would soon become her third husband. Michael Carey was the chef at Gorge's Grant, a motel owned by the same people who operated the Juniper Hill Inn just down the road in Ogunquit. Taber helped with banquets at Gorge's Grant and occasionally worked the front desk at its sister inn.

Although she loved her home state, Taber had not picked an auspicious time to enter Maine's tourist industry. The summer throngs from the big American cities hadn't returned to their pre-recession levels, and the battered Canadian dollar kept northerners away when the tourist agenda switched from the beaches to the state's famous ski hills.

It was from Wells that Taber called the author in the early autumn of 1993 with the news that it was "possible" that she had not actually seen Kelly throw his wife off the balcony, but may have "dreamed" the whole thing. On September 12, they met again, and walked the beach at Wells, buffeted by a chilly wind that hinted at the winter to come.

In the years since they'd last talked face-to-face, Dawn had conducted an investigation of her own to gain an understanding of how her evidence against Kelly had been obtained. Her former view that the whole truth had not come out had evolved in the intervening years into the conviction that she had been the dupe of the police, who had "manipulated the evidence" and her testimony "through fear and intimidation."

After talking to Kelly in 1990, she no longer believed that he had asked David Warriner to arrange her death; Warriner had probably been a police plant, and the authorities had told her about the alleged contract on her life only to keep her in line. Her decision to contact Kelly had been prompted partly by her desire to find out about Warriner, but also because she knew that to the extent that her evidence had been manipulated, Patrick, too, had suffered.

"I felt that, um, there were things that – that I was somewhat responsible for him being there under this first degree murder . . . I didn't understand how he was convicted, because I didn't know what they had done to me to gain this," she said.

Even though Dr. Peter Rowsell had denied it in a telephone conversation with Taber, she suspected that she had been hypnotised during their two-hour session just before she told police that she had witnessed the murder. Although his "white-hand, pink-hand" theory had seemed helpful at the time, she now thought it had been just another manipulation technique, "a bunch of hocus-pocus" designed to make her say things she would not otherwise have told detectives Stewart and Cziraky. Even though she knew that she was an "unfit" witness at the time and told police so, there had never been any question in her mind about what the detectives wanted to hear: "That, that I saw Pat throw Jeannette – and it – off the balcony. And it was important for them to get me out of the den and into the living room . . . I knew what they needed."

To get to the bottom of her own involvement, Taber had requested the tapes of her interviews with police and Rowsell. Listening to them, her theory that she had been manipulated took deeper root: the language seemed foreign. It struck her as a policeman's narrative that had become her own by the naïve act of reading his rendition of her words into a tape recorder. The one tape that she couldn't get was of her session with Rowsell. Since he had assured her that a recording had been made of their crucial session (he stressed that none of the evidence in the case had been discussed), she suspected that Ed Stewart was hiding something from her. That belief grew stronger when Joe Cziraky explained to her why his former partner had been so reluctant to assist her in gathering research for the book that she was writing. "He is still concerned that something is going to backfire somewhere down the line," Cziraky said, adding that the Kelly case was "a big thing on his plate." Cziraky was unaware that Taber was taping the call.

Taber believed that everyone's fate now hung on finding out what she actually knew about Jeannette Kelly's murder as opposed to what she had testified to in court. Unconcerned by the potential of being charged with perjury or conspiracy, she now knew what she had to do. "The issue now is to bring this to the forefront and address it and put things right."

When asked if that meant that she had not seen Kelly throw his unconscious wife over the balcony of apartment 1705, her reply was guarded: "I don't know what I know. I don't know what I *really* know, and what was told to me or what was put into my consciousness."

Taber said that she intended to find a reputable hypnotist to take her back to the time of the Rowsell interview to find out what had happened. Aware of the provisions of her immunity agreement, which could trigger a charge against her if she contradicted her sworn statement, the author told her he didn't think that was the kind of professional help she needed most.

"If you're thinking of publicly changing your story, Dawn, I think you had better see a lawyer first."

Two months after the interview in Wells, Dawn Taber finally revealed the truth about what she knew about the murder. Her confidante was Dan Brodsky, a Toronto lawyer she had retained to advise her of the possible legal consequences of recanting her previously sworn court testimony. Since she believed that her original part in the case had been badly mishandled, it was important to her that the record be set straight in a proper and responsible fashion. That way, the authorities could respond to her new information without having to perform in a three-ring media circus, the way Taber had been forced to back in 1984. After discussing the situation with Brodsky, who advised her of the risks that she was taking in changing her story, Taber agreed that the first step was the preparation of a new affidavit that stated the facts as she now knew them to be.

On November 10, 1993, the same day that Taber and Brodsky were preparing their legal strategy, the author interviewed Sgt. Ed Stewart. Stewart had moved up in the world and was now in charge of the homicide squad of the Metropolitan Toronto Police. Their brief discussion for the record focused on the allegations made by Taber in her Wells interview with the author. When asked if he had "pressured" Taber into giving her eyewitness testimony, Stewart leaned forward, the folds of his heavily lined face making him look like a wise and mournful hound.

"That's totally untrue. And that's completely false. I did a complete, fair investigation all the way through, like I do on any particular case. And I try to do my investigations as thoroughly as possible, and I find this new information absolutely – you know it's just not true at all. So therefore, I take it very seriously."

When the author asked to talk about the session with Dr. Rowsell, Stewart replied, "I don't think we'll talk any further about *that* particular aspect of the case, because what you are saying now to me is that there are certain allegations that it was improper. . . . As a result, I'm duty-bound to bring that new information to the attention of the attorney general, as well as whoever Patrick Kelly's new counsel is." He then terminated the interview, leaving the door open to carry it on at a later date, once he had dealt with the ethical issues he was facing.

Stewart then repeated that his request for a "proper" investigation of Taber's allegations would be on the attorney general's desk the next morning and explained that, since he had participated in the original investigation, the task of reviewing the case would have to go to another police force.

That night, the author met Taber and her fiancé for dinner to find out what she and Brodsky had decided to do. When the woman in the eye of the gathering legal storm learned of Stewart's vow to ask for an investigation into her allegations, she seemed relieved. She had finally learned enough of what had happened to her to be able to tell the truth as she knew it. Now that Brodsky had advised her of the possible legal consequences and she wasn't "flying blind," the time had come to let the chips fall where they may.

A month later, there was still no sign of Ed Stewart's impartial investigation, nor had Patrick Kelly's new lawyer, Clayton Ruby, heard from either the Attorney General's Office or the police about the new evidence in the Kelly case. Fretting that the system was ignoring her, Dawn Taber called the author and said that she wanted to do something public to breach the official wall of silence surrounding her new information.

They met again, this time at the Juniper Hill Inn, where over the next two days Taber told the story of what she had really seen in apartment 1705 on the last day of Jeannette Kelly's life. Her account began with the bombshell revelation that she had lied at the murder trial, a fact that she and Brodsky would be using as the centrepiece of her affidavit, though they would lay the blame for her false testimony squarely at the feet of the police.

"I did not see Pat Kelly drop Jeannette Kelly from the balcony of the seventeenth storey," she said.

On the day of the murder, Taber had gone to the Palace Pier to make amends with Jeannette over an old quarrel and to beg the Kellys to help her get out of her unhappy relationship with John Nascimento.

Although Patrick let her in, both the Kellys gave Taber a chilly reception, behaving almost as coldly towards her as they were to each other. While Jeannette packed for her trip to Italy, Taber waited in the den, intending to drive her to the airport.

She had heard the Kellys arguing before she knocked on the door, and they didn't stop after they let her in. In the bits and pieces Taber could make out, she got the gist of what they were fighting about, although Jeannette's "taunting" voice was the one she heard most clearly. Patrick wanted a divorce, but Jeannette refused to give him one, insisting that she wasn't about to give up her fashionable lifestyle and reminding him that she knew too much about his shady activities to force the issue. The confrontation was briefly interrupted by a telephone call that Taber suspected was from Marcello, who was awaiting Jeannette's arrival in Florence later that night. After Kelly fielded the call, the arguing had escalated. Taber suddenly heard Jeannette scream, "No, Pat, no!" Then she heard the sickening smack of a blow.

In the same instant, Taber's conversation with Kelly of the previous year before flashed through her mind and she knew what was about to happen. She came out of the den to find Jeannette lying motionless in the hallway, wearing a plaid T-shirt and a pair of blue jeans. There was blood near her head. Taber joined Kelly on the balcony, the only place he would talk because he still believed his apartment was bugged from the days of the arson investigation. If Taber had any doubts about her dread premonition, there could be none after Kelly's next words. "He told me that he was, that I was to say, if there were any questions, that what he was going to say was that Jeannette was, Jeannette fell trying to hang flower pots."

Kelly told Taber that he loved her, tenderly comforting her until she recovered from the physical collapse brought on by the grim scene in front of her. When Taber left the apartment with Kelly that afternoon, Jeannette was still lying on the floor, either dead or unconscious. It didn't really matter which, because she was about to go over the balcony in a body-imploding drop to the cement loading dock below, a horrible end that would mask any wounds that had been inflicted in the apartment. Patrick took Dawn to the twenty-fifth floor and put her on an express elevator that travelled to the ground floor without a stop. She was to go home and say nothing to anyone; he would take care of everything. Even though Jeannette did not go over the balcony until 3:45 P.M., Taber placed the deadly fight between the Kellys at around 1 P.M.

On her way home that day, the desperate woman attempted to borrow money from a friend to leave the country; unsuccessful, she returned to the apartment that she shared with John Nascimento and said nothing about the dreadful events at the Palace Pier. The next day, Luanne Rowbotham had called about the newspaper account of Jeannette's death and Taber had fallen apart. "Right then, I knew that he did it," she said. After Taber became hysterical, Nascimento called her mother in the United States and put her on the line. Crying so hard that her words were almost indecipherable, Taber told Starr Foster that Jeannette had fallen over the balcony trying to hang a flower pot, just as Kelly had told her to say. But Taber was no "cold-blooded friggin' murderer," and Kelly hadn't factored in her emotional reaction to Jeannette's death, a reaction that she later shared with her mother. "I told her that there were other things, and that I thought I should go to the police and she said, 'No, you shouldn't go to the police, because you were there and it would incriminate you.' . . . I didn't do anything. I didn't, and I couldn't have done anything. But I just – I didn't, I didn't help her."

Taber had waited all these years to come forward with the truth because she hadn't understood why she had given her false testimony in the first place. Now she did. "I was programmed, hypnotised, put into a state of relaxation with pictures to give me the information that they needed to convict Pat Kelly . . . I was shown pictures of the balcony and of the door and in that state of mind – I had had nightmares of Jeannette going over, I had had these nightmares because I knew what he did. And Rowsell basically implanted those things in my mind. . . . But I knew, even when I was saying it at times, I knew that it was not true. But I couldn't stop it."

When her patience was exhausted by the continuing official silence, Dawn Taber told her shocking story on national television in Canada just before Christmas 1993. Featured in the same show with her on "Sunday Edition," a weekly news and information program on the CTV network, were Patrick Kelly, his parents, and his lawyer, Clayton Ruby. The former eyewitness recanted her testimony in a single, devastating line. "I said that I saw Pat Kelly drop her from the balcony, and I did not." She acknowledged that she carried "a great shroud of moral guilt" for standing by the lie she claimed had been manipulated out of her by overzealous detectives and a police-supplied forensic psychiatrist.

Interviewed at William Head Institution, a gaunt Kelly was remarkably low-key in his reaction to the startling development in his case. He denied killing his wife, and said that his heart went out to Taber for finally coming forward to set the record straight. But he left no doubt about what he thought should happen next.

"I think I was arrested, charged, and convicted mainly on Dawn's evidence. I would say if Dawn is recanting, that this evidence must be immediately reviewed by the authorities, and I would hope they would order a new trial, my immediate release, and perhaps an inquiry."

Ruby said that "this kind of recantation is really shocking," and seconded his client's demand for the speedy redress of the obvious miscarriage of justice. The final clip of the program was devoted to Taber, as the interviewer tried to give the audience some idea of how strongly she felt about her clearly self-damaging recantation.

"If the cost of telling the truth is going to jail, are you prepared to stand by your story?" he asked.

"Yes."

"Perhaps you could explain why, why you're able to say that today?"

"There's no sense in being out here. I mean there's no sense in me trying to live day-to-day and trying to put this aside, because it doesn't go aside; it's inside . . . I'm wasting my life."

"Would you say that on the basis of what you have now acknowledged, that Patrick Kelly should be released from prison?"

"Because he was wrongfully convicted, yes."

When an inmate protesting his innocence has exhausted all his normal legal options, he still has one last hope. Under Section 690 of the Criminal Code of Canada, a convicted person may appeal to the federal justice minister for "Mercy of the Crown," a provision that permits a review of the case in the event that new evidence of a compelling nature emerges. Under this appeal of last resort, the minister can uphold the original conviction, order a new trial, or issue a pardon. There are approximately thirty-five "690s" a year on average in Canada, fewer than one of them is successful.

The day after Taber recanted her eyewitness testimony on "Sunday Edition," both Gary Botting and Clayton Ruby filed 690s on behalf of Kelly with Justice Minister Allan Rock. Botting based his appeal on two facts: Taber's admission that her eyewitness evidence was false, and the unscientific evidence of Eric Kreuger at Kelly's original trial, which Botting claimed "a dozen undoubted experts in the area of kinetics and physiology" had now refuted.

Ruby restricted his application to the fact that the woman who had testified that she had witnessed the murder was now saying she first learned of it from a friend the day after Jeannette Kelly died. He asked Rock to consider appointing an independent counsel to investigate the matter, bearing in mind that the royal commission inquiry into the Donald Marshall case had recommended such a procedure in the interests of a fair and impartial review of a potentially tainted judicial decision.

It would be weeks before the wheels of justice began their slow grind, but the media pounced on the sensational new development. There was wide coverage of Taber's retraction, including a frenzied response by the Scottish *Daily Record*, whose reporters beat a path to Lottie Arbuckle's door in Glasgow. "I just slammed it in their faces," the victim's angry mother said. Frank Jones, the crime columnist for the *Toronto Star*, stoutly proclaimed the ex-Mountie's guilt, dismissing the gaping flaw in the process that convicted him as being irrelevant.

"Spare no sympathy this season of goodwill for one Patrick Kelly. . . . Even if it turned out that Taber was at the other end of the earth the day Jeannette Kelly was murdered, it makes, in my view, no difference as far as guilt is concerned. The cases of Donald Marshall and David Milgaard have conditioned us to take very seriously any allegation of a miscarriage of justice. But in Kelly's case, I believe the facts convict him, even without Taber's evidence," Jones declared.

Jones had written about Kelly in his 1992 crime anthology, *Beyond Suspicion*, in which he portrayed the Jeannette Kelly murder as an example of an open-and-shut case. Predictably, his editorializing infuriated both Kelly and Taber. Kelly fumed that unless Jones was prepared to make public new information supporting the conviction, he should stop opining like a judge and jury of one. Taber, who had previously crossed swords with the eminent crime writer in June 1993, when he included her in one of his anthologies without interviewing her, scolded the columnist for not even spelling Jeannette's name correctly. (Jones spelled her name exactly as it appeared on her birth certificate. It was Jeannette herself who added the second "n.") She also reminded him that he had missed the point of her retraction; she was not saying that Kelly was innocent, only that she had been part of a flawed process that had wrongfully convicted him. Taber was not much happier with the CBC when one of its editors called to say that, since she had broken her story on the rival network, they would not be following the story until Canada's justice minister decided Kelly's fate.

It would be a long wait. The Justice Department took two months just to respond to Clayton Ruby's initial letter. The reply was written by a functionary from Allan Rock's office, and its mundane subject matter was hardly the stuff of profound reflection – a standard administrative request for trial transcripts, appeal documents, Taber's affidavit, and her address and phone number, a waiver of Kelly's solicitor-client privilege, and access to his prison records, including all medical assessments. Although it was "unusual," the minister would consider Ruby's request to appoint an independent investigator and his assessment of the 690 application would begin once the requested items were in his hands. Overjoyed at the prospect of finally getting his case reviewed, Kelly signed the requested consents on the anniversary of his eleventh year behind bars.

A year later, his good cheer had turned to frustrated despair.

For twelve long months, Clayton Ruby and the Justice Department engaged in a bitter procedural wrangle over the review of Kelly's murder conviction. Rock turned down the lawyer's request for an independent investigator and gave carriage of the case to Eugene Williams, the Justice Department lawyer who for several years had frustrated attempts by David Milgaard's lawyers to get his case reviewed. Ruby believed that Williams had prejudged the matter and was throwing up obstacles in the way of gathering the facts; the Justice Department lawyer thought that Ruby was acting as though he was conducting a trial rather than making a 690 application.

At the heart of their dispute was more than six thousand pages of documents from the original police investigation that the Metropolitan Toronto Police had never disclosed to Kelly or to his counsel. Since

Taber was now saying that the detectives of record had manipulated her evidence, Ruby wanted to examine the complete file to see if it contained evidence to support her allegation, and, therefore, his client's 690 application.

In a letter to the Justice Department, he wrote, "I want to make my own independent evaluation of what documents are helpful. In this way, I can ensure that documents which would support the innocence of Mr. Kelly or support an argument that we are going to bring before you are not left without the support that could be furnished from the police file which I have never seen."

Williams replied that officials from the Justice Department would examine the Metro police file and disclose any material they considered to be relevant to the issues Ruby had raised in his 690 application. In other words, the Justice Department wasn't about to sanction any fishing trips for new evidence on behalf of Patrick Kelly, a position Williams bluntly set out when Ruby objected to the minister's decision not to hand over the police files for his independent review: "While you may not agree with the disclosure procedure described by the Minister of Justice in his letter to you, that is the procedure that will govern this case."

Ruby was frustrated by what he saw as Williams's mean-spirited officiousness, but was hopeful when he was unexpectedly handed a chance to have him removed from the Kelly case by none other than Taber. Taber informed Ruby that Ed Stewart had contacted Det. Don Clark of the Portsmouth police in New Hampshire to set up an interview for Williams as part of his fact-finding mission in the United States. To Ruby, this was exactly the kind of tainted process that had consigned Donald Marshall, Jr., to eleven years in prison for a crime he did not commit. Like the doomed first reinvestigation of that landmark case, in which the RCMP was assisted by the original detectives who had botched it, Williams had used one of the police officers who now stood accused of manipulating a key Crown witness. It was enough to persuade Ruby that Williams had already made up his mind that Kelly's application had no merit. Allan Rock answered Ruby's request for Williams's removal with august silence, but Rock would not be able to play Pontius Pilate in the Kelly case for much longer.

After months had dragged by without any sign of official action, Patrick Kelly was ready to explode. When Dawn Taber had recanted, he had expected a speedy review of his case and a new trial. After all, the Crown's chief witness had admitted to perjury, and there was no doubt that her false testimony had anchored his conviction, just as her damning police statement had triggered his arrest. As for the fact that she still said that she'd seen Jeannette Kelly unconscious on the floor on the day of her death, it would be up to a new jury to see if they found her credible. In Kelly's opinion, there was "zero chance" that anything she now had to say would be believed, considering her lie on the crucial point of having witnessed the murder. The truth was, she hadn't even been in the apartment on the day of the accident, as he'd steadfastly claimed since his arrest more than a decade ago.

As the system continued to spin its procedural wheels, Kelly began a ferocious letter-writing campaign, bombarding MPs with missives about "one of the most horrendous injustices in Canadian history." On the thirteenth anniversary of Jeannette's "accident," he wrote to Reform MP Keith Martin that his tragic case was being given the "bureaucratic shuffle" by Justice Minister Allan Rock. It was "outrageous" that all these months later, no one from the Justice Department had even bothered to contact Dawn Taber, or that Ed Stewart hadn't been suspended pending the outcome of a full investigation of the allegations against him. In April 1994, Kelly's case finally reached the floor of the House of Commons, thanks mostly to his relentless campaign to pressure public officials into standing up for his cause.

"Not only is Patrick Kelly languishing in jail for a crime he did not commit," thundered the MP for Saskatoon–Clarks Crossing, Chris Axworthy, "but this also raises serious questions about the efficacy of the Canadian justice system."

Kelly's frustrations spilled over into his relationship with his own lawyer. He wanted Clayton Ruby to press perjury charges against Taber because of her admittedly false evidence. But as Ruby explained, that could no longer be done, since Taber had amended her recanting affidavit of December 17 to say that at the time that she had given her false evidence, she had believed it to be truthful. And then there was the stubbornness of the police in handing over information crucial to his review.

As furious as Kelly was at the official refusal to disclose the complete Metro police file, he instructed Ruby to proceed with the submissions for his 690 application without it. The stalemate could theoretically go on forever, and Kelly reminded his lawyer that he was the one "who remains incarcerated while the government fails to act."

Meanwhile, the system took action on another legal front. On May 31, 1994, Madam Justice Barbara Reed of the Federal Court took just ten minutes to dismiss Kelly's lawsuit against the CSC for wrongful placement and ordered him to pay costs of $30,000. In her written judgment, Judge Reed found that there was "not a shred of reliable evidence that would lead me to conclude that Correctional Service Canada was negligent in its handling of the plaintiff's incarceration." She found that the written argument filed on Kelly's behalf by Victoria lawyer Gary Botting contained "many slanted and distorted misstatements of the evidence . . . I want it to be absolutely clear that that document contains so many misconstructions of the facts, and errors, that it cannot be relied upon."

The second weakness the judge found in Kelly's lawsuit was highly personal. She wrote that "the plaintiff did not leave me with the impression that his evidence was accurate. Some individuals are good actors. Sometimes they are so good that they seem to be able to make themselves believe the embellishments that they make to the facts are true . . . I did not find him a reliable witness."

The third factor that bothered the judge was the absence of a "reliable, written, contemporaneous record mentioning any excessive abuse suffered by Mr. Kelly while he was at Kingston, particularly any such abuse which focussed on his ex-RCMP officer role." In fact, the written documentation demonstrated the exact opposite, and the judge doubted that Kelly would have refrained from reporting abuse had any happened, given his reputation as one of the most prolific complainers in the system. "He does not shrink from being very insistent and vigorous . . . in requesting action when he sees such to be in his best interest."

Kelly was livid when he learned of the decision and the subsequent countersuit against him by the CSC to recover its costs. In a withering judgement of his own, he blamed his loss in court on the lies of witnesses for the correctional service and an incompetent judge. "This lady should not be on a court bench but rather in a rocking chair knitting booties and sweaters for her grandchildren. . . . At least there, the mistakes she makes would not affect lives. . . . This court decision will not cause me to alter my ways. I shall continue with what I see as impeccable behaviour and I shall not lower my standards to that of either Madam Justice Reed or the CSC."

In keeping with his reputation for never taking a reversal sitting down, Kelly launched an appeal of Judge Reed's decision.

As the days slipped by without action from Allan Rock, Dawn Taber grew almost as frustrated as Patrick Kelly. Like him, she had expected the system to deal expeditiously with her new information, but eight long months after she went public, the Justice Department had yet to interview her. When she had learned from Det. Don Clark that Ed Stewart was arranging interviews for Eugene Williams, she was outraged. It appeared that the Canadian justice system was merely circling the wagons to preserve Kelly's conviction rather than dealing honestly with her attempt to set the record straight. For the second time, she felt like the victim of forces she couldn't control.

Adding to her frustration, Dr. Peter Rowsell had refused her request for a copy of her medical file. Rowsell justified his decision by pointing out that at the time of their 1983 interview, his real client had been the Metropolitan Toronto Police and Taber had never been his patient. Just as the police had refused Kelly access to the complete investigative file on his case, they declined to provide Taber with Rowsell's records of the crucial session. When Clayton Ruby complained about the Metro police's refusal to co-operate, one lawyer working on the case for Allan Rock had an idea of what might lay behind their reluctance to disclose. "Maybe they're afraid he [Kelly] will sue."

Whatever private agenda the police or others in the justice system might be pursuing, Taber's emotional reserves were stretched to the breaking point by the maddening realization that no one seemed to understand what she was doing. She had not come forward, she said, to help Kelly, but to face up to her true role in the dire events of March 29, 1981, and hopefully put them behind her. She still had the tear-stained handkerchief that Maria Nascimento had given her the night after Jeannette's death; when the memories hurt too much, she draped it over the framed picture she kept of her murdered friend. She had hoped that 1994 would be the year that she could throw it away, but if anything, the memories were becoming more unbearable as the law's delay dragged on.

Six weeks after appearing on "Sunday Edition," Taber had called the author, upset by a terrifying experience she had just had in Maine. While looking out her back window, she had seen a huge bird of prey appear out of nowhere and attack other birds in her yard. It killed two and injured a third. When Taber rushed outside to assist the injured bird, the predator flew at her; as she stared into the hawk's piercing eyes, it was as though Jeannette were looking back at her. Even after Michael Carey had driven the bird away, she remained shaken.

The old and nameless guilt seemed to be back, even though Taber had now made a clean breast of the matter, and the author wondered why. Since Taber had always maintained that she "didn't have a clue" that a murder was to take place on that March day long ago, what could have put Jeannette into the avenging eyes of the hawk? Was it possible, he asked, that Kelly had asked her to do something *after* the murder?

"From what my mother told me, I think the answer is yes, he asked me to do several things. But this is very dangerous ground and I'm afraid of going into it alone. The police asked me at the time if I carried anything out of the apartment, and that has always stuck with me, that I had the feeling that I might have. And for some reason that statue in the hall has always stuck in my mind."

Frustrated by the war of nerves the Justice Department seemed to be waging with her, and still troubled by private memories of the murder that wouldn't go away, Taber agreed to appear on "The Phil Donahue Show" along with Kelly and the author. If the system was trying to sweep the case under the rug, what better way of serving notice that she wasn't about to co-operate than placing the story in front of millions of viewers?

A hush fell over the audience when Phil Donahue directed his first question to a satellite image of Patrick Kelly from William Head Institution. Kelly's greying hair was closely cropped and his face was now heavily lined around the mouth and eyes. The curious audience searched his expression for a clue to his innocence or guilt.

"This murder happened in 1981, is that correct?" Donahue asked.

"That's correct," Kelly replied before adding his gentle correction. "My wife died in 1981."

After a brief exchange with Kelly, Donahue turned to Taber and cut to the heart of the matter – her testimony that she saw Kelly throw his wife off the balcony. "Ms. Taber, what would you like this audience to know about that testimony?"

"That I did not see him drop her," she answered softly.

"You did not."

"No."

"Were you there at the time that she fell or that her body toppled over the –"

"No."

"You weren't even in the apartment."

"No," she answered, touching off a disapproving murmur that rippled through the studio audience.

"And why then, would you testify that you had seen Patrick Kelly do this?"

Taber started to explain about the lengthy police interviews and the session with the forensic psychiatrist, but the words wouldn't come.

"So you're suggesting then it was by some kind of *hypnotic* power you were encouraged to make this damning statement against Mr. Kelly?" Donahue paused while the same disapproving buzz rose and fell in the audience behind him. "The audience – well wait a minute. The audience has already expressed its misgiving about that. Would you want to speak to this, Mr. Kelly? Why would Dawn Taber do this to you?"

The expressionless face on the television monitor answered without hesitation in a flat, unemotional voice. "I don't know, Phil. I've asked myself that question a thousand times, if not more. All I know is my wife died accidentally in 1981. In 1983, I was driving down the street and was arrested within twenty-four hours of Ms. Taber giving a statement to the police, and I've been in custody ever since."

When Donahue asked the author about Taber's explanation for her false testimony, he explained that it was very unusual for detectives to provide a prospective witness with a forensic psychiatrist and to then make her swear an affidavit in front of a judge to shore up her police statement. But in order that viewers not be misled, the author reminded Donahue that Taber was not completely deserting her trial testimony.

"Dawn Taber is saying today, in addition to withdrawing the evidence of the eyewitnessing of the murder, she heard a blow. She walked out of a den and saw Jeannette Kelly on the rug, with blood on the rug around her. So it's very important. . . . People who are unconscious, lying on rugs, don't go out and fall off balconies, generally."

Turning once again to Taber, Donahue used the new information to embark on his toughest line of questioning of the day.

"You did see her on the floor with blood around her?"

"Yes."

"And – and what did you do when you saw her with – on the floor with blood around her? Did you walk out?"

"No."

After a long pause, Donahue tried again to get an answer.

"May we know? It is not a court of law. You are free not to answer."

"I don't know what I did," Taber weakly replied. It was a question she had answered in detail on several occasions, but she could not repeat its unflattering particulars in front of the clearly disapproving audience.

After eliciting a brief synopsis of the forensic evidence from the author, Donahue returned to Taber and what he now understood was the essence of the tangled case.

"Okay. So you're recanting half the story."

"No, what I'm recanting is the key," Taber answered in her most passionate moment in the interview. "What I'm recanting is what the police needed to convict him."

"That sounds very contrived," Donahue shot back. "You're recanting what you believe to be the statement –"

"No, no."

"– that convicted him."

"That is what I've been told, that the police did not have enough to convict him of –"

"So you were hypnotically encouraged to say that he threw his wife – you saw him throw his wife over the side of the balcony. . . . You saw the body on the floor, surrounded by blood?"

"She wasn't surrounded by blood. I haven't – I didn't say that."

"But you did see —"

"There was blood."

"You saw a body on the floor."

"Yes."

Donahue was as puzzled as his audience. "Okay. Dawn, this is strange. You'll have to grant us that."

"Well, I think that you — I think that . . ."

"And we have a man doing time, here. He's doing life. And you're here saying, 'Well, I,' you know 'I did see this, but I didn't see this.' And we have a writer here who's saying that the constabulary or the officials in charge who oversee this kind of thing in Canada are looking the other way on this whole matter."

"Well they need to because they're the ones who put the words in my mouth," Taber answered defiantly.

A week after the "Donahue" show aired, adding the dithering of the Canadian justice system to the trivia bank of twenty million Americans, Justice Minister Allan Rock reversed himself and announced the appointment of an independent counsel in the Kelly case, though he made a point of saying that Eugene Williams continued to enjoy his "full confidence." Clayton Ruby was delighted with the choice of Michelle Fuerst, a crack Toronto criminal defence lawyer, and told reporters that Rock had made the decision because "his in-house counsel was biased." Several months later, when he was still fighting with Fuerst for disclosure of 6,238 pages of the Metro police file on the Kelly case, thirty-two audio cassettes, and four videotapes, he was decidedly less enthusiastic.

"This case has gone on far too long," he wrote to her. "Can we get the interview with Dawn Taber done? Can we get disclosure?"

20

DARK PASSAGE

News of the reopening of the Kelly case reached deep into the shadows. Edgar X arrived outside Toronto's Islington subway station in a chauffeur-driven, midnight-blue Lincoln Continental. As he later explained, he had expressly not told the author where they were lunching to prevent him from arranging surveillance of their meeting, just in case it turned out that he was working for the police.

Patrick Kelly had once described Edgar X as the most dangerous and powerful person he had ever met, but it was his chauffeur, a lean and leathery man in mirror-coated aviator sunglasses, whose every movement bespoke a coiled violence. They drove in silence until Edgar X pointed out a diner. The chauffeur edged the big car as close to the entrance as he could before coming to a stop.

It took Edgar almost a minute to extract his 350-pound frame from the front seat, swinging each leg into position with puffy hands. Once on his feet, he leaned against the limousine to catch his breath, then poked his head through the window and told his driver to pick him up in an hour and a half. It was obvious "John" disapproved of the unchaperoned meeting. Running a cold eye over the author, he synchronized his watch with his boss's and reluctantly pulled away, watching them in the rearview mirror until he turned onto the highway and merged smoothly into the afternoon traffic.

"A fine young man," Edgar wheezed. "He's a champion kick-boxer, you know."

The restaurant was nearly empty. Sipping on the first of several diet Pepsis, the big man launched into a description of his failing health, a commentary delivered in a mellifluous southern drawl. His ankles were grossly swollen from chronic heart trouble and his face was covered with acne from the medication he was taking. The root of his health problems was his enormous bulk, which had ballooned to more than 400 pounds before he was put on the diet that helped him to shed 50 of them. In happier times, his mother had been in charge of his well-being, but she was dead now and his care had fallen to relative strangers.

"She was a grand old dowager," he said with a catch in his voice, his brown eyes misting over. "I miss her terribly."

For a man who had just been released from the state correctional facility in Santa Barbara, California, Edgar was in surprisingly good spirits. He claimed that his legal difficulties had been caused by the RCMP, who were unhappy with him because of his attempt to help Patrick Kelly after he had been charged with his wife's murder. Edgar had offered authorities a unique defence of the former undercover operator, insisting that he was simply too well trained to kill Jeannette Kelly in such a "stupid" fashion as throwing her over a balcony in broad daylight. He also believed that the RCMP had used the Metro police, whose intelligence branch he claimed was "very, very dirty," to nail Kelly on the murder charge to make up for its own failure to convict him for burning down his Cookstown home. After visiting Kelly at the Metro West Detention Centre, Edgar was warned by a senior police acquaintance to "shut down" the relationship or face the consequences.

"The truth is," he said, dabbing at his mouth with a paper napkin, "Patrick was the best operator they ever had. They had two choices – promote him or warehouse him. Once they warehoused him, they blew smoke up anybody's ass who tried to help him, including mine."

Edgar claimed that because of his relationship with Kelly, the RCMP had branded him a homosexual in intelligence circles and "whispered" to the FBI about his so-called fraudulent dealings with a wealthy southern Baptist congregation in the United States. The force's vengeful intervention led directly to the charges against him for a scam centred around the "donation" of a rare pipe organ to the church. Authorities even had a tape recording of the swindler addressing the congregation he was later convicted of defrauding. Edgar insisted that his only crime in the tangled affair had been to try and realize his "mummy's" desire to have the priceless instrument dedicated to the Baptist church in her name. "That hasn't yet happened," he said. "Maybe now it never will."

After his arrest, Edgar had been extradited to the United States. Rather than become a pawn between the District Attorney's Office and the Baptist Church, which he pointed out was an unpleasant thing to be in a Louisiana election year, he had pleaded guilty to the "trumped up" charges against him and accepted a jail sentence. All told, he served thirty months in a prison reserved for wealthy or influential white-collar criminals. During his time at Santa Barbara, he had met several of the major players in the savings & loan scandal then rocking the U.S. financial community. The dinner conversation had been fascinating; not since the era of the great robber barons, Edgar said, had so many huge fortunes been amassed. The only other noteworthy episode behind bars had been a sexual overture from another inmate that he had parried in his characteristically ambiguous way.

"I said, 'If you want to give me a blowjob, okay, but my teeth don't fit well enough anymore to return the favour.'"

"Who got you into Santa Barbara?"

"I really don't know. I could have done it myself with a few phone calls, but you never use a juice card on a purely personal matter."

When the author turned to the subject of Patrick Kelly, Edgar rolled his eyes in mock horror as he listened to how Kelly had described their relationship, and denied paying the ex-Mountie for any clandestine operation.

"What did Kelly have that I could possibly have wanted?" he asked. "Is the boy losing touch with reality?"

Under more detailed questioning, Edgar admitted that he had given the former undercover operator several thousand dollars "out of Mummy's purse," but only because a mutual friend had said that he was a good fellow temporarily down on his luck. He also admitted that he had obtained Kelly's top-secret operational file from the RCMP by using a "juice card," though he wouldn't say why. Finally, he acknowledged that he had been involved in a plan to produce and market the Buzzsaw, a fully silenced machine gun that he had hoped to sell to the North Koreans. The prototype, he explained, had had to be manufactured outside the United States to get around laws forbidding the export of American technology to hostile countries.

When it came to his connections to the U.S. intelligence community, Edgar denied any links to the CIA, but added that he wouldn't admit to any even if they existed. He had been less coy with others. He had told a Toronto lawyer that he worked for the CIA; and his own brother, a respectable citizen, confirmed that Edgar was "associated" with the CIA. Just before he was to testify as a defence witness at Edgar's fraud trial, the brother suddenly died. Edgar had also turned up as a peripheral witness to a Mafia-style execution that had taken place on a stretch of railway tracks in Mississauga, Ontario. All in all, a strange and mysterious man.

Clearly uncomfortable talking about Kelly, Edgar returned to the subject of the CIA. The agency was the "bottom-dweller" of U.S. intelligence, he explained, compared to the "big dogs" at the National Security Agency and Naval Intelligence. But the real covert power in the world was a group called the Illuminati, an international secret society he claimed orchestrated all the truly "big events." It had been the Illuminati, whose American representatives controlled the U.S. Federal Reserve, which was behind the Davidian fiasco in Waco, Texas. The slaughter of the sect had been ordered to see how much force the public would tolerate authorities using to end such standoffs in the future. The Illuminati were extremely security conscious and frowned on anyone who delved too deeply into its activities, or "heaven forbid," who wrote about it.

"People have been known to wake up in Sweden and find that they've had a sex-change operation in their sleep," Edgar X said, smiling sweetly as he hoisted his empty tumbler towards the waitress, its half-melted ice cubes tinkling against the sides of the glass. "These guys can have your balls for breakfast anytime they want!"

Before leaving the restaurant, Edgar explained to the author that he had been "chastened" by his time in prison and was now trying to "frame up" his life. Although in his fifties, Edgar X had never had a social insurance number, a birth certificate, or a driver's licence, but was in the process of getting all the standard ID of a taxpaying citizen. Since he was honestly trying to play by the rules, he didn't want the authorities poking into his "heavy ship and airplane business," or bothering the "good Baptists" he was living with now that "Mummy" was gone.

Edgar drove the author to the Port Credit GO Station and walked him to the glass doors of the terminal. His "intuition" told him that the author should "watch out" for himself, a friendly warning that was offered just in case he had missed the allegory of the Illuminati. "If you see Pat," he said, arching his eyebrows, "tell him to keep his mouth shut."

They shook hands and Edgar X plodded back to his limousine on profoundly flat feet, a huge puppet animated by invisible strings. After arranging himself in the front seat, he turned his pale, moon-shaped face towards the author and brought his index finger to his lips, an indulgent father hushing a boisterous child.

Marshall Stern was arguably the best defence attorney in New England; he was certainly the most charismatic. Boasting a string of celebrity acquaintances from U.S. Attorney General Janet Reno to veteran Democratic powerbroker George Mitchell, he had made his legal reputation taking on controversial clients like Carol Manning, the so-called United Freedom Front bank robber, and clerical activist Rev. David Dumphy, who ran afoul of the law when he forcibly removed a teenage girl from what he believed was an abusive foster home. Earlier, Senator Edmund Muskie had been so impressed with the flamboyant and energetic Stern that he recruited him to run his Democratic campaign for the presidency. But it was not Stern's excellent political connections that made him the perfect choice to lead Dawn Taber out of the dark passage of the Jeannette Kelly murder, but rather his view of his role in a legal system where defence attorneys routinely ended up with clients who were guilty. "I don't judge my clients, I judge the government's conduct," he proudly declared. "Because if the rules aren't applied equally for all, then they fail for all."

Taber had turned to Stern in the spring of 1995 when she began to doubt that Toronto lawyer Dan Brodsky fully appreciated the legal dangers she was running in recanting her testimony. After reading the transcripts of the trial, including the Crown's assessment of Taber during

Lloyd Budzinsky's ominous jury address, Stern agreed that she was indeed at risk of being charged. Because Stern himself had been hypnotized in preparation for a previous case, and Taber claimed that her damning statement against Kelly may have been the result of her session with Dr. Peter Rowsell, the crack attorney agreed to represent her in her ongoing war of nerves with the Canadian justice system. Eighteen months after she had gone public with her recantation on national television, she had yet to be interviewed.

One of the first things Stern decided was that his client wouldn't return to the jurisdiction where the crime had been committed for any official interviews in connection with Patrick Kelly's 690 application. If Canadian authorities wanted to talk to Taber, they would have to come to Bangor, Maine, where he could more easily protect her rights as an American citizen. Nor did he want her talking to the author with whom she had already spent so much time discussing the Kelly murder case, though after eight years, numerous telephone conversations, and several lengthy interviews, Stern realized that there was probably not a lot left for Taber to say.

When the Canadian delegation, led by independent counsel Michelle Fuerst, finally showed up at the U.S. Attorney's Office in Bangor on May 18, 1995, for two days of preliminary talks, Taber had to smile at the antics of her American lawyer. Stern had strategically parked his Mercedes-Benz so that the Canadians couldn't help seeing it on their way in, a gleaming symbol calculated to serve notice that they weren't dealing with a legal-aid lawyer working on his first case. The prop was unnecessary. Fuerst impressed Taber and her lawyer with her professionalism and diplomacy in what were admittedly difficult circumstances for everyone.

Although it had taken nearly a year and a half for the interview to take place, it was obvious that the intervening time hadn't been wasted. The Justice Department had conducted a lengthy and detailed inquiry into Taber's past, and one of the people they had interviewed was her former husband, Victor Bragg.

Bragg had apparently told investigators that his ex-wife had once said that she could create interest in the book she was writing about the Kelly murder by repudiating her trial testimony. Taber was aghast. She admitted that she had once thought of writing a book as a means of putting the dread event behind her, but she adamantly denied that her recantation had been a publicity stunt. She explained that even though the book had never been written, her ex-husband had been so convinced of its monetary value, he had insisted that it be included on the list of matrimonial assets to be divided at the time of their divorce. Exasperated by what she saw as Bragg's greed, Taber had finally given him the couple's pickup truck in return for dropping all claims to her phantom murder memoir.

Taber was also nettled by Fuerst's assumption that she had recanted her testimony to help Kelly, a man she still believed had murdered her best friend. If Fuerst wanted to know why she had changed her story all these years later, her reason was much simpler than helping Kelly or trying to hype a nonexistent book with a marketing ploy that could just as easily send her to prison. Taber wanted the truth to be known, and by finally telling it, she hoped to lay the matter to rest.

As the interview progressed, Taber sensed that the Toronto lawyer seemed genuinely touched by her dilemma. Fuerst even told the troubled woman that she hoped that she would be "all right" when they finally reached the end of the legal road, wherever that might be. But professionally, Fuerst remained sceptical, commenting to Stern that Taber was either the smartest person in the world or the most foolish for doing what she had done.

During a break, Stern treated his Canadian colleagues to lunch at Miller's, a popular restaurant in downtown Bangor. Later that afternoon, they worked out the agenda for a second meeting slated for June 12, 1995. In that meeting, which was to be videotaped, Taber would be questioned in detail on her various accounts of the events of March 29, 1981, including her bombshell admission that she had not witnessed Jeannette Kelly's murder.

Both Stern and his client were shocked by what they learned during the May 18 meeting. Fuerst showed them notes written by Det. Joe Cziraky during Taber's morning session with Dr. Rowsell in March 1983, just before she gave what she now said was her false account of the murder to police. The notes had apparently never been disclosed to Kelly's lawyer, and since neither Cziraky nor Rowsell had testified at his trial, their contents had remained a secret since the day they had been written more than twelve years ago.

In Stern's opinion, at the very least, the notes proved that Taber should never have been a witness in 1984 because of her obviously unstable emotional state. In fact, he informed her after the first day of talks with the Canadian lawyers that she should she seek psychiatric counselling. According to Cziraky's observations, it was something Taber appeared to have realized at the time of the session with Dr. Rowsell; Taber had begun the interview by asking Rowsell if she was a "schizophrenic." Stern told Taber that, based on the notes, a case could be made that she had been hypnotized and that her subsequent statement to police had, in fact, been the result of post-hypnotic suggestion. Painful as it was to read the notes, which she believed authorities had suppressed the better to manipulate her evidence, Taber believed that they vindicated her. "I've been trying so hard to prove that I was crazy all these years and I've finally done it. There it is, the proof. . . . When I read them, [Cziraky's notes] I thought, 'God damn you guys, how could you do this to me.'"

With Taber's approval, Stern began preparing a civil suit against Rowsell, telling her that this was the most "mindboggling case" he had seen in twenty-five years as a criminal lawyer. Before leaving, Taber told Stern that she was worried about the fact that their next session with Canadian justice authorities would be videotaped. She didn't mind telling her story in order to set the record straight, but she didn't want clips of the video leaking out and appearing on the six o'clock news. Stern assured her that Fuerst's purpose in taping the second interview had nothing to do with drawing further attention to the already controversial murder case.

"He told me that the only reason they wanted the videotape was to preserve my evidence in case anything happened to me before Pat Kelly's new trial."

In this world, there were no guarantees.

Tall and raw-boned, twenty-year-old Russell Crouse slid into the seat of his red pickup truck and swung onto Route 2, heading north. Sitting beside the star university athlete and volunteer worker was eleven-year-old Jimmy Thorne, the foster child he had spent the day with at Old Town's YMCA in central Maine. They had had a good time together and they talked excitedly about the day's activities as they drove back to the County Foster Home in Lincoln.

It was windless, clear and brilliant, a typical Maine evening in early summer, the air tinct with the fragrance of pine trees. As he passed through the small community of Greenbush, Crouse realized he was running a little late and dialled his mother's number on the car phone. The sun was sinking, and he shielded his eyes from its brilliant rays as he listened to the ringing on the other end. His brother answered; while Crouse waited for his mother to come on the line, he pulled into the southbound lane to pass a slow-moving vehicle, pressing the accelerator to the floor.

An hour earlier, Marshall Stern had wheeled his Mercedes-Benz out of the parking lot of the courthouse in Millinocket and headed south on Route 2 for the sixty-mile drive back to Bangor. His twenty-two-year-old son Jason, who was entering George Washington Law School in the autumn, had made the trip to Millinocket that Wednesday to see his father in action. Stern was delighted that Jason had decided to uphold a family tradition by becoming a lawyer. At 5:45 P.M., as they cruised through the late afternoon sun towards Greenbush, Jason called his mother on the cellular phone to tell her that they would soon be home for supper.

The red truck loomed up so suddenly that Stern didn't have time to apply his brakes. Crouse had no reason to slow his vehicle, since he never saw the car he was about to hit head-on travelling at better than sixty miles an hour. On impact, the pickup truck exploded, sending an orange fireball into the clear summer sky, while the heavier Mercedes folded like an accordion, its dual air bags deploying like giant mushrooms. Russell Crouse and Marshall Stern died instantly, and shortly after rescue workers from Old Town and Milford arrived to drape tarpaulins over the mangled vehicles, so too did Jimmy Thorne. The victims were burned beyond recognition and would later be officially identified from dental records. Jason Stern was rushed by ambulance to the Eastern Maine Medical Centre, where he underwent the first of several operations for massive internal injuries.

Back at the Crouse household, Russell's worried mother wondered why the telephone had suddenly gone dead.

The day Marshall Stern was killed, Michelle Fuerst sent him a fax requesting that their June 12 interview with Dawn Taber begin at

8:30 A.M. at the U.S. Attorney's Office in Bangor. She asked that Taber review her preliminary and trial evidence, a transcript of a telephone conversation with OPP Insp. David Crane dating from his 1991 reinvestigation of the Kelly case, and the two affidavits in which she had recanted her 1984 court testimony. Fuerst also wanted to see all other relevant material that Taber had promised to produce, including a personal journal in which she had recorded her thoughts about Jeannette Kelly's murder over the years.

In the wake of Stern's death, the June 12 meeting was postponed. Fuerst still hoped to complete Taber's interview by the end of the month, but it was not to be. A few weeks after her lawyer's funeral, Taber called Fuerst to inform her that she could not continue with their interview. She had trusted and respected Stern and did not feel comfortable turning the matter over to his law partner, or to Dan Brodsky, who had previously represented her in Canada. There was also a financial consideration. Stern's firm had sent her a bill for $6,000 (later reduced to $3,500) that she couldn't pay, and there was just no way that she could afford further legal expenses arising out of the Kelly case.

Fuerst suggested that she attend the interview with a third party such as her husband rather than a lawyer, but Taber declined. Years earlier, she had made the mistake of dealing with Canadian authorities without legal representation and the results had been disastrous. Although she didn't tell Fuerst, Taber had also decided against showing investigators her journal. It would be too easy for others to "misinterpret" the entries relating to Jeannette Kelly's death and use them as the basis for laying a charge against their author. Reluctantly, Fuerst told Taber that she would inform Canada's justice minister of her decision, saying that she was sure Allan Rock would make "the appropriate decision."

While the country waited for the minister's decision, a few people had already made up their minds about the truth of the matter. John and Winnifred Kelly remain convinced of their son's innocence, and although they've had support over the years from family, friends, their minister, and psychiatrist, their suffering has been unrelieved since their daughter-in-law's death and the judicial fiasco they believe it touched off.

"This is the worst tragedy that we've ever faced, even with the death of our son [Timmy Kelly died in October 1990]. . . . But I'll face it until the day that Pat's released out that gate to me. I'm going to be out there to drive him home," Kelly's father says.

Eight thousand miles away, Lottie Arbuckle is heartsick at the possibility that Patrick Kelly may be released from prison, acquitted, or tried again for her daughter's murder. The seventy-two-year-old widow is as convinced of Kelly's guilt as his parents are of his innocence, and is bitter that no one in the Canadian justice system bothered to contact her about the new developments in the fourteen-year-old murder.

"I really don't think that the police or the lawyers in the case have been fair to me; after all, I brought Jeannette into this world and not for that evil bastard to take her life the way he did. Their difficulty has been to cover up as much of what happened as they could, and much more has been swept under the rug. I just feel so helpless. The years are flying past and I will never be able to go and visit my daughter's grave. This last fourteen years has been a complete nightmare for me."

Although still alive, Jimmy Hanlon is oblivious to the pain that his former wife feels now that the old wound of their daughter's death has been reopened. In 1992, he was institutionalized after suffering a massive stroke that left him paralysed and unable to recognize Lottie when she visits him. "What a wasted life," she wrote. "I feel that this has been all caused through Jeannette's murder."

Since the days when he helped Earl Levy defend Patrick Kelly, lawyer David McComb has seen a lot change in the Ontario legal community. The prosecutor on the famous case, Lloyd Budzinsky, is now a judge, Ed Stewart is chief of Homicide for the Metro Toronto Police, and Joe Cziraky has retired to Sooke, British Columbia, where he and his wife run a bed and breakfast. McComb has followed the twists and turns in the case over the years, and he has his doubts about Taber's claim that the police orchestrated her eyewitness evidence.

"I recall being dispatched to hear the tapes of Dawn's initial telephone calls to homicide," he wrote to Patrick Kelly after hearing about Taber's recantation. "No one would ever say there's anything coerced in those particular conversations. She may wish to descend into the murky world of 'false memory syndrome' and claim the shrink made her do it – lots of luck. The problem is – she's still not telling the *entire* truth. . . . There's an old saying about 'better 100 guilty men go free than one innocent man be convicted.' We don't really believe it or the law would never allow a case of one person's word against another without any independent confirmation to go to a jury. And I never thought the so-called independent evidence in your case qualified. The zeal with which 'they' went after you always bothered me."

Although he doesn't believe her new story, Dr. Peter Rowsell wasn't surprised when Taber recanted her trial testimony. Nor was he taken aback at her 1993 claim that she had given her false testimony against Kelly after being hypnotized by the police-supplied psychiatrist. When he interviewed her back in 1983, Dr. Rowsell had indeed detected signs of psychological distress in Taber's responses, a condition he believes the troubled woman still suffers from today. For whatever the reason, Taber needs to see herself as a "victim," or so the psychiatrist believes.

"As far as I could see at the time, she was not psychotic. She had a personality disorder and still has. Personality disorders reveal themselves in patterns. Hers was a total helplessness characteristic of a sex abuse pattern, which in turn creates a pattern of seeking out people who would treat her badly."

After their 1983 meeting, during which the psychiatrist said he had used relaxation therapy, not hypnosis, to get Taber to face what she knew about the case, Rowsell had returned to his home, where he dictated an unofficial account of their session. Included in the seven-page document was the fact that the subject suffered from a personality disorder. Aware that his assessment might help the defence to raise questions about the truthfulness of Taber's testimony, Rowsell had expected his report to be the subject of tough cross-examination at Kelly's 1984 trial; in fact, he was never called to testify.

"The thing that has always surprised me about this is that Patrick Kelly had a first-rate lawyer. Earl Levy certainly knew what he was doing, yet I was never subpoenaed by the defence."

When he raised this subject with the Justice Department after the Kelly case had been reopened, Rowsell was assured that his unofficial report had been an exhibit at Kelly's trial.

According to the list of exhibits, it was not.

While some people clearly doubt both Taber's recantation and the motive behind it, her mother isn't one of them. Starr Foster had her own reasons for believing that her daughter had not witnessed Jeannette

Kelly's murder from the very beginning. For one thing, Dawn had always told her that she "suspected" that Kelly had murdered Jeannette, hardly the language of an eyewitness. Knowing that it was her daughter's nature to "please people," Foster believes it is possible that she may have assisted police in a well-intentioned attempt to help them catch Patrick Kelly, since she was convinced from previous conversations that he had murdered Jeannette. As for Dawn's stubborn refusal to follow her mother's advice to "close it up, put it away, and forget about it," Foster thinks that if she really did come out of the den and see Jeannette on the rug, left the apartment without helping her, and then kept that terrible secret to herself for more than two years, "this could be the part that is killing her slowly inside." One thing Foster knows for certain is that her daughter's latest version of events is the truth. "Dawn is the type that lets things out to me gradually, a little at a time. She's always been honest with me, it's just a little slower coming out. I think anyone who knows Dawn believes her."

After years of research, the author had half-expected that Taber would some day change her story. Based on other elements of her testimony that the jury had chosen to disregard in favour of her dramatic eyewitness account of the murder, he had long since concluded that the crucial part of her trial evidence was false. Taber testified that she had been in the apartment for some time after Jeannette Kelly had gone over the balcony, and that after comforting her, Kelly had taken her to the express elevator on the twenty-fifth floor. As defence attorney Earl Levy tried to point out at the trial, these activities would have taken about twenty minutes – an interval that simply didn't exist after Jeannette Kelly had gone over the balcony.

Witnesses placed Patrick Kelly at his wife's side somewhere between three and five minutes after her fall, which meant that he could not have been with Taber. More importantly, the description of the apartment that Taber gave to police was riddled with major factual errors – she had seen no seventy-five-pound sheepdog, no stool on the balcony, and no kettle on the boil. She had also placed Jeannette's suitcases in the wrong location, and had the victim wearing a plaid T-shirt with buttons, not the long-sleeved, navy-blue cashmere sweater in which she was found.

Patrick Kelly has always maintained that the police investigators provided Taber with the details of the scene in the apartment that day because they wanted to frame him for his wife's murder. But if that was so, why would they give their star witness information that didn't square with the known facts? They clearly would not, so the question remains: how had she gotten so many things wrong if she had indeed been in the Kelly apartment on the afternoon of March 29, 1981?

In theory, there was an explanation for the inaccuracies in Taber's police statements and testimony that was consistent with other known facts and her 1993 admission that she had not witnessed the murder. Taber had always maintained that the events in apartment 1705 began much earlier than the established time for Jeannette's fall, somewhere between 1 P.M. and 2 P.M., rather than at 3:45 P.M. If Jeannette Kelly had indeed been murdered or rendered unconscious before being thrown over the balcony, Taber could have left the apartment before Patrick Kelly decided what to do with his wife's body. That would explain why Taber acted perfectly normally with John Nascimento on March 29 and was an emotional wreck the next day with her mother and girlfriends after learning of Jeannette Kelly's death from Luanne Rowbotham.

If Taber had, in fact, left before the drop, Kelly would have had time to retrieve his dog from wherever it had been while she had been in the apartment, redress his wife's body in different clothes, put on the kettle, move the suitcases, and place the kitchen stool on the balcony before hoisting Jeannette over the railing. If an overwrought Dawn Taber ever decided to go to the police after learning about Jeannette's "accident" in the press, her inability to describe the apartment or the victim accurately would make it appear as though she were lying. The point was simply this: if Taber's court testimony was true, and she and Kelly did spend fifteen to twenty minutes together after Jeannette's fall, where had he found time to return to the apartment and rearrange the evidence?

The other theory, of course, is that Taber was not in the Kellys' apartment at all that day. No evidence was ever presented at trial to confirm her claim that she was, and Kelly has always adamantly denied that she was present. But it is a theory with a curious snag that the court never saw. When police asked Taber what Jeannette Kelly had been wearing on the day of her death, she said a T-shirt. Since the victim's body was found in a long-sleeved cashmere sweater, it looked like Kelly was telling the truth when he insisted that Taber had not been in the apartment that day.

But when the author was going through Eddie Greenspan's preliminary interviews with Kelly, he discovered a puzzling fact. During discussions with the accused, one of Greenspan's assistants asked Kelly what his wife had been wearing on the day of her death. His recorded answer was "blue jeans and a plaid T-shirt that had buttons. She was probably wearing no underwear, and was wearing the same clothes as the clothes she was found in when she died." Since the defence is not required to disclose information to the Crown or police about its client, neither Lloyd Budzinsky nor Ed Stewart had ever known this detail. But Dawn Taber had. If she hadn't been in the Palace Pier that day, why did she mention the same article of clothing that Kelly had identified to his own lawyer in a privileged conversation? There were only two possibilities: she had randomly guessed the same article of clothing Kelly had described; or, two years after Jeannette Kelly's death, the accused had made a fatal slip and had answered his lawyer truthfully about what she had been wearing on the afternoon of March 29, 1981.

When the author asked Kelly about the T-shirt incident, he replied, "I have no explanation for that. All I can tell you is that on the day my wife died, she was wearing a blue cashmere sweater."

Fifteen years after his roller-coaster ride with Patrick Kelly, Victor Simpson practises family and criminal law from a basement office in his parents' suburban Victoria home. All told, being Kelly's closest friend cost him approximately $300,000, a debt that forced him and his wife to sell their home and most of their worldly goods. The Simpsons will be repaying Kelly's debts for a long time to come.

Although an RCMP investigation into Simpson's handling of funds belonging to Mina McIntosh did not result in criminal charges, his reputation suffered as much as his pocketbook from his friendship with Kelly. The B.C. Law Society found him grossly incompetent for recklessly investing his client's trust money, as well as for drawing up the Cameron Croll loan at criminally high interest rates and without proper security. The benchers found that the quality of Simpson's legal services was "so far below the standard required of the most minimally competent solicitor that his acts or omissions . . . constitute professional misconduct."

The Law Society also found Simpson guilty of professional misconduct for assisting Kelly in deceiving his first wife and others by creating the impression that he was employed by K&V Enterprises, for disclosing to Kelly that money from the McIntosh estate was available for investment purposes, and for encouraging Cameron Croll to make a loan to Kelly "for the purposes of reloaning these monies to the Central Intelligence Agency, when the Member knew, or ought to have known, Kelly's explanation of the purpose of such loan was incredible."

Despite its ringing denunciation, the Law Society stopped short of disbarring Simpson, concluding instead that he had been duped by his con-man friend and for that reason "should be given another chance." Simpson was suspended from the practise of law for thirty days, fined $3,000, and ordered to participate in a remedial program that the Law Society runs for lawyers who wrestle with their consciences and lose.

In order to pay his fine and other debts, Simpson was eventually forced to sell his practice. One of the conditions of the sale was that he was not to do solicitor's work relating to real estate transactions, wills, or estate planning, since these activities would take business away from the purchaser of his former firm.

In 1992, a few years into his fresh start, Simpson was called in front of the Law Society for breaking his agreement not to do any solicitor's work. The benchers found that he had, in fact, drafted a will for his secretary and acted for clients in two separate real estate transactions. He was cited, reprimanded, fined $1,000, and ordered to pay the costs of the professional hearing. Two years later, he was before the benchers again, this time as a result of a formal complaint by a former client. Patrick Kelly alleged that Simpson had defamed him and violated solicitor-client privilege in an interview with British Columbia journalist Jim Reid. In the article based on that interview which appeared in *Monday Magazine*, Reid quoted Simpson as describing Kelly as a "sociopath" and a master manipulator.

Despite all that has happened, Simpson looks back on his relationship with Kelly as "a positive friendship," remains unconvinced of his guilt in the death of his first wife, and believes that the RCMP may have been responsible for giving his friend's character a sinister twist: "I'm not sure exactly if that's his character to deceive and to try and make himself out to be the best person in the situation. I still hope that that's not the person that I was a friend to, but the more I hear about him, the more that comes out, maybe that is the way that he is. Not that he was always that way, but that he was trained to manipulate other people through his dealings with the RCMP, that he was trained to deceive, that he was trained to have a lifestyle that showed opulence, to deal with people in a very public way but have different feelings for them privately. . . . Basically, I believe he used other people because he was trained to use other people. He has the ability to use a lot of people and then dispense with them, as he dispensed with me."

The RCMP ignored the author's request for an interview about its former star agent, but the force has discreetly monitored Kelly's reappearance in the news.

In the years since his murder conviction, Canada's national police force has done its best to make sure that none of its approximately 150 present-day undercover operators, only 5 per cent of them women, follow in his footsteps. In fact, it uses Kelly's case as an object lesson in just how badly things can go wrong when a law officer of his ability and training crosses the line.

Thanks to Dr. Michael Girodo of the University of Ottawa, who was hired by the RCMP in the early 1980s as a consulting psychologist, agents are now alerted to the special perils of their profession from the very beginning of their training. During their three-week undercover course, trainees get fourteen hours of lectures by Girodo on the psychological pressures and pitfalls of covert police work.

On Girodo's advice, the RCMP has retained psychologists in cities across Canada to assist any agent who finds himself in mental difficulties during a mission. The consulting psychologist also teaches agents hypnotism and meditation, self-help techniques designed to prevent them from developing serious drinking problems or other destructive habits arising from the long stretches of boredom, loneliness, and chastity associated with real-life undercover work.

Girodo emphasizes the need for constant reality checks in the fantasy world that these men and women inhabit. Today's agents are actively encouraged by their cover men to remember who they really are, a far cry from Kelly's day, when they urged undercover operators to live their false identities to the hilt in order to be more convincing in the field. Agents are even permitted to telephone their spouses or lovers while working undercover, something Kelly was strictly forbidden to do, as anecdotes about normal life help to counterbalance their own exotic experiences. Girodo also counsels operators on how to deal with the depression that follows the emotional high of the "round-up," the moment when the undercover agent's deceptions lead to the arrest of the target. Patrick Kelly had often experienced such letdowns, but had received no understanding or assistance from his RCMP superiors. In the late 1970s, getting over the "operational blues" after spending months of living a lie was something that every agent was left to handle on his own.

But the biggest change in the way the RCMP conducts its covert business in the 1990s happens long before an agent finds himself in an actual operation, or even on an undercover training course. Girodo convinced the RCMP that many of its problems with agents originated with its recruitment of people who bordered on the psychopathic. It is no accident that these magnetic and dangerous individuals are attracted to undercover work, or that they often make the best agents.

According to the clinical profile worked up by Dr. Robert Hare, a psychologist at the University of British Columbia whose psychopathy checklist is used worldwide, the psychopath could have been designed by nature for the treacherous world of undercover police work. They normally live on the edge and obsessively seek out excitement. Lying, deceiving, and manipulating come naturally. Regardless of what they do to others, they never experience guilt or shame, largely because they see themselves as the walking centre of the universe, superior beings who play by their own rules in pursuit of complete self-gratification. In tandem with this towering sense of entitlement, they have an uncanny ability to find a person's weak spot and exploit it for their own purposes. As one psychopath quoted by Hare put it, "I look for an angle, an edge, figure out what you need and give it to you."

One of the reasons psychopaths make such good impostors is that they slip naturally into roles that give them power or prestige, a proclivity in keeping with their strong need to be "in charge" of people and events. In order to better manipulate others, they often make a formal study of psychology, as did serial killer Ted Bundy. Over and over again, the charming psychopath carefully studied his female victims and then lured the sympathetic young women into his car by pretending to be disabled.

When their crimes are financial, psychopaths seduce their victims with flattery, mock sympathy, and wildly inflated accounts of their financial position and social status. They can be fascinating companions, particularly for people with a dash of larceny in their own personalities. As con artists, psychopaths are also consummate opportunists, resorting to anything at hand to execute their often daring if improbable frauds.

In his book *Without Conscience*, Dr. Hare cites the case of a white-collar psychopath who defrauded financial institutions of over $23 million by using the stationery of a prestigious accounting firm to forge financial statements to support his loan applications. As a student, the same man had been caught embezzling money from his fraternity, but wasn't charged because the victim-organization wanted to avoid a scandal.

Although they are brilliant dissemblers, there are a few chinks in the psychopath's otherwise formidable social armour. Many observers have noted their intense and emotionless stare, which psychopaths often use to help them intimidate and control others. Although their victims often notice the gulf between the expressionless gaze and the emotion the psychopath is portraying, few realize the significance of those cold, unchanging eyes. Elated or depressed, loving or enraged, the psychopath surveys his world with the same detached and calculating stare, measuring the responses of others, constantly taking aim.

Occasionally, the psychopath will reveal himself in his skewed thought processes when presented with a situation where he has to choose between a range of options. One of their characteristic methods of resolving multiple choice dilemmas is to make lists. Hare wrote about a psychopathic lawyer who listed the possible courses of action to deal with his marital difficulties, including who would get custody of the couple's four children. "Do nothing; File for Paternity/Conciliation Court; Take girls without killing; Take girls, Killing 4; Kill girls and Justine." After reviewing the chilling list, the lawyer's probation officer concluded that it showed "the mind of a man who would contemplate killing his own children with the detachment of someone considering various auto-insurance policies. It is the laundry list of a man without a soul."

Hare notes that when psychopaths are caught for their crimes, they typically blame their misfortune on bad luck, dishonest companions, or corrupt institutions that have treated them unfairly. Even when they are convicted of capital offences like murder, they see their predicament as a temporary setback from which they will somehow rebound when the world finally sees the error of its ways. Despite their compelling personalities and often dazzling accomplishments, they are easily society's most dangerous members.

"Psychopaths are social predators who charm, manipulate, and ruthlessly plow their way through life, leaving a broad trail of broken hearts, shattered expectations, and empty wallets," Dr. Hare writes. "Completely lacking in conscience and feelings for others, they selfishly take what they want and do as they please, violating social norms and expectations without the slightest sense of guilt or regret."

Through his groundbreaking work with psychopaths, Hare has made some interesting discoveries. In most people, the two sides of the brain have different, highly specialized functions. The language centre, for example, is usually on the left side. But in some people, there are bilateral language centres – one in each side of the brain – an oddity that creates difficulties as the two centres compete for control. Hare's experiments have shown that certain forms of dyslexia and stuttering are associated with this brain configuration. "New experimental evidence suggests that bilateral language processes are also characteristic of psychopathy," he writes.

Similarly, for most of the population, the right side of the brain plays a central role in the normal workings of human emotion. But Hare has found that neither side of a psychopath's brain is proficient in the processes of emotion. "In the final analysis, their self-image is defined more by possessions and other visible signs of success and power than by love, insight, and compassion, which are abstractions."

But Dr. Michael Girodo was tasked with keeping psychopaths out of the RCMP, not divining the mysteries of their terrifying condition. To do that, he persuaded the force to steer away from flashy smooth-talkers like Patrick Kelly and recruit more mature and mentally stable candidates for its undercover activities. Although the Mounties have never formally taken any responsibility for Kelly's criminal exploits, Girodo's new regime for undercover agents suggests that the RCMP has now realized its terrible mistake and that the crushing pressures it routinely subjected its agents to without the slightest concern for their psychological well-being occasionally destroyed their characters and their lives.

For Patrick Kelly, the insight came too late.

For years, Patrick Kelly has paced up and down behind the walls of various prisons like a restless animal looking for a way out. His story remains the same: Jeannette Kelly accidentally fell to her death trying to fix a rattle in the flashing of the balcony above apartment 1705. Despite the Crown's expert evidence that his account of his own actions was not humanly possible, he insists that he did reach his wife at the precise moment she began to fall, but had been unable to hold on to her.

He explains his murder conviction as the work of corrupt and conspiratorial forces. Dawn Taber was not in his apartment on March 29, 1981, and witnessed absolutely nothing. Why she told such a dreadful lie about him, he cannot say, although he believes she may have been an unwitting tool of the police. The RCMP worked hand-in-glove with the Metro police to discredit him because he knew about their illegal practices. Even his alleged bank frauds, he claims, were trumped up by former police officers who controlled that industry's security operations. Victor Simpson betrayed their boyhood friendship, as well as their professional relationship, by stealing hundreds of thousands of dollars of Kelly's income instead of paying the ex-Mountie's bills. By his own account, Kelly is the victim of an elaborate and malevolent frame-up perpetrated by two police forces, the courts, old friends, and former lovers.

Before Dawn Taber recanted part of her damning testimony, Kelly had come up with a daring plan. He would ask to see a justice of the peace, then swear out an affidavit that Taber had not only been in the apartment that day, but that she had been the one who had murdered Jeannette Kelly. Since the Crown was publicly committed to charging Taber if evidence implicating her in the crime ever emerged from a source other than her own statements, authorities would have no alternative but to replay the proceedings of 1984 with a bizarre reversal of roles – Taber as the accused and Kelly, the eyewitness against her.

396 • THE JUDAS KISS

In the meantime, Kelly would mail letters to various people declaring his real purpose: making a false accusation to force Taber to admit that she wasn't in the apartment the day Jeannette died, something he was sure she would do when faced with the prospect of going to prison herself. Once she had recanted her false story, Kelly would produce his letters, and the authorities would have to admit their terrible mistake and compensate him for the years of imprisonment he had endured as an innocent man.

Taber's voluntary retraction of her eyewitness evidence made it unnecessary for Kelly to resort to this artful manipulation. With the key piece of evidence that led to his conviction so stunningly repudiated, Kelly believed that his case would be referred to an appeal court, where he would be swiftly exonerated, largely because nothing that Taber now said could be seen as credible. As the months turned into years, and his case remained unresolved, Kelly's stutter made a strange reappearance and some of his old confidence began to drain away. He stopped seeing visitors and put the word out in the prison population that he wanted to be left alone, withdrawing into an angry and contemplative isolation.

"My time in prison has been an adventure that I would not wish on any human being. I can only hope that my near future holds release, some form of compensation, and some form of inquiry to establish how this whole ordeal occurred in the first place."

The Palace Pier is still one of Etobicoke's finest addresses. Since the days when Patrick and Jeannette Kelly lived here, developers have built a second tower closer to the waterfront. An apartment like the Kellys' former residence, with its desirable southwest aspect, now sells for more than four times what the young couple paid when they moved to the new building from Cookstown in 1978. As Patrick Kelly predicted, the luxury condominiums have turned out to be an excellent investment.

The sales pitch is still aimed at the rich, people who can appreciate the five-piece marble baths with their jacuzzis for two, the mirrored walls, and, of course, the walk-out balconies. There is a shuttle bus to nearby Toronto, a valet to fetch their car if they decide to drive, a squash court, and the elegant pool where Kelly used to swim daily laps to keep himself fit for the dangerous world in which he made his living. When an apartment comes up for sale, the merely curious are kept at bay by the practice of restricting viewings to those who have prequalified for a mortgage. Money is the passport to the good life here; without it, as the Kellys knew, one need not apply.

Although it is still remembered, few Palace Pier residents speak of the sensational murder that once cast a pall over their posh address. Their urban castle, like the city whose skyline beckons just to the east, easily diverts the living from the dour consideration of a life so terribly taken. When they venture out of their luxury cocoons, there is tennis, the Pier's gourmet restaurant, or the adjoining nightclub. On hot summer evenings, after nightfall, a popular retreat is the rooftop observation deck. Standing by the edge, cooled by the onshore breeze, you can muse about the future and spin dreams, high above the glittering city and the wide and peaceful lake.